NINETY-SIX SERMONS

BY THE

RIGHT HONOURABLE AND REVEREND FATHER IN GOD,

LANCELOT ANDREWES,

SOMETIME LORD BISHOP OF WINCHESTER.

PUBLISHED BY HIS MAJESTY'S SPECIAL COMMAND.

VOL. III.

NEW EDITION.

WIPF & STOCK · Eugene, Oregon

Wipf and Stock Publishers
199 W 8th Ave, Suite 3
Eugene, OR 97401

Ninety-Six Sermons by the Right Honourable and Reverend Father in God,
Lancelot Andrewes, Sometime Lord Bishop of Winchester, Vol. III
By Andrewes, Lancelot
ISBN 13: 978-1-60608-125-9
Publication date 12/1/2009
Previously published by James Parker and Co., 1875

SERMONS

OF THE RESURRECTION

XIV.—XVIII.

OF THE SENDING OF THE HOLY GHOST,

PREACHED ON WHIT-SUNDAY.

EDITOR'S PREFACE.

THE present volume contains nineteen Discourses; the remainder of those preached on Easter-day, on our Lord's Resurrection, and the whole series preached on Whit-Sunday, on the Sending of the Holy Ghost.

Of those on the Resurrection, the first four were preached before King James I. at Whitehall, between the years 1620 and 1623, both inclusive; and the last was only prepared for delivery on Easter-day 1624, but was never actually preached.

With respect to the subject-matter of these Sermons little need be said. The first three are occupied with a consideration of the great love and devotion displayed by St. Mary Magdalene, at the tomb of her Divine Master; together with a particular examination of the probable grounds which induced our blessed Saviour to repress her ardent zeal, and through her to inculcate upon us the necessity of spiritualizing our affections, and at the same time of reposing with implicit confidence upon Him, Who is at once our Father and our God.

The two last discourses in this series, from different texts, enforce the same practical lesson, namely, the obligation which is laid upon every Christian of making a suitable and correspondent return for the great blessings of salvation.

The Sermons preached on Whit-Sunday, on the Sending of the Holy Ghost, come next under consideration.

They are fifteen in number, and, with the exception of the last, were all preached before King James I. at Greenwich, Whitehall, Windsor, and Holy-rood House, between the years 1606 and 1621, both inclusive. The last, which was just excepted, was only prepared to be preached on Whit-Sunday 1622.

This series is particularly valuable for the light which it throws upon some of the very highest and most mysterious—and it may be added the most essential—Articles of the Catholic Faith; and also for the arguments which it affords to the controversialist who combats the Socinian and other rationalistic heresies. Herein we have asserted, and established, the distinction of Persons and the unity of essence, in the Godhead,—the Divinity, personality, and agency of the Holy Spirit in particular—His procession from the Father and the Son,—His three-fold coming—His office, His works, His gifts, His place, in the economy of redemption—the power which He confers in Holy Orders—the danger of grieving Him—the necessity of receiving Him—His indwelling—the comfort He imparts, the meetness with which He endues the soul for the inheritance of the Saints in glory. These, and other points of a similar character, form the substance of the above sermons; and it will at once be perceived on perusal that they are not merely speculative, but that they abound in practical applications to the consciences of individual Christians, such indeed as cannot easily be resisted, except in cases where the mind is inveterately prejudiced against the reception of the truth.

On the whole, it is hoped that these discourses may, in the full depth of their meaning, be blessed to the edification of those whom a false philosophy, or perhaps the mere pride of intellect, has unhappily influenced against the mysteries of Revelation, by satisfactorily shewing that there is nothing in them to prevent a rightly-constituted mind from still embracing and holding them fast, as forming a part of that sacred deposit of faith once given to the Saints, and entrusted to us for transmission to succeeding generations.

The Hebrew Quotations have for the most part been revised and corrected by the Rev. C. Seager, M.A., late Scholar of Worcester College, to whom the Editor is glad of having an opportunity of thus recording his obligations.

The Variations between the texts heading the Sermons, and the same as they occur in the Genevan Bible, are given as before (the most important of them) in a note below [a].

It is not impossible but that, in the course of the volumes already published, a few obvious and literal misprints may be detected. The Editor hopes, however, that they are not numerous, or important, or indeed such as require particular notice. Any one, who is at all conversant with the press, is of course aware that occasional misprints are unavoidable in a work of this nature.

J. P. W.

Magdalene College,
Whit-Monday.

[a] The variations are distinguished by italics.

SERMONS ON THE RESURRECTION.

Serm. XIV. John xx. 11. . . . . stood *without at* . . . as she wept, she *bowed herself.* Ver. 14. . . . . she turned herself *back.*

Serm. XV. & XVI. No variation.

Serm. XVII. Isaiah lxiii. 1—3. . . . . in *His* strength. . . . . of all *the* people. . . . .

Serm. XVIII. Heb. xiii. 20, 21. . . . . our Lord Jesus *Christ.*

SERMONS ON THE SENDING OF THE HOLY GHOST.

Serm. I.—X. No variation of the slightest importance.

Serm. XI. Acts ii. 16—21. Ver. 18. . . . . I will pour out of My Spirit *in those days.* Ver. 19. . . . the *vapours.*

Serm. XII. No variation.

Serm. XIII. 1 John v. 6. . . . *that* Spirit that beareth witness. . . . *that* Spirit.

Serm. XIV. James i. 16, 17. . . . every good *giving* . . . . neither *shadow of* turning.

Serm. XV. No variation.

ERRATUM IN VOL. II. p. 119.

For Who. . . reporting the Passion, and the last act of the Passion—this opening of the side, and piercing of the heart—our Saviour Christ saith plainly,.. *read,* Who . . . reporting the Passion, and the last act of the Passion—this opening of the side, and piercing of the heart of our Saviour Christ—saith plainly, . . .

CONTENTS.

SERMONS OF THE RESURRECTION,

PREACHED UPON EASTER-DAY.

SERMON XIV.

(Page 3.)

Preached before the King's Majesty at Whitehall, on the Sixteenth of April, A.D. MDCXX., being Easter-day.

JOHN xx. 11—17.

But Mary stood by the sepulchre weeping; and as she wept, she stooped, and looked into the sepulchre,

And saw two Angels in white, sitting, the one at the head, the other at the feet, where the Body of Jesus had lain.

And they said to her, Woman, why weepest thou? She said to them, They have taken away my Lord, and I know not where they have laid Him.

When she had thus said, she turned herself about, and saw Jesus standing, and knew not that it was Jesus.

Jesus saith to her, Woman, why weepest thou? Whom seekest thou? She, supposing He had been the gardener, said to Him, Sir, if thou have borne Him hence, tell me where thou hast laid Him, and I will take Him thence.

Jesus saith to her, Mary. She turned herself, and said to Him, Rabboni, that is to say, Master.

Jesus said to her, Touch Me not; for I am not yet ascended to My Father: but go to My brethren, and say to them, I ascend to My Father and to your Father, and to My God and your God.

SERMON XV.

Preached before the King's Majesty at Whitehall, on the First of April, A.D. MDCXXI., being Easter-day.

JOHN xx. 17.

Jesus saith unto her, Touch Me not.

SERMON XVI.

Preached before the King's Majesty at Whitehall, on the Twenty-first of April, A.D. MDCXXII., being Easter-day.

JOHN xx. 17.

Jesus saith unto her, Touch Me not, for I am not yet ascended to My Father; but go to My brethren, and say unto them, I ascend unto My Father and your Father, and to My God and your God.

SERMON XVII.

Preached before the King's Majesty at Whitehall, on the Thirteenth of April, A.D. MDCXXIII., being Easter-day.

ISAIAH lxiii. 1—3.

Who is this That cometh from Edom, with red garments from Bozrah? He is glorious in His apparel and walketh in great strength; I speak in righteousness, and am mighty to save.

Wherefore is Thine apparel red, and Thy garments like him that treadeth in the winepress?

I have trodden the winepress alone, and of all the people there was none with Me; for I will tread them in Mine anger, and tread them under foot in My wrath, and their blood shall be sprinkled upon My garments, and I will stain all My raiment.

SERMON XVIII.

(Page 81.)

Prepared to be preached on Easter-day, A.D. MDCXXIV.

HEBREWS xiii. 20, 21.

The God of peace That brought again from the dead our Lord Jesus Christ, the great Shepherd of the sheep, through the blood of the everlasting testament,

Make you perfect in all good works to do His will, working in you that which is pleasant in His sight, through Jesus Christ; to Whom be praise for ever and ever! Amen.

SERMONS OF THE SENDING OF THE HOLY GHOST.

PREACHED UPON WHIT-SUNDAY.

SERMON I.

(Page 107.)

Preached before the King's Majesty at Greenwich, on the Eighth of June, A.D. MDCVI., being Whit-Sunday.

ACTS ii. 1—4.

And when the day of Pentecost was come (or, when the fifty days were fulfilled) *they were all with one accord in one place.*

And there came suddenly from Heaven the sound of a mighty wind, and it filled the place where they sat.

And there appeared tongues cloven as they had been of fire, and sat upon each of them.

And they were all filled with the Holy Ghost, and they began to speak with other tongues, as the Spirit gave them utterance.

SERMON II.

Preached before the King's Majesty at Greenwich, on the Twenty-fourth of May, A.D. MDCVIII., being Whit-Sunday.

ACTS ii. 4.

And they were all filled with the Holy Ghost, and began to speak with other tongues, as the Spirit gave them utterance.

SERMON III.

Preached before the King's Majesty at Whitehall, on the Twenty-seventh of May, A.D. MDCX., being Whit-Sunday.

JOHN xiv. 15, 16.

If ye love Me, keep My commandments.

And I will pray the Father, and He shall give you another Comforter, that He may abide with you for ever.

SERMON IV.

Preached before the King's Majesty at Windsor, on the Twelfth of May, A.D. MDCXI., being Whit-Sunday.

JOHN xvi. 7.

Yet I tell you the truth; it is expedient for you that I go away: for if I go not away, the Comforter will not come unto you; but if I depart, I will send Him unto you.

SERMON V.

Preached before the King's Majesty at Whitehall, on the Thirty-first of May, A.D. MDCXII., being Whit-Sunday.

ACTS xix. 1—3.

And it came to pass, &c. that Paul came to Ephesus, and found there certain Disciples,

And said unto them, Have ye received the Holy Ghost since ye believed? And they said unto him, We have not so much as heard whether there be an Holy Ghost.

And he said unto them, Unto what were ye then baptized? And they said, Unto John's baptism.

SERMON VI.

Preached before the King's Majesty at Whitehall, on the Twenty-third of May, A.D. MDCXIII., being Whit-Sunday.

EPHESIANS iv. 30.

And grieve not (or, be not willing to grieve) *the Holy Spirit of God, by Whom ye are sealed unto the day of redemption.*

SERMON VII.

Preached before the King's Majesty at Greenwich, on the Twelfth of June, A.D. MDCXIV., being Whit-Sunday.

PSALM lxviii. 18.

Thou art gone up on high, Thou hast led captivity captive, and received gifts for men; yea, even the rebellious hast Thou led, *that the Lord God might dwell there.*

SERMON VIII.

Preached before the King's Majesty at Greenwich, on the Twenty-ninth of May, A.D. MDCXV., being Whit-Sunday.

LUKE iii. 21, 22.

Now it came to pass, when all the people were baptized, and that Jesus also was baptized, and did pray, the heaven was opened,

And the Holy Ghost came down upon Him in a bodily shape like a dove, and there was a voice from Heaven, saying, Thou art My beloved Son, in Whom I am well pleased.

SERMON IX.

Preached before the King's Majesty at Greenwich, on the Nineteenth of May, A.D. MDCXVI., being Whit-Sunday.

JOHN xx. 22.

And when He had said that, He breathed on them, and said unto them, Receive the Holy Ghost.

SERMON X.

(Page 284.)

Preached before the King's Majesty at Holyrood-House, in Edinburgh, on the Eighth of June, A.D. MDCXVII., being Whit-Sunday.

Luke iv. 18, 19.

The Spirit of the Lord is upon Me, because He hath anointed Me, that I should preach the Gospel to the poor; He hath sent Me, that I should heal the broken-hearted, that I should preach deliverance to the captives, and recovering of sight to the blind, and that I should set at liberty them that are bruised,

And that I should preach the acceptable year of the Lord.

SERMON XI.

(Page 305.)

Preached before the King's Majesty at Greenwich, on the Twenty-fourth of May, A.D. MDCXVIII., being Whit-Sunday.

Acts ii. 16—21.

But this is that which was spoken by the Prophet Joel;

And it shall be in the last days, saith God, I will pour out of My Spirit upon all flesh: and your sons and your daughters shall prophesy, and your young men shall see visions, and your old men shall dream dreams:

And on My servants and on Mine handmaids I will pour out of My Spirit; and they shall prophesy:

And I will shew wonders in Heaven above, and tokens in the earth beneath; blood and fire, and the vapour of smoke:

The sun shall be turned into darkness, and the moon into blood, before that great and notable day of the Lord come:

And it shall be, that whosoever shall call on the name of the Lord, shall be saved.

SERMON XII.

Preached before the King's Majesty at Greenwich, on the Sixteenth of May, A.D. MDCXIX., being Whit-Sunday.

ACTS x. 34, 35.

Then Peter opened his mouth, and said, Of a truth I perceive that God is no accepter of persons:

But in every nation he that feareth Him, and worketh righteousness, is accepted with Him.

SERMON XIII.

Preached before the King's Majesty at Whitehall, on the Fourth of June, A.D. MDCXX., being Whit-Sunday.

1 JOHN v. 6.

This is that Jesus Christ That came by water and blood; not by water only, but by water and blood. And it is the Spirit That beareth witness, for the Spirit is truth.

SERMON XIV.

Preached before the King's Majesty at Greenwich, on the Twentieth of May, A.D. MDCXXI., being Whit-Sunday.

JAMES i. 16, 17.

Err not, my dear brethren.

Every good thing and every perfect gift is from above, and cometh down from the Father of lights, with Whom is no variableness, neither shadowing by turning.

SERMON XV.

(Page 382.)

Prepared to be preached on Whit-Sunday, A.D. MDCXXII.

1 Cor. xii. 4—7.

Now there are diversities of gifts, but the same Spirit.
And there are diversities of administrations, but the same Lord.
And there are diversities of operations, but God is the same, Which worketh all in all.
But the manifestation of the Spirit is given to every man to profit withal.

SERMONS

OF THE RESURRECTION,

PREACHED ON EASTER-DAY.

XIV.—XVIII.

A SERMON

PREACHED BEFORE

THE KING'S MAJESTY, AT WHITEHALL,

ON THE SIXTEENTH OF APRIL, A.D. MDCXX. BEING EASTER-DAY.

JOHN XX. 11—17.

But Mary stood by the sepulchre weeping; and as she wept, she stooped, and looked into the sepulchre,

And saw two Angels in white, sitting, the one at the head, the other at the feet, where the body of Jesus had lain.

And they said to her, Woman, why weepest thou? She said to them, They have taken away my Lord, and I know not where they have laid Him.

When she had thus said, she turned herself about, and saw Jesus standing, and knew not that it was Jesus.

Jesus saith to her, Woman, why weepest thou? Whom seekest thou? She, supposing He had been the gardener, said to Him, Sir, if thou have borne Him hence, tell me where thou hast laid Him, and I will take Him thence.

Jesus saith to her, Mary. She turned herself, and said to Him, Rabboni, that is to say, Master.

Jesus said to her, Touch Me not; for I am not yet ascended to My Father: but go to My brethren, and say to them, I ascend to My Father and to your Father, and to My God and your God.

[*Maria autem stabat ad monumentum foris, plorans: Dum ergo fleret, inclinavit se, et prospexit in monumentum;*

Et vidit duos Angelos in albis, sedentes, unum ad caput, et unum ad pedes, ubi positum fuerat corpus Jesu.

Dicunt ei illi, Mulier, quid ploras? Dicit eis, Quia tulerunt Dominum meum, et nescio ubi posuerunt Eum.

Hæc cum dixisset, conversa est retrorsum, et vidit Jesum stantem, et non sciebat quia Jesus est.

Dicit ei Jesus, Mulier, quid ploras? quem quæris? Illa existimans quia hortulanus esset, dicit ei, Domine, si tu sustulisti Eum, dicito mihi ubi posuisti Eum, et ego Eum tollam.

Dicit ei Jesus, Maria. Conversa illa, dicit Ei, Rabboni, quod dicitur Magister.

Dicit ei Jesus, Noli Me tangere, nondum enim ascendi ad Patrem Meum : vade autem ad fratres Meos, et dic eis, Ascendo ad Patrem Meum, et Patrem vestrum, Deum Meum, et Deum vestrum. Latin Vulg.]

[*But Mary stood without at the sepulchre weeping; and as she wept she stooped down and looked into the sepulchre,*

And seeth two Angels in white, sitting, the one at the head, and the other at the feet, where the body of Jesus had lain.

And they say unto her, Woman, why weepest thou? She saith unto them, Because they have taken away my Lord, and I know not where they have laid Him.

And when she had thus said, she turned herself back, and saw Jesus standing, and knew not that it was Jesus.

Jesus saith unto her, Woman, why weepest thou? whom seekest thou? She, supposing Him to be the gardener, saith unto Him, Sir, if thou have borne Him hence, tell me where thou hast laid Him, and I will take Him away.

Jesus saith unto her, Mary. She turned herself, and saith unto Him, Rabboni, which is to say, Master.

Jesus saith unto her, Touch Me not; for I am not yet ascended to My Father: but go to My brethren, and say unto them, I ascend unto My Father and your Father, and to My God and your God. Engl. Trans.]

This last verse was not touched.

SERM. XIV.

IT is Easter-day abroad, and it is so in the text. We keep Solomon's rule, *Verbum diei in die suo.* For all this I have
1 Kings 8. 59. read, is nothing else but a report of Christ's rising, and of His appearing this Easter-day morning, His very first appearing of all. St. Mark is express for it, that Christ was
Mark 16. 9. no sooner risen this day but "He appeared first of all to Mary Magdalene;" which first appearing of His is here by St. John extended, and set down at large.

The sum of it is, 1. The seeking Christ dead; 2. The finding Him alive.

The manner of it is, That Mary Magdalene staying still by the sepulchre, first she saw a vision of Angels; and after, she saw Christ Himself. Saw Him, and was herself made an Angel by Him, a good Angel to carry the Evangel, the first good and joyful tidings of his rising again from the dead. And this was a great honour, all considered, to serve in an Angel's place. To do that at His resurrection, His second birth, that at His first birth an Angel did. An Angel first published that, Mary Magdalene brought first notice of this. As he to the shepherds, so she to the Apostles, the Pastors of Christ's flock, by them to be spread abroad to the ends of the world. Acts 13. 33.

To look a little into it. 1. Mary is the name of a woman; 2. Mary Magdalene of a sinful woman.

That to a woman first—it agreeth well to make even with Eve; that as by a woman came the first news of death, so by a woman also might come the first notice of the Resurrection from the dead. And the place fits well, for in a garden they came both. [Conf. S. Greg. in Evang. lib. 2. Hom. 25.6 ad fin.]

That to a sinful woman first—that also agrees well. To her first that most needed it; most needed it, and so first sought it. And it agrees well, He be first found of her that first sought Him; even in that respect she was to be respected.

In which two there is opened unto us "a gate of hope," two great leaves, as it were; one, that no infirmity of sex—for a woman we see; the other, that no enormity of sin—for a sinful woman, one that had the blemish that she went under the common name of *peccatrix*, as notorious and famous in that kind; that neither of these shall debar any to have their part in Christ and in His resurrection; any, that shall seek Him in such sort as she did. For either of these *non obstante*, nay notwithstanding both these, she had the happiness to see His Angels—and that was no small favour; to see Christ Himself, and that first of all, before all others to see and salute Him; and to receive a commission from Him of *vade et dic*, to "go and tell," that is as it were to be an Apostle, and that to the Apostles themselves, to bring them the first good news of Christ's rising again. Hos. 2. 15. Lu. 7. 37. [Vid. S. Greg. ubi sup. s. 10.]

There are three parties that take up the whole text, and if I should divide it, I would make those three parties the three parts; I. Mary Magdalene, II. the Angels, III. and Christ our Saviour.

I. Mary Magdalene begins her part in the first verse, but she goes along through them all.

SERM. XIV. II. Then the Angels' part in the two verses next. 1. Their appearing, 2. and their speech to her; appearing in the twelfth, speech in the thirteenth.

III. And last, Christ's part in all the rest. 1. His appearing, 2. and speech likewise. Appearing first, unknown, in the fourteenth, and His speech then in the fifteenth.

After, His appearing and speech again, being known, in the sixteenth and seventeenth. 1. Forbidding her, *mane et tange*, to stay and to touch; 2. and bidding her, *vade et dic*, to get her quickly to His brethren, and tell them His resurrection was past, for *ascendo*, He was taking thought for His Ascension, and preparing for that. Thus lieth the order and the parts.

The use will be, that we in our seeking carry ourselves as she did;—and so may we have the happiness that she had to find Christ, as He is now to be found in the virtue of His resurrection!

Ver. 11. "But Mary stood by the Sepulchre weeping, and as she wept she stooped, and looked into the Sepulchre."

Of the favours vouchsafed this same *felix peccatrix*, as the Fathers term her, this day; 1. To see but Christ's Angels, 2. To see Christ at all, 3. To see Him first of all, 4. But more than all these, to be employed by Him in so heavenly an errand, reason we can render none that helped her to

Lu. 7. 47. these, but that which in a place Christ himself renders, *Quia dilexit multum*, "because she loved much."

"She loved much;" we cannot say, She believed much; for by her *sustulerunt* thrice repeated, the second, thirteenth, fifteenth verses, it seems she believed no more than just as much as the High Priests would have had the world believe, that "He was taken away by night."

[Vid. Origen. Hom. de Mar. Mag.] *Defectus fidei non est negandus, affectus amoris non est vituperandus*:—it is Origen; 'We cannot commend her faith, her love we cannot but commend,' and so do—commend it in her, commend it to you. Much it was, and much good proof gave she of it. Before, to Him living; now, to Him dead. To Him dead, there are divers; 1. She was last at His cross, and first at His grave; 2. Stayed longest there, was soonest here; 3. Could not rest till she were up to seek

Mat. 28. 1. Him; 4. Sought Him while it was yet dark, before she had light to seek Him by.

But to take her as we find her in the text, and to look no
whither else. There are in the text no less than ten, all
arguments of her great love; all as it were a commentary
upon *dilexit multum.* And even in this first verse there are
five of them.

The first in these words, *stabat juxta monumentum,* that 1.
"she stood by the grave," a place where faint love loves
not to stand. Bring Him to the grave, and lay Him in the
grave, and there leave Him; but come no more at it, nor
stand not long by it. Stand by Him while He is alive—so
did many; stand, and go, and sit by Him. But *stans juxta
monumentum,* stand by Him dead; Mary Magdalene, she did
it, and she only did it, and none but she. *Amor stans juxta
monumentum.*

The next in these, *Maria autem stabat,* "But Mary 2.
stood." In the *autem,* the "but"—that helps us to another.
"But Mary stood," that is as much to say as, Others did
not, "but" she did. Peter and John were there but even Joh. 20. 8.
now. Thither they came, but not finding Him, away they
went. They went, but Mary went not, she stood still. Their
going away commends her staying behind. To the grave
she came before them, from the grave she went to tell them,
to the grave she returns with them, at the grave she stays
behind them. *Fortior eam figebat affectus,* saith Augustine, [S. Aug. Tract. in
'a stronger affection fixed her;' so fixed her that she had Joan. 121.
not the power to remove thence. Go who would, she would init.]
not, but stay still. To stay, while others do so, while company stays, that is the world's love; but Peter is gone, and
John too; all are gone, and we left alone; then to stay is
love, and constant love. *Amor manens aliis recedentibus,*
'love that when others shrink and give over, holds out still.'

The third in these, "she stood, and she wept;" and not a 3.
tear or two, but she wept a good as we say, that the Angels,
that Christ Himself pity her, and both of them the first
thing they do, they ask her why she wept so. Both of them
begin with that question. And in this is love. For if, when
Christ stood at Lazarus' grave's side and wept, the Jews
said, "See, how He loved him!" may not we say the very [John 11.
same, when Mary stood at Christ's grave and wept, See, how 36.]
she loved Him! Whose presence she wished for, His miss

SERM. XIV. she wept for; Whom she dearly loved while she had Him, she bitterly bewailed when she lost Him. *Amor amare flens*, 'love running down the cheeks.'

4. The fourth in these, "And as she wept, she stooped, and looked in" ever and anon. That is, she did so weep as she did seek withal. Weeping without seeking, is but to small purpose. But her weeping hindered not her seeking, her sorrow dulled not her diligence. And diligence is a character of love, comes from the same root, *dilectio* and *diligentia* from *diligo*, both. *Amor diligentiam diligens.*

5. To seek, is one thing; not to give over seeking, is another. For I ask, why should she now look in? Peter and John had looked there before, nay, had been in the grave, they. It makes no matter; she will not trust Peter's eyes, nor
Joh. 20. 8. John's neither. But she herself had before this, looked in too. No force, she will not trust herself, she will not suspect her own eyes, she will rather think she looked not well before, than leave off her looking. It is not enough for love to look in once. [S. Greg. ubi supra, s. 2.] Thus we use, this is our manner when we seek a thing seriously; where we have sought already, there to seek again, thinking we did it not well, but if we now look again better, we shall surely find it then. [S. Aug. ubi sup.] *Amor quærens ubi quæsivit*, love that never thinks it hath looked enough. These five.

And, by these five we may take measure of our love, and of the true *multum* of it. *Ut prosit nobis ejus stare, ejus plorare et quærere*, saith Origen, [Origen. ubi supra, init.] 'that her standing, her weeping, and seeking, we may take some good by them.'

I doubt ours will fall short. Stay by Him alive, that we can, *juxta mensam*; but *juxta monumentum*, who takes up His standing there? And our love it is dry-eyed, it cannot weep; it is stiff-jointed, it cannot stoop to seek. If it do, and we hit not on Him at first, away we go with Peter and John; we stay it not out with Mary Magdalene. A sign our love is little and light, and our seeking suitable, and so it is without success. We find not Christ—no marvel; but seek Him as she sought Him, and we shall speed as she sped.

Ver. 16. "And saw two Angels in white, sitting, the one at the head, the other at the feet, where the body of Jesus had lain."

For what came of this? Thus staying by it, and thus looking in, again and again, though she saw not Christ at first, she sees His Angels. For so it pleased Christ to come by degrees, His Angels before Him. And it is no vulgar honour this, to see but an Angel; what would one of us give to see but the like sight?

We are now at the Angels' part, their appearing in this verse. There are four points in it: 1. Their place; 2. Their habit; 3. Their site; 4. and their order. 1. Place, in the grave; 2. Habit, in white; 3. site—they were sitting; 4. and their order in sitting, one at the head, the other at the feet.

The place. In the grave she saw them; and Angels in 1.
a grave, is a strange sight, a sight never seen before; not
till Christ's body had been there, never till this day; this
the first news of Angels in that place. For a grave is no
place for Angels, one would think; for worms rather:
blessed Angels, not but in a blessed place. But since Christ
lay there, that place is blessed. There was a voice heard
from Heaven, "Blessed be the dead:" "Precious the Rev. 14. 13.
death," "Glorious the memory" now, "of them that die in Ps. 116. 15.
the Lord." And even this, that the Angels disdained not
now to come thither, and to sit there, is an *auspicium* of
a great change to ensue in the state of that place. *Quid
gloriosius Angelo? quid vilius vermiculo?* saith Augustine.
Quid fuit vermiculorum locus, est et Angelorum. 'That which
was the place for worms, is become a place for Angels.'

Their habit. "In white." So were there divers of them, 2.
divers times this day, seen, "in white" all; in that colour.
It seems to be their Easter-day colour, for at this feast they
all do their service in it. Their Easter-day colour, for it is
the colour of the Resurrection. The state whereof when
Christ would represent upon the Mount, "His raiment was Mark 9. 3.
all white, no fuller in the earth could come near it." And
our colour it shall be, when rising again we "shall walk [Rev. 3. 4.] Rev. 7. 9.
in white robes," and "follow the Lamb whithersoever He [Rev. 14. 4.]
goeth."

Heaven mourned on Good-Friday, the eclipse made all
then in black. Easter-day it rejoiceth, Heaven and Angels,
all in white. Solomon tells us, it is the colour of joy. And Eccles. 9. 8.

SERM. XIV. that is the state of joy, and this the day of the first joyful tidings of it, with joy ever celebrated, even *in albis*, eight days together, by them that found Christ.

3. "In white," and "sitting." As the colour of joy, so the situation of rest. So we say, Sit down, and rest. And so is the grave made, by this morning's work, a place of rest. Rest, not from our labours only—so do the beasts rest when they die; but as it is in the sixteenth Psalm, a Psalm of the
Ps. 16. 9. Resurrection, a "rest in hope"—"hope" of rising again, the members in the virtue of their Head Who this day is
Heb. 4. 9. risen. So to enter into the "rest," which yet "remaineth for the people of God," even the Sabbath eternal.

4. "Sitting," and in this order "sitting;" "at the head one, at the feet another, where His body had lain."

1. Which order may well refer to Christ Himself, Whose
Col. 2. 9. body was the true ark indeed, "in which it pleased the Godhead to dwell bodily;" and is therefore here between
Ex. 25. 22. two Angels, as was the ark, the type of it, "between the two cherubims."

Mat. 26. 7. 2. May also refer to Mary Magdalene. She had anointed
Joh. 12. 3. His head, she had anointed His feet: at these two places sit the two angels, as it were to acknowledge so much for her sake.

3. In mystery, they refer it thus. Because *caput Christi*
1 Cor. 11. 3. *Deus*, "the Godhead is the head of Christ," and His feet which the serpent did bruise, His manhood; that either of
Gen. 3. 15. these hath his Angel. That to Christ man no less than to
[S. Greg. ubi supra, s. 3.] Christ God, the Angels do now their service. *In principio*
[Joh. 1. 1. 14.] *erat Verbum*, His Godhead; there, an Angel. *Verbum caro*
Heb. 1. 6. *factum*, his manhood; there, another. "And let all the Angels of God worship Him" in both. Even in His man-
Lu. 2. 13. hood, at His cradle, the head of it, a choir of Angels; at His grave, the feet of it, Angels likewise.

4. And lastly, for our comfort thus. That henceforth
Rev. 20. 6. even such shall our graves be, if we be so happy as to "have our parts in the first resurrection," which is of the soul from sin. We shall go to our graves in white, in the comfort and colour of hope, lie between two Angels there; they guard our bodies dead, and present them alive again at the Resurrection.

1. Yet before we leave them, to learn somewhat of the Angels; specially, of "the Angel that sat at the feet." That between them there was no striving for places. He that "sat at the feet," as well content with his place as he that "at the head." We to be so by their example. For with us, both the Angels would have been "at the head," never an one "at the feet;" with us none would be at the feet by his good will, head-Angels all.

2. Again, from them both. That inasmuch as the head ever stands for the beginning, and the feet for the end, that we be careful that our beginnings only be not glorious—O an Angel at the head in any wise—but that we look to the feet, there be another there too. *Ne turpiter atrum desinat*, 'that it end not in a black Angel,' that began in a white. And this for the Angels' appearing. [Hor. Ars Poet. init.]

Ver. 13. "And they said to her, Woman, why weepest thou? She said to them, They have taken away my Lord, and I know not where they have laid Him."

Their question.

Now to their speech. It was not a dumb show this, a bare apparition, and so vanished away. It was *visio et vox*, 'a vocal vision.' Here is a dialogue too, the Angels speak to her.

And they ask her, *Quid ploras?* Why she wept, what cause she had to weep. They mean she had none, as indeed no more she had. All was in error, *piæ lachrymæ sed cæcæ*, 'tears of grief but false grief,' imagining that to be that was not, Him to be dead that was alive. She weeps, because she found the grave empty, which God forbid she should have found full, for then Christ must have been dead still, and so no Resurrection. Gregory. [Lib. 2. Hom. 25. init.]

And this case of Mary Magdalene's is our case oftentimes. In the error of our conceit to weep, where we have no cause; to joy, where we have as little. Where we should, where we have cause to joy, we weep; and where to weep, we joy. Our *ploras* hath never a *quid*. False joys and false sorrows, false hopes and false fears this life of ours is full of—God help us!

Now because she erred, they ask her the cause, that she alleging it they may take it away, and shew it to be no cause. As the elench, *a non causâ pro causâ*, makes foul rule among us, beguiles us all our life long.

SERM. XIV.

Her answer. Will ye hear her answer to "Why weep you?" why? *sustulerunt,* that was the cause, her Lord was gone, was "taken away."

1. And a good cause it had been, if it had been true. Any have cause to grieve that have lost, lost a good Lord, so good and gracious a Lord as He had been to her.

But that is not all; a worse matter, a greater grief than
2. that. When one dieth, we reckon him taken away; that is one kind of taking away. But his dead body is left, so all is not taken from us; that was not her case. For in saying, "her Lord," she means not her Lord alive—that is not it; she means not they had slain Him, they had taken away His life—she had wept her fill for that already. But "her Lord," that is, His dead body. For though His life was gone, yet His body was left. And that was all she now had left of Him that she calls her Lord, and that "they had taken away" from her too. A poor one it was, yet some comfort it was to her, to have even that left her to visit, to anoint, to do other offices of love, even to that. *Etiam viso cadavere recalescit amor,* at the sight even of that will love revive, it will fetch life of love again. But now here is her case; that is gone and all, and nothing but an empty grave now left to stand by. That St. Augustine saith well, *sublatus de monumento* grieved her more than *occisus in ligno,* for then something yet was left; now nothing at all. Right *sustulerunt,* taken away quite and clean.

[S. Aug. Tract. in Joann. 121. 1.] Ambros. [Origen. ubi sup.] [S. Aug. ubi supra init.]

3. And thirdly, her *nescio ubi.* For though He be taken away, it is some comfort yet, if we know where to fetch Him again. But here, He is gone without all hope of recovery or getting again. For "they"—but she knew not who, "had carried Him," she knew not whither; "laid Him," she knew not where; there to do to Him, she knew not what. So that now she knew not whither to go, to find any comfort. It was *nescio ubi* with her right. Put all these together, His life taken away, His body taken away, and carried no man knows whither; and do they ask why she wept? or can any blame her for it?

[S. Aug. ubi supra ad fin.]

Her error. The truth is, none had "taken away her Lord" for all this; for all this while her Lord was well, was as she would have had Him, alive and safe. He went away of Himself, none carried Him thence. What of that? *Non credens suscitatum, credidit sublatum,* 'for want of belief He was risen, she believed He was carried away.' She erred in so believing; there was error in her love, but there was love in her error too.

And, give me leave to lay out three more arguments of her love, out of this verse, to make up eight, towards the making up of her *multum.* Yet her love.

1. The very title she gives Him, of *Dominum meum,* is one; "My Lord," that she gives Him that term. For it shews her love and respect was no whit abated by the scandal of His death. It was a most opprobrious, ignominious, shameful death He suffered; such, as in the eyes of the world any would have been ashamed to own Him, or say of Him, *Meum;* but any would have been afraid to honour Him with that title, to style Him *Dominum.* She was neither. *Meum,* for hers; *Dominum meum,* for her Lord she acknowledgeth Him, is neither ashamed nor afraid to continue that title still. *Amor scandalo non scandalizatus.*

2. Another, which I take to be far beyond this, That she having looked into the grave a little before, and seen never an Angel there, and of a sudden looking in now and seeing two, a sight able to have amazed any, any but her, it moves not her at all. The suddenness, the strangeness, the gloriousness of the sight, yea, even of Angels, move her not at all. She seems to have no sense of it, and so to be in a kind of ecstacy all the while. *Domine, propter Te est extra se,* saith Bernard. *Amor extasin patiens.*

3. And thirdly, as that strange sight affected her not a whit, so neither did their comfortable speech work with her at all. Comfortable I call it, for they that ask the cause why, "why weep you?" shew they would remove it if it lay in them. Neither of these did or could move her, or make her once leave her weeping—she wept on still: Christ will ask her, *quid ploras?* by and by again. If she find an Angel, if she find not her Lord, it will not serve. She had rather find His dead body, than them in all their glory. No man in earth, no Angel in Heaven can comfort her; none but He that is taken away, Christ, and none but Christ; and till she find Him again, her soul refuseth all manner of comfort, yea

SERM. XIV. even from Heaven, even from the Angels themselves; these three. *Amor super amissum renuens consolari.*

Thus she, in her love, for her supposed loss or taking away. And what shall become of us in ours then? That lose Him 1. not once, but oft; 2. and not in suppose as she did, but in very deed; 3. and that by sin, the worst loss of all; 4. and that not by any other's taking away, but by our own act and wilful default; and are not grieved, nay not moved a whit, break none of our wonted sports for it, as if we reckoned Him as good lost as found. Yea, when Christ and the Holy Ghost, and the favour of God, and all is gone, how soon, how easily are we comforted again for all this! that none shall need to say, *quid ploras?* to us rather, *quid non ploras?* ask us why we weep not, having so good cause to do it as we then have? This for the Angels' part.

Ver. 14. "When she had thus said, she turned herself about, and saw Jesus standing, and knew not that it was Jesus."

Always the Angels, we see, touched the right string, and she tells them the wrong cause, but yet the right, if it had been right.

Now to this answer of hers they would have replied, and taken away her error touching her Lord's taking away; that if she knew all, she would have left her seeking, and set her down by them, and left her weeping, and been in white as well as they.

But here is a *supersedeas* to them, the Lord himself comes in place. Now come we from the seeking Him dead, to the finding Him alive. For when He saw no Angels, no sight, no speech of theirs would serve, none but her Lord could give her any comfort, her Lord comes. *Christus adest.*

Adest Christus, nec ab eis unquam abest a quibus quæritur, saith Augustine; 'Christ is found, found by her; and this case of hers shall be the case of all that seriously seek Him.' This woman here for one, she sought Him we see. They that went to Emmaus to-day, they but talked of Him sadly,
Isa. 65. 1. and they both found Him. Why, He is found of them that seek Him not; but of them that seek Him, never but found.
Ps. 9. 10. "For Thou, Lord, never failest them that seek Thee."

"God is not unrighteous, to forget the work and labour of Heb. 6. 10.
their love that seek Him."

So find Him they shall, but happily not all so fully at first, no more than she did. For first, to try her yet a little farther, He comes unknown, stands by her, and she little thought it had been He.

A case that likewise falls out full oft. Doubtless, "He is
not far from every one of us," saith the Apostle to the Athe- Acts 17. 27.
nians. But He is nearer us many times than we think;
even hard by us and we not aware of it, saith Job. And Job 9. 11.
O si cognovisses et tu, O if we did know, and it standeth us Lu. 19. 42.
in hand to pray that we may know when He is so, for that
is "the time of our visitation." Lu. 19. 44.

St. John saith here, the Angels were sitting; St. Luke
saith, they stood. They are thus reconciled. That Christ Lu. 24. 4.
coming in presence, the Angels which before were sitting stood up. Their standing up made Mary Magdalene turn her to see who it was they rose to. And so Christ she saw, but knew Him not.

Not only not knew Him, but mis-knew Him, took Him for the gardener. Tears will dim the sight, and it was not yet scarce day, and she seeing one, and not knowing what any one should make in the ground so early but he that
dressed it, she might well mistake. But it was more than Lu. 24. 16.
so; her eyes were not holden only that she did not know
Him, but over and beside He did appear ἑτέρᾳ μορφῇ, in Mark 16. 12.
some such shape as might resemble the gardener whom she took Him for.

Proper enough it was, it fitted well the time and place, this person. The time, it was the spring; the place, it was the garden: that place is most in request at that time, for that place and time a gardener doth well.

Of which her so taking Him, St. Gregory saith well, *pro-* [S. Greg. in Evang. lib. 2. Hom. 25. 4. ad fin.]
fecto errando non erravit. She did not mistake in taking Him for a gardener; though she might seem to err in some sense, yet in some other she was in the right. For in a sense, and a good sense, Christ may well be said to be a gardener, and indeed is one. For our rule is, Christ as He appears, so He is ever; no false semblant in Him.

1. A gardener He is then. The first, the fairest garden

SERM. XIV. that ever was, Paradise, He was the gardener, it was of His planting. So, a gardener.

2. And ever since it is He That as God makes all our gardens green, sends us yearly the spring, and all the herbs
[1 Cor. 3. 6.] and flowers we then gather; and neither Paul with his planting, nor Apollos with his watering, could do any good without Him. So a gardener in that sense.

3. But not in that alone; but He it is that gardens our "souls" too, and makes them, as the Prophet saith,
Jer. 31. 12. "like a well-watered garden;" weeds out of them whatsoever is noisome or unsavory, sows and plants them with true roots and seeds of righteousness, waters them with the dew of His grace, and makes them bring forth fruit to eternal life.

But it is none of all these, but besides all these, nay over and above all these, this day if ever, most properly He was a gardener. Was one, and so after a more peculiar manner might take this likeness on Him. Christ rising was indeed a gardener, and that a strange one, Who made such an herb grow out of the ground this day as the like was never seen before, a dead body to shoot forth alive out of the grave.

I ask, was He so this day alone? No, but this profession of His, this day begun, He will follow to the end. For He it is That by virtue of this morning's act shall garden our bodies too, turn all our graves into garden plots; yea, shall one day turn land and sea and all into a great garden, and so husband them as they shall in due time bring forth live bodies, even all our bodies alive again.

Long before, did Esay see this and sing of it in his song,
Isa. 26. 19. resembling the resurrection to a spring garden. "Awake and sing," saith he; "ye that dwell for a time are as it were sown in the dust, for His dew shall be as the dew of herbs, and the earth shall shoot forth her dead." So then, He appeared no other than He was; a gardener He was, not in show alone, but *opere et veritate*, and so came in His own likeness. This for Christ's appearing. Now to His speech, but as unknown still.

Ver. 15. "Jesus saith to her, Woman, why weepest thou? whom seekest thou?" She, supposing He had been the gardener, said to Him, "Sir, if thou have borne Him hence, tell me where thou hast laid Him, and I will take Him thence."

Still she weeps; so He begins with *Quid ploras?* asks the same question the Angels had before; only quickens it a little with *quem quæris,* "whom seek you?" So, *Quem quæris quærit a te, Quem quæris?* Whom she sought, He asks her "Whom she sought." *Si quæris, cur non cognoscis? si cognoscis, cur quæris?* saith Augustine. If she seek Him, why knows she Him not? If she know Him, why seeks she Him still? A common thing with us, this also; to seek a thing, and when we have found it, not to know we have so, but even *Christum a Christo quærere,* 'to ask Christ for Christ.' Which however it fall in other matters, in this seeking of Christ it is safe. Even when we seek Christ, to pray to Christ to help us to find Christ; we shall do it full evil without Him.

Christ's question unknown.

[Origen. ubi sup.]

This *quid ploras?* it comes now twice. The Angels asked it, we stood not on it then. Now, seeing Christ asks it again the second time, we will think there is something in it, and stay a little at it. The rather, for that it is the very opening of His mouth, the very first words that ever came from Him, that He spake first of all, after His rising again from death. There is sure some more than ordinary matter in this *quid ploras?* if it be but even for that.

Thus say the Fathers; 1. That Mary Magdalene standing by the grave's side, and there weeping, is thus brought in to represent unto us the state of all mankind before this day, the day of Christ's rising again, weeping over the dead, as do the heathen "that have no hope;" comes Christ with His *quid ploras,* "Why do you weep?" As much to say, as *ne ploras;* "Weep not, why should you weep?" there is no cause of weeping now. Henceforth none shall need to stand by the grave to weep there any more. A question very proper for Easter-day, for the day of the Resurrection. For if there be a rising again, *quid ploras* is right, why should she, why should any weep then?

1 Thes. 4. 13.

So that this *quid ploras* of Christ's wipes away tears from all eyes, and as we sing in the thirtieth Psalm, whose title is, the Psalm of the Resurrection, puts off our "sackcloth," [Ps. 30. 11.]

SERM. XIV. that is our mourning weeds, girds us "with gladness," puts us all in white with the Angels.

Ploras then, leave that for Good-Friday, for His Passion; weep then, and spare not. But *quid ploras?* for Easter-day is in kind the feast of the Resurrection, why should there be any weeping upon it? Is not Christ risen? Shall not He raise us with Him? Is He not a gardener, to make our bodies sown to grow again? *Ploras,* leave that to the heathen that are without hope; but to the Christian man, *quid ploras?* Why should he weep? he hath hopes; the Head is already risen, the members shall in their due time follow Him.

I observe that four times this day, at four several appearings, 1. at the first, at this here, He asked her, *quid*
Lu. 24. 17. *ploras?* why she wept. 2. Of them that went to Emmaus, *quid tristes estis?* "Why are ye sad?" 3. Within a verse
[Luke 24. 36.] following, the nineteenth, He saith to the Eleven, *Pax vobis,* "Peace be to them:" 4. And to the women that met
Mat. 28. 9. Him on the way, *χαίρετε*, that is, "rejoice, be glad." So, no weeping, no being sad; now, nothing this day, but peace and joy; they do properly belong to this feast.

And this I note the more willingly now this year, because the last Easter we could not so well have noted it. Some wept then; all were sad, little joy there was, and there was a *quid*, a good cause for it. But blessed be God That hath now sent us a more kindly Easter, of this, by taking away the cause of our sorrow then, that we may preach of *quid ploras?* and be far from it. So much for *quid ploras?* Christ's question. Now to her answer.

[The Queen's death is probably meant.]

Her answer. She is still where she was; at *sustulerunt* before, at *sustulisti* now—*si tu sustulisti:* we shall never get that word from her.

But to Christ she seems somewhat more harsh than to the Angels. To them she complains of others; "they have taken." Christ she seems to charge, at least to suspect of the fact, as if He looked like one that had been a breaker up of graves, a carrier away of corpses out of their place of rest. Her *if* implies as much. But pardon love; as it fears where it needs not, so it suspects oft where it hath no cause. He, or any that comes in our way, hath done it, hath taken Him away, when love is at a loss. But Bernard speaks to Christ for her; *Domine, amor quem habebat in Te, et dolor quem* [Origen. ubi supra, ad fin.] *habebat de Te, excuset eam apud Te, si forte erravit circa Te:* that 'the love she bare to Him, the sorrow she had for Him, may excuse her with Him, if she were in any error concerning Him in her saying,' *Si tu sustulisti.*

And yet see how God shall direct the tongue! In thus charging Him, *prophetat et nescit,* 'she says truer than she was aware.' For indeed, if any took Him away, it was He did it. So she was not much amiss. Her *si tu* was true, though not in her sense. For, *quod de Ipso factum est, Ipse fecit,* 'All that was done to Him, He did it Himself.' His taking away, *virtus fuit, non facinus,* 'was by His own power, Chrysologus. not by the act of any other;' *et gloria, non injuria,* 'no other man's injury it was, but His own glory,' that she found Him not there. This was true, but this was no part of her meaning.

I cannot here pass over two more characters of her love, that so you may have the full ten I promised.

One, in *si tu sustulisti Eum,* in her *Eum,* in her "Him." 1.
Him? Which Him? Her affections seem so to transport [N. Clar. Vall. ad calc. S. Bern. in Fest. B. M. Magd. ad fin.] her, as she says no man knows what. To one, a mere stranger to her, and she to him, she talks of one thrice under the term of "Him;" "if thou hast taken Him away, tell me where thou hast laid Him, and I will fetch Him;" Him, Him, and Him, and never names Him, or tells who He is. This is *solœcismus amoris,* an irregular speech, but love's own dialect. "Him" is enough with love: who knows not who that is? It supposes every body, all the world bound to take notice of him whom we look for, only by saying "Him," though we never tell his name, nor say a word more. *Amor, quem ipse cogitat, neminem putans ignorare.*

The other is in her *ego tollam:* if he would tell her where 2.
he had laid Him, she would go fetch Him, that she would. Alas, poor woman, she was not able to lift Him. There are more than one, or two either, allowed to the carrying of a corpse.

As for His, it had more than a hundred pound weight of Joh. 19. 39.
myrrh and other odours upon it, beside the poise of a dead [N. Clar. Vall. ap. S. Bern. ubi supra.] body. She could not do it. Well, yet she would do it

SERM. XIV. though. *O mulier, non mulier,* saith Origen, for *ego tollam* seems rather the speech of a porter, or of some lusty strong fellow at least, than of a silly weak woman. But love makes women more than women, at least it makes them have νοῦν ὑπὲρ ἰσχὺν, 'the courage above the strength,' far. Never measures her own forces, no burden too heavy, no assay too hard for love, *et nihil erubescit nisi nomen difficultatis,* 'and is not ashamed of any thing but that any thing should be too hard or too heavy for it.' *Affectus sine mensurâ virium propriarum.* Both these argue *dilexit multum.* And so now, you have the full number of ten.

[Origen. ubi sup.]

Christ's second speech.

Ver. 16. "Jesus saith to her, Mary; she turned herself, and said to Him, Rabboni, that is to say, Master."

Now *magnes amoris amor;* 'nothing so allures, so draws love to it, as doth love itself.' In Christ specially, and in such in whom the same mind is. For when her Lord saw there was no taking away His taking away from her, all was in vain, neither men, nor Angels, nor Himself, so long as He kept Himself gardener, could get any thing of her but her Lord was gone, He was taken away, and that for the want of Jesus nothing but Jesus could yield her any comfort, He is no longer able to contain, but even discloses Himself; and discloses Himself by His voice.

For it should seem before, with His shape He had changed that also. But now He speaks to her in His known voice, in the wonted accent of it, does but name her name, Mary—no more, and that was enough. That was as much to say, *Recognosce a Quo recognosceris,* 'she would at least take notice of Him That shewed He was no stranger by calling her by her name;' for whom we call by their names, we take particular notice of. So God says to Moses, *Te autem cognovi de nomine,* "thou hast found grace in My sight, and I know thee by name." As God Moses, so Christ Mary Magdalene.

[S. Greg. in Evang. lib. 2. Hom. 25. 5.]

Exod. 33. 17.

And this indeed is the right way to know Christ, to be known of Him first. The Apostle saith, now we "have known God," and then correcteth himself, "or rather have been known of God." For till He know us, we shall never know Him aright.

Gal. 4. 9.

And now, lo Christ is found; found alive, That was sought dead. A cloud may be so thick we shall not see the sun

through it. The sun must scatter that cloud, and then we may. Here is an example of it. It is strange a thick cloud of heaviness had so covered her, as see Him she could not through it; this one word, these two syllables, Mary, from His mouth, scatters it all. No sooner had His voice sounded in her ears but it drives away all the mist, dries up her tears, lightens her eyes, that she knew Him straight, and answers Him with her wonted salutation, "Rabboni." If it had lain Her answer.
in her power to have raised Him from the dead, she would not have failed but done it, I dare say. Now it is done to her hands.

And with this all is turned out and in; a new world now. Away with *sustulerunt;* His taking away is taken away quite. For if His taking away were her sorrow, *contrario-* Augustine.
rum contraria consequentia. Si de sublato ploravit, de suscitato exultavit, we may be sure; 'if sad for His death, for His taking away, then glad for His rising, for His restoring again.' Surely if she would have been glad but to have found but His dead body, now she finds it and Him alive, what was her joy, how great may we think! So that by this she saw *Quid ploras* was not asked her for nought, that it was no impertinent question, as it fell out. Well now, He That was thought lost is found again, and found, not as He was sought for, not a dead body, but "a living soul;" nay, "a quickening Spirit" then. And that might Mary 1 Cor. 15. 45.
Magdalene well say. He shewed it, for He quickened her, and her spirits that were as good as dead. You thought you should have come to Christ's resurrection to-day, and so you do. But not to His alone, but even to Mary Magdalene's resurrection too. For in very deed a kind of resurrection it was was wrought in her; revived as it were, and raised from a dead and drooping, to a lively and cheerful estate. The gardener had done His part, made her all green on the sudden.

And all this by a word of His mouth. Such power is there in every word of His; so easily are they called, whom Christ will but speak to.

But by this we see, when He would be made known to her after His rising, He did choose to be made known by the ear rather than by the eye. By hearing rather than by

SERM. XIV. appearing. Opens her ears first, and her eyes after. Her
Lu. 24. 16. "eyes were holden" till her ears were opened; comes *aures*
Ps. 40. 6. *autem aperuisti mihi,* and that opens them.

With the philosophers, hearing is the sense of wisdom. With us, in divinity, it is the sense of faith. So, most meet. Christ is the Word; hearing then, that sense, is Christ's
Ps. 48. 8. sense; *voce quam visu,* more proper to the word. So, *sicut audivimus* goes before, and then *sic vidimus* comes after. In matters of faith the ear goes first ever, and is of more use, and to be trusted before the eye. For in many cases faith holdeth, where sight faileth.

This then is a good way to come to the knowledge of
Ps. 95. 7. Christ, by *hodie si vocem,* to "hear His voice." Howbeit, it is not the only way. There is another way to take notice of Him by besides, and we to take notice of it. On this very day we have them both.

For twice this day came Christ; unknown first, and then known after. To Mary Magdalene here, and to them at Emmaus. To Mary Magdalene unknown, in the shape of a gardener. To those that went to Emmaus unknown, in the likeness of a traveller by the way-side. Comes to be known to her by His voice, by the word of His mouth. Not so to them. For many words He spake to them, and they
Lu. 24. 32. 35. felt them warm at their hearts, but knew Him not for all that. But "He was known to them in the breaking of the bread." Her eyes opened by speaking a word; their eyes opened by the breaking of bread. There is the one and the other way, and so now you have both. And now you have them, I pray you make use of them. I see I shall not be able to go farther than this verse.

It were a folly to fall to comparisons, *committere inter se,* to set them at odds together these two ways, as the fond fashion now-a-days is, whether is better, Prayer or Preaching; the Word or the Sacraments. What needs this? Seeing we have both, both are ready for us; the one now, the other by-and-by; we may end this question soon. And this is the best and surest way to end it; to esteem of them both, to thank Him for both, to make use of both; having now done with one, to make trial of the other. It may be, who knows? if the one will not work, the other may. And if by

the one or by the other, by either if it be wrought, what harm have we? In case it be not, yet have we offered to God our service in both, and committed the success of both to Him. He will see they shall have success, and in His good time, as shall be expedient for us, vouchsafe every one of us as He did Mary Magdalene in the text, "to know Him Phil. 3. 10.
and the virtue of His resurrection;" and make us partakers of both, by both the means before remembered, by His blessed word, by His holy mysteries; the means to raise our souls here, the pledges of the raising up of our bodies hereafter. Of both which He make us partakers, Who is the Author of both, "Jesus Christ the Righteous," &c. [1Joh. 2. 1.]

A SERMON

PREACHED BEFORE

THE KING'S MAJESTY AT WHITEHALL,

ON THE FIRST OF APRIL, A.D. MDCXXI., BEING EASTER-DAY.

JOHN xx. 17.

Jesus saith unto her, Touch Me not.

Dicit ei Jesus, Noli Me tangere.

[*Jesus saith unto her, Touch Me not.* Engl. Trans.]

SERM. XV.

MARY MAGDALENE, because she loved much, and gave divers good proofs of it, had this morning divers favours
Joh. 20. 12. vouchsafed her: to see a vision of Angels; to see Christ
14. 16. Himself; to see Him before any other, first of all. He spake to her, "Mary;" she spake to Him, "Rabboni." Hitherto all was well. Now here, after all this love, after all these favours, even in the neck of them as it were, comes an unkind word or two, a *noli Me tangere*, and mars all; turns all out and in. Make the best of it, a repulse it is; but a cold salutation for an Easter-day morning.

Joh. 20. 15. A little before He asked why she wept. This is enough to set her on weeping afresh. For if she wept for *sustulerunt Dominum*, that others had taken away her Lord; much more now, when her Lord takes away Himself from her, that she may not so much as touch Him.

We observed that this morning Christ came in two shapes, and at either of them spake a speech. At first He came unknown, taken for a gardener; the latter, He spake in His own voice, and became known to her. I know not how, but unknown Christ proves better to her than when He came to be known; better for her, He had kept Himself unknown still, for then unknown He asked her kindly why she wept; as much to say as, Weep not, *noli te angere, noli Me plangere;*—there is some comfort in that. But known, He grows somewhat strange on the sudden, and asks her what she means to come so near Him, or offer to touch Him; which must needs be much to her discomfort, to be forbidden once to come near or touch her Saviour, and to be forbidden by His own mouth.

But there is good use of *noli Me plangere,* and *noli Me tangere,* both. One we have touched already; of the other, now. One would little think it, but they sort well, *Quid ploras?* and *noli Me tangere. Quid ploras?* To rejoice at His rising; *noli Me tangere,* to do it with reverence. They amount to *exultate in tremore.* Ps. 2 11.

The verse of itself falls into two parts. We may divide it, as the Jews do the Law, into Do not, and Do; somewhat forbidden there is, and somewhat bidden. Forbidden—do not, not touch Me; bidden—but do, "go your ways and tell." The forbidding part stands of two points; 1. a restraint, and 2. a reason. I. The restraint in these; *noli Me tangere, &c.* II. The reason in these; *nondum enim, &c.* "for I am not yet ascended," &c. (The division. I. II.)

The bidding part, of three. 1. A mission or commission, to go do a message, *vade et dic.* 2. The parties to whom; "to My brethren," that is, to His Disciples. 3. The message itself, "I ascend to My Father," &c. And this latter is as it were an amends for the former; that the text is like the time of the year—the morning somewhat fresh, but a fair day after. *Noli Me tangere,* the repulse, is the sharp morning; *vade et dic,* the welcome message, the fair day we spake of, that makes all well again.

Either of these will serve for a sermon; the former, *noli Me tangere, &c.* it is so full of difficulties, but withal, of good and needful caution. The latter, of the message, it is so fraught with high mysteries, and beside, with much heavenly comfort. They call it Mary Magdalene's Gospel, for glad tidings it contains; and what is the Gospel else? The first Gospel or glad tidings after Christ's resurrection. The very Gospel of the Gospel itself, and a compendium of all the

SERM. XV. four. Of which, if God will, at some other time. Now I will trouble you no farther but with, "Touch Me not, for I am not yet ascended to the Father."

I. The restraint. *Noli Me tangere.* No sooner had Christ's voice sounded in her ears, but she knew straight—"Rabboni," it was He; and withal, as it may be gathered by this *noli Me, &c.*, she did that which amounted to a *volo Te tangere;* that is, she made toward Him, stretched forth her hand, and offered, would have touched Him, but for this "Touch Me not." "Touch not?" why "not?" What harm had there been if He had suffered her to touch Him? The speech is strange to be spoken either by Him or to her; the reason, the "for," yet more strange; many difficulties in both: God send us well through them! There be but three words, 1. *Noli,* 2. *Me,* and 3. *tangere:* "touch" at which of these three you will—*tangere* the thing; *noli* and *Me,* the two parties; *Me,* Him, Christ; *noli,* her, Mary Magdalene; you will find somewhat strange this speech of His.

1. *Tangere,* the thing forbidden. Mat. 9. 21. *Tangere,* the thing. Not "touch?" Why, it is nothing to touch, and because it is nothing, might have been yielded to. And yet to touch Christ, is not nothing. Many desired, yea strove, to touch Him; there went virtue from Him, even while He was mortal; but now He is immortal, by all likelihood much more. That was not her case, to draw aught from Him; it was for pure love, and nothing else, she desired it. To love, it is not enough to hear or see; it is carried farther, to touch and take hold; it is *affectus unionis,* and the nearest union is *per contactum.*

2. The parties. Secondly, the parties. *Me;* not *Me,* not Christ. Why not Him? Christ was not wont to be so dainty of it. Divers times, and in divers places, He suffered the rude multitude to throng and to thrust Him. What speak we of that, when not three days since He suffered other manner of touches and twitches both? Then, *noli Me tangere* would have come in good time; would have done well on Good-Friday. Why suffered He them then? why suffered He not her now? She, I dare say for her, would have done Him no hurt, she. *Noli*
Mark 14. 3. Lu. 7. 46. is to her; not she, not Mary Magdalene. She had touched Him before now; touched His head, touched His feet, anointed them both; what was done she might not now?

She hath even now, this morning, brought odours in her hand to embalm Him; and with these, and with no other hands doth she offer to touch Him at this time:—she might have been borne with. It was early; as early as it was, Mark 16. 1.
she had this morning given many good proofs of her love. 1. That she was so early up; 2. came to the grave first; 3. stayed there last; 4. had been at such cost; 5. had taken such pains; 6. had wept so many tears; 7. would not be comforted, no not by Angels, till she had found Him; and now she hath found Him, not to touch Him? All these might have pleaded for as much as this comes to. For all these, one poor touch had been but an easy recompense. Of all other, this prohibition lay not against her; of all times, not at this. The more we look into it, the farther off we find it, to be spoken either by Him, or to her.

II. The reason.

But if we go farther, and look the reason, we shall find it yet more strange; it will increase the doubt. "Touch Me not, for I am not yet ascended." What a reason is this! As who should say; when He was ascended, she should then. But then when He was ascended, one would think she should be farther off than now. *Si stans in terrâ tam prope non tangitur, receptus in cœlum quomodo tangitur?* [Vid. S. August. Serm. 245. 2.] 'If standing on earth by her, He is not to be touched, when He is taken up into Heaven, no arm will then reach Him'—past touching then. That if not till then, never. The reason makes it yet farther from reason. No remedy, but we must pray a consultation, as they call it, upon this prohibition.

It cannot be denied, but for *noli me* there is a time and place. It is worth the noting; the world began with a *noli me tangere*—both the worlds. The old world; the first words in a manner God spake then were a kind of a *noli me tangere*, Touch not the forbidden fruit. And as in the old, so here at the beginning this new, for with Christ's rising began the new creature, it is Christ's first speech we see. Christ rising, it is His first precept, His first law is negative; it is the first thing He forbiddeth us, the first He thought good to warn us of. Of His first words we will have special care, I trust. The rule is; things that will hurt us, best not touch. Best not touch? nay sound and good

SERM. XV. was Arsenius the Eremite's advice touching those: *Impera Evæ et cave serpentem, et tutus eris; tutior autem, si arborem non aspexeris,* 'Can you command Eve, can you so? and can you beware the serpent? well; do so then, and you shall be safe. But, hear you, *tutior,* you shall be yet more safe, if you see not, look not upon, come not within the reach, nay not within the sight of the forbidden tree.' But Christ is
Joh. 11. 25. not the forbidden tree; the tree of life rather, to be touched and tasted, that we may live by Him. No place in Christ for a *noli me tangere.*

Of those that hurt us, some we have no sense of at the first. Such are all things unlawful and forbidden; which, though for the time they seem pleasant, yet they have their stings in their tail; sooner or later we shall find they will hurt us, any fruit of the forbidden tree.

Other things we feel hurt us, we forbear easily. An angry inflammation there is, the name of it is a *noli me tangere;* and not that only, but any boil or sore endures not the touching. What? had Christ any sore place about Him,
Joh. 20. 27. since His Passion? No; for St. Thomas put his finger, nay, his whole hand into the place of His wounds, and put Him to no pain at all. No place in Christ, for this *noli me tangere* neither.

1. Not on Christ's part.

Not to hold you longer, *noli Me tangere* can rise but one of these ways; either out of 1. *noli,* or 2. out of *Me; ex parte tacti,* or *ex parte tangentis;* Him that was touched, or hers that did touch Him. 1. "Touch Me not," you will hurt Me, I am sore—*ex parte tacti:* 2. or, "touch Me not," I shall hurt you, I am hot or sharp—*ex parte tangentis.* Fire, I shall scorch you; an edge tool, I shall wound you; pitch, I shall defile you; some contagious thing, I shall infect you. Every one of these cries, *noli me tangere.* But neither of these hath place in Christ. Christ rising was not now in state to receive any hurt, and neither now, nor ever in case to do any, to prick or to burn the fingers of any that touch Him.

2. But on Mary Magdalene's.

We resolve then, it was not on Christ's part, this "touch Me not." It should then more properly have been *nolo Me tangi;* but it is, *noli Me tangere,* and so on hers. No let in Him but He might be touched; the let in her, she might not touch Him. That it was never Christ's meaning, after He was risen, He would not be touched of any at all, it is evident. This very day, at even, appearing to the eleven, He not only suffered, but invited them to touch Him; nay more, *palpate Me*, which is, "touch Me throughly." This very chapter at the twenty-seventh verse, He calls to St. Thomas, *infer digitum*, "put in your finger;" nay, *affer manum*, "hand" and all; which is to touch, and touch home I am sure.

Lu. 24. 39.

[John 20. 27.]

[S. August. Serm. 244. in dieb. Pasch.]

How then? would He have men touch Him, and not women? nor that, neither. This is His first appearing; at His second, and next to this, certain women met Him on the way; He suffered them to touch Him, and take Him by the feet. Some virtuous woman it may be, but Mary Magdalene had been a notorious sinner, and so unworthy of it. No, nor that; for that, of the women that so met Him, and so touched Him, she was one. Mary Magdalene touch, and Mary Magdalene not touch! the difficulties grow still. For I ask, if at the second appearing, why not at the first? Why after, and not now? Why there, touch and spare not; and here, *noli Me tangere*, not come thither?

Mat. 28. 9.

Lu. 7. 47.

See Mat. 28. 9.

Let me tell you what we have gained yet; these three things. 1. The prohibition is not real; the touch, the thing is not forbidden, it is but personal. 2. Nay, not personal neither absolutely; not she simply, but not she as now at this time. She might touch it seems, for she did not long after. Mary Magdalene might, but not this Mary Magdalene. 3. And last, that it is not final; there is life, there is hope in it. Not never to touch, but not *stando in his terminis*, 'standing in the terms she doth.' What terms are those? And now, lo, we are come to the point, to that we search for.

Three senses I will give you, and they have great authors all three, Chrysostom, Gregory, Augustine. I will touch them all three, and you may take your choice of them; or, if you please, take them all, for they will stand well together.

One is, it is Chrysostom's, that all was not well—somewhat amiss; she something to blame in the manner of her offer, which was not all as it should. The most we can make

To correct her want of due reverence;

SERM. XV.

S. Chrysostom's sense. [Hom. 86. *al.* 85. in Joan.] she failed in somewhat. Not that she did it in any immodest or indecent manner; God forbid! never think of that. But only a little too forward it may be, not with that due respect that was meet.

We see by that is past, how the world went. Christ said, "Mary;" she answers Him with her wonted term, with a "Rabboni." And as she saluted Him with her wonted term, so after her wonted fashion she made toward Him, to have touched Him; not in such manner as was fit to have been observed, nor with that regard which His new glorified estate after His resurrection might seem justly to require. It is in "Me;" not the same "Me" He was. That that was enough to Christ a few days ago, was nothing near enough to-day for Him. He that three days since endured so much, the day is now come He will be touched after another fashion. Phil. 2. 9. *Propter hoc exaltavit Eum Deus,* "For to this end God so highly exalted Him." I tell you plainly I did not like her "Rabboni," it was no Easter-day salutation, it would have been some better term expressing more reverence. So her offer would have been in some more respective manner, her touch no Easter-day touch; her *tangere* had a tang in it, as we say. The touch-stone of our touching Christ, is with all regard and reverence that may be. Bring hers to this, and her touch was not the right touch, and all for want of expressing more regard; not for want of *toto* but *tanto:* not of reverence at all, but of reverence enough.

Two causes they give of this fail. One, a defect in her judgment; the other, an excess in her affection. Her amiss in the manner grew out of her amiss in the mind; a misconceit, He had been but even Rabboni still. As it should seem, it seemeth to her, it was with Him no otherwise than with her brother Lazarus; that Christ had risen *idem Qui prius,* neither more nor less, but just the same He was before. To be saluted, approached, touched, as formerly He had been. Formerly, He might have been touched; she thought He might have been even so still. Whereas, with Him the case was quite altered, He risen in a far other condition than so; 1 Cor. 15. 53. His corruptible had now put on incorruption, and His mortal immortality. He died in weakness and dishonour, rose again in power and glory. And as in another state, so to another end; not to stay upon earth or converse here any longer, but to ascend up into Heaven. There was no *ascendi* in her mind.

His reason imports as much. You touch Me not as if I were upon ascending, but as if to stay here still. For in saying "I am not yet," His meaning is, ere long He should. *Nondum ascendi,* "yet I am not;" but *ascendo,* "presently I am to do it," to leave this world and all here beneath, and to go up and take possession of My kingdom of glory. To this new glorious condition of His there belonged more than "Rabboni," another manner approach than *more solito.* He being so very highly exalted, and far otherwise than He was, her access to have been according: not being so, it made her unmeet to touch Him now. Nay, if you be but at "Rabboni," and make toward Me in no other sort than thus, *Noli Me tangere,* "Touch Me not."

Hence we learn, that when He sees we forget ourselves, Christ will take a little state upon Him; will not be saluted with "Rabboni," but with some more seemly term. St.
Thomas', "My Lord, and my God," a better far than "Rab- Joh. 20. 28.
boni." Nor be approached to after the old accustomed
fashion, but with some more seemly respect, *sicut decet* Eph. 5. 3.
sanctos. They that so press to touch Him, and be somewhat too homely with Him, they are in Mary Magdalene's case. Her *noli Me tangere* touches them home. And their punishment shall be, that touch Him they shall not.

It is no excuse to say, all was out of love; never lay it upon that. Love, Christ loves well; but love, if it be right,
οὐ περπερεύεται, nihil facit perperam, saith the Apostle, *οὐκ* [1 Cor. 13. 5.]
ἀσχημονεῖ "doth nothing uncomely," keeps decorum; forgets not what belongs to duty and decency, carries itself accordingly. And such love Christ loves. Otherwise, love may, and doth forget itself otherwhile; and then, in that case, the heathen man's saying is true, *importunus amor parum distat a simultate,* 'such love is not love.' A strange kind of love, when for very love to Christ we care not how we use Him, or carry ourselves towards Him. Which being her case, she heard, and heard justly, *Noli Me tangere;* you are not now in case, till you shall have learned to touch after a more regardful fashion.

SERM. XV. This may truly be said; she was not before so carried away with sorrow—that passion, but she was now as far gone in the other of joy, and so like enough to forget herself in offering to touch Him no otherwise than *heri* and *nudiustertius*, as 'two or three days ago' she might have done. St. Peter's
Mark 9. 6. case in the Mount was just her case here: "he knew not what he said," nor she, what she did; so surprised with the sudden joy, as she had no leisure to recollect herself, and to weigh the wonderful great change this day wrought in Him.

Out of which our lesson is, that in the sudden surprise of any passion *Christus non est tangibilis*, 'no touching Christ then.' But when the passion is over and we come to ourselves, it will be with us as with her; her affection calmed, her judgment settled better than now on the sudden it was as it seemed, she will be then fit, and then she may be admitted; and so she was, and did touch Him; but that time,
Mat. 28. 9. when she did so touch Him, she was upon her knees, down at His feet, another manner of gesture than here she offered.

Say she were unfit, yet hangs there a cloud still, all is not clear. For why then did others touch, to our seeming as unfit as she? Thomas with his faith in his fingers' ends? The rest, in whose teeth He cast their unbelief and hardness of heart—they touched Him at first; why not she as well as they? They were unfit, I grant, but their unfitness grew *ex alio capite*, 'another way than did hers.' They believed not, were in doubt; thought He had been but a ghost. To rid
Lu. 24. 37-40. them of that doubt, that they might be sure it was He, and
1 Joh. 1. 1. be able to say another day, "which our hands have handled of the Word of life," they were suffered to touch Him. Touching was the proper cure for their disease. So was it not for hers. She never doubted a whit, was sure He Whose voice she heard was "Rabboni." She had no need to be confirmed in that, her disease grew another way. Not from want of faith—of fear rather; from want of due regard. To touch would not have cured her disease, but made it worse. So, they touched because they believed not; she touched not because she misbelieved, believed not of Him aright. They touched, that they might know He was risen; she touched not, that she might know He was not so risen as she wrongly imagined, that is, as in former times she had known Him.

Out of that hath been spoken we learn, that they be not
so well advised who, if they hear one speak of *noli me tangere,*
imagine straight it must needs be meant of a boil, ulcer, or
some dangerous sore. Every *noli me tangere* is not so;
Christ's here is not so. Learn here, there doth to excellency
belong a *noli me tangere,* inducing reverence, no less than to
boils or sores procuring indolency. "Touch me not," come
not near me, I am "unclean," saith the leper. Stand back, Lev. 13. 45.
touch not my skirts. "I am holier than you," saith one, Isa. 65. 5.
Esay the sixty-fifth; that is, touch me not, I am so pure
and clean; as if to his excellent holiness there belongeth
this privilege, not to be touched.

The truth is, in the natural body the eye is a most excellent
part, but withal so tender, so delicate, it may not endure to
be touched, no, though it ail nothing, be not sore at all. In
the civil body the like is: there are in it both persons and
matters, whose excellency is such they are not familiarly to
be dealt with by hand, tongue, or pen, or any other way.
The persons, they are as the apple of God's own eye, *christi* Ps. 105. 15.
Domini. They have a peculiar *nolite tangere,* by themselves.
Wrong is offered them, when after this, or in familiar or
homely manner, any touch them. The matters likewise,
Princes' affairs, secrets of state, David calleth them *magna* Ps. 131. 1.
et mirabilia super se, and so *super nos;* points too high, too
wonderful for us to deal with. To these also, belongs this
"Touch not."

And if of Kings' secrets this may truly be said, may it not
as truly of God, of His secret decrees? May not they, for
their height and depth, claim to this *noli* too? Yes sure; and
I pray God, He be well-pleased with this licentious touching,
nay tossing His decrees of late; this sounding the depth of
His judgments with our line and lead, too much presumed
upon by some in these days of ours. *Judicia Ejus abyssus* Ps. 36. 6.
multa, saith the Psalmist, "His judgments are the great
deep." St. Paul, looking down into it, ran back and cried, Rom. 11. 33.
"O the depth!" the profound depth! not to be searched,
past our fathoming or finding out. Yet are there in the
world that make but a shallow of this great deep, they have
sounded it to the bottom. God's secret decrees they have
them at their fingers' ends, and can tell you the number

SERM. XV. and the order of them just with 1, 2, 3, 4, 5. Men that sure must have been in God's cabinet, above "the third
2 Cor. 12. 2. heaven," where St. Paul never came. Mary Magdalene's touch was nothing to these.

1. This was but on the by. The main of the text, that it beareth full against, *ex totâ substantiâ*, is undue and undutiful carriage, and against them that use it. Not that Mary Magdalene's was such; hers was but Tekel, certain grains too light, *minus habens;* not altogether without regard, but not altogether so full of regard as it might and ought to have been. Make it as little as you will, Christ saith *noli* to it; and *noli* is a word of unwillingness. Christ is not unwilling with aught that is good; what He saith *noli* to, is *eo ipso* not good, would be forborne, would not be offered Him, be it no more than hers was. She, it may be, shewed more regard than we; yet, if we shew not more regard than she, we shall hardly escape this *noli Me tangere.*

2. But from this we rise. If Christ said *noli* to her that failed but in *tanto*, what shall He say to them that fail both *in tanto* and *in toto?* The *noli* to her given, reacheth them in an higher degree. Greater must their fault be now, than hers was then. She had no *noli* to warn her; they have hers to warn them, and will take no warning by it. Christ, as He saw she was, so He foresaw others would be as, yea more defective, this way. The *noli* that was given to her, was in her given to them all. Even to this day Christ crieth still, *noli Me tangere,* even to this day there is use of it, to call upon us for a better touch.

3. If the text be against rudeness, to restrain it, then it is for reverence to enjoin it. If He say *noli* to the want of regard, we know what He will say *volo* to; that the more respectively[1], the better we carry ourselves, the better He will like us. This is sure: He will be approached to in all dutiful and decent sort, and He will not have us offer Him any other. Whatsoever is most or best in that kind, if there be any one better than other, be that it. The best we have I am sure is not too good for Christ. It is better to render account to Him of a little too much, than of a good deal too little.

4. Take this with you: Christ can say *noli*, then. For I

[1] [i. e. respectfully.]

know not how, our carriage, a many of us, is so loose; covered we sit, sitting we pray; standing, or walking, or as it takes us in the head, we receive; as if Christ were so gentle a person, we might touch Him, do to Him what we list, He would take all well, He hath not the power to say *noli* to any thing. But He hath we see and saith it, and saith it to one highly in His favour; and saith it but for a touch a little awry, otherwise than it should.

As the heathen said *vultu,* so the text saith, *tactu lædi* 5.
pietatem. One may offend Christ only by touching Him,
such the touch may be. We will allow Him greater than
the ark; that would not endure Uzzah's touch, he died for 2 Sam. 6. 7.
it. We will hold us to our text: if we touch Him unduly,
we shall do it *nolenti,* it shall be much against His will, He
likes it not; witness this *noli* here.

Which, though it go but to the touch, yet *a paritate* 6.
rationis it reacheth to all the body, and to every member of
it. To our very "feet," saith Solomon; we to look to them Ecc. 5. 1.
when we draw near to Him. To our very fingers, saith "a
greater than Solomon," we to look to them when we touch Lu. 11. 31.
Him. And as not with the foot of pride, nor the hand
of presumption, so along through the rest; neither with
a scornful eye, nor a stiff knee; all are equally forbidden
under one, all to be far from us.

It reacheth to all, but yet for all that, the native word 7.
of the text, the touch, is to have a kind of pre-eminence.
Most kindly, to that. To Christ it is every way, but most
of all, to Christ as He is *tangibilis,* 'comes under our touch.'
To all parts of His worship, but other parts will not come
under *tangere* so fitly as the Sacrament. So as the use
may seem properly to have relation to that, and we there to
shew our highest reverence. If we do so, *dicite justo quia* Isa. 3. 10.
bene, we do well. But divers have too much of Mary Magdalene in them. I know not how they would touch Christ,
if they had Him; that which on earth doth most nearly represent Him, His highest memorial, I know not how many
both touch and take otherwise than were to be wished.

But thus are we now come to the day, the very day it was given on. Christ gave this *noli Me tangere,* that it might be *verbum diei,* 'a watch-word for this day.' Take heed

SERM. XV. how you touch, for He easily foresaw this would be *tempus tangendi*, 'the time whereon touch we must;' nay, more
Joh. 6. 56. than touch Him we must, for "eat His flesh, and drink His blood" we must; and that can we not do, but we must touch Him. And this we must do by virtue of another
Mat. 26. 26. precept, *Accipite et manducate.*

How will *Accipite et manducate*, and *noli Me tangere* cleave together? "Take, eat," and yet "touch not?" If we take we must needs touch, one would think; if we eat, *gustus est sub tactu,* saith the philosopher; so that comes under touching too.

It seems the text was not so well chosen, these points considered. Nay, set the day aside, we have no need, God wot, to be preached to of not touching; we are not so for-
Joh. 20. 27. ward that way. It would rather have been that of St. Thomas, *affer manum.* This is now out of season.

But you will remember still, I told you, this *noli* was not general. It was but to Mary Magdalene; and to her but till she had learned a little better manners. Not to any, but such as she, or worse than she, that in unbeseeming manner press and proffer to touch Him—the only cause of
Mat. 28. 9. her repulse. But at another time, when she was on her knees, fell down at His feet, then did she touch Him without any check at all. Be you now but as she was then, and this *noli Me tangere* will not touch you at all.

It is the case of the Sacrament right. There is place in the taking it, for *noli Me tangere;* so is there for *affer manum.* To them that with St. Thomas, in a feeling of the defect of their faith, or of any other spiritual grace, cast
Joh. 20. 27. themselves down and cry, "My Lord, and my God," *affer manum* to them; I set them free, I give them a discharge from this *noli Me tangere.* But for them that are but at "Rabboni," and scarce so far, bold guests with Him; base in conceit, and homely in behaviour; to them, and to them properly, belongs this *noli Me tangere,* more properly than ever it did to her. And so that point reconciled. Thus far for St. Chrysostom, and his taking.

2. To hasten the message. S. Gregory's sense. There is a second, and it is St. Gregory's, that the *vade et dic*, was the cause of *noli Me, &c.*, and that all was but to save time, that she was not permitted it. Christ was

not willing to spend time in these compliments—it was no other, but to dispatch her away upon an errand better pleasing to Him, that required more haste. As if He should have said, Let us have no touching now, there is a matter in hand would be done out of hand; and therefore for this time, Hands off, "Touch Me not."

And the reason will follow well so; *nondum enim ascendi,* [S. Greg. in Evang. lib. 2. Hom. 25. 6.] You need not be so hasty, or eager to "touch Me, I am not yet ascended;" though I be upon going, yet I am not gone. You may do this at some other time, at some other meeting; *et quod differtur non aufertur,* at better leisure you may have your desire—forbear it now.

Why, what haste was there of doing this errand? Might she not have touched Him, and done it time enough? Peradventure she might think so; she knew Christ was risen, she was well. But they that sat in fear and sorrow, that knew not so much, they would not think so;—not to them. To them *nihil satis festinatur,* 'no haste was too much,' all delay too long.

Nor to Christ neither, Who was, we see, so desirous to have notice given with all speed, that He would not take so much time from it, as wherein Mary Magdalene might have had but a touch at Him. So careful they might receive comfort with the first that He saith, Go your ways with all speed, get you to them, the first thing you do; it will do them more good to hear of My rising, than it will do you to stand and touch Me.

Yet a touch and away, would not have taken up so much time. True; but He easily foresaw, in the terms she stood, if He suffered her to touch, that would not serve the turn, she would have taken hold too. And if she had taken hold once, nor that neither; she would have come to a *non dimittam* with her in the Canticles, *tenui Eum et non dimittam;* Cant. 3. 4. she would not have let Him go, or been long ere she had; so much time spent in impertinencies, which neither He nor she the better for. So she to let her touching alone, and put it off till another time, being to be employed in a business of more haste and importance.

3. To wean her from

The third place is St. Augustine, that Christ in these words had a farther meaning; to wean her from all sen-

SERM. XV.

sensual touching. St. Augustine's sense. [Serm. 243—246.] sual and fleshly touching, and teach her a new and a true touch, truer than that she was about. This sense groweth out of Christ's reason: "Touch Me not, for I am not yet ascended," as if till He were ascended, He would not be touched, and then He would. As much to say, Care not to touch Me here, stand not upon it, touch Me not till I be ascended; stay till then, and then do. That is the true touch, that is it will do you all the good.

And there is reason for this sense. For the touch of
Acts 1. 3. His body which she so much desired, that could last but forty days in all, while He in His body were among them. And what should all since, and we now, have been the better? He was to take her out a lesson, and to teach her another touch, that might serve for all to the world's end; that might serve when the body and bodily touch were taken from us.

[Joh. 6. 62.] Christ Himself touched upon this point in the sixth chapter, at the sixty-second verse, when at Capernaum they stumbled at the speech of eating His flesh. "What," saith He, "find you this strange, now? How will you find it then, when you shall see the Son of man ascend up where He was before?" How then? And yet then you must eat, or else there is no life in you.

So it is a plain item to her, that there may be a sensual touching of Him here; but that is not it, not the right, it avails little. It was her error this, she was all for the corporal presence, for the touch with the fingers. So were His disciples, all of them, too much addicted to it. From which
[2 Cor. 5. 16.] they were now to be weaned, that if they had before known Christ, or touched Him after the flesh, yet now from henceforth they were to do so no more, but learn a new touch; to touch Him, being now ascended. Such a touching there is, or else His reason holds not; and best touching Him so, better far than this of hers she was so eager on.

Do but ask the Church of Rome: even with them it is not the bodily touch in the Sacrament, that doth the good. Wicked men, very reprobates, have that touch, and remain reprobates as before. Nay, I will go farther; it is not that
Mark 5. 31. that toucheth Christ at all. Example "the multitude that thronged and thrust Him," yet for all that, as if none of

them all had touched Him, He asks, *Quis Me tetigit?* So that one may rudely thrust Him, and yet not touch Him though, not to any purpose so. [S. Aug. Hom. 26. in S. Joan.]

Christ resolves the point in that very place. The flesh, the touching, the eating it, profits nothing. "The words He spake, were spirit;" so the touching, the eating, to be spiritual. And St. Thomas and Mary Magdalene, or whosoever touched Him here on earth, *nisi fælicius fide quam manu tetigissent,* 'if they had not been more happy to touch Him with their faith than with their fingers' end,' they had had no part in Him; no good by it at all. It was found better with it to "touch the hem of His garment," than without it to touch any part of His body. Joh. 6. 63. Matt. 9. 20.

Now, if faith be to touch, that will touch Him no less in Heaven than here; one that is in Heaven may be touched so. No ascending can hinder that touch. Faith will elevate itself, that ascending in spirit we shall touch Him, and take hold of Him. *Mitte fidem et tenuisti*—it is St. Augustine. It is a touch to which there is never a *noli,* fear it not. [Conf. S. Aug. Hom. 25. in S. Joan.]

So do we then; send up our faith, and that shall touch Him, and there will virtue come from Him; and it shall take such hold on Him, as it shall raise us up to where He is; bring us to the end of the verse, and to the end of all our desires; to *ascendo ad Patrem,* a joyful ascension to our Father and His, and to Himself, and to the unity of the Blessed Spirit. To Whom, in the Trinity of Persons, &c.

A SERMON

PREACHED BEFORE

THE KING'S MAJESTY, AT WHITEHALL.

ON THE TWENTY-FIRST OF APRIL, A.D. MDCXXII., BEING EASTER-DAY.

JOHN xx. 17.

Jesus saith unto her, Touch Me not, for I am not yet ascended to My Father; but go to My brethren, and say unto them, I ascend unto My Father and your Father, and to My God and your God.

[*Dicit ei Jesus, Noli Me tangere, nondum enim ascendi ad Patrem Meum; vade autem ad fratres Meos, et dic eis, Ascendo ad Patrem Meum, et Patrem vestrum, Deum Meum, et Deum vestrum.* Latin Vulg.]

[*Jesus saith unto her, Touch Me not, for I am not yet ascended to My Father; but go to My brethren, and say unto them, I ascend unto My Father and your Father, and to My God and your God.* Engl. Trans.]

SERM. XVI.

OF *noli Me tangere,* the former part, you have formerly heard. Mary Magdalene might not touch; at least-wise not as thus, not as now.

The reason: 1. On her part, she forgat herself a little in her touch, as in her term toward Him. Who, though *nondum,* He were 'not yet,' was presently to ascend, and be taken up into Heaven, and would be touched in some better manner. And till she had learned so to touch, *noli Me tangere.*

2. On Christ's part. She need not be so eager, *nondum enim ascendi;* that is, though He were going, yet He was not gone. Some other time might serve her, to touch Him in. Now, He had matter of more haste to send her about, and

would have no time taken from it. And so, for saving of time, *noli Me tangere.*

3. On the touch itself. He was "not yet ascended;" and, to touch Him before He were so, was not the true touch, not the touch that would do her, or us, any good. For these all, or some of these, *noli Me tangere,* no touching now.

But what, shall she be quite cast off in the mean time? Denied touching; denied it, granted nothing for it? That were hard. Nothing to comfort her in lieu of it? Yes; Christ is not unrighteous, that He should forget the work Heb. 6. 10.
and labour of her love, which she this day made so many ways to appear. Somewhat He deviseth to comfort her, somewhat; in that He will have her do somewhat for Him. So, the old rule was, *quem non honoro non onero.* He will employ her in a message, and such a message as was to the present joy of them it was sent to, and should be to the general joy and good, not of them only, but of us all.

Now then, this must needs be reckoned as a special favour shewed her by our blessed Saviour. For otherwise He could as easily Himself have appeared to them He sent her, as to her He did; but that His will was to vouchsafe her the honour of the first bearing of these so joyful tidings to them, and in and by them to the whole world. When time was, Joh. 12. 3.
"she brake her box of precious ointment, and the scent of [Mar. 14. 3.]
it filled the whole house:" the breaking of this box now, of 2 Cor. 2. 16.
the tidings of Christ and His rising, with the sweet "savour of life unto life" hath filled, and still filleth the whole world, from one end to the other.

The sum of the text is, a dispatch of Mary Magdalene by The sum.
Christ, to deliver a message to His disciples. It is in effect as if He should have said, You know I am risen now, you are well for your part; there be others that know not so much, and because they know it not, sit in sorrow, heavy and half dead at home. It would comfort them much, revive them, put life into them again, to know what you know. Now you are well, think upon them that are not. Remember what was your own case but even now; you cannot do a better deed than carry comfort to the comfortless. I would they knew of it, I wish them well, they be "My brethren," however they forgat themselves when time was.

SERM. XVI.

But this is not all, that they might know of it, but they must know of it with all speed. For that she may the sooner go tell them, she must not touch. For if you mark it, it is not *vade et dic*, but *sed vade et dic;* it is not, barely, "go and tell them;" it is, "touch Me not, but go and tell them;" that is, instead of touching, she must be gone in all haste to tell them. As if He should say, Go to, let us have no touching now, get you to them the first thing you do, and tell them of it. It will do them more good to be told of this, than it will do you to stay here and touch Me never so oft.

This so great haste of the carrying it, is much for the credit of the message, much for it; I cannot but note it. That Christ thought the notice of it so necessary, the bearing of it so every way important, as we see He is careful no time be taken from it; but with all possible speed, with the very first, they acquainted with it. So careful as He would not take so much, or rather so little time from it, as wherein Mary Magdalene might have had but a touch at Him; but takes her off, and sends her away in all haste. As if some matter had lain in it, if they should not have heard of His rising before the sun-rising.

Much for the honour of the feast on which it was done, that He would for ever have a feast celebrated in memory of this day, whereon these tidings came to the world first.

Most of all, for His own honour, Who sheweth Himself so desirous that they that are in heaviness may receive comfort, as He thinketh no haste too much, no haste enough till they
Ps. 143. 8. hear of it, till they "hear of His loving-kindness betimes in the morning."

The division. To take the text in sunder. The parts be two; 1. a commission to carry a message, 2. and the message itself.

I. The Commission: *Vade ad fratres Meos et dic eis.* II. The Message: *Ascendo ad Patrem Meum, &c.*

In the Commission again there are two: 1. the parties first; 2. and then, the charge. 1. The parties, *fratres Meos;* 2. the charge, *vade et dic eis.*

In the message, two likewise: 1. First, that He is upon ascending; 2. then, the party to Whom. That party to Whom is but one, yet represented here under two names, 1. Father, and 2. God. And that which to us is the capital point of all, and which we to lay hold of specially, His Father but ours withal, and His God but ours as well as His; the last and best part of the message, for in it lieth the joy that cometh to us this morning.

On which four, 1. "My Father, and 2. your Father," and 3. "My God, and 4. your God," as it were so many wheels, is His *ascendo* drawn. Upon the same is ours likewise to be, and is therefore the *consummatum est* of the text and of the feast, and of this, yea I dare add of the whole Gospel.

And let not this move you a whit, that His Father and our Father, His God and our God, Who are the end to which we ascend, are made the chariot by which we ascend. This is no strange thing in divinity. *Ad Christum non itur nisi per Christum,* saith St. Augustine, and so neither *ad Deum nisi per Deum.* With us nothing is more certain, than that the end of our way which we come unto, is also the way itself whereby we come thither. One and the same, *ad Quem* and *per Quem ascenditur.*

We shall make four stands. 1. One at *fratres Meos,* the parties. 2. Another, at *dic eis,* the commission. 3. The third, at *ascendo,* the motion. 4. And the last, at "My Father and your Father, My God and your God," the *terminus ad quem,* which giveth the perfection to all our motions, and so to this, the last end of all our motions; for after *ascendo* we shall move no more, but rest for ever.

I. *Fratres Meos.* The parties.

Vade ad fratres Meos, "go to My brethren." Our first stand is to be at *fratres Meos,* "My brethren," the parties sent to.

Who be they? They she went to. To whom went she? To His "disciples," in the next verse. They then the parties He meant, they His "brethren." John 20.18.

A strange term to begin with, considering how they had dealt with Him, scarce like brethren, not long before. We shall therein do the work of the Sabbath, which is "to tell of His loving-kindness betimes in the morning," and this morning more than ever any. Ps. 59. 16.

Ere then we go any farther, let us touch a little at this term He gives them. It is no *noli me tangere,* this, it is a word to be touched and taken hold of; it was so, when time was, by Benhadad's servants, this very word. "Is Benhadad 1 Kings 20. 32, 33.

SERM. XVI. alive," saith the King of Israel, *frater meus est*, "he is my brother;" which they presently caught hold of, "Yea, thy brother Benhadad is yet living." So they.

And so we, *fratres Meos.* Let us not let this word fall to the ground, but say with Bernard, *Salvum sit verbum Domini mei*, 'God save this word,' blessed be the lips that spake it. Yea Thy brethren, good Lord, if so Thou wilt vouchsafe to call them.

Out of it first I note, here is nothing that savours of any displeasure, of remembering any old grudge. Not so much as an harsh term in all the message, no mention they had fled from Him, forsook Him, forswore Him, full un-brotherly. He hath forgotten it all, all is out of His mind; casts not them off as they did Him, but sends to them, and by the name of brethren sends to them; they be "My brethren," and I theirs, and by that name commend Me to them. Nothing here that savours of any anger.

Nor nothing that savours of any pride. But even as Joseph in the top of his honour, so He in this, the day of His glorious exalting from the dead, claims kindred of them, a sort of poor forlorn men; and as the Apostle expresseth it,
Heb. 2. 11. *non est confusus vocare*, is not a whit "ashamed" of them that were ashamed of Him. Disdains not, poor as they were, unkind as they were, but vouchsafes to call them "brethren" for all that.

Which word "brethren" implies two things: 1. First, identity of nature. His nature is not changed by death. The nature He died in, in the same He rises again. Thereby lies a matter. For if He rose as man, then man also may rise; if one be risen, there is hope for others; if the nature be risen, the persons in it may. So it was with the first Adam. In his person was our nature, and in him it died, and we in it. So is it in the second. In His person our nature is risen, in our nature we all. This first; risen in the same nature He had before—not changed it.

2. And second, risen with the same love and affection He had before—not changed it neither. Yes, changed it; I said not well in that, but changed it for the better. Before
Joh. 15. 15. this when He said most, He said but, "I will call you My friends"—the highest term He came to before. But here,

being risen, He riseth we see higher, as high as love can rise, to count them and style them *fratres Meos.* And so much for that, " Go to My brethren."

Well, when she comes to His brethren, what then? *Et dic eis,* " and say to them," or tell them. By which words He gives her a commission. *Vade* is her mission, *dic eis* her commission. A commission, to publish the first news of His rising, and as it falls out, of His ascending too. *Dic eis.* The commission.

The Fathers say that by this word she was by Christ made an Apostle, nay *Apostolorum Apostola,* 'an Apostle to the Apostles themselves.'

An Apostle; for what lacks she? 1. Sent first, immediately from Christ Himself; and what is an Apostle but so? 2. Secondly, sent to declare and make known; and what difference between *Ite prædicate,* and *Vade et dic,* but only the number? the thing is the same. 3. And last, what was she to make known? Christ's rising and ascending. And what are they but *Evangelium,* 'the Gospel,' yea the very Gospel of the Gospel? Mat. 28. 19.

This day, with Christ's rising, begins the Gospel; not before. Crucified, dead and buried, no good news, no Gospel they in themselves. And them the Jews believe as well as we. The first Gospel of all is the Gospel of this day, and the Gospel of this day is this Mary Magdalene's Gospel, πρωτευαγγέλιον, 'the prime Gospel' of all, before any of the other four. That Christ is risen and upon His ascending, and she the first that ever brought these glad tidings. At her hands the Apostles themselves received it first, and from them we all.

Which, as it was a special honour, and " wheresoever this Gospel is preached, shall be told for a memorial of her," so was it withal not without some kind of enthwiting[1] to them, to the Apostles, for sitting at home so drooping in a corner, that Christ not finding any of them is fain to seek Him a new Apostle; and finding her where He should have found them and did not, to send by the hand of her that He first found at the sepulchre's side, and to make Himself a new Apostle. And send her to them, to enter them as it were, and catechize them in the two Articles of the Christian Faith, the Resurrection and Ascension of Christ. To her, they and we both owe them, the first notice of them. Mat. 26. 13.

[[1] *i. e.* reproaching.]

SERM. XVI. And by this, lo, the amends we spake of is made her for her *noli Me tangere,*—full amends. For to be thus sent, to be the messenger of these so blessed tidings, is a higher honour, a more special favour done here, a better good turn, every way better, than if she had been let alone, had her desire, touched Christ, which she so longed for, and so eagerly reached at. Better sure, for I reason thus. Christ we may be sure, would never have enjoined her to leave the better, to take the worse; to leave to touch Him, to go to tell them, if to go to tell them had not been the better.

So that hence we infer, that to go and carry comfort to them that need it, to tell them of Christ's rising that do not know it, is better than to tarry and do nothing but stand touching Christ. Touching Christ gives place to teaching Christ. *Vade et dic* better than *mane et tange.* Christ we see is for *vade et dic.* That if we were in case where we might touch Christ, we were to leave Christ untouched, and even to give ourselves a *noli me tangere,* to go and do this; and to think ourselves better employed in telling them, than in touching Him.

Will you observe withal how well this agrees with her offer a little before of *ego tollam Eum?* She must needs know of Joh. 20. 15. the gardener, "Tell me where you have laid Him," *et ego tollam,* and she "would take Him and carry Him," that she would. Why, you that would so fain take and carry Me being dead, go take and carry Me now alive; that is, carry news that I am alive, and you shall better please Me with this *ego tollam* a great deal; it shall be a better carrying, *ego tollam* in a better sense than ever was that. Stand not here then touching Me, go and touch them; and with the very touch of this report you shall work in them a kind of that you see in Me, a kind of resurrection from a doleful and dead, to a cheerful and lively estate.

"Tell them" what? "Tell them that I ascend," that is, am about to ascend, am upon the point of it, am very shortly to do it. *Quod prope abest ut fiat, habetur pro facto,* 'that that is near done, we reckon as good as done.'

II. *Ascendo.* The motion. "Tell them that I ascend." Why how now, what day is to-day? It is not Ascension day; it is Easter, and but early

Easter yet. His ascension is forty days off. This were a text for that day. Why speaks He of that now? Why not rather, tell them that I am risen—more proper for this day? Why, He needs not tell her that, she could tell that of herself, she saw it. And besides, in saying "I ascend," He implies fully as much. Till He be risen, ascend He cannot; He must ascend out of the grave ere He can ascend up to Heaven, *resurrexit* must be past ere *ascendo* can come. *Ascendo* then puts His resurrection past all peradventure; He needs say no more of that, of His rising. But as she saw by His rising that He had "the keys of hell and death," Rev. 1. 18.
had unlocked those doors and come out from thence; so by *ascendo* He tells her farther, that He hath the keys of Heaven-gates also, which He would now unlock, and so set open the kingdom of Heaven to all believers.

And yet, there is a farther matter in *ascendo*, to shew us 2.
what was the end of His rising. Christ did not rise, to rise; no more must we. The Resurrection itself is for an end, it is not the end; it is but a state yet imperfect, but an entry to a greater good, which unless it lead us and bring us to, *non habetur propositum*, 'it is short, short of that it should be.' We must not then set up our rest upon our rising. There is somewhat more required than barely to rise. What is that? *Ascendo*, Christ rose to ascend; so are we to do. And rising is no rising, no right rising, we rise not on our right sides as we say, if that follow not upon it, if we ascend not withal. For to rise from the bottom of the grave to the brink of it, to stand upon our feet again and tread on the grave-stone, and no more, is but half a rising, is but Lazarus' rising. To rise up, up as high as Heaven, that is to rise indeed, that is Christ's rising; and that to be ours. As to rise is nothing but to ascend out of the grave, so to ascend is nothing but to rise as high as Heaven; and then we are truly risen, when so risen. Before I said, there was no Gospel till the Resurrection; I now say, the Resurrection itself is no Gospel, not of itself, unless *ascendo* follow it. *Resurrexit*, tell that to all the world. All that die in Adam shall rise in Christ—miscreants, Jews, Turks and all—no Gospel that, properly. Tell the Christian of more than so; tell him of *ascendo* too, that goes withal, that pertains to it. You must take that

SERM. XVI. with you too, if it be Christ's, if it be the right rising, the Resurrection to life and not to condemnation.

Mark this well, it is a material point. Better lie still in our graves, better never rise, than rise and rising not to ascend. Of them that shall rise, they that see they shall not ascend, shall wish themselves in their coffins again;
Lu. 23. 30. nay, they shall pray "the mountains to fall on them, and the hills to cover them," and bury them quick. So much doth this concern us, that these two part not, that *ascendo* attends us at our rising. And therefore, this you shall observe, that in all this speech or text Christ doth not so much as mention, as once name the word *rising* or *resurrection,* as if He made no great reckoning of it; but in this one short verse here, in these few words, He is at *ascendo* twice; speaks of that, mentions that over and over again. All to teach us, *ascendo* is all in all. That *resurrexit* is nothing, if it be nothing but *resurrexit;* nor any account to be made of it, if *ascendo* go not with it; but if *ascendo* go with it, then it is. And, that it may go with it, that to be all our care. Never take care for *resurrexit,* that will come of itself without any thought taking; never trouble yourselves with that. Take thought for *ascendo,* set your minds there. *Ascendo,* look well to that; *resurrexit,* let that go.

3. A third reason there is of *ascendo;* for He saw upon these tidings, as she did think, so they would say;—O is He risen, then shall we have His company again, as heretofore we had! But by sending them word of His ascending, He gives them warning betimes; He rose not to make any abode with them, or to converse with them on earth as formerly He had; that so they might have timely notice of it, and know what they were to look for. For this He knew would be a hard lesson. His rising they would like well, but His ascending be against; would not abide to hear of that, to lose His company at any hand. It was a conceit that troubled them much; they were still and ever addicted to His bodily being with them. Here they would
Mat. 17. 4. have kept Him, built Him a Tabernacle here; and by their
Lu. 24. 29. good-will never have let Him gone from hence. All for
Joh. 11. 32. *mane nobiscum,* and for *Domine si Tu fuisses hic;* all in

Mary Magdalene's case, had Him here to see Him and to touch Him, and then all had been well as they thought.

This was their error, and to rid them of it, of this earthly mind of theirs thus striving to affix and keep Him here on earth, and that then all should be well, He shews them that they were quite wrong, and sets them right. That for Him to be here below on earth, that is not it; but for them to be with Him there above in Heaven, that is it, there it is right. And never shall they or we be well, till there we be with Him. And thither would He raise them and us, with this His *ascendo*.

Yet one more. For this very point, that Christ riseth with *ascendo* in His mouth, that no sooner risen but makes ready for His ascending straight; this I say, if there were nothing but this, the so immediate joining it so close upon His rising, one hard to the other, no mean between, were of itself enough to make the idle dream of the old and new Chiliasts to vanish quite; that fancy to themselves I wot not what earthly kingdom here upon earth, somewhat like Mahomet's paradise, and will not hear of *ascendo* after they be risen, till a thousand years at least. This is none of Christ's rising, I am sure; so, to be none of ours. As with Him, so with us, rising and ascending are to follow straight one upon the other.

Christ then doth ascend. And out of what Christ did, we learn what we to do. Seeing Christ stayed not here, we not to set up our stay here neither, not to make earth our Heaven, not to place our felicity here below.

The Gospel is, we see, when Christ was risen His mind was upon *ascendo* presently. The Epistle is framed fit for it, that "if we be risen with Christ, we would set our Col. 3. 1. minds and seek the things above where Christ is;" that is, if we be risen with Him, make no more ado but ascend with Him also.

All things in Heaven and earth do so; rising, they ascend presently. In Heaven the stars, they be no sooner risen above the horizon, but they are in their ascendant *eo ipso*, and never leave ascending 'till they be in the highest point over our heads, in the very top of the sky. In earth, the little spires that peep out of the ground, now at this time,

SERM. XVI. nature's time of her yearly resurrection, they be no sooner out but up they shoot, and never leave to aspire till they have attained the full pitch of their highest growth they can ascend to. In ourselves, though I know for earthly men to have earthly minds it is not strange, πηλὸν ἔχοντες πατέρα, 'having clay to our father,' and προπάτερα χοῦν, 'dust to our sire,' we should have χαμερπῆ νοῦν, 'our souls should cleave to the dust,' as Nazianzen excellently saith. Not strange, I say, that so it is with us; yet, so it should not be. The very Heathen saw that though we be made of the earth, yet we are not made for the earth; that the heavenly soul was not put into the earthly body to the end the earthly body should draw it down to the earth, but rather to the end the soul should lift it up to Heaven. And
[Ovid. Met. 1. 85. 86.] so much they gathered out of our *os sublime*, and *vultus ad sidera*, the very frame of our body that bears up thitherward, and bodes as it were a kind of ascending whither it looks, and gives naturally. Nature doth teach this.

But grace by Christ's example much better. If Christ rise, that we rise with Christ; not in body yet, but to
[Rom. 6. 11.] "count ourselves dead to sin," and rise from that "and
Rev. 20. 5. live to God"—"the first Resurrection." And if Christ ascend, we likewise to ascend; not to part with Him, but to follow Him as we may. Not yet in body, it cannot be *sursum corpora* yet; it may be *sursum corda*, we may lift up our hearts thither, though. There "our treasure is," if
[Mat. 6. 21.] Christ be our treasure; there "our hearts to be," there we in heart to be at least, which is the first ascension, the προπαίδευμα of it, the *prœludium* so.

There are two words in the text, 1. *nondum ascendi*, "I am not yet ascended," and 2. *ascendo*, yet "I ascend" though; which will very well fit us, if while we are not at *ascendi* yet, that is in body ascended, we be for all that at *ascendo*, that is, ascend in mind, even as Christ here did. And blessed is the man, saith the Psalm, *cui in corde ascen-*
Ps. 84. 5. *siones*, "that hath the ascension in his heart," or his heart on it; that while it is *nondum ascendi* with him, yet at times it is *ascendo*, lifts up his eyes, sends up his sighs, exalts his thoughts otherwhile, represents as Christ doth, anticipates the ascension, *voto et desiderio* 'in will and desire,' before

the time itself come of the last and final ascension. Thus much for *ascendo*.

Ascendo is a motion. Every motion hath an *unde* and a *quo*, a 'whence' and 'a whither;' a *terminus a quo*, and a *terminus ad quem*. The *ad quem* is here *ad Patrem*. *Ad Patrem Meum.* The *Ad Quem.*

To ascend is to Christ His natural motion, Heaven is His natural place. Thence He came, thither He is to go again. Specially, His work being done He came for. That Joh. 19. 30.
was *consummatum est* with us, three days since. But till He be in Heaven again, it is not *consummatum est* with Him. So the motion is natural.

And the *ad quem*, *ad Patrem*, no less. Seeing for the Son to go to the Father is very kindly too, we may not be against it. Christ said, "If you loved Me, you would verily Joh. 14. 28.
rejoice because I said, I go to the Father." For very love to Christ, we cannot but rejoice with Him. In the *ad quem* all is well, if we consider that. But so is not in the *a quo*. For when all is said, make the best of it we can, *ascendo* is *discedo*, to go up is to go from—from them; and this is no good news. For Him no sooner to come, but gone again, and leave them to the wide world, it might trouble them for all "Tell My brethren." For by "brethren" He might mean false brethren that had left Him, and so would He them now; and peradventure do their errand in Heaven to His Father, and make them have but little thanks for it at His hands. So that, this *ascendo* implying a *nolo manere* in a manner, was as evil to them, as *noli Me tangere* was to her.

What is then become of the Gospel we spake of? where, or what is their comfort or ours, in these tidings? To deal plainly, when we seek it in *ascendo*, we find it not; nor in *ad Patrem*, nor in *ad Patrem Meum*. None of these is it. But in His *et ad Patrem vestrum*, there we find it, there it is. There was you will say as much as this comes to, in *fratres Meos*. It is true, it implied no less. But Christ would not deliver this *implicite*, 'by way of implying,' but *explicite*, as 'explicate and plainly,' as He could. And not once but twice. And it is a happy turn for us He did so, for this point can never be too plainly spoken to, too often repeated, too much stood upon. All the joy of the morn- *Et Patrem vestrum.*

SERM. XVI. ing is in this *vestrum*. "Tell them, I go to the Father"—that is not all; "Tell them" this too, as I go to the Father, so the Father I go to is their Father as well as Mine; not Mine alone, but theirs also. And tell them again, that if *Patrem Meum* be the cause of My ascending, as here is none other set down, if I go to Him thus because He is My Father; because He is theirs also, they also shall come after Me the same way, to the same place, upon the same reason.

And He doth express here the *terminus ad quem* by the party to Whom, rather than by the place to which, because the party will soon bring us to the place, and to somewhat besides. To the place; for you shall see what will follow
[John 14. 2.] of this, that His house, that Heaven is now become *Paterna domus* to us, as "our Father's house." And who shall keep
[Eph. 2. 19.] us from our Father's house? No more strangers now, but of the household of God. And in the household, not servants but children; and have thereto as good right and title, shall be as welcome thither every way, as any child to his own father's house here useth to be. God, through Him, standing no otherwise affected to us, than as a father to his child; as well disposed, as willing, as ready to receive
Mat. 3. 17. us. Christ His "beloved Son, in Whom He is" so absolutely "well pleased" as He always hears Him, hath prayed
Joh. 14. 3. to Him, and obtained of Him that "where He is, we may
Mic. 2. 13. be also," and, in due time, ascend up, whither He is now ascended, *pandens iter coram nobis*, "opening the passage for us to follow Him."

But I told you there was somewhat in the Person, more than in the place. For by virtue of this *Patrem vestrum*,
Rom. 8. 15. while we are here, if we cry "Abba Father" as now we may, He is ready to receive our prayers; and when we go hence, ready to receive our persons. While we are here, if
Lu. 15. 18. at any time we repent and say, *Ibo ad Patrem*, with the child in the Gospel, ready to receive us to grace; and when we go hence, we may say with Christ, *Vado ad Patrem*, ready to receive us to glory. So of *ad Patrem vestrum*, there is use here and there both.

And all this by means of Christ's resurrection; besides the general virtue whereof to make all men rise, all in the second Adam that die in the first, there is farther a second special virtue for us Christians, to make us rise, not only from the grave, but rise higher than so, even as high as to Heaven itself. And that we may have good right so to do, to make His Father ours, and His Father's house ours, that there we may dwell together *fratres in unum.* On [Ps. 133. 1.] which dependeth, and from whence riseth, all our hope of happiness for ever. And this is the joy of the feast we celebrate, the "loving-kindness of this morning," the glad tidings of Mary Magdalene's Gospel. It is *evangelium parvum,* so they call it, but 'a little one,' but it hath in it, in these few words couched, much matter both of high mystery and of heavenly comfort.

There be of the Fathers that telling the words of the message, which are fifteen in number, make them as so many steps or rongs, as it were, of Jacob's ladder, which we to ascend by. There be others that more properly, and to the text more agreeable, observe these four, 1. *Patrem Meum,* 2. *Patrem vestrum,* 3. *Deum Meum,* 4. *Deum vestrum,* as so many wheels, as it were, of Elias' chariot, in which "he was carried up to Heaven." *Ascendo,* the chariot; 2 Kings 2. 11. these, the four wheels of it.

The truth is, there lie fair before us in it, four pairs or combinations, by which four *ascendo* is here drawn in the text. 1. Two single: *Patrem* and *Deum,* one; 2. *Meum* and *vestrum,* the other. Two double: 3. *Patrem Meum,* and *Patrem vestrum,* one; and 4. *Deum Meum, Deum vestrum,* the other. I will but touch them briefly.

1. *Patrem Deum:* The first pair.

"Father" and "God" at large first, without any pronouns put to them at all. It was not so, *stylo veteri.* There in the Law, it was *Dominus Deus.* To change this, and to make it *stylo novo, Pater Deus;* in place of *Dominus* putting Exod. 20. 2. *Pater,* making of God a Lord, God a Father, is worth the while. It mends the term, and it mends the matter much, as much as a Father is better than a Lord. *Bonum pascha bonus transitus,* and we bound to our blessed Saviour for making this Passover, for working but this change or alteration in God's style.

"A Father:" how a Father? For a Father in a sense, we know, He may be said and is, to all things whatsoever.

SERM. XVI. "Father of the rain and of the drops of dew," in Job. But of us men, of mankind, more specially, in that we bear His
Job 38. 28. Image. But that is not it neither that here is meant. That is here meant is *ascendo ad Patrem*, a Father to ascend to. Not for our prayers only, but even also for our persons to ascend to. So a Father He is to none, but to Christ, and to the true Christian.

And this now, a Father to ascend to, is it that puts the difference between Him and all other fathers beside Him. Fathers to ascend to, such fathers there are none; none such here. Our fathers here we descend to, go down to them—down, down to the grave. Him, and Him only, we
Heb. 10. 12. go up to, up to Heaven, up even where Christ "is sitting at the right hand of God;" and He to that end a Father, even to make us ascend thither to Him.

Why would not "Father" suffice? Why is "God" added? Father is a name of much good will; but many a good father wants good means to his good will. God is added, that He may not be defective that way, have means to His meaning. For if He be a Father, first it is the voice of a father to his
Lu. 15. 31. son in the Gospel, *omnia mea tua sunt*. Now then, if this Father be also God, and all His be ours, what can we desire more than all God hath, all that ever God is worth; able to satisfy never so vast a desire, this. For so, if Heaven and the joys of it be His, they be ours too; and then there lacks nothing but *ascendo*, to go up and take possession of them; and here lo, it is, *ascendo ad Patrem*.

2. *Meum, vestrum*: The second pair. Bound to Him for this first, *Patrem Deum*. No whit less bound for the second, for putting to these pronouns possessives, *Meum* and *vestrum*, which is the second single combination. For till they came, till they in this wise were put to, *Meum* was *Meum*, and *vestrum* was *vestrum*; His was His, and ours was ours; His, His own, and ours to ourselves, and there an end. No relation either to other, no interest either in other. But now *Meum* is made *vestrum*, and *vestrum Meum*. His, ours; and ours His, interchangeably. A blessed change may we say; His great *Meum* for our little *vestrum*, little ours for great His. Every one will see the odds between these. That indeed we are as much bound for *Meum* and *vestrum*, as for *Patrem* and *Deum*. Nay more: For as there

is no comfort in Heaven without God, nor in God without a Father, so is there not any either in Father, Heaven, or God, without "ours" to give us a property in them. This then for the second single. Now to the two double.

Patrem Meum stands first, and is first every way. But *Patrem Meum* will do us no good. That which must do us the good, is the second in place, but to us the first. *Patrem vestrum*, that will serve; that alone will serve us, we need no more. *Ostende nobis Patrem et sufficit*, saith St. Philip. But how that should be compassed, and His *Meum* should be our *vestrum*, that He should be ours, *hic labor est*, 'that is all the matter.' 3. *Patrem Meum: Patrem vestrum:* The third pair. Joh. 14. 8.

This leads us to the other, the last combination of all, of *Deum Meum* and *vestrum*. For that His Father may be our Father, no remedy but our God must first be His God. So this fetches in that. One would not serve, there behoved to be twain, else the chariot will not go. *Deum Meum: Deum vestrum:* The fourth pair.

It will be best, *ante omnia*, to set forth in these terms, what is proper and what not; what Christ's and what ours. Much light we shall receive thereby.

Christ on His part saith, "My Father;" and He saith also, "My God." For Him to say, "My Father," is proper; we see reason for it. But for Him to say, "My God," no reason at all, altogether improper. For how can God have a God? *Patrem Meum. Deum Meum.*

Christ on our part saith, *Deum vestrum*, "your God." Right and true, that; we are His poor creatures, He our God; so known, so acknowledged to be. But He saith further, *Patrem vestrum*, "your Father;" how that can be said, we see not. Alas, we are but dust and ashes, our lineage is well set forth by Job; we must say "to rottenness, Thou art my father; and to the worms, Ye are my mother, ye are my sister." No Father of ours He, not properly. *Deum vestrum. Patrem vestrum.* Job 17. 14.

In exact propriety of speech then, "Father" here refers to Christ, God to us. "His Father," is right; so is "our God." We will never spend a word on them, let them go. But "His God," no way right; no more than, "our Father." These two, it is sure, are improper both. And if ever they shall be verified one of the other, it must be brought about by some other ways and means. And so it is, and by the *Patrem Meum: Deum vestrum.*

SERM. XVI. same way that the one, by the very same the other. "His Father," "our Father" by His means. "Our God," "His God" by ours.

Deum Meum. To set them in right method, in their true order, *erunt novissimi primi*, the last is to be first; we to begin at *Deum vestrum*, the very last word of all, as it were the foot of the ladder, or the two smaller wheels that go before. To make *Meum vestrum*, His ours, *vestrum* is to be made *Meum*, ours to be made His. Our God to become His God first, that His Father may become our Father after. Him That was our God, we to make His God, that Him That was His Father, He may make to be our Father.

That this might proceed, He That doth here ascend was to descend. Descend whither? Even to be one of us; and we were creatures, and so being one of us, He to be a creature as well as we. So He was, and so He is. For even the soul and body of Christ are in the rank of creatures; and relation had to them, a creature He is, a God He hath, the same That we, for there is but one; and so we might truly say *Deum Meum*, our God is His God. That we might ascend to the
Eph. 4. 9. highest Heaven, "He was to descend" εἰς κατώτερα τῆς γῆς, "to the lowest parts of the earth;" and so did. *Descendo ad matrem* with Him, that *ascendo ad Patrem* with us. That we
Rom. 8. 15. might cry "Abba Father," He was content to cry that strange
Mat. 27.46. cry, *Eli, Eli*, "My God, My God," on the cross.

So Christ might then say, and truly say, "My God," no less than "My Father;" His Father as God, His God as man. As the Son of God, a God He hath not, a Father He hath; as the Son of man, a Father He hath not, a God He hath. A God I say then He hath, but never till then; never till He meddled with us. But then He had, and since He hath. He That was ours not His, is now His as well as ours. These two wheels are set right.

Patrem vestrum. We have brought it to this, that Christ may say *Deum Meum*. After we have brought Him to *Deum Meum*, we are half way, our God is His. But now, how shall we get His Father to have Him to be our Father? First, His Father He was from all eternity; He, and none but He can say, and say properly, *Patrem Meum*. But He is content to quit that 'none but He,' and to take us in; and He being our brother before, to make us His now. Ours, in our estate of this mortal; His, in His estate of immortal life. For here now rising, and upon His ascending, He adopts us; and, by adopting, makes us; and by making, pronounces us His brethren, and so children to His Father. Us, His children; Him, our Father—witness *fratres Meos,* and *Patrem vestrum,* both from His own mouth. *Salvum sit verbum Domini mei,* by virtue whereof it is now *Abba Pater* with us. Now, *Vado ad Patrem,* we a Father of God, even as Christ That spake it, to pray to, to go to. *Meum* and *vestrum* both now in one. Then we had a Father of Him, and since we have; but till then, a God we had, but not a Father; at least, not such a Father of Him as since we have. This, the *bonum pascha,* the *felix transitus,* the blessed interchange we spoke of.

Deum Meum. Patrem vestrum.

Who gets by this? *Deum Meum,* His, His God, was His humiliation. He as low as we, nay lower than the lowest of us when He cried, "My God, My God." *Deum Meum,* His humiliation, and *Patrem vestrum* our exaltation; by it we are made in case as He, to rise, to ascend; to go whither, to be where He is for ever; to say *ibo ad Patrem;* to say *vado ad Patrem;* to say with Him, "Father, forgive;" and again, "Father, into Thy hands I commend My Spirit." In *Patrem vestrum* are all these. Lu. 23. 34. 46.

So by this time we see the necessity of both these combinations, of both pair of wheels; and that to our great comfort.

Meum and *vestrum,* not *nostrum.*

But we are not so to look to our own comfort, but that withal we be careful to preserve His honour; that so, both may go hand in hand together. And there is order taken for that too, by severing of each pair; that it is not *nostrum* in one word, 'ours,' but *Meum* and *vestrum* in two words, "Mine," and "yours;" yet otherwise His, and otherwise ours, both as Father and as God.

As Father. His by nature, by very generation; ours by grace, by mere adoption. As God, and there we are before Him, our God by nature. His no otherwise than as He took upon Him our nature.

But His honour thus set safe, by this partition kept on foot, then let the wheels run, pursue the rest as far as you please, make of it the most you can, for your best avail. That one

SERM. XVI. and the same is both His and ours. One Father, one God, Him and us both. Father to Him, God to us; God to Him, Father to us. If we a God, He one. If He a Father, we one. Our God Christ's God, Christ's Father our Father. There is *ascendo* your chariot, and these are the four wheels on which it moveth, and is carried up to Heaven.

But where is Easter-day, what is become of it all this while? For methinks, all the time we are thus about Father and Son, and taking our nature and becoming one of us, it should be Christmas by this, and not Easter as it is; that this a meeter text one would think for that feast, and that now it comes out of season.

Not a whit. It is Christ That speaketh, and He never speaketh but in season; never but to the purpose, never but on the right day.

A brotherhood, we grant, was begun then at Christmas by
[Ps. 87. 4.] His birth, as upon that day, for "lo then was He born." But so was He now also at Easter; born then too, and after a better manner born. His resurrection was a second birth, Easter a second Christmas. *Hodie genui Te*, as true of this day as of that. The Church appointeth for the first Psalm
Ps. 2. 7. this day the second Psalm, the Psalm of *hodie genui Te*. The
Acts 13. 33. Apostle saith expressly, when He rose from the dead, then was *hodie genui Te* fulfilled in Him, verified of Him. Then
Col. 1. 18. He was *primogenitus a mortuis*, "God's first-begotten from the dead." And upon this latter birth doth the brotherhood of this day depend.

There was then a new begetting this day. And if a new begetting, a new paternity, and fraternity both. By the *hodie genui Te* of Christmas, how soon He was born of the Virgin's womb He became our brother, sin except, subject to all our infirmities; so to mortality, and even to death itself. And by death that brotherhood had been dissolved, but for this day's rising. By the *hodie genui Te* of Easter, as soon as He was born again of the womb of the grave, He begins a new brotherhood, founds a new fraternity straight; adopts us we see anew again by His *fratres Meos*, and thereby He That was *primogenitus a mortuis* becomes
Rom. 8. 29. *primogenitus inter multos fratres;* when "the first-begotten
Rev. 1. 5. from the dead," then "the first-begotten" in this respect

"among many brethren." Before He was ours, now we are His. That was by the mother's side;—so, He ours. This is by *Patrem vestrum,* the Father's side;—so, we His. But half-brothers before, never of whole blood till now. Now by Father and mother both, *fratres germani, fratres fraterrimi,* we cannot be more.

To shut all up in a word, that of Christmas was the fraternity rising out of *Deum Meum, Deum vestrum;* so then brethren. This of Easter, adopting us to His Father, was the fraternity of *Patrem Meum, Patrem vestrum;* so brethren now.

This day's is the better birth, the better brotherhood by far; the fore-wheels are the less, the hinder the larger ever. For first, that of ours was when He was mortal; but His adoption He deferred, He would not make it while He was mortal; reserved it till He was risen again, and was even upon His ascending, and then He made it. So mortal He was, when He ours; but now when we His, He is immortal, and we brethren to Him in that state, the state of immortality. Brethren before, but not to *ascendo;* now to *ascendo* and all. Death was in danger to have dissolved that, but death hath now no power on Him, or on this; this shall never be in danger of being dissolved any more. That without this is nothing.

But we shall not need to stand in terms of comparison, since then it was but one of these; now it is both. His Father is now become our Father, to make us joint-heirs with Him of His Heavenly Kingdom; His God likewise become our God, to make us "partakers" with them both "of the Divine nature." *Patrem Meum* and *Patrem vestrum,* [2 Pet. 1. 4.] *Deum Meum* and *Deum vestrum,* run both merrily together, and *ascendo* upon them both.

Whereof, I mean of the partaking of His divine nature, to give us full and perfect assurance, as He took our flesh and became our Brother, flesh of our flesh then, so He gives us His flesh, that we may become His brethren, flesh of His flesh, now; and gives it us now upon this day, the very day of our adoption into this fraternity. By taking our flesh—so begun His; by giving His flesh—so begins ours. For requisite it was, that since we drew our death

SERM. XVI.

from the first Adam by partaking his substance, semblably and in like sort we should partake the substance of the second Adam; that so we might draw our life from Him; should be ingrafted into Him, as the branches into the vine, that we might receive His sap—which is His similitude; should be flesh of His flesh, not He of ours as before, but we of His now; that we might be vegetate with His Spirit, even with His Divine Spirit. For now in Him the Spirits are so united, as partake one and partake the other withal.

And it hath been, and it is therefore an ordinance in the Church for ever, that as upon this day, at the returning of it continually, His flesh and blood should be in Sacrament exhibited to us; as to make a yearly solemn renewing of this fraternity, so likewise to seal to us the fruit of it, our rising; and not rising only, but so rising as *ascendo* go withal. A badge of the one, a pledge of the other. For which cause, as it is called "the living Bread," for that it shall restore us to life and raise us up in the last day, so is it also "the Bread that came down from Heaven;" came down from thence, to make us go up thither, and in the strength of it to ascend into God's holy hill, and there rest with Him in His tabernacle for ever. That so the truth of the feast, and of the text both, may be fulfilled in us everlastingly with God (*Patrem vestrum*) our Father; and with Christ (*fratres Meos*) our Brother, and with the blessed Spirit, the love of them both one to the other, and of them both to us.

[John 6. 51.]

A SERMON

PREACHED BEFORE

THE KING'S MAJESTY, AT WHITEHALL,

ON THE THIRTEENTH OF APRIL, A.D. MDCXXIII., BEING EASTER-DAY.

Isaiah lxiii. 1—3.

Who is this That cometh from Edom, with red garments from Bosrah? He is glorious in His apparel, and walketh in great strength; I speak in righteousness, and am mighty to save.

Wherefore is Thine apparel red, and Thy garments like him that treadeth in the winepress?

I have trodden the winepress alone, and of all the people there was none with Me; for I will tread them in Mine anger, and tread them under foot in My wrath, and their blood shall be sprinkled upon My garments, and I will stain all My raiment.

[*Quis est iste Qui venit de Edom, tinctis vestibus de Bosra? Iste formosus in stolâ Suâ, gradiens in multitudine fortitudinis Suæ. Ego, Qui loquor justitiam, et propugnator sum ad salvandum.*

Quare ergo rubrum est indumentum Tuum, et vestimenta Tua sicut calcantium in torculari?

Torcular calcavi solus, et de gentibus non est vir Mecum; calcavi eos in furore Meo, et conculcavi eos in irâ Meâ; et aspersus est sanguis eorum super vestimenta Mea, et omnia indumenta Mea inquinavi. Latin Vulg.]

[*Who is this That cometh from Edom, with dyed garments from Bozrah? this That is glorious in His apparel, travelling in the greatness of His strength? I That speak in righteousness, mighty to save.*

Wherefore art Thou red in Thine apparel, and Thy garments like him that treadeth in the winefat?

I have trodden the winepress alone, and of the people there was none with Me; for I will tread them in Mine anger, and trample them in My fury; and their blood shall be sprinkled upon My garments, and I will stain all My raiment. Engl. Trans.]

Ever when we read or hear read any text or passage out of this Prophet, the Prophet Esay, it brings to our mind the

SERM. XVII. nobleman that sitting in his chariot, read another like passage out of this same Prophet. Brings him to mind, and
Acts 8. 34. with him his question, "Of whom doth the Prophet speak this? of himself or of some other?" Not of himself, that's once; it cannot be himself. It is he that asks the question. Some other then it must needs be of whom it is, and we to ask who that other was.

The tenor of Scripture that nobleman then read was out of the fifty-third chapter, and this of ours out of the sixty-third, ten chapters between. But if St. Philip had found him reading of this here, as he did of that, he would likewise have begun at this same Scripture as at that he did, and preached to him Christ—only with this difference; out of that, Christ's Passion; out of this, His Resurrection. For
Isa. 53. 7. He That was led "as a sheep to be slain," and so was slain there, He it is and no other That rises and comes here back like a lion "from Bozrah," imbrued with blood, the blood of His enemies.

I have before I was aware disclosed who this party is—it was not amiss I so should; not to hold you long in suspense, but to give you a little light at the first, whom it would fall on. Christ it is. Two things there are that make it can be no other but He. 1. One is without the text, in the end of
Isa. 62. 11 [See the Vulgate.] the chapter next before. There is a proclamation, "Behold, here comes your Saviour;" and immediately, He That comes is this party here from Edom. He is our Saviour, and besides Him there is none, even Christ the Lord. 2. The other is in the text itself, in these words; *Torcular calcavi solus,* "I have trod the winepress alone." Words so proper to Christ, so every where ascribed to Him, and to Him only, as you shall not read them any where applied to any other; no, not by the Jews themselves. So as if there were no more but these two, they shew it plainly enough it is, it can be, none but Christ.

And Christ when? Even this day of all days. His coming here from Edom, will fall out to be His rising from the dead; His return from Bozrah, nothing but His vanquishing
Ps. 16. 10. of hell. We may use His words in applying it, "Thou hast
[Ps. 71. 20.] not left My soul in hell," "but brought Me back from the deep of the earth again;" nothing but the act of His rising

again. So that this very morning was this Scripture fulfilled in our ears.

The whole text entire is a dialogue between two, 1. the I.
Prophet, and 2. Christ. There are in it two questions, and to the two questions two answers. 1. The Prophet's first question is touching the party Himself, who He is, in these words, "Who is this?" to which the party Himself answers in the same verse these words, "That am I, one That," &c.

The Prophet's second question is about His colours, why II.
He was all in red, in the second verse; "Wherefore then is Thy apparel," &c. The answer to that is in the third verse in these; "I have trodden," &c. "For I will tread them down."

Of Christ; of His rising or coming back, of His colours, of the winepress that gave Him this tincture, or rather of the two winepresses; 1. the winepress of redemption first, 2. and then of the other winepress of vengeance.

The Prophets use to speak of things to come as if they saw I. The first question touching the party: Who it is.
them present before their eyes. That makes their prophecies be called visions. In his vision here, the Prophet being taken up in Spirit sees one coming. Coming whence? From the land or country of Idumæa or Edom. From what place there? From Bozrah, the chief city in the land, the place of greatest strength. "Who will lead me into the strong city?" that is, Bozrah. "Who will bring me into Edom?" Ps. 60. 9.
He that can do the first, can do the latter. Win Bozrah, and Edom is won.

There was a cry in the end of the chapter before; "Behold, here comes your Saviour." He looked, and saw [Isa. 62. 11. See the Vulgate.]
one coming. Two things he descries in this party: 1. One, His habit, that He was *formosus in stolâ*, "very richly arrayed;" 2. The other, His gait, that He "came stoutly marching," or pacing the ground very strongly. Two good familiar notes, to descry a stranger by. His apparel, whether rich or mean, which the world most commonly takes notice of men by. His gait; for weak men have but a feeble gait. Valiant strong men tread upon the ground so, as by it you may discern their strength.

Now this party, He came so goodly in His apparel, so stately in His march, as if by all likelihood He had made

SERM. XVII. some conquest in Edom, the place He came from; had had a victory in Bozrah, the city where He had been. And the truth is, so He had. He saith it in the third verse, "He had trodden down His enemies," had trampled upon them, made the blood even start out of them; which blood of theirs had [Jud. 9. 53.] all to stained His garments. This was no evil news for Esay's countrymen, the people of God; Edom was the worst enemy they had.

With joy then, but not without admiration, such a party sees the Prophet come toward him. Sees Him, but knows Him not, thinks Him worthy the knowing; so thinking, and not knowing, is desirous to be instructed concerning Him. Out of this desire asks, *Quis est?* Not of Himself, he durst not be so bold, Who are you? but of some stander by, Whom have we here? Can you tell who this might be? The first question.

What is meant 1. by Edom. But before we come to the question, a word or two of the place where He had been, and whence He came. "Edom" and "Bozrah," what is meant by them? For if this party Mat. 2. 14. be Christ, Christ was in Egypt a child, but never in Edom that we read, never at Bozrah in all His life; so as here we are to leave the letter. Some other it might be the letter might mean; we will not much stand to look after him. For however possibly some such there was, yet it will plainly Rev. 19. 10. appear by the sequel, that "the testimony of Jesus," as it is of each other, so it "is the spirit of this prophecy."

Go we then to the kernel and let the husk lie; let go the dead letter, and take we to us the spiritual meaning that hath some life in it. For what care we for the literal Edom or Bozrah, what became of them; what are they to us? Let us compare spiritual things with spiritual things, that is it must do us good.

I will give you a key to this, and such like Scriptures. Familiar it is with the Prophets, nothing more, than to speak to their people in their own language; than to express their ghostly enemies, the both mortal and immortal enemies of their souls, under the titles and terms of those nations and cities as were the known sworn enemies of the commonwealth of Israel. As of Egypt where they were in bondage; as of Babylon, where in captivity; elsewhere, as of Edom here,

who maliced them more than both those. If the Angel tell us
right, Revelation the eleventh, there is "a spiritual Sodom Rev. 11. 8.
and Egypt where our Lord was crucified;" and if they, why
not a spiritual Edom too whence our Lord rose again? Put
all three together, Egypt, Babel, Edom, all their enmities,
all are nothing to the hatred that hell bears us. But yet if
you ask, of the three which was the worst? That was Edom.
To shew, the Prophet here made good choice of his place,
Edom upon earth comes nearest to the kingdom of darkness
in hell, of all the rest. And that, in these respects:

First, they were the wickedest people under the sun. If
there were any devils upon earth, it was they; if the devil of
any country, he would choose to be an Edomite. No place
on earth that resembled hell nearer; next to hell on earth
was Edom for all that naught was. Malachi calls Edom, Mal. 1. 4.
"the border of all wickedness," "a people with whom God
was angry for ever." In which very points, no enemies so
fitly express the enemies of our souls, against whom the
anger of God is eternal, and "the smoke of whose torments Rev. 14. 11.
shall ascend for ever." Hell, for all that naught is. That
if the power of darkness, and hell itself, if they be to be
expressed by any place on earth, they cannot be better
expressed than in these, "Edom" and "Bozrah."

I will give you another. The Edomites were the posterity 2.
of Esau; "the same is Edom." So they were nearest of kin Gen. 36. 1.
to the Jews, of all nations; so should have been their best
friends. The Jews and they came of two brethren. Edom
was the elder, and that was the grief, that the people of
Israel coming of Jacob the younger brother, had enlarged
their border; got them a better seat and country by far than
they, the Edomites had. Hence grew envy, and an enemy
out of envy is ever the worst. So were they, the most cankered enemies that Israel had. The case is so between us
and the evil spirits. Angels they were we know, and so in
a sort elder brethren to us. Of the two intellectual natures,
they the first created. Our case now, Christ be thanked! is
much better than theirs; which is that enraged them against
us, as much and more than ever any Edomite against Israel.
Hell, for rancour and envy.

Yet one more. They were ready to do God's people all 3.

SERM. XVII. the mischief they were able, and when they were not able of themselves, they shewed their good-wills though, set on
Ps. 137. 7. others. And when they had won Jerusalem, cried "Down with it, down with it, even to the ground;" no less would serve. And when it was on the ground, insulted and rejoiced above measure: "Remember the children of Edom." This is right the devil's property, *quarto modo*. He that hath but the heart of a man, will even rue to see his enemy lying in extreme misery. None but very devils, or devils incarnate, will do so; corrupt their compassion, cast off all pity; rejoice, insult, take delight at one's destruction. Hell for their ἐπέχαιρε κακίᾳ, 'insulting over men in misery.'

4. But will ye go even to the letter? none did ever so much
1 Sam. 22. 9. mischief to David, as did Doeg; he was an Edomite. Nor none so much to the Son of David, Christ, none bore more malice to Him first and last than did Herod; and he was an Edomite. So, which way soever we take it, next the kingdom of darkness was Edom upon earth. And Christ coming from thence, may well be said to come from Edom.

2. By Bozrah. But what say you to Bozrah? This; that if the country of Edom do well set before us the whole kingdom of darkness or region of death, Bozrah may well stand for hell itself. Bozrah was the strongest hold of that kingdom, hell is so of this. The whole country of Idumea was called and known by the name of Uz, that is, of strength; and what of such strength as death? all the sons of men stoop
Ps. 60. 9. to him. Bozrah was called "the strong city;" hell is strong as it every way. They write, it was environed with huge high rocks on all sides, one only cleft to come to it by. And when you were in, there must you perish; no getting out again. For all the world like to hell, as Abraham de-
Lu. 16. 26. scribes it to him that was in it, "they that would go from this place to you cannot possibly, neither can they come from thence to us;" the gulf is so great, no getting out. No *habeas corpus* from death, no *habeas animam* out of hell;
Ps. 49. 8. you must "let that alone for ever."

Now then we have the Prophet's true Edom, his very Bozrah indeed. By this we understand what they mean. "Edom," the kingdom of darkness and death; "Bozrah," the seat of the prince of darkness, that is, hell itself. From

both which Christ this day returned. "His soul was not Ps. 16. 10.
left in hell, His flesh saw not," but rose from, "corruption."

For "over Edom," strong as it was, yet David "cast his Ps. 108. 9.
shoe;" "over" it, that is, after the Hebrew phrase, set his foot upon it and trod it down. And Bozrah, as impregnable a hold as it was holden, yet David won it; was led "into the strong city," led into it, and came thence again. So did the Son of David this day from His Edom, death,
how strong soever, yet "swallowed up in victory" this day. 1 Cor. 15. 54.
And from hell His Bozrah, how hard soever it held, as he that was in it found there was no getting thence, Christ is got forth we see. How many souls soever were there left, His was not left there.

And when did He this? when *solutus doloribus inferni*,
"He loosed the pains of hell," trod upon the serpent's head, Acts 2. 24.
and all to[1] bruised it, took from death his "sting," from 1 Cor. 15. 55.
hell his "victory," that is his standard, alluding to the Roman standard that had in it the image of the goddess
Victory. Seized upon the *chirographum contra nos*, the Col. 2. 14, 15.
ragman roll[2] that made so strong against us; took it, rent it, and so rent "nailed it to His Cross;" made His banner of it, of the law cancelled, hanging at it banner-wise. And having thus "spoiled principalities and powers, He made an open show of them, triumphed over them" in *Semetipso*, "in His own person,"—all three are in Colossians the second,—and triumphantly came thence with the keys of Edom and Bozrah both, "of hell and of death" both, at His girdle, as He shews Himself. And when was this? if ever, on this very day. On which, having made a full and
perfect conquest of death, "and of him that hath the power Heb. 2. 14.
of death, that is, the devil," He rose and returned thence Judges 5, 21.
this morning as a mighty Conqueror, saying as Deborah did in her song, "O my soul, thou hast trodden down strength," thou hast marched valiantly!

And coming back thus, from the debellation of the spiritual Edom, and the breaking up of the true Bozrah indeed, it is wondered who it should be. Note this; that nobody knew
Christ at His rising, neither Mary Magdalene, nor they that Joh. 20. 14.
went to Emmaus. No more doth the Prophet here. Lu. 24. 16.

Now there was reason to ask this question, for none would 1.

[1 i. e. entirely]

[2 *Literally*, a Statute which respected complaints of injuries, and also such letters as contained self-accusations of crimes committed against the state. *Jamieson.*]

SERM. XVII. ever think it to be Christ. There is great odds it cannot be He. 1. Not He; He was put to death, and put into His grave, and a great stone upon Him, not three days since. This party is alive and alives-like. His ghost it cannot be; He glides not as ghosts they say do, but paces the ground very strongly.

2. Not He; He had His apparel shared amongst the soldiers, was left all naked. This party hath gotten Him on "glorious apparel," rich scarlet.

3. Not He; for if He come, He must come in white, in the linen He was lapped in, and laid in His grave. This party comes in quite another colour, all in red. So the colours suit not.

4. To be short, not He, for He was put to a foil, to a foul foil as ever was any; they did to Him even what they
Lu. 22. 53. listed; scorned, insulted upon Him. It was then "the hour and power of darkness." This Party, whatsoever He is, hath gotten the upper hand, won the field; marches stately, Conqueror-like. His, the day sure.

The first answer. That Party is Christ. Well, yet Christ it is. His answer gives Him for no other. To His answer then. The Party, it seems, overheard the Prophet's asking, and is pleased to give an answer to it Himself; we are much bound to Him for it. No man can tell so well as He Himself, who He is. Some other might mistake Him, and misinform us of Him; now we are sure we are right. No *error personæ.*

His name indeed He tells not, but describes Himself by two such notes as can agree to none properly but to Christ. Of none can these two be so affirmed, as of Him they may. That by these two we know this is Christ, as plainly as if His name had been spelled to us. 1. "Speaking righteousness;" and righteousness referred to speech, signifieth truth
1 Pet. 2. 22. ever. "No guile to be found in His mouth;" and *omnis*
Ps. 116. 11. *homo* is—you know what. 2. "Mighty to save;" and *vana*
Ps. 60. 11. *salus hominis,* "vain is the help of man." Who ever spake so right as He spake? Or who ever was so "mighty to save" as He? And this is His answer to *quis est iste.*

"That am I." One "that speak righteousness, and am mighty to save." Righteous in speaking, mighty in saving, Whose word is truth, Whose work is salvation. Just and true of My word and promise; powerful and mighty in performance of both. The best description, say I, that can be of any man; by His word and deed both.

And see how well they fit. Speaking is most proper; that 1. His nature.
refers to Him, as the Word—"in the beginning was the Joh. 1. 1.
Word"—to His Divine nature. Saving, that refers to His
very name Jesus, given Him by the Angel as man, for that
"He should save His people from their sins," from which Mat. 1. 21.
none had ever power to save but He. There have you His
two natures.

Speaking refers to His office of Priest: "the Priest's lips 2. His offices.
to preserve knowledge;"—the law of righteousness to be re- Mal. 2. 7.
quired at his mouth. Saving, and that mightily, pertains
to Him as a King, is the office, as Daniel calls Him, of Dan. 9. 25.
"Messias the Captain." Righteousness He spake, by His
preaching. Saving, that belongs first to His miraculous
suffering, it being far a greater miracle for the Deity to
suffer any the least injury, than to create a new world, yea
many. But secondly, which is proper to the text and time,
in His mighty subduing and treading down hell and death,
and all the power of Satan. *Prophetiza nobis,* they said at Lu. 22. 64.
His passion, "Speak, who hit you" there; and *Ave Rex* Mat. 27. 29.
they said too;—both in scorn, but most true both.

You may refer these two, if you please, to His two main 3. His benefits.
benefits redounding to us from these two. Two things there are that undo us, error and sin. From His speaking we receive knowledge of His truth, against error. From His saving we receive the power of grace against sin, and so are saved from sin's sequel, Edom and Bozrah both. This is His description, and this is enough. A full description of His Person, in His natures, offices, benefits; in word and in deed. He it is, and can be none but He. To reflect a little on these two.

You will observe that His speaking is set down simply, 1. "Mighty," not in speaking.
but in His saving He is said to be "mighty," or, as the word is, *multus ad servandum.* So, mark where the *multus* is. He is not *multus ad loquendum,* 'one that saith much,' and *paucus ad servandum,* 'and then does little,' as the manner of the world is. *Multus* is not there at His speech, it is put to *servandum;* there He is much, and His might much; "much of might to save."

SERM. XVII.

2. But "in saving." Isa. 55. 7. That His might is not put in treading down or destroying. No, but *multus ad ignoscendum*, in the fifty-fifth chapter before; and *multus ad servandum*, here. "Mighty" to shew mercy, and to save. Yet "mighty" He is too, to destroy and tread down; else had He not achieved this victory in the text. "Mighty to save," implieth ever mighty to subdue; to subdue them whom He saves us from. Yet of the twain He chooseth rather the term of saving, though both be true, because saving is with Him *primæ intentionis;* so, of the twain, in that He would have His might appear rather. Mighty to destroy He will not have mentioned, or come in His style; but "mighty to save," that is His title, that the quality He takes delight in; delights to describe Himself, and to be described by.

3. Yet He teacheth too; and that first. You will yet mark also, as the coupling of these two in the description of Christ, for not either of these alone will serve, but between them both they make it up, so that they go together, these two ever. He saves not any but those He teaches. And note the order of them too. For that that stands first, He doth first, first teaches. "Mighty to save" He is, but whom to save? whom He "speaks righteousness" to, and they hear Him, and return not again to their former folly. There is no fancying to ourselves we can dispense with one of these, never care whether we deal with the former or no, whether we hear Him speak at all, but take hold of the latter, and be saved with a good will. No; you cannot, but if you hear Him speak first. He saith so, and sets them to Himself.

We to be like Him in both. And put this to it, and I have done this point. That such as is Himself, such if we hear Him will He make us to be. And the more true and soothfast any of us is of His word, the more given to do good and save, the liker to Him, and the liker to have our parts in His rising. We know *quis est iste* now. This for the first part.

II. The second question: Why His apparel is red. Now, the Prophet hearing Him answer so gently, takes to him a little courage to ask Him one question more, about His colours; he was a little troubled with them. If you be so "mighty to save" as you say, how comes it then, what ails your garments to be so red? and adds, what kind of red. And he cannot tell what to liken them better to, than as if He had newly come out of some winepress, had been treading grapes, and pressing out wine there. He calls it wine, but the truth is it was no wine, it was very blood. New wine in show, blood indeed that upon His garments. So much appeareth in the next verse following, where He saith Himself plainly that blood it was that was sprinkled upon His clothes, and had stained them all over. We know well, our reason leads us, there could be no vintage at this time of the year, the season serves not; blood it was.

But because the Prophet made mention of a "winepress," had hit on that simile, taking occasion upon the naming it, He shapes him an answer according; that indeed He had been in a "winepress." And so He had. The truth is, He had been in one; nay, in two then. In one He had been before this here. A double winepress—we lose nothing by this—we find; Christ was in both. We cannot well take notice of the one, but we must needs touch upon the other. But thus they are distinguished. In that former it was *In torculari calcatus sum solus;* in this latter it is, *Torcular calcavi solus.* In the former, He was Himself trodden and pressed; He was the grapes and clusters Himself. In this latter here, He that was trodden on before, gets up again, and doth here tread upon and tread down, *calcare* and *conculcare* (both words are in the verse) upon some others, as it might be the Edomites. The press He was trodden in, was His Cross and Passion. This which He came out of this day, was in His descent and resurrection, both proper to this feast; one to Good-Friday, the other to Easter-day. The answer.

To pursue this of the winepress a little. The press, the treading in it, is to make wine; *calcatus sum* is properly of grapes, the fruit of the vine. Christ is the "true Vine," He saith it Himself. To make wine of Him, He and the clusters He bare must be pressed. So He was. Three shrewd strains they gave Him. One, in Gethsemane, that made Him sweat blood; the wine or blood,—all is one, came forth at all parts of Him. Another, in the Judgment hall, Gabbatha, which made the blood run forth at His head, with the thorns; out of His whole body, with the scourges; out of His hands and feet, with the nails. The last strain at Golgotha, where He was so pressed that The first wine-press. Christ's *calcatus sum.* Joh. 15. 5. Mat. 26. 36. &c. Joh. 19. 13. &c.

SERM. XVII. they pressed the very soul out of His body, and out ran
Joh. 19. 34. "blood and water" both. *Hæc sunt Ecclesiæ gemina Sacra-*
[S. Aug. in Joan. Tract. 120.] *menta*, saith St. Augustine, out came both Sacraments, 'the
twin Sacraments of the Church.'

Out of these pressures ran the blood of the grapes of the
true Vine, the fruit whereof, as it is said in Judges the
Judges 9. 13. ninth, "cheereth both God and man." God, as a *libamen*
or drink-offering to Him; man, as "the cup of salvation"
[Ps. 116. 13.] to them. But to make this wine, His clusters were to be
cut; cut, and cast in; cast in, and trodden on; trodden
and pressed out; all these, before He came to be wine in
the cup. As likewise, when He calls Himself *granum fru-*
Joh. 12. 24. *menti*, "the wheat-corn," these four, 1. the sickle, 2. the
flail, 3. the millstone, 4. the oven, He passed through; all
[Exod. 25. 30.] went over Him before He was made bread; "the shew-
[John 6. 48.] bread" to God, to us "the Bread of life."

But to return to the winepress, to tell you the occasion or
reason why thus it behoved to be. It was not idly done;
what need then was there of it, this first pressing? We
1 Cor. 10. 21. find *calix dæmoniorum*, the devil hath a cup. Adam must
Gen. 3. 5. needs be sipping of it; *Eritis sicut Dii* went down sweetly,
but poisoned him, turned his nature quite. For Adam was
by God planted a natural vine, a true root, but thereby,
Isa. 5. 4. by that cup, degenerated into a wild strange vine, which,
instead of good grapes, "brought forth" *labruscas*, "wild
Deut. 32. 32. grapes;" "grapes of gall," "bitter clusters," Moses calls
2 Kings 4. 39, 40. them; *colocynthidas*, the Prophet, *mors in olla*, and *mors in
calice*; by which is meant the deadly fruit of our deadly sins.

But, as it is in the fifth chapter of this prophecy, where God planted this vine first, He made a winepress in it, so the grapes that came of this strange vine were cut and cast into the press: thereof came a deadly wine, of which saith
Ps. 75. 8. the Psalmist, "in the hand of the Lord there is a cup, the
wine is red, it is full mixed, and He pours out of it; and
the sinners of the earth are to drink it, dregs and all."
Mat. 26. 27. Those sinners were our fathers, and we. It came to *Bibite
ex hoc omnes*; they and we were to drink of it all, one after another, round. Good reason to drink as we had brewed, to drink the fruit of our own inventions, our own words and works we had brought forth.

About the cup went, all strained at it. At last, to Christ
it came; He was none of the sinners, but was found among Isa. 53. 12.
them. By His good will He would have had it pass; *trans-* Mat. 26. 39.
eat a Me calix iste,—you know who That was. Yet, rather
than we, than any of us should take it—it would be our
bane, He knew—He took it; off it went, dregs and all.
Alas, the myrrh they gave Him at the beginning, the vinegar
at the ending of His Passion, were but poor resemblances
of this cup, such as they were. That, another manner
draught. We see it cast Him into so unnatural a sweat
of blood all over, as if He had been wrung and crushed in
a "winepress" it could not have been more. This, lo, was
the first "winepress," and Christ in it three days ago; and
what with the scourges, nails and spears, besides so pressed
as forth it ran, blood or wine, call it what you will, in such
so great quantity, as never ran it more plenteously out of
any winepress of them all. Here is *Christus in torculari,*
Christ's *calcatus sum.*

Of which wine so pressed then out of Him came our cup,
the cup of this day, "the cup of the New Testament in His Lu. 22. 20.
blood," represented by the blood of the grape. Wherein
long before old Jacob foretold Shiloh should "wash his Gen. 49. 11.
robe," as full well He might have done, there came enough
to have washed it over and over again. So you see now
how the case stands. That former, our cup due to us and
no way to Him, He drank for us that it might pass from
us, and we not drink it. Ours did He drink, that we might
drink of His. He "the cup of wrath," that we "the cup Isa. 51. 22.
of blessing," set first before God as a *libamen,* at the sight 1 Cor. 10. 16.
or scent whereof He smelleth a savour of rest, and is ap-
peased. After reached to us, as a sovereign restorative to
recover us of the devil's poison, for we also have been sipping at *calix dæmoniorum* more or less, woe to us for it!
and no way but this to cure us of it.

By this time you see the need of the first press, and of His being in it. Into which He was content to be thrown and there trodden on, all to satisfy His Father out of His justice requiring the drinking up of that cup by us or by some for us, and it came to His lot. And never was there lamb so meek before the shearer, nor worm so easy to be

SERM. XVII. trodden on; never cluster lay so quiet and still to be bruised as did Christ in the press of His passion. Ever be He blessed for it!

The second winepress, Christ's 1. *Calcavi.* Now come we to the other of this day in the text. This is not that we have touched but another, wherein the style is altered; no more *calcatus sum*, but *calcavi* and *conculcavi* too. Up it seems He gat, and down went they, and upon them He trod. His enemies of Edom lay like so many
Ps. 108. 9. clusters under His feet; and "He cast His shoe" over them, set His foot on them, and dashed them to pieces.

If it had meant His passion, it had been His own blood; but this was none of His now, but the blood of His enemies. For when the year of redemption was past, then came the day of vengeance; then came the time for that, and not before.

Mat. 3. 15. For after the *consummatum est* of his own pressure, *sic oportuit impleri omnem justitiam*, and that all the righteous-
Isa. 51. 9. ness He spake had been fulfilled; then "rise up, rise up thou arm of the Lord," saith the Prophet, and shew thyself mighty to save: He took Him to His second attribute, to be avenged of those that had been the ruin of us all, the ruin everlasting, but for Him. To Edom, the kingdom of death, He went, whither we were to be led captives; yea
Isa. 45. 2. even to Bozrah, to hell itself, and there "brake the gates of brass, and made the iron-bars fly in sunder." He That was weak to suffer, became "mighty to save." Of *calcatus*, He became *calcator*. He That was thrown Himself, threw them now another while into the press, trod them down, trampled upon them as upon grapes in a fat, till He made the blood spring out of them, and all to sprinkle His garments, as if He had come forth of a winepress indeed. And we before, mercifully rather than mightily by His passion, now mightily also saved by His glorious resurrection.

Thus have you two several vines, the natural and the strange vine, the sweet and the wild; two presses, that in Jewry, that in Edom; two cups, the cursed cup, and the cup of blessing; of wine or blood. His own, His enemies' blood; one, *sanguis Agni*, 'the blood of the Lamb' slain;
Rev. 12. 3. the other, *sanguis draconis*, 'the blood of the dragon,' "the red dragon" trod upon. One of His passion, three days

since; the other of His victory, as to-day. Between His burial and His rising some doing there had been, somewhat had been done; somewhere He had been, in some new winepress, in Bozrah, that had given a new tincture of red to His raiment all over.

Both these shall you find together set down in one and the same chapter, in two verses standing close one to the
other; 1. Christ represented first as a Lamb, "a Lamb v. 5. 5,6.
slain," dyed in His own blood: this is the first press. 2. And immediately in the very next verse, straight represented again in a new shape, as "a Lion" all be-bloody with the blood of His prey—"a Lion of the Tribe of Judah;" which
comes home to this here. For Judah, it is said, he should Gen. 49. 9—11.
"wash his robe in the blood of the grape." And so much for *tornular calcavi.*

We must not leave out *solus* in any wise; that both these 2. *Solus*, "alone."
He did "alone," so "alone" as not any man in the world with Him in either.

Not in the first; there pressed He was "alone." All Mat. 26. 56.
forsook Him; His disciples first; "alone" for them. Yet then He was not "alone," His Father was still with Him;
but after, Father and all, as appeared by His cry, "Why Mat. 27. 46.
hast Thou forsaken Me?" Then was He all "alone" indeed.

Not in the second neither. The very next verse, He complains how that He looked about Him round, and could not see any would once offer to help Him. Out of Bozrah He got "alone;" from death He rose, conquered, triumphed
in *Semetipso,* "Himself alone." The Angel indeed rolled Joh. 20. 1.
away the stone; but He was risen first, and the stone rolled away after.

Accordingly we to reckon of Him, that since in both these presses He was for us, He and none but He; that His, and none but His, be the glory of both. That seeing neither we for ourselves, nor any for us, could bring this to pass, but He and He only; He and He only might have the whole honour of both, have no partner in that which is only His due, and no creature's else at all, either in Heaven or earth.

And is Christ come from Bozrah? then be sure of this,

SERM. XVII. that He returning thus in triumph, as it is in the sixty-eighth Psalm, the Psalm of the Resurrection, He will not
Ps. 68. 22. leave us behind for whom He did all this, but "His own will He bring again as He did from Basan;" as from Basan, so from Bozrah; as "from the deep pit of the sea,"
2 Cor. 4. 14. so from the deep pit of hell. "He That raised Jesus, shall by Jesus raise us up also" from the Adama of Edom, the red mould of the earth, the power of the grave; and from the Bozrah of hell too, the gulf whence there is no scaping
Rom. 8. 37. out. Will make us in Him, saith the Apostle, "more than conquerors," and tread down Satan under our feet.

Christ's garments, why "red." You see how Christ's garments came to be "red." Of the winepress that made them so we have spoken, but not of the colour itself. A word of that too. It was His colour at His Passion. They put Him in purple; then it was His weed in derision, and so was it in earnest. Both "red" it was itself, and so He made it more with the dye of His own blood. And the same colour He is now in again at His rising. Not with His own now, but with the blood of the wounded Edomites, whom treading under His feet, their blood bestained Him and His apparel. So one and the same colour at both; dying and rising in red; but with difference as much as is between His own and His enemies' blood.

The spouse in the Canticles, asked of her Beloved's colours,
Cant. 5. 10. saith of Him, "My Beloved is white and red." "White," of His own proper: so He was when He shewed Himself in
Mat. 17. 2. Mark 9. 3. kind, "transfigured" in the Mount; His apparel then so "white," no fuller in the earth could come near it. "White" of Himself; how comes He "red" then? Not of Himself that, but for us. That is our natural colour, we are born
Lam. 4. 14. "polluted in our own blood." It is sin's colour that, for
Isa. 1. 18. shame is the colour of sin. Our sins, saith Esay, "are as crimson of as deep dye as any purple." This, the true
[Gen. 25. 30.] tincture of our sins, the Edomites' colour right, for Edom is red. The tincture, I say, first of our sin original, dyed in the wool; and then again of our sins actual, dyed in the cloth too. Twice dyed; so was Christ twice. Once in His own, again in His enemies', right *dibaphus*, a perfect full colour, a true purple, of a double dye His too. So was it

meet for crimson sinners to have a crimson Saviour; a Saviour of such a colour it behoved us to have. Coming then to save us, off went His white, on went our red; laid by His own righteousness to be clothed with our sin. He to wear our colours, that we His; He in our red, that we in His white. So we find our "robes" are not only "washed clean," but dyed a pure white in the blood of the Lamb. Yea, He died and rose again both in our colours, that we might die and rise too in His. We fall now again upon the same point in the colours we did before in the cups. He to drink the sour vinegar of our wild grapes, that we might drink His sweet in the cup of blessing. O cup of blessing, may we say of this cup! *O stolam formosam,* of that colour! *Illi gloriosam, nobis fructuosam;* 'glorious to Him, no less fruitful to us.' He in Mount Golgotha like to us, that we in Mount Tabor like to Him. This is the substance of our rejoicing in this colour. Rev. 7. 14.

One more; how well this colour fits Him in respect of His two titles, *loquens justitiam,* and *multus ad servandum.* *Loquens justitiam,* is to wear red; *potens ad servandum* is so too. The first. To whom is this colour given? Scarlet is allowed the degree of Doctors. Why? for their speaking righteousness to us, the righteousness of God, that which Christ spake. Nay, even they which speak but the righteousness of man's law, they are honoured with it too. But Christ "spake so as never man spake," and so call ye none on earth Doctor but One; none in comparison of Him. So of all, He to wear it. This ye shall observe in the Revelation; at the first appearing of the Lamb, there was a book with seven seals. No man would meddle with it; the Lamb took it, opened the seals, read it, read out of it a lecture of righteousness to the whole world; the righteousness of God, that shall make us so before Him. Let Him be arrayed in scarlet: it is His due, His Doctor's weed.

From *loquens justitiam,* as a Doctor.

Joh. 7. 46.

Rev. 5. 1-7.

This is no new thing. The heathen king propounded it for a reward to any that could read the hand-writing on the wall. Daniel did it, and had it. *Sed ecce major Daniele hic.* Thus was it in the Law. This colour was the ground of the Ephod, a principal ingredient into the Priest's vesture. Why? For, "his lips were to preserve knowledge," all to

Dan. 5. 7

Mal. 2. 7.

SERM. XVII. require the law from his mouth. And indeed, the very lips themselves that we speak righteousness with, are of the same

Cant. 4. 3. colour. In the Canticles it is said, "His lips are like a scarlet thread." And the fruit of the lips hath God created peace, and the fruit of peace is sown in righteousness; and till that be sown and spoken, never any hope of true peace.

2. From *potens ad servandum*, as a Captain.

Enough for speaking. What say you to the other, *potens ad servandum*, which of the twain seems the more proper to this time and place? I say that way it fits Him too, this colour. Men of war, great captains, "mighty to save" us from the enemies, they take it to themselves, and their colour it is of right. A plain text for it, Nahum the second.

Nahum 2. 3. "Their valiant men," or captains, "are in scarlet." And

Dan. 9. 25. I told you Christ by Daniel is called "Captain Messias," and so well might. So in His late conflict with Edom He shewed Himself, fought for us even to blood. Many a bloody wound it cost Him, but returned with the spoil of His enemies, stained with their blood; and whoso is able so to do, is worthy to wear it. So in this respect also, so in both; His colours become Him well.

Shall I put you in mind, that there is in these two, in either of them, a kind of winepress? In "mighty to save," it is evident; trodden in one press, treading in another. Not so evident in "the speaking of righteousness." Yet even in that also, there is a press going. For when we read, what do we but gather grapes here and there; and when we study what we have gathered, then are we even *in torculari*, and press them we do, and press out of them that which daily you taste of. I know there is great odds in the liquors

Judges 8. 2. so pressed, and that "a cluster of Ephraim is worth a whole vintage of Abiezer;" but for that, every man as he may. Nay, it may be farther said, and that truly, that even this great title, "Mighty to save," comes under *loquens justitiam*. There

Jas. 1. 21. is in the word of righteousness a saving power. "Take the word," saith St. James, "graft it in you, it is able to save your souls;" even that wherein we of this calling in a sort

1 Tim. 4. 16. participate with Christ, while "by attending to reading and doctrine we save both ourselves and them that hear us;" we

[Wisd. 1. 12.] tread down sin, and save sinners from "seeking death in the error of their life."

But though there be in the word a saving power, yet is not all saving power in that, nor in that only; there is a press beside. For this press is going continually among us, but there is another that goes but at times. But in that, it goes at such times as it falls in fit with the winepress here. Nay, falls in most fit of all the rest. For of it comes very wine indeed, the blood of the grapes of the true Vine, which in the blessed Sacrament is reached to us, and with it is given us that for which it was given, even remission of sins. Not only represented therein, but even exhibited to us. Both which when we partake, then have we a full and perfect communion with Christ this day; of His speaking righteousness in the word preached, of His power to save in the holy Eucharist ministered. Both presses run for us, and we to partake them both.

I may not end till I tell you there remaineth yet another,
a third winepress; that you may take heed of it. I will but
point you to it; it may serve as sour herbs to eat our Pas-
chal lamb with. The sun, they say, danced this morning at
Christ's resurrection; the earth trembled then I am sure, Mat. 28. 2.
there was an earthquake at Christ's rising. So there is
trembling to our joy; *exultate in tremore,* as the Psalmist Ps. 2. 11.
wills us. The vintage of the earth, when the time of that
is come, and when the grapes be ripe and ready for it, one
there is that crieth to him with the "sharp sickle" in his Rev. 14.
hand to "thrust it in," cut off the clusters, "and cast them 18—20.
into the great winepress of the wrath of God." A dismal
day that, a pitiful slaughter then. It is there said, "the
blood shall come up to the horse-bridles by the space of a
thousand six hundred furlongs." Keep you out, take heed
of coming in that press.

We have a kind item given us of this, here in the text, in
the last verse. There be two acts of Christ; one of being
trodden, the other of treading down. The first is for His
chosen, the other against His enemies. One is called "the Isa. 63. 4.
year of redemption," the other "the day of vengeance."
"The year of redemption" is already come, and is now;
we are in it; during which time the two former winepresses
run, 1. of the word, and 2. Sacrament. "The day of vengeance" is not yet come, it is but in His heart—so the text

SERM. XVII. is—that is, but in His purpose and intent yet. But certainly come it will that day; and, with that day comes the last wine-press with the blood to the bridles: ere it come, and during our "year of redemption," that year's allowance, we are to endeavour to keep ourselves out of it; for that is "the day of vengeance," of *ira ventura*, God's wrath for ever. So as all we have to study is, how we may be in at the first two, out at the last press; and the due Christian use of the first, will keep us from the last.

While then it is with us "the year of redemption," and before that day come; while it is yet time of speaking
Ps. 95. 7. righteousness, that is, "to-day if ye will hear His voice;"
[1 Cor. 10. 16.] while "the cup of blessing" is held out, if we will take it, lay hold on both. That so we may be accounted worthy to escape in that day, from that day and the vengeance of it;
[Jas. 1. 21.] and may feel the fulness of His saving power in "the word engrafted, which is able to save our souls;" and in "the
[Ps. 116. 13.] cup of salvation" which is joined with it, and that to our endless joy. "The year of redemption" is last in the verse; with that the Prophet ends. With that let us end also; and to that end, may all that hath been spoken arrive and bring us!

A SERMON

PREPARED TO BE

PREACHED ON EASTER-DAY,

ON THE TWENTY-EIGHTH OF MARCH, A.D. MDCXXIV.

HEBREWS xiii. 20, 21.

The God of peace, That brought again from the dead our Lord Jesus Christ, the great Shepherd of the sheep, through the blood of the everlasting testament,

Make you perfect in all good works to do His will, working in you that which is pleasant in His sight, through Jesus Christ: to Whom be praise for ever and ever! Amen.

[*Deus autem Pacis Qui eduxit de mortuis Pastorem magnum ovium, in sanguine testamenti æterni, Dominum nostrum Jesum Christum,*

Aptet vos in omni bono, ut faciatis Ejus voluntatem, faciens in vobis quod placeat coram Se, per Jesum Christum, Cui est gloria in sæcula sæculorum! Amen. Latin Vulg.]

[*Now the God of peace, That brought again from the dead our Lord Jesus, that great Shepherd of the sheep, through the blood of the everlasting covenant,*

Make you perfect in every good work to do His will, working in you that which is wellpleasing in His sight, through Jesus Christ; to Whom be glory, for ever and ever! Amen. Engl. Trans.]

THESE words, "who hath brought Christ again from the dead," make this a text proper for this day; for as this day was Christ "brought again" from thence.

And these words, "the blood of the everlasting testament," make it as proper every way for a Communion; for there, at a Communion, we are made to drink of that blood.

SERM. XVIII. Put these together, 1. The bringing of Christ from the dead, 2. and "the blood of the Testament," and they will serve well for a text at Communion on Easter-day.

I will touch in a word, 1. the nature of the text, 2. the sum, and 3. the partition of it.

1. The nature of the text. For the nature, it is a benediction. The use the Church doth make of it and such other like, is to pronounce them over the congregation by way of a blessing. For not only the power to pray, to preach, to make and to give the Sacrament; but the power also to bless you that are God's people, is annexed, and is a branch of ours, of the Priests' office. You may plainly read the power committed, the act enjoined, and the very form of words prescribed, all in the sixth of Numbers. [Num. 6. 23.] There God saith, "Thus shall you bless the people;" that is, do it you shall, and thus shall you do it, *in hæc verba.* Neither was this act Levitical, or then first taken up, it was long before: "while Levi was yet in the loins of Abraham," [Heb.] even then it was a part of Melchisedek's Priesthood, and, if the bread and wine were no more but a refreshing, the only part that we read of, to say *Benedictus* over Abraham, as great a patriarch as he was. There is nothing else mentioned to shew he was a priest, but that.

This blessing they used first and last, but rather last. For lightly[1] then the people were all together. They be not so at first, but only a few then. And here, you see, the Apostle makes it his farewell. With this he shuts up his Epistle, and with some other such, all the rest. And that, by Christ's example. The last thing that Christ did in this world, was; "He lift up His hands to bless His disciples," and so went away to Heaven. [Lu. 24 50.] And so you shall find it was the manner in the Primitive Church, at the end of the Liturgy, ever to dismiss the assembly with a blessing. Which blessing they were then so conceited of, they would not offer to stir, not a man of them, till bowing down their heads they had the blessing pronounced over them. As if some great matter had lain in the missing of it; as if they had been of Jacob's mind, *Non dimittam Te nisi benedixeris mihi:* they would neither let the Priest depart, nor depart themselves, till they had their blessing with them; such a virtue they held in it. [Gen. 32. 26.] The blessing pronounced, they had then leave to go with [See Bingham, vol. 4. 80. new ed.]

[1] [i. e. usually.]

λαοῖς ἄφεσις, in the Greek, *missa est fidelibus,* in the Latin, Church; and none went away before.

An evil custom hath prevailed with our people; away they go without blessing, without leave, without care of either. Mark if they run not out before any blessing, as if it were not worth the taking with them.

I marvel how they will be "inheritors of the blessing," that Heb. 12. 17.
seem to set so little by it. If they mean to hear, "Come, ye Mat. 25. 34.
blessed," they should methinks love it better than by their running from it they seem to do.

This would be amended. We are herein departed from the Primitive Christians, with whom it was in more regard. Sure, there is more in the neglect of it than we are aware of.

This blessing could not be delivered in better terms than in those that came from the Apostles themselves, which accordingly have been sought up here and there in their writings, and by the Church sorted to several days which they seemed best to agree with. As this here, having Easter-day in it, was made an Easter-day benediction. For the special mention in it of Christ, "brought again from the dead," doth in a manner appropriate it to this feast. Utter it but thus; "The God of peace Who did now, as upon this day, bring again Christ from the dead"—do but utter it thus, and it will appear most plainly how well they suit, the time, and the text.

For the sum. It is no more in effect but shortly this. 2 The sum.
That God would so bless them and us, as to make us fit for, and perfect in, all good works. A good wish at any time. But why at this time specially, upon mention of Christ's rising, he should wish it, is not seen at first. Yet there is some matter in it, that at Christ's rising he doth not wish our faith increased, or our hope strengthened, or any other grace or virtue revived; but only, that good works might be perfected in us, and we in them. Surely, this sorting them thus together seems to imply as if Christ's resurrection had some more peculiar interest in good works, as indeed it hath. And there hath ever been, and still are, more of them done now at this time, than at any other time of the year.

A general reason may be given. That what time Christ doth for us some principal great work, as at all the feasts He

SERM. XVIII. doth some, and now at this time sensibly, we to take occasion by it at that time to do somewhat more than ordinary in memory and honour of it. More particularly, some such as may in some sort suit with and resemble the act of Christ then done. As it might be, when Christ died, sin to die in us; when Christ rose again, good works to rise together with Him. Christ's passion, to be sin's passion; Christ's resurrection, good works' resurrection. Good-Friday is for sin, Easter for good works. Good-Friday to bring sin to death, Easter to bring good works from the dead. And we that were dead before to good works, by occasion of this to revive again to the doing of them; and not as the manner is with us, sin to have an Easter, to rise and live again, and good works to be crucified, lie dead and have no resurrection.

3. The division. For the partition. Two verses there are, and two parts accordingly. 1. The premises, and 2. the sequel. The premises are God, and the sequel good works. The former verse is nothing but God, with His style or addition; "The God of peace Who hath brought again," &c. The latter is all for good works, "Make you perfect," &c. We may consider them thus. Of the two, 1. one a thing done for us, in the former verse; 2. the other, a thing to be done by us, in the latter verse. The bringing back Christ, the benefit done us by God; the applying good works, our duty to be done to Him for it.

The thing done is an act, that is, a bringing back. Which act is but one, but applieth another precedent necessarily. For ἀναγαγὼν, which is a "bringing back," implieth ἀγαγὼν, which is a 'bringing thither.'

1. To this act there is a concurrence of two agents. 1. One,
2. the party that brought; 2. the other, the party that is brought. The party that brought is God, under the name or title of "the God of peace." The party that was brought is Christ, set forth here under the metaphor of a Shepherd, "the great Shepherd of the sheep."

"The God of peace" did bring again this "Shepherd;"
3. from whence and how? 3. From whence? "From the dead."
Then among the dead He was first. First, brought thither.
4. 4. How from thence? by what means? "By the blood of a
Testament everlasting." All which is nothing else but the

resurrection of Christ extended at large through all these points.

The thing to be done. That God would so bless them as II.
"to make them," 1. first, "fit to do;" 2. and then "to do good works." 1. "Fit to do," in the word *καταρτίσαι*. "To do." Wherein we consider two things; 1. the doing. To which doing there is a concurrence of two agents, 1. *εἰς τὸ ποιῆσαι ὑμᾶς*, what we to do; 2. and *ποιῶν ἐν ὑμῖν*, what He to do. 2. And then the work itself expressed in two words, 1. *θέλημα*, and 2. *εὐάρεστον*: *θέλημα*, that is, "His will;" *εὐάρεστον*, "that which is well pleasing" in His sight. These two be holding for two degrees; and the latter of the twain to have the more in it.

And last of all, the sequel. Where is to be shewed, how III.
these two hang together and follow one upon the other. First, the "God of peace," and the bringing of Christ from death. Then, how the bringing of Christ from death concerns our bringing forth good works. Which being shewed, what this feast of Easter hath to do with good works will fall in of itself. That with Christ now rising they also should now rise—they are thought as good as dead—that there may be a resurrection of them at Christ's resurrection.

"The God of peace," &c. Here is a long process. What I. The thing done for us. 1. The party by whom.
needs all this setting out His style at length? Why goes He not to the point roundly? And seeing good works'-doing is His errand, why saith He not shortly, God make you given to good works! and no more ado? but tells us a long tale of Shepherds and Testaments, and I wot not what, one would think to small purpose? But sure to purpose it is, the Holy Ghost useth no waste words, nor ever speaks but to the point we may be sure.

Let us see, and begin with His first title, "the God of His title. "The God of peace."
peace." God's titles be divers, as be His acts; and His acts are, as His properties be they proceed from. And lightly, the title is taken from the property which best fits the act it produceth. As when God proceedeth to punish, He is called the "righteous God;" when to shew favour, "the Exod. 9. 27. 2 Cor. 1. 3. Ps. 89. 8.
God of mercy;" when to do some great work, "the God of power." Now then this seems not so proper; should it not rather have been, 'the God of power Which brought

SERM. XVIII. again,' &c. To bring again from death seems rather an act of power than of peace. One would think so. But being well looked into, it will be found to belong rather to peace. No power of His will be set on working, will ever bring again from death, unless He be first pacified and made the Lord of peace. Of His power there is no question; of His peace there may be some. I shall tell you why. For all the Old Testament through you shall observe God's great title is "the Lord of Hosts," which in the New you shall never read; but ever since He rose from the dead it is, instead of it, "the God of peace." To the Romans, Philippians, Thessalonians, &c. and now here to the Hebrews; and still, "the God of peace." It is not amiss for us, this change. For if the Lord of Hosts come to be at peace with us, His hosts shall be all for us, which were against us, while it was no peace. So as make but God "the God of peace," and more needs not. For His peace will command His power straight.

[1 Sam. 1. 11. Isai. 1. 24. Jer. 46. 18. Hab. 2. 13. Mal. 1. 14.] Rom. 15. 13. Phil. 4. 9. 1 Thes. 5. 23. 2 Thes. 3. 16.

When His hosts were so about Him, it seemed hostility; how came He then to lay away that title of "the Lord of Hosts," to become *Deus pacis?* That did He by thus doing; He brought again one from the dead, and that bringing brought peace, and made this change *stylo novo,* "the God of peace."

2. The second party, "Our Lord Jesus." *Pastorem,* "The Shepherd."

This brings us to the other, the second party; He is not named till all be done, and then He is in the end of the verse; "our Lord and Saviour Jesus Christ." But at first He is brought in as a Shepherd. Think never the meaner of Him for that. Moses and David, the founders of the monarchy of the Jews; Cyrus and Romulus, the founders, one of the Persian, the other of the Roman monarchy, were taken all from the sheepfolds. The heathen poet calls the great ruler of the Grecian monarchy but *ποιμένα λαῶν,* that is, the 'Shepherd of the people.' Christ gives it to Himself, and God doth not disdain it in the eightieth Psalm. And the name, howsoever it falls to us of the Clergy now, *ab initio non fuit sic.* Secular men, Joseph, Joshua, and David, were first so termed, and are more often so termed in the Bible than we.

[Hom. Iliad. B. 243.] Ps. 80. 1.

The term of "Shepherd" is well chosen as referring to "the God of peace." Peace is best for shepherds and for

sheep. They love peace: then they are safe, then they feed quietly. Yet not so but that shepherds have ventured far to rescue the sheep from the bear and from the lion, as did
King David; and as the Son of David here That ventured 1 Sam. 17.
farther than any, Who is brought in here *in sanguine,* 36.
'bleeding,' howsoever it comes.

But this title was not so much for God as for us—*Pastorem ovium;* and in *ovium* are we, there come we in, we hold by that word. For so there is a mutual and reciprocal relation between Him and us; that we thereby may be assured by this very term relative, whither, and whensoever He was brought, all He did or suffered, it was not for Himself. For then an absolute name of His own would have been put. All for His correlative, for *ovium,* that is, for us. He is no ways considered in all this, as absolutely put or severed from us, His flock, but still with reference and relation unto us.

But because others enter common in this and other His *Pastorem*
names with Him, He bears it with a difference; *Pastor* *magnum,* "the great
Magnus, "the great Shepherd." Not, as Diphilus said to Shepherd."
Pompeius Magnus, *Nostrâ miseriâ magnus es,* 'great by making others little;' but *misericordiâ suâ magnus,* 'by making Himself little to make us great.'

The gradual points of His greatness, in respect of others, 1.
are these. Great first, for *totum* is *parte majus;* greater is He That feeds the whole, than they that but certain parcels of the flock. All else feed but pieces; so they be but petty shepherds to Him. But He, the whole, main entire flock; He and none but He. So He "the great Shepherd" of the great flock.

Again, greater is He That owns the sheep He feeds, than 2.
they that feed the sheep they own not. All others feed His
sheep; none can say, *pasce oves Meas.* His they be; and Joh. 21. 16.
reason. For "He made them," they be "the sheep of His Ps. 95. 7.
hands;" He feeds them, so the sheep of His hands, and of
"His pasture" both. Ps. 100. 3.

But this is not the greatness here meant. But *Ecce quan-* 3.
tam charitatem, "see the great love" to His sheep! Others 1 Joh. 3. 1
sell and kill theirs. He is so far from selling or killing, as He, this Shepherd, was sold and slain for them, though they were His own. Paid for them, bought them again,

SERM. XVIII. and then He "brought them again." It may be there were others had ventured their lives, but not lost them and so lost them as He did. Which makes Him not only great, but *primæ magnitudinis,* that is, simply the greatest that ever was.

Of which greatness, two great proofs there are in the two words, 1. *sanguis,* and 2. *testamentum. Sanguis,* a great price; *testamentum,* a great legacy. *Sanguis,* what He suffered; *testamentum,* what He did for them.

In sanguine, "through the blood." The next word is *in sanguine,* a Shepherd "in His blood." So this Shepherd sweat blood, ere He could bring them back. It was no easy matter, it cost blood; and not any blood, such as He could well spare, but it cost Him His life-blood. It could not be the blood of the testament, but there must be a testament, and a testament there cannot be but the Testator must die. So He died, He was brought to the dead for it. This blood brought Him to His testament, which is further than blood.

The two acts. We said there were two acts; 1. one expressed, "brought Him thence," ἀναγαγών. The other implied, 'brought Him thither,' ἀγαγών. But first, 'brought thither,' before "brought thence." We will touch them both. 1. Why brought thither, and how? 2. And why brought thence, and how?

1. Brought thither. If when He was "brought thence" it was peace, when He was 'brought thither' it was none. How came it there was none? What made this separation? That did sin, sin brake the peace.

2 Cor. 5. 21. Why, sin touched not Him, "He knew no sin." True; it was not for Himself nor any sin of His. Whose then? here are but two, 1. *Pastor,* and 2. *ovium; Pastor* He, *ovium* we. If not the Shepherd's then the sheep's sin; if not His, ours. And so it was; *peccata vestra,* saith God in Isa. 59. 2. Esay, and speaks it to us. No quarrel He had to the Shepherd; nothing to say to Christ, as Christ. But He would needs be dealing with sheep, and His sheep fell to straying, and light into the wolves' den; and thither He must go to fetch them, if He will have them.

For *ovium* then is all this ado, and that is for us. For Isa. 53. 6. "all we, as sheep, had gone astray." I may say further; all we, as sheep, were appointed to the slaughter. So it was we should have been carried thither, and "the Lord laid upon Him the transgressions of us all," and so He was carried for us. This Pastor became *tanquam ovis*, "as a sheep" for His sheep, and was brought thither, and the wolves did to Him whatsoever they would.

As if God had said; Away with these sheep, *incidant in lupos, quia nolunt regi a Pastore*, 'to the wolves with them, seeing they will be kept in no fold.' But that the Shepherd endured not; but rather than they should, He would. When it came to this, who shall go thither, *Pastor* or *ovium*, the sheep or the Shepherd? *Sinite hos abire*, they be His own words, "Let them go their way," let the sheep go, and "smite the Shepherd," sentence Him to be carried thither. The sheep were to be, they should have been; but the Shepherd was. *In sanguine nostro* it should have been; *in sanguine Suo*, "His blood," it was. So to spare ours, He spilt His own. Joh. 18. 8. [Zech. 13. 7.]

2. "Brought again" thence.

Thither now He is brought, brought thither by His own blood-shedding. We can understand that well, but not how He should be brought thence by His blood. Yet the text is plain, how He was brought again, *in sanguine*, "by His blood."

First then, let us make God "the God of peace;" and when He is so, you soon see Him "bring Him back" again. That which broke the peace as we said, the very thing that carried Him to the cross, took Him down thence dead, carried Him to His grave, and there lodged Him among the dead, was sin. Away with sin then, that so there may be peace. But there is no taking away sin but by "shedding of blood"—the blood either of *Pastor* or of *ovium*, one of them. Heb. 9. 22.

3. *In sanguine*, "By the blood."

Why then here is blood, even the Shepherd's blood; and shed it is, and by the shedding of it sin is taken away, and with sin God's displeasure. It is the Apostle's own word. "Hatred was slain," and so hatred being slain, peace followed of her own accord. "He was our Peace," saith the Apostle, in one place; "He made our peace," or pacified all "by His blood," in another. Eph. 2. 14—16. Col. 1. 20.

Now then, upon this peace, He That was before carried away was brought back again, and so well might be. For

SERM. XVIII. all being discharged, He was then to be *inter mortuos liber*,
Ps. 88. 5. no longer bound, but "free from the dead;" not to be kept in prison any longer, but to come forth again. And by His very blood to come forth again. For it was the nature of a ransom, which being laid down, the Prisoner that was brought thither is to go thence, whither He will. For a
1 Sam. 2. 6. ransom hath *potestatem eductivam* or *reductivam*, "a power to bring forth, or bring back again" from any captivity.

In both these bringings, God had His hand; God bringeth to death, and bringeth back again. True, if ever, in this Shepherd. Brought Him to the dead, as "the Lord of Hosts;" brought Him from the dead, as being now pacified, and "the God of peace." Out of His justice, God smote the Shepherd; out of His love to His sheep, the Shepherd was smitten. But *Quem deduxit iratus, reduxit placatus*; 'Whom of His just wrath against sin He brought thither, now having fulfilled all righteousness He was to bring thence again.' And so brought back He was, and the same way that He was carried thither. Carried the way of justice, to satisfy for them He had undertaken for. And having fully satisfied for them, was in very justice to be brought back again. And so He was; God accepted His passion in full satisfaction, gave present order for His raising again.

And let not this phrase of God's bringing back, or of Christ's coming back, of God's raising Him, or of Christ's rising, any-thing trouble you. The resurrection is one entire act of two joint Agents, that both had Their hands in it. Ascribed one while to Christ Himself, that He rose, that
Joh. 10. 18. He came back; to shew that He had "power to lay down His life, and power to take it again." Another while to God, that He raised Him, that He brought Him back; to shew that God was fully satisfied and well-pleased with it, reach Him His hand, as it were, to bring Him thence again.

To shew you the benefit that riseth to us by this His rising. Brought thither He was to the dead: so, it lay us upon; if He had not, we should. We were even carrying thither; and that we might not, He was. Brought thence He was, from the dead: so it stood us in hand; if He had not been brought thence, we should never have come thence, but been left to have lain there world without end.

Brought thither He would be—He, and not we; He without us. So careful He was not to spare Himself that we might be spared. Brought thence He would not be, not without His sheep we may be sure; He would bring us thence too, or He would not be brought thence without us. You may see Him in the parable, coming with His lost sheep on His shoulders. That one sheep is the image of us all. So careful He was, as He laid him on His own neck, to be sure; which is the true portraiture or representation of His *ἀναγωγή*. That if "the God of peace" bring Him back, He must bring them also, for He will not come back without them. Upon His bringing back from death, is ours founded; in Him all His were brought back. In His person our nature, in our nature we all.

Lu. 15. 5.

Think you after the payment of such a price He will come back Himself alone, He will let the sheep be carried thither, and not see them brought back again? He did not suffer all this we may be sure, to come away thence, and leave them behind Him. It was never seen that any that paid after so high a rate for any, be it what it will, that when He had done would not see it brought away, but lose all His labour and cost. No; as sure as Himself was brought, so sure He will bring them whom He would not part from, He will die first. Nothing shall part them now. *Pastor* and *ovium*, "sheep" and "Shepherd" now, or no bargain. He with His flock, and His flock with Him; it with Him and He with it; He and they, or not He Himself; both together, or not at all. Will you hear Himself say as much? "Father, My will is, that whither I go," whence I come, where I am, thither, thence, and there, "these be also."

[John 17. 24.]

4. *Sanguine testamenti,* "the blood of the testament."

But when He had brought us thence, what shall become of us trow? Will He leave us at random to wander in the mountains? No; but *ubi desinit Pastor, ibi incipit Testator;* 'where the Shepherd goes out, the Testator comes in.' Which we find plainly in the word "testament." For though peace be a fair blessing in itself, if no more but it; and bringing back be worth the while, yet here is now a greater matter than so. There is more in the blood than we are aware of. This is also meant; that there is the

SERM. XVIII. blood of a testament, which bodeth some further matter. There should need no testament, if it were for nothing but to make peace. A covenant would serve for that; "My covenant of peace would I make with thee," saith God. *Sanguis fœderis* would have done that, if there had been no more but so. But here it is the blood of a testament.

Ezek. 37. 26.

It is *sanguis cum testamento annexo*, 'blood with a testament annexed.' Beside the pacification and back-bringing, this Scripture "offereth more grace;" even a testamentary matter to be administered for our further behoof.

[James 4. 6.]

For I ask. Every drop of this blood is more worth than many worlds: shall this blood then so precious, of so great a Person as the Son of God, be spent to bring forth nothing but pardon and peace? Being of so great a value, shall it produce but so poor an effect? Pity it should be shed, to bring forth nothing but a few sheep from death. There is enough in it to serve further to make a purchase, which He may dispose of to them He will vouchsafe to bring again from the dead. For when He hath brought them thence, how He will dispose them, that would be thought on too.

I find then ascribed to His blood, a price; not only of ἀπολύτρωσις, that is, a "redemption or ransom," but also περιποίησις, that is, of "perquisition or purchase." And I find them both in one verse. So that this blood availed, as to pay our debt, so over and above to make a purchase; served not only to procure our peace, but to state us in a condition better than ever we were before. Not only brought us, but bought us; nay not only bought us and brought us back, but bought for us further an everlasting inheritance, and brought us to it.

Eph. 1. 14.

Two powers were in it; 1. as *sanguis fœderis*, "the blood of the covenant," the covenant of peace, for in blood were the covenants made; that with Abraham in Genesis fifteen, that with Moses in Exodus twenty-four, in blood both; and among the heathen men, never any covenant of peace but in blood. 2. Now for peace this were enough; but it is *sanguis testamenti* too, "the blood of a testament," which is founded upon better promises, bequeaths legacies, disposeth estates—matter far of a higher nature than bare peace. As the blood of the covenant, so it pacifieth and

[Heb. 10. 29.]

Gen. 15. 9, 10.

Exod. 24. 8.

[Heb. 13. 20.]

appeaseth; as the blood of the testament, so it passeth over and conveyeth besides.

But say it did not, it were for nothing else but our peace, yet it is much better for us, that our peace go by testament rather than by a covenant. Leagues, covenants, edicts of pacification, have oft been, and are we see daily broken. Small hold of them; a stronger hold than so behoved us. A stronger hold there is not than that of a testament. That is holden inviolable, never to be reversed. Nothing *in rebus humanis* is held more sacred; so as peace by a testament is far the surer of the twain.

Of which testament, and the greatness of it, there is much to be said, for it is not as other testaments, to be fully administered; this shall never be so, it is "everlasting." "Everlasting," for so is He That made it; "His goings out are from everlasting." "Everlasting," for so is the testament itself; though it be executed in time, it was made *ab æterno,* and lay by Him all the while. "Everlasting," for so is the blood wherewith it is sealed, the virtue and vigour thereof doth still continue as a fountain in-exhaust, never dry, but flowing still as fresh as the very first day His side was first opened. We that now live, come to it of even hand with the Apostles themselves, that were then at the opening. And they that come after us, shall not come too late, but to full as good a match as either they or we. "Everlasting," for the legacies of it are so. Not as with us, of things temporal; nor as of the former testament of the land of Canaan, now grown a barren wilderness; but of eternal life and joy and bliss, of eternity itself. And lastly, "everlasting," that we may look for no more; our Gospel is *Evangelium æternum,* none to come after it. This is the last, and so to last for ever.

Testamenti æterni, "O the everlasting testament." Mic. 5. 2.

Rev. 14. 6.

Now lay these together, and tell me, Was He not "the great Shepherd" indeed, That endured this carrying thither, whence this day He came? That paid this great ransom, purchased this great estate, made this great will, disposed these great legacies, even His heavenly kingdom to His little flock? Was He not every way as good as great?—which is the true greatness, ἐν τῷ εὖ τὸ μέγα. Here with us, men be good because they be great; with God they be great because

[Luke 12, 32.]

SERM. XVIII.

they be good. For this His great love, His great price, His great testament, was He not worthy to wear His title of *Pastor magnus*, of *Pastor* and of *Testator* both? For so both He was, and we not only His sheep but His legataries, both in His Pastorship, and in His Testatorship; in His bringing forward and in His bringing backward, no ways to be severed from us. He procured no peace, shed no blood, made no testament; was neither brought to the dead nor from the dead for Himself, but for His flock, for us still. All He did, all He suffered, all He bequeathed, all He was, He was for us.

And now when all is done, then now, lo, He is the "Lord Jesus Christ." Till then a Shepherd, wholly and solely; the more are we beholden to Him. Then lo, He tells us His name, that He is "the great Shepherd," He That was brought back; the blood His, His the testament. Truly called "the testament;" there can no inventory be made of this. It hath not entered in the heart of man to conceive what things God hath prepared for those that have their part in this testament, above all that we can desire or imagine. Upon earth there is no greater thing than a king-
Lu. 12. 32. dom; and no less than a "kingdom it is His Father's will to dispose unto us." But a kingdom eternal, all glorious and blessed, far above these here.

II. The thing to be done by us, 1. The fitting or doing.

All this is a good hearing; hitherto we have heard nothing but pleaseth us well. God at peace; the Shepherd brought to death, that we might not; and brought from death, that we also might be brought from thence; and not brought and left to the wide world, but farther to receive those good things which are comprised in His testament. This is done, done by Him for us. Now to that which is to be done, to be done by us. Not for Him—I should not do well to say so—but indeed for ourselves. For so, for us in the end it will prove; both what He did, and what we do ourselves.

That which on our part the Apostle wishes us is, that we may be so happy as that God would in effect do the same for us He did for Him, that is, bring us back; back from our sinful course of life to a new, given to do good works.

The Resurrection is here termed ἀναγωγὴ, "a bringing

back." So that any bringing back from the worse to the better carrieth the type, is a kind of a resurrection, refers to that of Christ Who died and rose that sin might die, and that good works might rise in us. Both the time and the text lay upon us this duty, to see if good works that seem to be dead and gone, we can bring life to them and make them to rise again.

The rule of reason is, *Unumquodque propter operationem suam,* 'every thing is, and hath his being for the work it is to do.' And these are the works which we were born, and came into the world to do. The Apostle speaks it plainly; "we were created for good works, to walk in them." And Eph. 2. 10
again, "That we were redeemed to be a people zealously Tit. 2. 14.
given to good works." So they come doubly commended to us, as the end of our creation and redemption both.

In this text we see, it is God's will, it is His good pleasure we do them, if we any thing regard either His will or pleasure.

In this text, the Apostle prays that we may "be made perfect in them." So, imperfect we are without them; imperfect we, and our faith both. For, "by works is our Jas. 2. 22.
faith made perfect," even as Abraham's faith was. And the faith that is without them, is not only imperfect, but stark dead; so as that faith needs a resurrection, to be brought from the dead again.

And whatsoever become of the rest, in this text it is that He hath not left them out, nor unremembered in His testament. They are in it, and divers good legacies to us for them. Which, if we mean to be legataries, we must have a care of. For as His blood serveth for the taking away of evil works, so doth His testament for the bringing again of good. And as it is good philosophy, *unumquodque propter operationem suam,* so this is sure, it is sound divinity, *unusquisque recipiet secundum operationem suam.* At our coming back from the dead whence we all shall come, we shall be disposed of according to them; receive we shall, every man "according to his works." And when it comes to going, Mat. 16. 27.
they that have done good works shall go into everlasting life; and they, not that have done evil, but they that have not done good, shall go—you know whither. Let no man

SERM. XVIII. deceive you; the root of immortality, the same is the root of virtue—but one and the same root both. When all is said that can be, naturally and by very course of kind, good works, you see, do rise out of Christ's resurrection.

Καταρτίσαι, "to make perfect." Ps. 51. 3. "Make you perfect"—so we read it; which shews we are, as indeed we are, in a state of imperfection till we do them. Nay, if that be all, we will never stick for that; *cognoscimus imperfectum nostrum*, we yield ourselves for such, for imperfect; and that is well. But we must so find and feel our imperfection, that as the Apostle tells us in the sixth chapter Heb. 6. 1. before, "we strive to be carried forward to perfection" all we may. Else, all our *cognoscimus imperfectum* will stand us in small stead.

Why, is there any perfection in this life? There is: else, how should the Apostle's exhortation there, or his blessing here, take place. I wot well, absolute, complete, consummate perfection, in this life, there is none; it is agreed of all Phil. 3. 13. hands, none may be out of it. *Non puto me comprehendisse*, saith St. Paul, "I count not myself to have attained?" No more must we. Not "attained?" What then? "But this I do," saith he, and so must we; "I forget that which is behind, and endeavour myself, and make forward still, to that which is before." Which is the perfection of travellers, of wayfaring men; the farther onward on their journey, the nearer their journey's end, the more perfect; which is the perfection of this life, for this life is a journey.

Now good works are as so many steps onward. The Rom. 4. 12. Apostle calls them so, "the steps of the faith of our father Abraham," who went that way, and we to follow him in it. And the more of them we do, the more steps do we make; the further still shall we find ourselves to depart from iniquity, the nearer still to approach unto God in the land of the living; whither to attain, is the total or *consummatum est* of our perfection.

Καταρτίσαι, "To make fit or even.' But not to keep from you the truth, as it is, the nature of the Apostle's word καταρτίσαι is rather to "make fit" than "to make perfect." Wherein this he seems to say, that to the doing of good works, there is first requisite a fitness to do them, before we can do them; καταρτίσαι and ποιῆσαι are both in the text. Fit to do them, ere we can do them. We may not think to do them hand over head, at the first dash. In an unfit and indisposed subject, no agent can work; not God Himself, but by miracle. Fit then we must be.

Now of ourselves, as of ourselves, we are not fit so much
as "to think" a good thought; it is the second of Co- 2 Cor. 3. 5.
rinthians, the third chapter, verse five. Not so much as
to will, "for it is God That worketh in us to will." If not Phil. 2. 13.
these two, 1. neither "think," 2. nor "will," then not to
work. No more we are; neither to begin, nor, having be- Phil. 1. 6.
gun, to go forward, and bring it to an end. Fit to none of these. Then made fit we must be, and who to reduce us to fitness but this "God of peace here, That brought again Christ from the dead."

Now, if I shall tell you what manner of fitness it is the Καταρ-
Apostle's word καταρτίσαι here doth import, it is properly τίσαι, "To set
the fitness which is in setting that in which was out of joint, in join..."
in doing the part of a good bone-setter. This is the very true and native sense of the word; "set you in joint" to do
good works. For the Apostle tells us that the Church and Eph. 4. 1
things spiritual go by joints and sinews whereof they are Col. 2. 19.
compact, and by which they have their action and motion. And where there are joints, there may be, and otherwhiles there is a disjointing or dislocation, no less in things spiritual than in the natural body. And that is when things are missorted, or put out of their right places.

Now that our nature is not right in joint is so evident, that the very heathen men have seen and confessed it.

And by a fall things come out of joint, and indeed so they did; Adam's fall we call it, and we call it right. Sin which before broke the peace, which made the going from or departure which needed the bringing back; the same sin, here now again, put all out of joint. And things out of joint are never quiet, never at peace and rest, till they be set right again. But when all is in frame, all is in peace; and so it refers well to "the God of peace" Who is to do it.

And mark again. The putting in joint is nothing but a bringing back again to the right place whence it slipped, that still there is a good coherence with that which went

SERM. XVIII.

before; the peace-maker, the bringer-back, the bone-setter, are all one.

The force or fulness of the Apostle's simile, *out of joint*, you shall never fully conceive till you take in hand some good work of some moment, and then you shall for certain. For do but mark me then, how many rubs, lets, impediments, there will be, as it were so many puttings out of joint, ere it can be brought to pass. This wants, or that wants; one thing or other frames not. A sinew shrinks, a bone is out, somewhat is awry; and what ado there is ere we can get it right! Either the will is averse, and we have no mind to it; or the power is shrunk, and the means fail us; or the time serves not: or the place is not meet; or the parties to be dealt with, we find them indisposed. And the misery is, when one is got in, the other is out again. That the wit of man could not have devised a fitter term to have expressed it in. This for the disease.

What way doth God take to set us right? First, by our ministry and means. For it is a part of our profession under God, this same καταρτισμὸς, to set the church in, and every member that is out of joint. You may read it in this very
Eph. 4. 12. term, πρὸς καταρτισμόν. And that we do, by applying outwardly this testament and the blood of it, two special splints
Heb. 13. 22. as it were, to keep all straight. Out of the testament, by "the word of exhortation," as in the next verse he calls it, praying us to suffer the splinting. For it may sometimes pinch them, and put them to some pain that are not well in joint, by pressing it and putting it home. But both by denouncing one while the threats of the Old Testament, another while by laying forth the promises of the New, if by any means we may get them right again. This by the Testament, which is one outward means. The blood is another inward means. By it we are made fit and perfect, (choose you whether,) and that so, as at no time of all our life we are so well in joint, or come so near the state of perfectness, as when we come new from the drinking of that blood. And thus are we made fit.

Εἰς τὸ ποιῆσαι, "The first agent."

Provided that καταρτίσαι do end, as here it doth, in ποιῆσαι and ἐν ἔργῳ; that all this fit-making do end in doing and in a work, that some work be done. For in doing it is to end, if it end aright; if it end, as the Apostle here would have it. For this fitting is not to hear, learn, or know, but "to do His will." We have been long at 'Teach me Thy will,' at that lesson. There is another in Psalm one hundred and forty-three, "Teach me to do Thy will;" we must take out that also. 'Teach me Thy will,' and "Teach me to do Thy will," are two distinct lessons. We are all our life long about the first, and never come to the second, to εἰς τὸ ποιῆσαι. It is required we should now come to the second, εἰς τὸ ποιῆσαι. We are not made fit, when we are so, to do never a whit the more; καταρτίσαι is to end in ποιῆσαι, which is doing, and in ἔργον, that is, in 'a work.' [See Ps. 27. 11.] Ps. 143. 10.

'Εν παντὶ ἔργῳ. "In all good works."

In work, and "in every good work." We must not slip the collar there, neither. For if we be able to stir our hand but one way and not another, it is a sign it is not well set in. His that is well set, he can move it to and fro, up and down, forward and backward; every way, and to every work. There be that are all for some one work, that single some one piece of God's service, wholly addicted to that, but cannot skill of the rest. That is no good sign. To be for every one, for all sorts of good works, for every part of God's worship alike, for no one more than another, that sure is the right. So choose your religion, so practise your worship of God. It is not safe to do otherwise, nor to serve God by Synecdoche; but ἐν παντὶ, to take all before us.

Ποιῶν ἐν ὑμῖν. "The second agent."

But in the doing of all or any, beside our part, εἰς τὸ ποιῆσαι, here is also ποιῶν ἐν ὑμῖν, a worker besides. For when God hath fitted us by the outward means, there is not all. He leaves not us to ourselves for the rest, but to that outward application of ours joins His ποιῶν ἐν ὑμῖν, an inward operation of His own inspiring, His grace, which is nothing but the breath of the Holy Ghost. Thereby enlightening our minds, inclining our wills, working on our affections, making us *homines bonæ voluntatis;* that when we have done well, we may say with the Prophet, *Domine universa opera nostra operatus es in nobis,* "Lord, all our good works Thou hast wrought in us." Our works they be, yet of Thy working. And with the Apostle, "we did them, yet not we, but the grace of God that was with us." Both ways, it is true: what He works by us He works in us, and what He works [Lu. 2. 14. Vulg.] Isa. 26. 12. 1Cor.15.10.

SERM. XVIII. in us He works by us. For ἐνεργεῖ, συνεργεῖ, take not away one the other, but stand well together. This for the doing.

2. The work. Now for the work. In every good work we do His will; yet, it seemeth, degrees there are. For here is mention of θέλημα, "His will;" and besides it, of εὐάρεστον, "His good pleasure," and this latter sounds as if it did import more than a single will. One's good pleasure is more than his
Heb. 12. 28. bare will. So in the chapter before he wisheth, λατρεύσαι εὐαρέστως, that is, we may serve and please; that is, may so serve as that we may please. Acceptable service then is more than any, such as it is. There is no question but that, as of evil works some displease God more than other, so of good works there are some better pleasing, and that He takes a more special delight in.

And if you would know what they be, above at the six-
[Heb. 13. 16.] teenth verse it is said, that "to do good and to distribute," that is, distributive doing good, it is more than an ordinary service; it is a sacrifice, every such work. It is of the highest kind of service, and that with that kind (εὐαρεστεῖται, our word here) "God is highly pleased." So doth St. Paul call the bounteous supplying of his wants from the Philippians, θυσίαν δεκτὴν, "a sacrifice right acceptable and pleas-
Phil. 4. 18. ing to God," and ὀσμὴν εὐωδίας, "a most delightful sweet savour." And that you may still see He looks to the Resurrection, He saith, the Philippians had lain dead and dry a great while, as in winter trees do use. But when that work of bounty came from them, they did ἀναθάλλειν, that
[Phil. 4. 10.] is, "shoot forth, wax fresh, grow green again," as now at this season plants do. That so the very virtue of Christ's resurrection did shew forth itself in them; so fitting nature's resurrection-time, the time of bringing things as it were from the dead again, with this of Christ. Which time is therefore the most pleasing time, the time of the greatest pleasure of all the times of the year. So we know how to do that is pleasing in His sight.

Yet even this pleasing and all else is to conclude, as here it doth, with "through Jesus Christ our Lord:" He is in here too. In, at the doing; in, at the making them to please God, *ut faciat quisque per Christum, quod placeat per*

Christum, 'that what by Christ is done, by Christ may please when it is done.' In at the doing, *infundendo gratiam, gratiam activam,* 'by infusing or dropping in His grace active;' making us able and fit to do, and so to do them. In at the pleasing, *affundendo gratiam, gratiam passivam,* 'by pouring on His good grace and favour passive,' as it might be some drops of His blood, whereby it pleaseth being done. Gracing His work, as we use to say, in God's sight; that so He of His grace may crown it.

We have gone through with both points. Now comes the hardest point of all, the sequel, to couple them and make them hang well together. III. The sequel.

First then, they be ascribed to "the God of peace." There are but three things to be done in the text, and peace doth them all. And if peace, then God by no other title than "the God of peace." 1. Peace bringeth from death; for war, I am sure, bringeth to death many a worthy man. There is little question to be made of this; that "the God of peace" doth the one, but the devil of discord doth the other. 1.

Secondly, peace sets in joint, war brings all out of joint; war is not good for the joints as we see daily, peace doth them no hurt. 2.

Thirdly, peace makes us fit for good; war for all manner 3.
of evil works, saith St. James in the third chapter, verse [Jam. 3.
sixteen. Therefore "the God of peace," say we. And if 16.]
He take it from us for a time, that He bring it quickly back to us again. For when He was first brought into the world, among the living, at His birth, Janus was shut; the
Angels, they sung "peace upon earth." And when He was Lu. 2. 14.
"brought again from the dead" this day, He was no sooner risen but the first news was, the soldiers ran all away—a sign of peace. And indeed, when He had slain hatred, it was most kindly then to bring peace. As this evening with
His own mouth He spake it once and twice, *Pax vobis,* over Joh. 20. 19
and over again. Which is the Apostle's benediction here. 21.
So resurrection and peace, they accord well.

Now for the sequel of good works, upon Christ's bringing from the dead. Being to infer good works, He would never put in all this, of Christ's bringing back again from the dead, if there had not been some special operative force to, or toward them, in Christ's resurrection. If Christ's rising made not for them, had not some special reference to them, some peculiar interest in them, all this had not been *ad idem*, but idle, and beside the point quite. We must take heed of this error, to think the passion or resurrection of Christ, though it be *actus transiens*, that with the doing passeth away, that it hath not a virtue and force permanent; that it left not behind it a virtue and force permanent to work continually some grace in us; as to think His resurrection to be *actus suspensus*, an act to have his effect at the latter day, and in the mean time to serve for nothing but to hang *in nubibus*, as they say. But that this day it hath an efficacy continuing, that sheweth forth itself; and, as the rule is, in the soul, before it doth on the body. We will leave the heathen to their habits and habitualities, but with us Christians this is sure: whatsoever in us, or by us is wrought, that is pleasing to God, it is so wrought by the virtue of Christ's resurrection. We have not thought of it perhaps, but most certain it is it is so. So God hath ordained it. Whatsoever evil is truly mortified in us, it is so by the power of Christ's death, and thither to be referred properly. And whatsoever good is revived or brought again anew from us, it is all from the virtue of Christ's rising again. All do rise, all are raised, thence. The same power that did create at first, the same it is that makes a new creature. The same power that raised Lazarus the brother from his grave of stone, the same raised Mary Magdalene the sister from her grave of sin. From one and the same power both. Which keepeth this method; worketh first to the raising of the soul from the death of sin; and after, in the due time, to the raising of the body from the dust of death. Else, what hath the Apostle said all this while?

Now this power is inherent in the Spirit as the proper subject of it, even the eternal Spirit, Whereby Christ offered Himself first unto God, and after raised Himself from the dead. Now as in the texture of the natural body ever there goes the spirit with the blood; ever with a vein, the vessel of the one, there runs along an artery, the vessel of the other, so is it in Christ; His blood and His Spirit always go together. In the Spirit is the power; in the power virtually every good work it produceth, which it was ordained for. If we get the Spirit, we cannot fail of the power. And the Spirit, That ever goes with the blood, which never is without it.

This carries us now to the blood. The very shedding whereof upon the cross, *primum et ante omnia* was the nature of a price. A price, first, of our ransom from death due to our sin, through that His satisfaction. A price again of the purchase He made for us, through the vail[1] of His merit, which by His testament is by Him passed over to us. [[1] i. e. avail.]

Now then, His blood, after it had by the very pouring it out wrought these two effects, it ran not waste, but divided into two streams. 1. One into "the laver of the new birth" —our baptism, applied to us outwardly to take away the spots of our sin. 2. The other, into "the Cup of the New Testament in His blood," which inwardly administered serveth, as to purge and "cleanse the conscience from dead works" that so live works may grow up in the place, so to endue us with the Spirit That shall enable us with the power to bring them forth. *Hæc sunt Ecclesiæ gemina Sacramenta;* 'these are,' not two of the Sacraments, but 'the two twin-Sacraments of the Church,' saith St. Augustine. And with us there are two rules. 1. One, *Quicquid Sacrificio offertur, Sacramento confertur;* 'what the Sacrifice offereth, that the Sacrament obtaineth.' 2. The other, *Quicquid Testamento legatur, Sacramento dispensatur;* 'what the Testament bequeatheth, that is dispensed in the holy mysteries." Tit. 3. 5. Lu. 22. 20. Heb. 9. 14. [Vid. S. Aug. Tract. in Joan. 9. 10. 15. 8. 120. 2. De Civ. Dei 15. 26. 22. 17.]

To draw to an end. If this power be in the Spirit, and the blood be the *vehiculum* of the Spirit, how may we partake this blood? It shall be offered you straight in "the Cup of blessing, which we bless in His name. For "is not the Cup of blessing which we bless, the communion of the blood of Christ?" saith St. Paul. Is there any doubt of that? In which blood of Christ is the Spirit of Christ. In which Spirit is all spiritual power; and namely, this power that frameth us fit to the works of the Spirit, which Spirit we are all made there to drink of. 1 Cor. 10. 16. [1 Cor. 12. 13.]

And what time shall we do this? What time is best? What time better than that day in which It first shewed forth the force and power It had in making peace, in bring-

SERM. XVIII. ing back Christ That brought peace back with Him, That made the Testament, That sealed it with His blood, That died upon it, that it might stand firm for ever? All which were as upon this day. This day then somewhat would be done, somewhat more than ordinary, more than every day. Let every day be for every good work, to do His will; but this day to do something more than so, something that may be well-pleasing in His sight. So it will be kindly, so we shall keep the degrees in the text, so we shall give proof that we have our part and fellowship in Christ, in Christ's resurrection;—grace rising in us, works of grace rising from it. That so, there may be a resurrection of virtue, and good works at Christ's resurrection. That as there is a reviving, *ἀναθαλία* in the earth, when all and every herbs and flowers are "brought again from the dead," so among men good works may come up too, that we be not found fruitless at our bringing back from the dead, in the great Resurrection, but have our parts as here now in the blood, so there then in the testament, and the legacies thereof, which are glory, joy and bliss, for ever and ever.

SERMONS

OF THE

SENDING OF THE HOLY GHOST,

PREACHED UPON WHIT-SUNDAY.

A SERMON

PREACHED BEFORE

THE KING'S MAJESTY AT GREENWICH,

ON THE EIGHTH OF JUNE, A.D. MDCVI., BEING WHIT-SUNDAY.

Acts ii. 1—4.

When the Day of Pentecost was come, (or, when the fifty days were fulfilled,) *they were all with one accord in one place.*

And there came suddenly from Heaven the sound of a mighty wind, and it filled the place where they sat.

And there appeared tongues cloven as they had been of fire, and sat upon each of them.

And they were all filled with the Holy Ghost, and they began to speak with other tongues, as the Spirit gave them utterance.

[*Et cum complerentur dies Pentecostes, erant omnes pariter in eodem loco.*

Et factus est repente de Cœlo sonus, tamquam advenientis spiritus vehementis, et replevit totam domum ubi erant sedentes.

Et apparuerunt illis dispertitæ linguæ tamquam ignis, seditque supra singulos eorum;

Et repleti sunt omnes Spiritu Sancto, et cœperunt loqui variis linguis, prout Spiritus Sanctus dabat eloqui illis. Latin Vulg.]

[*And when the day of Pentecost was fully come, they were all with one accord in one place.*

And suddenly there came a sound from Heaven as of a rushing mighty wind, and it filled all the house where they were sitting.

And there appeared unto them cloven tongues like as of fire, and it sat upon each of them.

And they were all filled with the Holy Ghost, and began to speak with other tongues, as the Spirit gave them utterance. Engl. Trans.]

We are this day, beside our weekly due of the Sabbath, to renew and to celebrate the yearly memory of the sending down the Holy Ghost. One of the *magnalia Dei*, as they Acts 2. 11.

SERM. I. be termed after in the eleventh verse; one of "the great and wonderful benefits of God;" indeed, a benefit so great and so wonderful as there were not tongues enough upon earth to celebrate it withal, but there were fain to be more sent from Heaven to help to sound it out throughly, even a new supply of tongues from Heaven. For all the tongues in earth were not sufficient to magnify God for His goodness in sending down to men the gift of the Holy Ghost.

This we may make a several benefit by itself, from those
Gal. 4. 4. 6. of Christ's. And so the Apostle seemeth to do. First, "God sent His Son," in one verse; and then, after, "God sent the Spirit of His Son," in another.

Or we may hold our continuation still, and make this the last of Christ's benefits; for *ascendit in altum* is not the last,
Ps. 68. 18. there is one still remaining, which is, *dona dedit hominibus*. And that is this day's peculiar; wherein were given to men many and manifold both graces and gifts, and all in one gift, the gift of the Holy Ghost.

Howsoever we make it, sure it is that all the rest, all the feasts hitherto in the return of the year from His incarnation to the very last of His ascension, though all of them be great and worthy of all honour in themselves, yet to us they are as nothing, any of them or all of them, even all the feasts in the Calendar, without this day, the feast which now we hold holy to the sending of the Holy Ghost.

Christ is the Word, and all of Him but words spoken or words written, there is no seal put to till this day; the Holy
Eph. 4. 30. Ghost is the seal or signature, *in Quo signati estis*. A testament we have and therein many fair legacies, but till this
1 Cor. 12. 5. day nothing administered. "The administrations are the Spirit's." In all these of Christ's there is but the purchase made and paid for, and as they say, *jus ad rem* acquired; but *jus in re, missio in possessionem*, livery and seizin, that is reserved till this day; for the Spirit is the *arrha*,
2 Cor. 5. 5. "the earnest" or the investiture of all that Christ has done for us.

These, if we should compare them, it would not be easy to determine, whether the greater of these two: 1. that of the
Isa. 9. 6. Prophet, *Filius datus est nobis*; 2. or that of the Apostle,
Rom. 5. 5. *Spiritus datus est nobis*; the ascending of our flesh, or the

descending of His Spirit; *incarnatio Dei*, or *inspiratio hominis;* the mystery of His incarnation, or the mystery of our inspiration. For mysteries they are both, and "great mysteries of godliness" both; and in both of them, "God manifested in the flesh." 1. In the former, by the union of His Son; 2. In the latter, by the communion of His Blessed Spirit. 1 Tim. 3. 16.

But we will not compare them, they are both above all comparison. Yet this we may safely say of them: without either of them we are not complete, we have not our accomplishment; but by both we have, and that fully, even by this day's royal exchange. Whereby, as before He of ours, so now we of His are made partakers. He clothed with our flesh and we invested with His Spirit. The great promise of the Old Testament accomplished, that He should partake our human nature; and the great and precious promise of the New, that we should be *consortes divinæ naturæ*, "partake His divine nature," both are this day accomplished. That the text well beginneth with *dum complerentur*, for it is our complement indeed: and not only ours, but the very Gospel's too. It is Tertullian; *Christus Legis, Spiritus Sanctus Evangelii complementum;* 'the coming of Christ was the fulfilling of the Law, the coming of the Holy Ghost is the fulfilling of the Gospel.' 2 Pet. 1. 4.

Of which coming of the Holy Ghost the report is here set down by St. Luke; both of the 1. time, and 2. the manner of it. 1. The time, in the first words, "when the day of Pentecost was come." 2. The manner, in all the rest of the four verses. The division. I. II.

And the manner, first, on their parts to whom He came; of the preparation for His coming, in the first verse. And then the manner of His coming, in the other three.

On their parts to whom He came, how they stood prepared, how they were found framed and fitted to receive Him when He came, in these three: 1. "They were all of one accord;" 2. "They were all in one place;" 3. And both these, *dum complerentur*, "even so long, till the fifty days were fulfilled." 1.

On His part the manner of His coming to them thus prepared. 1. First, as it is propounded in type or figure, in the 2.

SERM. I.

second and third verses; 2. And then, as it is expounded in truth and in deed, in the fourth.

1. In type or figure, *symbolice;* and that is two ways, agreeable to the two chief senses, 1. the hearing, and 2. the sight. 1. To the hearing, by "a sound," in the second verse; 2. to the sight, by a show, in the third.

1. To the hearing, by "a sound," in the second. "A sound of a wind"—"a wind," 1. "sudden," 2. "vehement," 3. "that came from Heaven," and 4. "filled that place where they sat."

2. To the sight, by a show, in the third. There appeared 1. "tongues;" 2. "cloven;" 3. "as it were of fire;" 4. "which sat upon each of them." Thus far the figure.

2. Then in the fourth, followeth the thing itself. Which verse is, as it were, a commentary of the two former. 1. Of the wind inward, in the first part of it, and these words; "They were filled with the Holy Ghost." 2. Of the tongues outward, in the latter, and these words, "They began to speak with other tongues, as the Spirit gave them utterance."

The one, to represent the inward operation. The other the outward manifestation of the Spirit. Thus standeth the order, these are the parts.

1. The time. "When the day of Pentecost was come."

The first point is the time of His coming, that is, "The day of Pentecost."

1. Why that day? The day of Pentecost was a great feast under the Law, and meet it was this coming should be at some great feast. 1. The first dedication of Christ's Catholic Church on earth, 2. the first publishing the Gospel, 3. the first proclaiming the Apostles' commission, were so great matters as it was not meet they should be obscurely carried, stolen as it were, or "done in a corner." Much lay upon them: and fit it was they should be done in as great an assembly as might be. And so they were; even in a concourse, as in the fifth verse it is, "of every nation under Heaven;" that so notice might be taken of it, and by them carried all over the world, even to the utmost corners of the earth. St. Paul said well to King Agrippa: "This is well enough known, this was not done in a corner." Acts 26. 26.

2. At a great feast it was meet, but there were many great feasts; why at this feast, the feast of Pentecost?

It is agreed by all interpreters old and new—Cyprian is the first we find it in—that it was to hold harmony, to keep correspondency between the two Testaments, the Old and the New. So it was at Christ's death we see. He was slain, not only as the Lamb was, but even when the Lamb was slain too: on the feast of the Passover, then, was "Christ our Passover" offered for us.

2. At the feast of giving the Law. [Vid. edit. Baluz. App. cxlvi.] Cyprian. Ser. de Spiritu. 1 Cor. 5. 7.

Now, from that feast of the Passover, reckoning fifty days they came to Sinai; and there on that day, the day of Pentecost, received they the Law—a memorable day with them, a high feast, even for so great a benefit; and is therefore by them called the feast of the Law.

And even the very same day, reckoning from "Christ our Passover" fifty days, that the Law was given in Sinai, the very same day doth the new "Law" here "go out of Sion," as the Prophet Esay foretold, *exibit de Sion Lex;* which is nothing else but the promulgation of the Gospel. "The royal Law," as St. James calleth it, as given by Christ our King: the other but by Moses, a servant, and savoureth therefore of "the spirit of bondage," the fear of servants; as this doth of the princely spirit, "the spirit of ingenuity and adoption," the love of children.

Isa. 2. 3. Jas. 2. 8. Ps. 51. 12. Rom. 8. 15.

On the feast of Pentecost, then, because then was given the Law of Christ, written in our hearts by the Holy Ghost.

To this doth Chrysostom join a second harmony. That as under the Law, at this feast, they first put their sickle to the corn—harvest, in that climate, beginning with them in this month—the first-fruits whereof they offered at Easter, and was called therefore by them *festum messis;* in like sort we see that this very day, the Lord of the harvest so disposing it, Who not long before "lifting up His eyes and looking on the regions round about saw them white and ready to the harvest," His first workmen, the Apostles, did put in their first sickle into the great harvest, *cujus ager est mundus,* "whereof the world is the field," and the several furrows of it "all the nations under Heaven." On the feast of Pentecost then second, because then began the great spiritual harvest.

2. The feast of beginning of Easter. [Chrysost. Hom. 4. in Act. Apost. init.] Joh. 4. 35. Mat. 13. 38. Acts 2. 5.

To these two doth St. Augustine add a third, taken out of the number in the very name of Pentecost, and that is

The feast of Jubilee. August. ep. 119. [55. B.]

SERM. I. fifty. Which being all along the Law the number of the Jubilee, which was the time of forgiving of debts and restoring men to their first estates, it falleth fit with the proclaiming of the Gospel, done presently here in the thirty-eighth verse of this chapter, which is an act of God's most gracious general free pardon of all the sins of all the sinners in the world.

Cyril. Cat. 17. Ps. 104. 30. [De Sanc. Trin. Dial. 7. post. med.] And no less fit falleth it for our restitution, whereunto Cyril applieth excellently the thirtieth verse of the hundred and fourth Psalm, *emitte Spiritum Tuum et creabuntur, et renovabis faciem terræ.* Shewing there was first an emission of the Spirit into man at his creation, which being since choked with sin and so come to nothing, this day there is here a second emission of the same Spirit into man, fully to restore and renew him, and in him the whole mass of the creation. On the day of Pentecost then last, because therein is the true number and force of the true Jubilee. This for the choice of the time.

II. The manner. 1. On their parts. Their preparation. The number thus settled, we descend to the second point, of the manner. And first, on their parts on whom the Holy Ghost came; how He found them framed, and fit to receive such a guest. It is called by the Fathers *parasceue Spiritus,* 'the preparation;' as there was one for the Passover, so here for Pentecost.

It is truly said by the philosopher, that *actus activorum sunt in patiente disposito;* 'if the patient be prepared aright, the agent will have his work, both the sooner and the better.' And so consequently the Spirit in His coming, if the parties to whom He cometh be made perspirable.

And this is three-fold, set down in these words: 1. "They were all with one accord;" 2. "They were all in one place." A double unity: 1. unity of mind, (so is ὁμοθυμαδὸν, θυμοῦ,) or of hearts, (so is "accord," *cordium.* 2. And secondly, unity of place. 3. And thirdly, these two, *dum complerentur;* patiently expecting, while the fifty days were accomplished.

"1. They were all of one accord." Unity is the first—unity of mind. And for it, take but any spirit that is to give life to a natural body; can any spirit animate or give life to members dismembered, unless they be first united and compact together? It cannot: unity must prepare the way to any spirit, though but natural.

A fair example we have in Ezekiel, chapter the thirty-seventh. Ezek. 37, 7-9.
A sort of scattered dead bones there lay; they were to be revived. First, "the bones came together, every bone to his bone;" then, "the sinews grew and knit them;" then, "the flesh and skin, and covered them;" and then, when they were thus united, then and not before called He for the spirit from the four winds, to enter into them and to give them life. No spirit, not the ordinary natural spirit, will come, but where there is a way made and prepared by accord and unity of the body.

Now then take the Holy Ghost, the Spirit of spirits, the third Person in Trinity; He is the very essential unity, love, and love-knot of the two Persons, the Father and the Son; even of God with God. And He is sent to be the union, love, and love-knot of the two natures united in Christ; even of God with man. And can we imagine that He will enter, essential Unity, but where there is unity? The Spirit of unity, but where there is unity of spirit? Verily there is not, there cannot possibly be a more proper and peculiar, a more true and certain disposition, to make us meet for Him, than that quality in us, that is likest His nature and essence, that is, unanimity. Faith to the Word, and love to the Spirit, are the true preparatives. And there is not a greater bar, a more fatal or forcible opposition to His entry, than discord, and dis-united minds, and such as are "in the Acts 8. 23.
gall of bitterness;" they can neither give nor receive the Holy Ghost. *Divisum est cor eorum, jamjam interibunt*, saith Hos. 10. 2.
the Prophet; "their heart is divided," their "accord" is gone, that cord is untwisted; they cannot live, the Spirit is gone too.

And do we marvel, that the Spirit doth scarcely pant in us? that we sing and say, "Come, Holy Ghost," and [See the Ordering of Priests.]
yet He cometh no faster? Why, the day of Pentecost is come, and we are not "all of one accord." "Accord" is wanting; the very first point is wanting, to make us meet for His coming. Sure, His after-coming will be like to His first; to them that are, and not to any but them that are, "of one accord."

And who shall make us "of one accord?" High shall be his reward in Heaven, and happy his remembrance on

SERM. I. earth, that shall be the means to restore this "accord" to the Church; that once we may keep a true and perfect Pentecost, like this here, *erant omnes unanimiter*. I pass to the second.

2. "In one place." But suppose we were of "one accord," is not that enough? May we not spare this other, of "one place?" If our minds be one, for the place it skills not; it is but a circumstance or ceremony; what should we stand at it? Yes sure; seeing the Holy Ghost hath thought it so needful as to enter it, we
Rom. 15. 6. may not pass it over, or leave it out. Not only "of one mind," that is, unanimity, but also "in one place" too, that
Eph. 4. 3. is, uniformity. Both "in the unity of the Spirit," that is inward, and "in the bond of peace" too, that is outward. An item for those whom the Apostle calleth *filii subtractionis*, that forsake the congregation, as even then in the
Heb. 10. 39. Heb. 10. 25. Apostles' times "the manner of some" was, "and do withdraw themselves to their perdition," to no less matter. God's will is, we should be, as upon one foundation, so under one
Ps. 68. 6. [Pr. B. ver.] roof; that is His doing, *Qui facit unanimes, &c.* "He that maketh men of one mind to dwell in one house." Therefore it is expressly noted of this company here, in the text,
Acts 4. 24. where they prayed, "they prayed all together;" when they
Acts 8. 6. Acts 2. 46. heard, "they heard all together;" when they brake bread, they did it all together. All together ever: not in one place some, and some in another; but all ἐπὶ τὸ αὐτὸ, all "in one and the self-same place." For say what they will, division of places will not long be without division of minds. This must be our ground. The same Spirit, That loveth unanimity, loveth uniformity; unity even in matter of circumstance, in matter of place. Thus the Church was begun, thus it must be continued.

3. "While the fifty days were fulfilled." To these do the Fathers join a third, which they raise out of the words, *dum complerentur*. A disposition in them whereby they held out, and stirred not even till the fifty days were fulfilled. That former, unanimity; this latter, longanimity. There is in us a hot hasty spirit, impatient of any delay: what we would have, we would have out of hand; and these same *dum* and *donec*, and such like words, we love them not. This spirit was even in these here, the Apostles themselves, at the first, as we may see in the last

chapter, verse the sixth, where they shew it; *Domine jamne* Acts 1. 6.
vis? "Lord, wilt Thou now?" even now? by and by? But that spirit He cast out, with *non est vestrum, &c. Manete* Acts 1. 7.
vos dum. After which charge given, though at the instant of His ascending He promised He would send them the Holy Ghost, yet they did not look for Him the same afternoon; nor stayed but till the morrow after Ascension-day; nor, as the Bethulians' stint was, four or "five days" at the Judith 7. 30.
farthest, and then waxed weary, and would wait no longer; but as He willed them to wait, so they did wait; not five days, but five and five; and so continued waiting, even *usque dum complerentur,* till they were accomplished; and then brake not up neither, to keep holy-day, but held on their waiting, holy-days and all.

We said before, this feast had divers names; 1. The feast of the law, 2. "The feast of harvest," 3. The feast of Pentecost; we may put to a fourth out of Deuteronomy, chapter Deu. 16. 10.
sixteen, verse ten. It is there called 4. "the feast of weeks." [Comp. Lev. 23. 15. &c. with Acts 2. 1.] [Ex. 23. 16.]
It is not hours will serve the turn, nor yet days; it must be weeks, and as many weeks as be days in a week, to make it Pentecost, that is, fifty days. Thus long they sat by it, as it is in the next verse, and tarried patiently the Lord's leisure, till He came unto them. *Qui crediderit ne festinet,* saith the Isa. 28. 16.
Prophet Esay, "he that believeth let him not be hasty;" and, *si moram fecerit, expecta Eum,* saith Habakkuk, "if He Habak. 2. 3.
happen to stay, stay for Him." And so we shall, if we call to mind this, that He hath waited for us and our conversion more years than we do days for Him. And this withal, *veniendo veniet;* stay He may for a time, but, if we wait, come He will certainly; and when He cometh, *manebit vobis in æternum,* "He will never forsake us, but continue with us for ever." Joh. 14. 16.
Dum complerentur shall have his accomplishment.

And in this manner doth the Scripture bear witness of them they were prepared, and that they sped of the Spirit; and let us of like preparing look for like success.

The manner, on His part. 1. His coming in type.

And now we come to the manner of His coming. And that, first in type sensibly, thus described. 1. "There came a sound;" 2. "There were seen tongues," which is a sensible kind of coming.

And that is a coming rare, and nothing usual with the

SERM. I. Holy Ghost, Which as an invisible Spirit cometh for the most part invisibly. So saith Job: "He cometh to me, and
Job 9. 11. I see Him not; He passeth hard by me, and I perceive Him not." It was thus here for this once; but after we see, in
Acts 10. 44. the tenth chapter, He came upon Cornelius and his com-
Acts 19. 6. pany; and after that, upon the twelve at Ephesus, in the nineteenth chapter. But on neither, that aught could be seen or heard; only discerned by some effect He wrought in them. He that best knew the Spirit, Christ, sets us down the manner of His coming: *Spiritus spirat, sed nescis*
Joh. 3. 8. *unde aut quo*, "He doth come and inspire, but how or which way, that know you not."

Yet here in this present case, for this once, it was meet He should thus come in state; and that there should be a solemn, set, sensible descending of it.

1. Meet, that no less honour done to this law of Sion, than to that of Sinai, which was public, and full of Majesty; and so was this to be.

2. Meet, that having once before been, and never but once, upon Christ the Head, it should be so once more on the Church too, the Body. It pleased Him to vouchsafe to grace the Church, His Queen, with like solemn inauguration to that of His own, when the Holy Ghost descended on Him in likeness of a dove; that she might, no less than He Himself, receive from Heaven like solemn attestation.

3. Lastly, meet it was it should remain to the memory of all ages testified, that a day there was when even apparently to sense mankind was visited from on high; and that this wind here, and these tongues came not for nought, at so high a feast, in so great an assembly.

This coming then of His, thus in state, is such as it was both to be heard and seen, to the ear and the eye both.
Acts 2. 33. So saith St. Peter of it after: "Being thus exalted," saith he of Christ, "and having received the promise of the Father, He hath shed forth this which you now both see and hear." And with good reason both: to both senses is the Holy Ghost presented. To the ear, which is the sense of faith; to the eye, which is the sense of love. The ear, that is the ground of the word, which is audible; the eye, which is the ground of the Sacraments, which are visible.

To the ear in a noise, to the eye in a show; a noise of a mighty wind, a show of fiery tongues. The noise serving as a trumpet, to awake the world, and give them warning He was come. The fiery tongues, as so many lights to shew them, and to let them see the day of that their visitation.

To begin with the first. "There came a sound." Which "There
very sound is to shew that the Spirit, Whereof it is the fore- came a sound."
runner, is no dumb Spirit but vocal. And so it is. "The Rom. 10.
sound Thereof is not only gone into all lands," but hath 18.
been heard in all ages: before the flood it sounded in "Enoch Jude 14.
a Prophet," and "Noah a preacher of righteousness." All 2 Pet. 2. 5.
the law long it sounded in them, by whom "Moses was Acts 15. 21.
preached every Sabbath day." The very beginning of the
Gospel was with a sound, *Vox clamantis;* and, but for this Mat. 3. 3.
sound, St. Paul knoweth not how we should do. "How Rom. 10.
should they believe," saith he, "in Him of Whom they have 14.
not heard?" and without a sound, there is no hearing. But
we shall come to this again in the apparition of the tongues.

"There came a sound," and not any sound. It will not "A sound"
be amiss to weigh what kind of sound is expressed in the echo-wise.
word here used, ἦχος. You know what sound an echo is; a sound at the second hand, a sound at the rebound. *Verbum Domini venit ad nos;* "The word of the Lord cometh to us:" there is the first sound, to us; and ours is but the echo, the reflection of it to you. God's first, and then ours second. For if it come from us directly, and not from Him to us first, and from us then to you, echo-wise, it is to be suspected. A sound it may be, the Holy Ghost cometh not with it; His forerunner it is not, for that is ἦχος.

"There came a sound," and it was "the sound of a "A sound
wind;" and this too, very fitly. For the wind, which is here of a wind."
the type of the Holy Ghost, of all the creatures doth best express It.

1. For first, of all bodily things it is the least bodily, and cometh nearest to the nature of a spirit, invisible as it is.

2. And secondly, quick and active as the Spirit is. Of the wind it is said, *Usque adeo agit, ut nisi agat non sit;* so active it is as, no stirring the air, no action, no wind: even so, no operation, no Spirit. So like, as both have but one name;, nay, all three but one. 1. The wind in the wide

SERM. I. world, 2. the breath in our bodies, 3. and the Spirit in the mystical body, the Church. And much ado we have to distinguish them in many places, they be taken so one for another.

1. It came "suddenly." Now, this "wind" that came and made this sound, is here described with four properties. 1. It fell "suddenly;" 2. it was "mighty" or violent; 3. it came "from Heaven;" 4. "it filled that place where they sat"—that place and no other. Of which, the two first are ordinary, and, like the wind, common: 1. To be sudden, 2. and to be violent. The other two not so, but dislike: 3. To come from Heaven, 4. and to keep itself within one place, and that of no great compass.

"A wind." 1. That "came suddenly." It fell suddenly, ἄφνω φερομένη. So doth the wind. It riseth oftentimes in the midst of a calm, giveth no warning, but rusheth up of a sudden; and even so doth the Spirit.
Lu. 17. 20. For that "cometh not by observation" neither, saith our Saviour, you can make no set rules of it; you must wait for It as well when It cometh not, as when It comes. Many
Isa. 65. 1. times It is "found of them that seek It not," and therefore little account make of It, and therefore little deserve It.
1 Sam. 10. 10; 16. 13. Acts 10. 44. *Cecidit super eum Spiritus*, is so common in both the Old and New Testament, as we can make no doubt of this. Which sheweth It falls suddenly, It creeps not: *serpentis est serpere.* Commonly, motions that come from the serpent, creep upon us; but, *nescit tarda molimina Spiritus*
Ps. 147. 15. *Sancti gratia*, saith Ambrose. *Velociter currit sermo Ejus*,
Ps. 18. 10. "His word runneth very swiftly," and "His Spirit cometh with the wings of the wind." And therefore sudden, saith Gregory, because things, if they be not sudden, awake us not, affect us not; but, *repentina valde mutant*, 'sudden things start us and make us look up.' And therefore sudden, saith he again, that men may learn not to despise present motions of grace, though suddenly rising in them, and though they can give no certain reason of them, but take the wind while it bloweth, and the water while the Angel moveth it, as not knowing when it will, or whether ever it will blow again, or stir any more. It is ἄφνω φερομένη, it fell on a sudden.

2. "A vehement wind." It was "a mighty" or vehement "wind." The wind is so, and the Spirit is so; both in this, well sorted together.

Of the wind it is a common observation, that being nothing else but a puff of air, the thinnest, the poorest, and to our seeming of the least force of all creatures, yet groweth it to that violence, and gathereth such strength, as it "rattles together the great ships of Tarshish," as it "rents and rives in sunder mountains and rocks," pulls up trees, blows down huge piles of building, hath most strange and wonderful effects, which our eyes have often seen; and all this, but a little thin air.

Ps. 48. 7. 1 Kings 19. 11.

And surely no less observable, or admirable, nay much more have been and are the operations of the Spirit. Even presently after this, this Spirit, in a few poor weak and simple instruments, God knoweth, waxed so full and forcible, as it "cast down strong holds, brought into captivity many an exalting thought," made "a conquest of the whole world," even then when it was bent fully in main opposition against it, as it hath set all men in a maze to consider, how so poor a beginning should grow to such might, that wisdom and learning, and might and majesty, and all have stooped unto it; and all was but God's little "finger," all "the breath of His mouth." Verily the wind was never so vehement, as the Spirit hath been and is in His proceeding.

2 Cor. 10. 4. 1 Joh. 5. 4. Lu. 11. 20. 2 Thes. 2. 8.

These two are common with the wind; and for these two it might have been no more, but even a common wind. The other two are not so, but shew it to be more than a wind: 3. The coming from Heaven, 4. the filling but of that one place. In these two it is dislike, as in the former two like, ordinary wind that bloweth.

3. It "came from Heaven."

It "came from Heaven." Winds, naturally, come not from thence, but out of the caves and holes of the earth; they blow not downward, but move laterally from one coast or climate to another. To come directly down, not only *de sursum*, 'from above,' (so it may be from the middle region of the air,) but *de cœlo*, "from Heaven" itself; that is supernatural sure, that is "a wind out of God's own treasury" indeed, that points us plainly to Him That is ascended up into Heaven, and now sendeth it down from thence.

Ps. 135. 7.

And therefore sendeth it "from Heaven," that it may fill us with the breath of Heaven. For as the wind is, so are the blasts, so is the breath of it; and as is the

SERM. I. Spirit, so are the motions It useth, so are the reasons It is carried by.

To distinguish this wind from others, is no hard matter. If our notions come from above, if we fetch our grounds there, *de cœlo,* "from Heaven," from religion, from the sanctuary, it is this wind; but those that come from earthly respects, we know their cave, and that there is nothing but natural in them. This wind came thence to make us hea-
Col. 3. 1. venly minded, *sapere quæ sursum,* to "set our affections on
Phil. 3. 20. things heavenly," and to frame the rules of "our conversation agreeable unto Heaven." So we shall know what wind blows, whether it be *de cœlo,* or *de hominibus,* whether
Mat. 21. 25. it be *defluxus cœli,* or *exhalatio terræ;* "from Heaven or of men,"—a breath from Heaven, or a terrene exhalation.

4. "It filled that place" only.

And like to this is the fourth: "it filled that place where they sat." "That place where they;" "that place," not the places about. That place it filled, the other felt it not. And this is another plain *dissimile,* To blow but in one place; and sheweth it to be more than ordinary. The common wind, all places within his circuit, it aireth all alike; one as well as another, indifferently. This here seemeth to blow *elective,* as if there were sense in it, or it blew by discretion. For it blew upon none of the neighbour houses, none of the places adjacent, where these men were not. That, and only that room it filled, where they were sitting.

And this, of blowing upon one certain place, is a pro-
Joh. 3. 8. perty very well fitting the Spirit: *Ubi vult spirat.* To blow in certain places where Itself will, and upon certain persons, and they shall plainly feel It, and others about them not a whit. There shall be an hundred or more in an auditory: one sound is heard, one breath doth blow. At that instant, one or two and no more; one here, another there; they shall feel the Spirit, shall be affected and touched with It sensibly; twenty on this side them, and forty on that, shall not feel It, but sit all becalmed, and go their way no more moved than they came. *Ubi vult spirat,* is most true.

And that *ubi* is not any where, but where these men sat; that is, it is a peculiar wind, and appropriate to that place where the Apostles are, that is, the Church. Elsewhere to

seek it, is but folly. The place it bloweth in, is Sion; and in Sion, where men be so disposed as we shewed ere-while, that is, where there is concord and unity, the dew of Sion, *ibi mandavit Dominus benedictionem;* there God sendeth this Ps. 133. 3.
wind, and "there He sendeth His blessing" with this wind, which never leaveth us till it bringeth us to life for evermore, to eternal life. So doth Solomon describe the nature of the wind; that it goeth forth, and that it "compasseth Eccl. 1. 6.
round about," and then, last, that it returneth *per circuitus suos.* So doth this: it cometh from Heaven, and it bloweth into the Church, and through and through it, to fill it with the breath of Heaven; and as it came from Heaven to the Church, so it shall return from the Church into Heaven again, *per circuitus suos;* and whose sails it hath filled with that wind, it shall carry with it along *per circuitus suos;* even to "see the goodness of the Lord in the land of the [Ps. 27. 13.]
living," there to live with Him and His Holy Spirit for ever.

So we have, briefly, the four properties of this wind, and of the Spirit Whose type it is: 1. That it is "sudden" in the first coming; 2. That it is "mighty" in proceeding; 3. That it cometh "from Heaven;" 4. That it cometh into the Church; to fill it with the Spirit of Heaven, and to carry it thither whence itself cometh. Thus much for the second, the first type.

2. To be seen. "There appeared tongues," &c.

This wind brought down with it tongues, even *imbrem linguarum,* 'a whole shower of them,' which is in the next point of the show which appeared. By which appearing it appeareth plainly, that the wind came not for themselves only, but for others too beside; in that here is not only sent a wind which serveth for their own inspiration, but there be also sent tongues with it, which serve for elocution, that is, to impart the benefit to more than themselves.

It sheweth that the Holy Ghost cometh and is given here, rather as *gratia gratis data,* to do others good; than as *gratia gratum faciens,* to benefit themselves. *Charitas diffusa in* Rom. 5. 5.
corde would serve them, "charity poured into their hearts;" but *gratia diffusa in labiis,* "grace poured into their lips," Ps. 45. 2.
that is not needful for themselves, but needful to make others beside them partakers of the benefit. The wind alone, that is to breathe withal, the grace of the Holy Ghost

SERM. I. whereby ourselves live; but the wind and tongues, that is to speak withal, the grace of the Holy Ghost whereby we make others live, and partake of the same knowledge to life. An union of the wind and tongue here on earth, expressing the unity of the Spirit and Word in Heaven; that as the wind or breath in us is to serve the tongue, so is the Spirit given to set forth the Word, and the Holy Ghost to spread abroad the knowledge of Christ.

Where it is not unworthy your observing neither, that as, in the natural body, one and the same breath of ours is *organon* both *vitæ* and *vocis*, 'is the instrument both of life and voice,' the same that we live by, is the same that we speak by; even the very like is in the body mystical, and both the vital breath and the vocal come both, as we here see, from the Holy Ghost.

This also standeth of four parts, as did the former. For there appeared, 1. "tongues," 2. "cloven," 3. "as it were of fire," 4. "sitting upon each of them."

1. 'Tongues.' The tongue is the substantive and subject of all the rest. It is so; and God can send from Heaven no better thing, nor the devil from hell no worse thing than it. "The best member we have," saith the Prophet; the worst member we have, saith the Apostle:—both, as it is employed. [Ps. 108. 1. Pr. B. vers. Jas. 3. 6.]

"The best," if it be of God's cleaving; if it be of His lightening with the fire of Heaven; if it be one that will sit still, if cause be. The worst, if it come from the devil's hands. For he, as in many other, so in the sending of tongues, striveth to be like God; as knowing well they are every way as fit instruments to work mischief by, as to do good with. There be "tongues of Angels" in 1 Cor. 13. 1: and if of good Angels, I make no doubt but of evil; and so, the devil hath his tongues. [1 Cor. 13. 1.]

And he hath the art of cleaving. He shewed it in the beginning, when he made the serpent, *linguam bisulcam*, 'a forked tongue,' to speak that which was contrary to his knowledge and meaning—they should not die; and as he did the serpent's, so he can do others. [Gen. 3. 4.]

There is fire in hell, as well as in Heaven; that we all know.

Only in this they agree not, but are unlike: his tongues

cannot sit still, but fly up and down all over the world, and spare neither Minister nor Magistrate, no nor God Himself.

But if we shall say to our tongue, as David did to his, "Awake up my glory," that is, make it the glory of all the rest of our members, it can have no greater glory than this, to be the organ of the Holy Ghost, to set forth and sound abroad the knowledge of Christ, to the glory of God the Father. And so used, it is heavenly, no time so heavenly as then; in no service so heavenly as in that. Ps. 108. 2. [Ps. 57. 8.]

Not to enlarge this point further, there is no new matter in it. This here, of the "tongues," is as that before of the "sound:" both are to no other end but to admonish them of their office, whereto they here received ordination; even to be tongues, to be trumpets of the counsel of God, and of His love to mankind, in sending His Son to save them.

Here is wind to serve for breath, and here are tongues now, and what should let them to do it? That which before they received in charge audibly, *Ite, prædicate,* the very same they here received visibly in this apparition, which is after expounded thus: *Cœperunt loqui,* by virtue of these tongues "they began to speak." Mar. 16. 15. [Acts 2. 4.]

2. "Cloven tongues."

"Tongues" and "cloven tongues." And that very cleaving of right necessary use to the business intended. For that of theirs was but one whole entire tongue that could speak but one poor language, the Syriac, they were bred in. There was not a cleft in it. So could they speak their mind to none but Syrians; and by that means should the Gospel have been shut up in one corner of the world.

Τὸ κοινωνικὸν is the goodness of all that is good; even the imparting it to the good of the common. To the end then this great good of the knowledge of the Gospel might be dispersed to many nations, even to every nation under Heaven—to that end clove He their tongues; to make many tongues in one tongue, to make one man to be able to speak to many men of many countries, to every one in his own language. If there must be a calling of the Gentiles, they must have the tongues of the Gentiles wherewith to call them. If they were "debtors," not only "to the Jews, but to the Grecians;" nay, not only "to the Grecians, but to the Barbarians too;" then must they have the tongues not only Acts 20. 21.

SERM. I. of the Jews, but of the Grecians and of the Barbarians too, to
Rom. 1. 14. pay this debt, to discharge the duty of *Ite, prædicate,* to all.
Mar. 16. 15. And this was a special favour from God, for the propagation of His Gospel far and wide, this division of tongues, and it is by the ancient writers all reckoned a plain reversing of the curse of Babel, by this blessing of Sion, since they account it all one, and so it is, either as at the first for all men to speak one language, or as here one man speak all. That is here recovered, that there was lost; and they enabled for the building up of Sion in every nation, to speak so as all might understand them of every nation.

But this withal we are to take with us; that with their
Rom. 15. 6. many tongues they spake one thing, and that *univoce.* "With
Acts 4. 24. one mouth," "with one voice."

With divers tongues to utter one and the same sense, that is God's cloven tongue; that is the division of Sion, serving to edification.

With one tongue, *æquivoce,* to utter divers senses, divers meanings; that is none of God's, it is the serpent's forked tongue, the very division of Babel, and tendeth to nothing but confusion.

"Tongues cloven," and, "as they had been of fire." "As they had been;" to keep a difference in these as before in the wind, and to shew that they were not of our elementary fire. For it is added, "sat upon them;" which they could not have done without some hurt, without scorching them at least, if it had been such fire as it is in our chimneys. But it was ὡσεὶ, "as it were" ours; that is, in show, earthly, indeed celestial. And as the wind, so the fire from Heaven; of the nature of that, in the third of Exodus, which made
Exod. 3. 2. "the bush burn, and yet consumed it not."

Where, first, we are to observe again the conjunction of the tongue and fire. The seat of the tongue is in the head,
Eph. 1. 22. and the "Head of the Church" is Christ. The native place of heat, the quality in us answering to this fire, is the heart, and the Heart of the Church is the Holy Ghost. These two join to this work, Christ to give the tongue, the Holy Ghost to put fire into it. For as in the body natural the next, the immediate instrument of the soul is heat, whereby it worketh all the members over, even so in the mystical

body, a vigour there is like that of heat, which we are willed to cherish, to be "fervent in the Spirit," "to stir" and to blow it up; which is it that giveth efficacy to all the spiritual operations. Rom. 12. 11. 1 Thes. 5. 19. 2 Tim. 1. 6.

To express this quality, it appeareth in the likeness of this element; even to shew there should be an efficacy or vigour in their doctrine resembling it; *quod igneus est illis vigor*, that the force of fire should shew forth itself in their words; both in the splendour which is the light of knowledge to clear the mist of their darkened understanding, and in the fervour which is the force of spiritual efficacy, to quicken the dulness of their cold and dead affections. [Virg. Æneid. 6. 730.]

And indeed the world was then so overwhelmed with ignorance and error, and so overgrown with dross and other bad matter, by paganism, it long had been that their lips did need to be touched with "a coal from the altar." Tongues of flesh would not serve the turn, nor words of air, but there must be fire put into the tongue, and spirit and life into the words they spake, a force more than natural, that is, the force of the Spirit; even to speak sparks of fire instead of words, to drive away the darkness, and to refine the dross of their heathenish conversation so long continued. Isa. 6. 6.

Our Saviour Christ saw this and said, Every sacrifice then had need to be seasoned with fire, but there was no fire to do it with. Therefore He added in another place, "I came to send fire upon earth," and this day He was as good as His word, and sent it. Mark 9. 49. Lu. 12. 49.

And with such a tongue spake He Himself when they said of Him, "Did not our hearts burn within us, while He spake unto us by the way?" With such a tongue St. Peter here, in this chapter; for sure there fell from him something like fire on their hearts, when they were pricked with it and cried, "Men and brethren, what shall we do?" Lu. 24. 32. Acts 2. 37.

And even to this day yet, in them that move the dead and dull hearts of their hearers, and make them to have a lively apprehension of things pertaining to God, there is a remainder of that which this day was sent; and they shew plainly, that yet this fire is not clean gone out.

But this is not always, nor in all, with us—no more was it with them; but in those of their hearers which had some

SERM. I. of "the anointing," and that will easily take the fire, in
1 Joh. 2. 27. them good will be done; or at least, where there was some
Mat. 12. 20. "smoking flax," some remainder of the Spirit, which without any great ado will be kindled anew. Them it doth good—the rest it did not. This for the fire.

4. "And sat on each of them." These "sat upon each of them." In which sitting is set down unto us their last quality, of continuance and constancy. The virtue is προσεδρεύειν, fiery tongues "sitting;" the vice opposite ἐπιπολάζειν, fiery tongues 'flitting.' They did not light and touch, and away, after the manner of but-
Acts 2. 2. terflies, but both they sat themselves, in the former verse,
Acts 2. 3. [and] "the tongues sat on them," that is, they abode still, and continued staid and steady, without stirring or starting
Ps. 78. 57. aside, saith the Psalmist, "like a swerving bow."

Of our Saviour Christ Himself, how to know Him, God Himself gave St. John Baptist a privy sign, and it was this:
Joh. 1. 33. "On whomsoever thou seest the Spirit lighting, and abiding on Him," that is He. Lighting is not it, though it be the Holy Ghost; but lighting and abiding, that is the true sign.

The same [of] our Saviour is this day said, that "ascend-
Ps. 68. 18. ing on high, He gave gifts unto men;" and to what end? "that the Lord their God might dwell among them." Mark that "dwell;" not, might stay and lodge for a night, as in an inn or hostelry, and then be gone in the morning, but "dwell," that is, have His habitation, take up His residence among them.

The God, or that Person of the Deity, he there saith shall "dwell," is the Holy Ghost; one of whose chief attributes
Ps. 51. 10. in the Psalm is that He is רוח נכון, "a constant Spirit"—and if *Sanctus* come of *sancio,* there is as much said in the Latin word as in the Hebrew—"constant," not desultory; and His fire not like the foolish meteor, now in, now out,
Lev. 6. 12. but permanent still, like "the fire on the altar."

So in vigour, as His vigour is not brunts only or starts, *impetus,* but *habitus,* that it holdeth out habit-wise. Not only like the sparks before which will make a man stir for the present, but leaving an impression, such an one as iron red-hot leaving in vessels of wood: a fire-mark never to be got out more. Such doth the Holy Ghost leave in the memo-
Ps. 119. 93. ries: *In æternum non obliviscar,* "I shall never forget it."

And such did it leave in the hearts of the first Christians, that could never be got out of their hearts by their persecutors, till they plucked out hearts and all.

With this salt, as well as with that fire, saith Christ, must Mar. 9. 49.
every sacrifice be seasoned; not only with that fire to stir it up, but with this salt to preserve it. By this virtue, in the former verse, they were disposed to the Spirit; and now here, you see, again by the Spirit they are disposed to this virtue; and not only disposed to it, but rooted, and more and more confirmed in it; that we may learn to esteem of it accordingly.

And thus have we, as before heard what the sound, so now seen what the sight can shew us, even all four: 1. "Tongues," that they might preach; 2. "Cloven," that they might preach to many; 3. "Fire," that they might do it effectually; 4. and "Sitting," that so effectually as not flittingly, but that it might be an efficacy, constant, abiding, and staying still with them; so forcible, that continual.

Now are we to know what all this amounts to, what is the *signatum* or 'thing signified' of both these signs; what was wrought in them by inward concurrence with this outward resemblance. And that followeth in the fourth verse, wherein there is a commentary of this wind, and a gloss of these tongues. Of the wind in the forepart: "they were all filled with the Holy Ghost." Of the tongues in the latter: "they began to speak with other tongues, as the Spirit gave them utterance."

But the time being already spent, I will not so far presume as to enter into it, it would ask too long a treaty.

It remaineth now that first we offer up our due praise and unfeigned hearty thanks, giving to Him That is ascended up on high for sending this day this blessing upon that His Church, the mother of us all. The fruit whereof, even of this wind, and of these tongues, in the effect of them both, the blowing of the one, and the speaking of the other, we all feel to this day so far as Christendom is wide. It is the duty of the day.

First then this; and then withal secondly, to endeavour that we may have this day some feeling of this day's benefit ourselves, and some way find ourselves visited with the same Spirit.

SERM. I. I told you, after this first there is no more visible coming to be looked for, but that after His accustomed usual manner invisibly He ceaseth not to come still, nor will not to the world's end.

Even in this book, after this time here three several times, [Acts 4. 31; 10. 44; 19. 6.] in the fourth, tenth, and nineteenth chapters; and at three several places, Jerusalem, Cæsarea, Ephesus, the same Spirit came upon the faithful people, and yet nothing heard nor seen; only discerned after, by the impression it left behind it. And this coming is still usual with Him, and this we may hope for; hope for and have, if we labour and dispose ourselves for it.

And we may direct ourselves how to do this, by those three places I even now alleged. 1. In the fourth chapter, [Acts 4 31; 10. 44; 19. 6.] the thirty-first verse; "As they prayed," the Spirit came upon them 2. In the tenth, verse the forty-fourth; "While Peter yet spake, the Spirit fell upon them." 3. In the nineteenth chapter, verse the sixth; As they received the Sacrament, the Spirit was sent on them. In which three are plainly set down to us, these three means to procure the Spirit's coming: 1. Prayer, 2. the Word, 3. the Sacraments.

I know well it was the Sacrament of Baptism in the place last alleged; but that is all one. In one verse doth the Apostle name them both, as of equal power, both for the 1 Cor. 12. 13. purpose: *Uno Spiritu baptizati estis;* and before he ends the verse, *et uno Spiritu poti.* "Baptized in the Spirit"—there is theirs at Ephesus; but "made drink of the same Spirit"—that is this of ours here. For *ex similibus sumus et alimur.* Ours here, I say, where we do "drink of the Spirit," if aright we 1 Cor. 10. 4. receive it; in which respect he calleth it "the spiritual drink," because we do even drink the Spirit with it.

And even in this very chapter, before the end, it is noted by St. Luke, as a special means whereby they invited the [Acts 2. 46.] Spirit to them again and again, "their continuing in the Temple with one accord, and breaking of bread." Of "one accord," we spake at the first, as an effectual disposition thereto; and this Sacrament of "breaking of bread" is the Sacrament of "accord," as that which representeth unto us 1 Cor. 10. 17. perfect unity in the many grains kneaded into "one loaf," and the many grapes pressed into one cup; and what it representeth lively, it worketh as effectually.

Howsoever it be, if these three, 1. Prayer, 2. the Word, 3. the Sacraments, be every one of them as an artery to convey the Spirit into us, well may we hope, if we use them all three, we shall be in a good way to speed of our desires. For many times we miss, when we use this one or that one alone; where, it may well be God hath appointed to give it us by neither, but by the third. It is not for us to limit or appoint Him, how, or by what way, He shall come unto us and visit us, but to offer up our obedience in using them all; and, using them all, He will not fail but come unto us, either as a wind to allay in us some unnatural heat of some distempered desire in us to evil, or as a fire to kindle in us some luke-warm, or some key-cold affection in us to good. Come unto us, either as the Spirit of truth, lightening us with some new knowledge; or, as the Spirit of holiness, reviving in us some virtue or grace; or, as the Comforter, manifesting to us some inward contentment, or joy in the Holy Ghost; or, in one or other certainly He will come. For a complete obedience on our part in the use of all His prescribed means never did go away empty from Him, or without a blessing; never did nor never shall.

Never; but not on this day, of all days; the day wherein *dona dedit hominibus*, "He gave gifts unto men." It is *dies* [Ps. 68. 18.]
donorum, 'His giving day, His day of donatives.' Some gift He will give, either from the wind, inward, or from the tongue, outward; some gift He will give.

There be nine of them set down, nine "manifestations 1 Cor. 12. 7.
of the Spirit"—some of them nine. There be nine more
set down, nine "fruits of the Spirit"—some of them nine— Gal. 5. 22.
some gift He will give.

Only let us dispose ourselves by the use, not of this one or that one, or two, but of all the means, to receive it by. Inwardly, by unity and patient waiting His leisure, as these here; outwardly, by frequenting those holy duties, and offices, all which, we see, succeeded with those there in the three places remembered.

And in these, the blessed Spirit so dispose us, and in them

so bless us, as we may not only by outward celebration, but by inward participation, feel and find in ourselves, that we have kept to Him, this day, a true feast of the coming of His Spirit, of the sending down the Holy Ghost! Which Almighty God grant, &c.

A SERMON

PREACHED BEFORE

THE KING'S MAJESTY, AT GREENWICH,

ON THE TWENTY-FOURTH OF MAY, A.D. MDCVIII., BEING WHIT-SUNDAY.

Acts ii. 4.

And they were all filled with the Holy Ghost, and began to speak with other tongues, as the Spirit gave them utterance.

Et repleti sunt omnes Spiritu Sancto, et cœperunt loqui variis linguis, prout Spiritus Sanctus dabat eloqui illis.

[*And they were all filled with the Holy Ghost, and began to speak with other tongues, as the Spirit gave them utterance.* Engl. Trans.]

This day hold we holy to the Holy Ghost, by Whom all holy days, persons, and things, are made holy. And with good reason hold we it; He That maketh all holy days, it is meet should be allowed one Himself. And if we yield this honour to this and that Saint, much more to the Saint-maker, to Him That is the only true Canonizer of all the Saints in the Calendar.

2. This honour were we bound to yield Him, if there were nothing besides; but seldom shall ye find a feast wherein with His honour there is not joined the remembrance of some memorable benefit then vouchsafed us; as here this feast is not to the Holy Ghost simply, but to the sending or coming of the Holy Ghost; to the Holy Ghost sent.

3. Sent; not, as in former times, qualified or by measure, but even *in plenitudine*, 'in plenteous manner,' fully. It is said, "They were filled with the Holy Ghost."

4. "Filled;" not to hold, but to set over. For so many tongues, so many pipes to derive it to others, that by preaching they might impart the Spirit they received; preaching being nothing else, as the Fathers observe out of the eleventh

SERM. II. Nu. 11. 25. of Numbers, but "the taking of the spirit" of the preacher, and putting it on the hearer; or, to express it by the type of fire, the lighting of one torch by another, that so it might pass from man to man, till all were lightened.

For this Holy Spirit thus sent, plenteously sent, sent to them, and by them to all and to us, are we here met to render our thanks to God, even to imitate Him; to send this day tongues into Heaven, there to laud and magnify Him Who as this day sent these tongues into earth.

At Pentecost, A.D. 1606. Now, of this benefit, so far as the two types in the former verses, hath formerly been treated; and we are now to supply what was then left in remainder.

The sum. This fourth verse then is nothing else but a commentary of the former; what in them was set forth in figure, is here expressed in plain terms. The types were of two sorts, according to the two chief senses: 1. Audible to the ear, in the sound of wind; 2. Visible to the eye, in the show of tongues. These two are expounded in the two moieties of this verse. The former, the commentary of the wind, in these words: "They were filled with the Holy Ghost." The latter, the gloss of the tongues, in these; "And they began to speak with other tongues, as the Spirit gave them utterance."

The division. For the first. The place was filled with a wind from Hea-
I. ven. The filling of the place was a sign of the filling the persons in the place; the wind was a sign of the Spirit—the wind from Heaven, of the Holy Spirit; which Spirit filled the persons, no less than did the wind the room they sat
1. in. Two points there be in it: 1. One of the gift itself, in
2 *Spiritu Sancto;* 2. The other of the measure of the gift, in *repleti sunt.*

II. For the latter, four things were in the type; 1. "tongues,"
1-4. 2. "cloven," 3. "sitting," 4. "of fire;" all four here expressed, and suited. 1. "Tongues;" "they began to speak." 2. "Cloven;" "with other tongues." 3. "Sitting;" "as the Spirit gave them." 4. "Fire;" *ἀποφθέγγεσθαι*, "utterance," it is turned, it is more. These are the heads. But for that there is no speaking of the Spirit without the Spirit, no hearing neither; to the end that speaking and hearing of Him, He may help our infirmities, &c.

The truth answering the type *per omnia,* as there were in that, two, 1. the wind, and 2. tongues; so are there here two, 1. the spirit, 2. and speech. Spirit, because speech without spirit is but a dead sound like the "tinkling of a cymbal." Speech, because spirit without speech is but as the spirit that Christ cast forth, *et illud erat mutum,* "a dumb spirit," none the better for it. Which made the Holy Ghost come in spirit and speech; not in spirit only, but in spirit and speech.

I. The commentary of the wind. Of both parts jointly: spirit and speech both. 1 Cor. 13. 1. Lu. 11. 14. But spirit first in order.

But in spirit first, and then speech. So is the order. The Holy Ghost begins within, *a centro,* and worketh outward; alters the mind, before it change the speech; gives another heart, before another tongue; works on the spirit, before on the phrase or utterance; ever so. It is preposterous, and all out of order, to have the tongues come before the wind: where they do, it commonly falls out in such, all their religion is in common phrases and terms well got by heart, and nothing else. This for their joining, and for their order.

Now of either, apart. Of the Spirit first, Which they were filled with; after, of their filling: that is, 1. first, of the gift itself: 2. then, of the measure. That they were filled with is set down in two words; 1. *Spiritu* and 2. *Sancto.* First, that it was a "spirit;" then, that that spirit was "holy." A "spirit," for men may be filled, and not with the "Spirit;" "holy," for there is a *spiritu* and *sancto.* We must needs put the difference: "spirit and "holy" are two diverse things

I. Of the parts severally. 1. The gift. 1. It was a spirit.

"With the Spirit;" for men may be "filled," and not with the "Spirit." That which enforceth this note, is a speech at the thirteenth verse; there they stick not, some, this that was the Spirit indeed to reproach with the term of new wine. "These men are full," say they; "full," they grant; but with "wine," a liquor though full of spirit, yet no spirit though. It was false, as it fell out; yet this it worketh, that if the Spirit may be taken for a humour, why not a humour for the Spirit likewise? And not the humour of the vine only; but the philosopher in his problems tells us, that look whatsoever operation wine hath, the same have some humours in our bodies, with a little fermenting. The Prophet Esay seemeth to say the same in two places, that men

A spirit, not an humour.

Isa. 29. 9; 51. 21.

SERM. II. may be "drunk, and not with wine," their own humour will do it as well.

I wish it were not true, this; that humours were not sometimes mistaken, and mistermed the Spirit. A hot humour flowing from the gall, taken for this fire here, and termed, though untruly, the spirit of zeal. Another windy humour proceeding from the spleen, supposed to be this wind here, and they that filled with it, if nobody will give it them, taking to themselves the style of the godly brethren. I wish it were not needful to make this observation, but you shall easily know it for an humour; *non continetur termino suo*, 'its own limits will not hold it.' They are ever mending churches, states, superiors—mending all, save themselves; *alieno, non suo*, is the note to distinguish an humour.

2. "The Holy Spirit." Not our own spirit. "With the Spirit;" yet, not every spirit. I told you, there was a *spiritu* without *sancto;* and I mean not the wicked spirit—away with him, we will not once mention him—but, two other. 1. There is a "spirit" in a man, saith
Job 32. 8. Elihu, that is, our own spirit; and many there be, *qui se-*
Ezek. 13. 3. *quuntur spiritum suum*, "that follow their own ghost," instead of the Holy Ghost; for even that ghost taketh upon
Mat. 16.17. it to inspire, and "flesh and blood," we know, have their revelations.

2. Not the world's spirit. The other is, that the Apostle calleth *spiritum mundi*, "the world's spirit," or worldly spirit, *qui posuit mundum in corde*
1 Cor. 2. 12. Eccl. 3. 11. *suo*, saith Solomon, hath set up and shrined the world in his heart; thence rise all his reasons, by them he frames and measures religion. Up shall the golden calves, to uphold
Joh. 11. 48. the present estate; down shall Christ, *ne veniant Romani*, "that the Romans come not," and carry us all away. Either
[Virg. Æn. 3. 57.] of these is peradventure *sacer spiritus*, as the Poet calleth
2 Pet. 1. 20. *auri sacra fames;* but neither is *sanctus*. St. Peter opposeth the first, "of private resolution," to the Holy Ghost; St. Paul
2 Cor. 1. 12. the second, of "worldly wisdom," to the Spirit of God. The wind before had four qualities: two of them, 1. suddenness, and 2. vehemency, are passed by. Every wind, every spirit hath them. And commonly, other spirits are more violent, and make a greater noise, than the true Spirit. The other two, 1. of coming from Heaven, 2. coming for the Church; from the holy Heaven to the holy Church, are both in *sancto;*

and *sapere quæ sursum*, being wise from thence, and regard to religion and the Church, are the two best characters to discern the Holy Spirit by.

Now ye will understand of yourselves, I shall not need to tell you, when we speak of the Holy Spirit as It filleth us, we mean not the Essence or Person of the Holy Ghost— That "filleth Heaven and earth," saith the Prophet; and "there is no going from It," saith the Psalmist—but only certain impressions of the Spirit. The Psalmist calleth them "gifts," the Apostle "graces," which carry the name of their cause; so that, in the dialect or idiom of the Scriptures, to be filled with them, is to be filled with the Spirit. To shew this, otherwhile they be joined; "the spirit and power of Elias," that is, the power of the Spirit; "the wisdom and spirit of Stephen," that is, the wisdom of the Spirit.

The Holy Spirit, that is, His Graces.

Jer. 23. 24. Ps. 139. 7. Ps. 68. 18. 1 Cor. 12. 4. Lu. 1. 17. Acts 6. 10.

And because these "gifts" and "graces" be of many points, more points of this wind than there be of the compass, and as it were many Spirits in One; six, saith Esay; "seven," saith St. John; they are all recapitulate under these two:—1. Under the wind is represented the saving grace which all are to have so to serve God that they may please Him, as necessary to all, and without which we can be no more in our spiritual life than we can without our breath in our natural. This is general to all. It is said, *repleti sunt omnes;* the hearer must have it, as well as the speaker. It must air and dry up the superfluity of our nature; else the fire will not kindle in us, but turn all to smoke. Of this Spirit are those nine points, Galatians, the fifth chapter, and the twenty-second verse. 2. The other, represented in the tongues, set forth unto us another kind of grace, principally meant and sent for the benefit of others; given therefore in tongues which serve to teach, and in fire which serveth to warm others; to shew they are given and received for the good of others rather than of themselves. And of this Spirit are the points reckoned up, the first of Corinthians, twelfth chapter, and the seventh verse.

Isa. 11. 2. Rev. 1. 4. Rev. 3. 1. Gal. 5. 22. [1 Cor. 12. 7, &c.]

And now we know what it was they were filled with, let us come to the measure—*repleti sunt*. It was not *spiritus transiens*, but *implens;* a wind, not that blew through them, as it doth through many of us, I know not how oft, but that

2. The measure; *Repleti sunt.*

SERM. II. filled them; they were the fuller for it. Which word, of filling, wanteth not his special force: refer we it to their estate now, compared with what it was before, *repleti sunt;* or to their estate in this point compared with other since, and namely with ourselves, *repleti sunt illi.*

1. *Repleti sunt* compared with their former estate. With their own estate first. For there is no question they were not empty or void of the Spirit before this coming. They had not been baptized by Christ, He had not breathed Joh. 20. 22. on them, and bid them "receive the Holy Ghost," in vain. If before this they had died, none would have doubted of the estate of their souls. This filling then, first, sheweth us there be divers measures of the Spirit; some single, some 2 Kings 2. 9. double portions, as appeareth by Elisha's petition; not all of one size or scantling. That as there are degrees in the wind, *aura, ventus, procella,* 'a breath, a blast, a stiff gale,' so are there in the Spirit. One thing, to receive the Spirit as on Easter-day; another, as on Whit-Sunday. Then but Joh. 20. 22. "a breath," now "a mighty wind;" then but "received" it, now "filled" with it. Sprinkled before as with a few drops— Ezek. 20. 46. [36. 25.] Joel 2. 28. Ezekiel's *Stillabo Spiritum;* but now comes Joel's *Effundam Spiritum,* which very text is alleged at the twenty-eighth verse after by St. Peter, "poured out plenteously," and they baptized, that is, plunged in It. *Imbuti Spiritu,* covered with some part of It—so were they before; here now they be *in-* Lu. 24. 49. *duti Spiritu,* "clothed all over with power from above," as Christ promised. To conclude: the Holy Ghost came here, [S. Leon. de Pentecost. Serm. 3. 1.] saith Leo, *cumulans, non inchoans; nec novus opere, sed dives largitate;* 'rather, by way of augmenting the old, than beginning a new.' Though, to say the truth, both ways He came here. The rule of the Fathers is—Hierome and Cyril have it—where the Holy Ghost was before, and is said to come again, it is to be understood one of these two ways:— 1. either of an increase of the former, which before was had; 2. or, of some new, not had before, but sent now for some new effect. Breath they had before; breath and wind are both of one kind, differ only *secundum magis et minus;* to be "filled," is but to receive only in a greater measure; therefore greater, because their work was now greater. Before, Mat. 1. 6. Joh. 10. 16. but "to the lost sheep of Israel;" now to all the stray sheep in all the mountains of the whole earth.

But beside that increase, here is a new form too. Which is a sign of a new gift, utterly wanting in them before, and wherewith now, and never till now, they were furnished; to speak to all nations, of all tongues under heaven. Thus far, compared with themselves.

Now, *repleti sunt illi. Illi,* with reference to others since, and if you will, to ourselves. They, in the succeeding ages, and we to this day, receive the Spirit too, or else it is wrong with us. But both they before us, short of the Apostles; and we short of them, by much. It fareth herein, as it doth in the pouring forth of an "ointment"—the Psalm so likeneth it. No ointment at the skirts or edges of a garment, doth run so fresh and full as on the head and beard, where it was first shed; ever, the farther it goeth, the thinner and thinner the streams be. Therefore it is said, *Repleti sunt illi;* and even *illi* wants not his force, they were filled, they. We, but a hin to their ephah; but an handful, to their heap; but a rantism[1], to their Baptism. They "filled;" had as much as they could hold. We have our measure, such as it is; but full we are not. None of us so full, but we could hold more.

2. *Repleti sunt illi,* with reference to others.

Ps. 133. 2.

[[1] *i. e.* a sprinkling.]

And two reasons there are rendered: 1. One, such a Pentecost as this, never was but this; never the like before, nor since. It was Christ's coronation day, the day of placing Him in His throne, when He "gave these gifts unto men." That day, all magnificence was shewed, the like not to be looked for ever after.

1. Reason.

Ps. 68. 18. Eph. 4. 8.

Then again, to say truth, our task-work is not so great, that we need require such a filling. We have to deal but with an handful of men, in comparison; and those brought up in religion, and, as it were, broken to our hands. They, with the "fulness of the Gentiles," all mankind; wild as then, and enraged; filled full of malice against them, and their doctrine by the evil spirit; that they need the good Spirit, to fill, to encounter such opposition. The case, you see, differs much. It was happy for the world, they had this overflowing fulness of the Spirit. It is enough for us, we have the measure spoken of—the second of Corinthians, the twelfth chapter, and the ninth verse—*sufficit tibi gratia,* "grace sufficient" for us; and let that content us. And

2. Reason.

[Rom. 11. 25.]

[2 Cor. 12. 9.]

SERM. II.

thus much for the commentary of the wind. Now, to the gloss of the tongues.

The gloss of the tongues.

And they spake.

Ps. 39. 3.

"They were filled;" and in sign they were filled it is added, they ran over. The "fire was kindled in them" by this wind; and in sign thereof, "they spake with their tongue." Indeed, pity they should be thus full, and have no means to vent it; have a spirit to fill, and not a tongue to empty or impart it. Therefore the tongues were requisite. The wind would have served them, if they had been to be Christians only; but they were to be Apostles, that is, ambassadors, and such must have tongues, needs. But two imperfections were in their tongues. 1. They were but single: He cleft them, and made them able to deal with many. 2. Their tongues were waterish and weak: He gave them the force and operation of fire, to kindle such a light as should burn to the world's end. In a word, where they knew neither how nor what to speak, He gave them both; both *sicut*, how, and ἀποφθέγγεσθαι, what: He gave them both, and so made them perfect Apostles. These four, 1. Courage; 2. Language; 3. Discretion; and 4. Learning.

The dependence of *repleti*, and *locuti*, their skill.

First, a word of the dependence of *repleti* and *locuti*: they were filled, and then "they began to speak." It is well they began not before, but were filled first and then spake after. This is the right order. Somewhere, some fall a speaking, I will not say before they be full or half full, but while they be little better than empty, if not empty quite. There is not *repleti sunt, et cœperunt loqui; cœperunt loqui* begins the verse with them, *repleti sunt* is skipped over. Ever, emptying pre-supposeth filling; *repleti* hath reference to the cistern, *locuti* to the cock. The cistern would be first looked to, that it have water store, before we be too busy to ply the cock; else follow we not the Holy Ghost's method. Else it may be *cœperunt loqui*, but not *sicut dedit Spiritus;* He giveth leave to none to speak empty.

It is but a grammar note, that of Hierome's, but it is to
Isa. 28. [9.] the purpose, upon the word *quem docebo scientiam*, that *doceo*, if it have his right, would have a double accusative; not only *quem*, 'whom,' that is, an auditory; but *scientiam*, what, that is, "knowledge." So as he that hath not *scientiam*, should not have *quem;* and they that get themselves whom to

teach, and have not *scientiam* what to teach, go they never so oft into the pulpit, it is not *sicut dedit Spiritus*, the Holy Ghost gave them neither mission nor commission. He ever taketh order for *repleti* before He giveth license for *cœperunt loqui.*

1. *Cœperunt loqui.* Their courage.

And this for their skill. But he that reads the Fathers' writings, shall find they refer this *cœperunt loqui* no less to their boldness, than to their ability; "began," not only *posse*, 'to be able,' in respect of their skill, but *audere*, 'to dare,' in regard of their courage. Before, neither courage nor skill; now, both; that any man might see there was a new spirit come into them. In saying, "they began," it is as if before they had been tongue-tied, had never spoken. No more they had; never, as they spoke now; never, with that confidence. Before, they did not speak out, they durst not; they spake between the teeth, hoarsely, as if they had lost their voice. A poor damsel did but ask St. Peter a question;—he faltered presently, could not speak a right word. Every thing then took away their voice. But after this mighty wind had filled them and blown up the fire, and they warmed with it, then, saith Augustine, *in omni prætorio, in omni consistorio*, 'in every judgment-place, in every consistory,' then, they spake what they had heard and seen, even before kings, and were not abashed. It confirmed them, it gave them sides and strength. Which so sudden change, from so great pusillanimity to so great courage and constancy, was sure *mutatio dexteræ Excelsi*, 'a change wrought by' "the hand of the Most High." No hand could work it.

Mat. 26. 69.

[S. Aug. Serm. 182. Append.]

Ps. 77. 10.

2. *Linguis, &c.* Their language.

And that we may know, that not only the tongues wrought in them, but even the cleaving also had his effect, "they began," not only "to speak;" but, "with other tongues;" "other," than ever they had learned. For look, what tongue soever it was beside the Syriac, it was another tongue, it was not theirs, they had but one till now; any other they could not skill of. But now, on a sudden, Greek, Latin, Arabic, Persian, Parthian, none came amiss; yet never were they taught them, but came to them, as it were with a cleft only. A great miracle in itself, and a great enabling to them. For by this means every Apostle, look how many tongues

SERM. II. he could speak, so many Apostles was he, as serving for so many sundry men as must else have been used for the speaking so many sundry tongues to so many sundry
Ps. 19. 4. nations. Whereby, as the "line" of the Creator is said to
Rom. 10. 18. have gone "into all lands," so is the "sound" of the Apostles said likewise to have gone as far. The one, to proclaim the creation; the other, the redemption of the world. And so, by speaking all tongues, they have gathered a Church that speaketh all tongues; a thing much tending to the glory of God. For being now converted to Christ, they send up daily to Heaven so many tongues, there to praise His Name, as He this day sent down to earth, to convert them withal to His truth. And indeed, it was not meet one tongue only should be employed that way, as before but one was. It was too poor and slender, like the music of a monochord. Far more meet was it that many tongues, yea, that all tongues should do it; which, as a concert of many instruments, might yield a full harmony. In which, we behold the mighty work of God; that the same means of
Gen. 11. 7. divers tongues, which was the destroying of Babel, the very same is here made to work the building of Sion; that means that scattered them from the tower of confusion, the very same to reduce them to the fold of unity; that so the curse might be taken away, and a blessing come in place, the confused tongues being united into God's glory; and there
[Ps. 19. 3.] "being neither speech nor language, but His praise is heard among them." The nations being once converted to the faith, most of them, this gift is ceased; ceased so far as by immediate inspiration, though in part to attain it by our endeavours, and God's blessing upon them, is found still of good use. For, even to this day, it is holden for requisite, there be one cleft at least in the tongue; and we able to speak one tongue more than our mothers taught us. Better yet, if the cleft, which God hath made in His word, in the tongues of the Old and New Testament, be in our tongues too. That hath still a necessary service, and maimed are we without it; for we must else receive the embassage from God by an interpreter, which is not so convenient. But enough of the cleft of the tongues.

Now, that this might not prove to vain-glory, as it did

after in some at Corinth, it is well added, ***sicut dedit Spiritus,*** which is the third; that "they began to speak," not as their own vanity carried them, but as the Holy Ghost directed them. Their "tongue" was but "the pen;" He, the "Writer." His wind blew the fire, slaked it, and made it more or less, as need was. "The tongues sat on them," and He in the tongues, holding, as it were, the reins in His hand; guiding and moderating their speech; making them keep time, measure, and manner: time, when; measure, how much; manner, how to speak. Which *sicut* is the gift of discretion, many times as much worth as *dedit,* the gift itself. Sure, these are two: 1. *dedit* is one thing, the gift; 2. *sicut* another, the use of the gift. To many is given to speak, but not with the right *sicut.* Two distinct things be they; and howsoever we do with the one, we shall find a needful use of prayer to obtain the other. We may begin to speak when we please; but who shall give us our *sicut?* Sure, none but the Spirit. Of Him we must receive this, or else we shall never have. Let that suffice.

Their discretion. *Sicut dedit Spiritus.*

Ps. 45. 1.

Last then, that we mistake not what it was He gave them to speak; for all this while it is not said what. That "they began to speak" is said; and wherewith, "with other tongues;" and how, "as the Spirit gave them utterance." Lest therefore we might mistake, it was *quicquid in buccam,* 'any thing that took them in the head,' it skilled not what, he tells us what it was in the last word, that He gave them *ἀποφθέγγεσθαι,* 'utterance,' we read; it is of larger contents, a more pregnant word, and more full of significancy.

4. Their learning. "as the Spirit gave them utterance."

"They began to speak as the Spirit gave them." Why not there stay, what needed any more? Yes; more it seems needed; there goeth more unto it than so. Speaking will not serve the turn; else, *λαλῆσαι* had been enough, and not any word more put to it. He foresaw that to speak, and only to speak, would be enough for some. So we go up for an hour and speak, be it to the purpose or no, it is all one. For the common man it skills not, it contents him well enough; but the Holy Ghost is not content with *λαλῆσαι,* it is not every speaking, but a kind of speaking it must be, and that kind is *ἀποφθέγγεσθαι.*

SERM. II.

The word I wish well weighed. Chrysostom, Œcumenius, the interpreters, all weigh it; and assure us, it is no slight, or light word, but *verbum talenti*, 'a word of weight, of a talent weight.' To tell you what it is. You have heard of apophthegms; (so doth both Greeks and Latins call wise and weighty sententious speeches:) that word, apophthegms, is the true and proper derivative of this ἀποφθέγγεσθαι here. Such the Spirit gave them to utter. Not the crudities of their own brain, idle, loose, undigested gear, God knoweth; no, but pithy and wise sentences; those be *sicut dedit Spiritus*, "such as the Holy Ghost gave them." It is after said in the second verse, that by virtue of this, when they spake, they spake *magnalia*; *magnalia*, "great and high points;" not *trivialia*, 'base and vulgar stuff,' not worth the time it wasteth, and taketh from the hearer. Yet now, all is quite turned, and we are come to this, that this kind of speaking is only from the Spirit of God; and the other, said here to be given by the Holy Ghost, is study, or affectation, or I wot not what: but *Spiritus non dedit*, that is certain.

[S. Chrysost. in Act. Apost. Hom. 4. in loc.] [Œcumen. in loc.]

Well, St. Luke saith ἀποφθέγγεσθαι is that the Spirit
Tit. 1. 9. giveth. So saith St. Paul, λόγος κατὰ διδαχὴν, "speech
according to learning." So St. Peter, such speech as may
1 Pet. 4. 11. seem, or beseem the very "oracles of God," as may work
light in the understanding, or fervour in the affection; those
Isa. 6. 7. two shew it fire. The fire of the Old Testament, "the burning coal," wherewith the Seraphim touched Esay's mouth,
Isa. 50. 4. and gave him as he saith, *linguam eruditam*, "a learned
tongue;" not only a tongue, but "a learned tongue." As
the fire of the Old, so of the New. So, I am sure, was our
Lu. 21. 15. Saviour's promise, *Dabo vobis os et sapientiam*, He would give them "a mouth and wisdom." Not "a mouth" only, but "a mouth and wisdom." Put these two together, 1. "a mouth and wisdom," 2. and "a learned tongue," and you know what is ἀποφθέγγεσθαι, and you know what is meant by a tongue of fire. For fire cannot speak chaff, it consumes it we see; therefore if it be chaff, it is no fiery tongue that speaks it.

And where it is required that not only the tongue have this fire, but that it sit and bide by us, sure it is that volu-

bility of utterance, earnestness of action, straining the voice in a passionate delivery, phrases and figures, these all have their heat, but they be but blazes. It is the evidence of the Spirit in the soundness of the sense, that leaves the true impression; that is the tongue that will sit by us, that the fire that will keep still alive. The rest come in passion; move for the present, make us a little sermon-warm for the while; but after they flit and vanish, and go their way—true mark leave they none. It is only *verba sapientium clavi,* Ecc. 12. 11.
saith the Wise Man; "the wisdom of the speech," that is "the nail," the nail red-hot, that leaveth a mark behind, that will never be got out. Enough, I trust, to sever them that do *λαλῆσαι,* as their own spirit, from them that do *ἀποφθέγγεσθαι,* as the Spirit of God giveth them: and to stop their mouths for ever, that call it not speaking by the Spirit, unless never a wise word be spoken. So have we the gloss of the tongues:—1. The "tongues" themselves, in *cœperunt loqui;* 2. "cloven," in *linguis aliis;* 3. "sitting," in the Spirit's *sicut;* 4. "fire," in *ἀποφθέγγεσθαι,* the truth answering the type in every point; shewing us what was in them, and what they should be that hold their places; able to speak more tongues than one, to speak discreetly, and to speak learnedly.

And now to draw to an end. Let us return to our Pen- The application.
tecost duty, to glorify God for the Holy Ghost thus sent these two ways:—1. as the Spirit within, filling; 2. as the tongues without, uttering. The tongues, they are a peculiar to one kind of men, though all now invade them, and talk even too much. Of them first. Where the Apostle expoundeth that of the Psalm, "Going up on high, He gave Eph. 4. 8. 11, &c.
gifts unto men," he tells us what those gifts were: "He gave some Apostles, some Prophets, some Evangelists;" and he says not there, but tells us that part of that gift were "Pastors and Teachers," whereof there were none at Christ's ascension, but they were ordained after, for the succeeding ages. Intending, as it seemeth, a part of our Pentecostal duty should be, not only to give thanks for them He first sent on the very day, but even of those He sent ever since; and for those He still sendeth, even in these days of ours. To thank Him for the Apostles; thank Him for

SERM. II. the ancient Doctors and Fathers; thank Him for those we have, if we have any so much worth. And are these the "gifts" which Christ sent "from on high?" Was St. Paul well advised? Must we keep our Pentecost in thanksgiving for these? Are they worth so much, trow? We would be loath to have the Prophet's way taken with us, that it should be said to us as there it is; If you so reckon of them indeed, let us see the wages you value them at; and when we shall see it is but eight pound a year, and having once so much, never to be capable of more, may not then the Prophet's speech there well be taken up, "A goodly price" these high gifts are valued at by you! And may not He justly, instead of Zachary and such as he is, send us a sort of foolish shepherds; and send us this senselessness withal, that speak they never so fondly, so they speak, all is well, it shall serve our turn as well as the best of them all? Sure, if this be a part of our duty this day to praise God for them, it is to be a part of our care too, they may be such as we may justly praise God for. Which, whether we shall be likely to effect by some courses as of late have been offered, that leave I to the weighing of your wise considerations.

Zech. 11. 13.

But leaving this which is peculiar but to some, let us return to the Holy Spirit common to all, and how to be filled with It. A point which importeth every one of us, this day especially; when first, certain it is we are not to content ourselves, as Bernard well saith, *quibusvis angustiis*, 'with every small beginning,' and there to stick still; to think, if we have never so small a breath of It and that but once in all our life, that that is enough, we may sit us down securely, and take no more thought, but rely upon that, for that will do it; but to aspire still as we may, nearer and nearer, to this measure here, and know that *repleti sunt* was not said for nothing. Which how to do, we may take some light from the text. The two types He came in being bodily, serve to teach us we are not to seek after means merely spiritual for attaining it, but trust, as here He visited these, so will He us, and that *per signa corporea*, saith Chrysostom. For had we been spirit, and nothing else, God could and would immediately have inspired us that way; but consisting of bodies also as we do, it hath seemed to His wisdom most agreeable, to make bodily signs the means of conveying the graces of His Spirit into us. And that, now the rather, ever since the Holy One Himself and Fountain of all holiness, Christ, the Son of God, partaketh of both body and Spirit, is both Word and flesh. Thus it is; that "by the word we are sanctified," *et per linguam verbi patrem,* saith Chrysostom, even by those tongues here; but no less, by His flesh and body. And indeed, this best answereth the term filling, which is proper to food; *et Spiritus est ultimum alimenti,* 'the uttermost perfection of nourishment.' In which respect He instituted *escam spiritualem,* "spiritual food," to that end; so called spiritual, not so much for that it is received spiritually, as for that being so received it maketh us, together with it, to receive the Spirit, even *potare Spiritum*—it is the Apostle's own word.

1 Tim. 4. 5 John 17. 17 Heb. 10. 10. 1 Cor. 10. 3. Joh. 6. 63. 1 Cor. 12. 13.

In a word; our Pentecost is to be as these types here were. They were for both senses; 1. the ear, which is the sense of the word; 2. and the eye, which is the sense of the Sacrament, *visibile verbum,* so it is called. Meant thereby, that both these should ever go together, as this day; and as the type was, so the truth should be. And for our example, we have themselves and their practice, in this very chapter, who on this feast joined together the word, at the fourteenth, and the breaking of bread, at the forty-second verse. And so let us too; and trust that, by filling up the measure of both types, we shall set ourselves in a good way to partake the fulfilling of His promise, which is to be "endued with power from above," as they were; at least, in such sort, as He knoweth meet for us. Which Almighty God grant we may!

[Acts 2. 14. 42.] [Luke 24. 49.

A SERMON

PREACHED BEFORE

THE KING'S MAJESTY AT WHITEHALL,

ON THE TWENTY-SEVENTH OF MAY, A.D. MDCX., BEING WHIT-SUNDAY.

JOHN xiv. 15, 16.

If ye love Me, keep My commandments.
And I will pray the Father, and He shall give you another Comforter, that He may abide with you for ever.

[*Si diligitis Me, mandata Mea servate,*
Et Ego rogabo Patrem, et alium Paracletum dabit vobis, ut maneat vobiscum in æternum.]

[*If ye love Me, keep My commandments,*
And I will pray the Father, and He shall give you another Comforter, that He may abide with you for ever. Engl. Trans.]

SERM. III.

THEY are Christ's words to His Apostles; they touch the coming of the Holy Ghost. Of Whose coming this text is a promise; a promise of a prayer to procure "the Comforter" sent them. Which "Comforter," Who it is, is told us, verse the twenty-sixth, "the Comforter which is the Holy Ghost." Let this be said to the honour of it. An angel served to annunciate Christ's coming: no angel would serve for this annunciation; Christ Himself did it; thought not Himself too good to do it. A special high benefit therefore it is, we may be sure. And this "Comforter, the Holy Ghost," was by the Father sent, and by them received; and so the prayer heard, and the promise performed, all as this day. Which day we yearly hold holy in thankful remembrance of the Holy Ghost promised to be sent, and sent.

The Holy Ghost is the Alpha and Omega of all our

solemnities. In His coming down all the feasts begin; at His annunciation, when He descended on the Blessed Virgin, whereby the Son of God did take our nature, the [Lu. 1. 35.] nature of man. And in the Holy Ghost's coming they end, even in His descending this day upon the sons of men, whereby they actually become "partakers," *θείας φύσεως*, 2 Pet. 1. 4. "of His nature, the nature of God." Of which His last and great coming, in this text is the promise, and at this time the performance; that as promise and performance, so the text and time agree.

Every promise is glad tidings, but every promise is not gospel; nor is it good to make a text of it while it is in suspense. But when it is *dixit et factum est*, "so said and so [Ps. 33. 9.] done," then it is a gospel, and may be preached on. Being then made good this day, the Church hath made it the Gospel of this day; it being *festum solutionis*, 'the feast whereon it was to be, and whereon it was paid.'

This promise grew thus. They were to be deprived of Christ's presence; He to be gone. They were troubled with it, troubled at the very heart. In that state they needed comfort. A "Comforter" He promiseth them. His promise is in manner of a deed; not absolute, but as it were with articles on both parts, *per modum syngraphæ*. A covenant on His part, a condition on theirs. He covenants two things; the one supposed, love—"If ye love Me." The other imposed—then "keep My commandments." These two on their part well and truly performed and kept, He stands bound to pray, and praying to procure them a "Comforter," another in His stead. And that they might not be every other while to seek for a new one, that should not leave them as He did, but "abide with them for ever."

Many are the benefits that come to us by the Holy Ghost, and so His titles many. He is here expressed in the title of a "Comforter." Comfort never comes amiss, but it is most welcome to men in their estate here, troubled in mind. It may be, our estate is not yet as theirs was, and we have our *terrenas consolatiunculas*, which yet serve our turn well enough. But there is none of us but the day will come, when we shall need Him and His comfort. It will be good to look after Him; and the sooner the better. He came

SERM. III. here, we see, before "the third hour of the day," that is,
Acts 2. 15. nine in the morning: let us not put Him off till nine at night. It will be too late to seek for our oil when the
Mat. 25. 9. bridegroom is coming.

Those articles were here drawn for them; but he that liketh the same conditions, may have title to the same covenant to the world's end. For to the world's end this covenant here holdeth; and the Holy Ghost offered to be sent—though not in visible manner as this day; it was meet it should be with some solemnity at His first coming, for the more credit, yet—sensibly to them that receive Him. No day excepted; yet this day pleadeth a special interest.

It will then not be amiss if we take instructions what is required on both parts, so many as are desirous to be partakers of His heavenly comfort, which I trust is the desire of us all, that so with comfort we may celebrate this *festum Paracleti*, 'this feast of the Comforter.'

The division. Thus they will rise to be treated of. I. The condition
I. first: 1. their love; 2. their looking to His commandments'
II. keeping. II. Then the covenant: 3. Christ's intercession 4. His Father's giving; 5. giving "the Comforter;" 6. "another Comforter." Where both will come to be touched; but His diversity. 7. At last His perpetuity, or abode with them for ever.

I. The condition. 1. Their love. The condition stands first, as first commended to our care. For of our part we had need have care; on His, we need not. And let me say this of it: No condition could have been devised more proper and fit for this feast—both parts of it. First, "If you love Me"—"love;" and this is *festum charitatis*, 'the feast of love;' and He Whose the feast is, the Holy Ghost, love itself, the essential love and love-knot of the two Persons of the Godhead, Father and Son. The same, the love-knot between God and man, and yet more specially between Christ and His Church. Properly, as faith referreth to Christ the Word, so doth love to the Spirit, and comfort to love. It is the Apostle; *Si quod*
Phil. 2. 1. *solatium charitatis*, "If there be any comfort, it is in love." What condition could be more fit?

And the second is like to it, as fit every way: "keep My
[Exod. 19. 1. et sq.] commandments." For ye shall read in Exodus, that at this

Feast of Pentecost the commandments were given. The very Feast itself institute in remembrance of the Law then given: then very meet they be remembered of them at this Feast. And the Holy Ghost sent, *inter alia,* that they may be written not in stone, but in their hearts; not with the letter, but with the spirit; and the spirit not of fear, but love, as by Whom the love of God is shed abroad in our hearts. Which love is the fulfilling of the commandments, and they all abridged in this one word *diliges.* So, whether Rom. 13. 9.
we regard the Feast, or the Person, or the office of Him to Whom we hold the Feast, the condition is well chosen.

To begin then with the first; "If ye love Me." "Love" 1. Love.
is not so fit here, as "if" is unfitting. For "if" is as if there were some *if,* some doubt in the matter; whereof, God forbid there should be any. It would be without "if." Thus rather: 'forasmuch as you love Me, keep My,' &c. That they and we love Him, I trust, shall not need to be put *in hypothesi; et erat tam dignus amari,* 'seeing He is so well worthy our love,' that we to blame, if we endure any "if," any question to be made of it.

It grieveth me to stand long on this condition, to make an *if* of it at Pentecost. Take the feasts all along, and see if by every one of them it be not put past "if." Christmas-day;
for us, and for our love, He "became flesh," that we might Joh. 1. 14.
love Him, because like us He took our nature on Him. New
year's-day: "knowing no sin, He was made sin for us," 2 Cor. 5. 21.
sealed the bond with the first drops of His blood, wherewith
the debt of our sin light upon Him. Candlemas-day: He
was presented in the Temple, offered as a live oblation for us, Lu. 2. 22.
that so the obedience of His whole life might be ours. Good-Friday: made a slain sacrifice on the cross, that we might be redeemed by the benefit of His death. Easter-day: opened
us the gate of life, "as the first fruits of them" that rise again. 1 Cor. 15. 20.
Ascension-day: opened us the gate of Heaven; thither, as
"our forerunner entered," to prepare a place for us. And this Heb. 6. 20.
day seals up all by giving us seisin of all He hath done for us, by His Spirit sent down upon earth. And after all this, come ye in with "If ye love Me?" Shall we not with *si* strike out "if," and make the condition absolute? Shall
we not to St. Paul's "if," "If any man love not the Lord 1 Cor. 16. 22.

SERM. III. Jesus, let him be anathema maranatha," all say, let him be so?

Mat. 5. 46. "If we love them that love us, what singular thing do we, since the very publicans do the like?" That if our love be but as the publicans, there would be no "if" made of it, for He loved us.

And not because we loved Him, but He loved us first. *Et nulla major ad amorem provocatio, quam prævenire amando; nimis enim durus est, qui amorem etsi nolebat impendere, nolit rependere;* 'No more kindly attractive of love, than in loving to prevent; for too hard metal is he of, that though he like not to love first, will not requite it and love again, either first or second.'

Specially, since His love was not little, but such as St. John
1 Joh. 3. 1. makes an *ecce quantam charitatem* of, "see how great love!"
Joh. 15. 13. How great? So, as none greater. "For, greater love hath no man than this, to give his life for his friends." No man greater but He, for His was beyond. To give His life, is
[Phil. 2. 8.] but to die any sort of death; but *morte crucis,* to die as He died, that is more. And for such as were His friends is
Rom. 5. 10. much; but, *cum inimici essemus* is a great deal more. And
Isa. 5. 4. yet is it "If?" Put it to the Prophet's question, *quid debuit facere?* And add to it, if ye will, *quid debuit pati?* What should He have done, and what suffered? If He did it not, if He suffered not, make an "if" of His love; but if He did both, out with it.

But the publican will be the publican, and the world the world, their love is mercenary sale ware; *si nihil attuleris,* no profit, no love. To take away that "if," even thither He will follow us, and apply Himself to that. And if we will make port-sale of our love, and let it go by Who gives more? He will outbid all. All, by the last word, *in æternum.* For whatsoever we may have here, if it were a kingdom, it is not for ever. But this "Comforter" That "shall abide with us," is but a pledge of that bliss and kingdom of His wherein we shall abide with Him eternally. Let any offer more for our love, and carry it.

Verily, *bonum, si non amatur, non cognoscitur,* said the Heathen. But more true of Christ, if we love Him not, we know Him not. If we did but know what He is in Himself, what to us; what He hath already done, what He is ready to do for us still, we would take it evil a case should be put, and yield to it without more ado.

Why so we do; take it evil an *if* is made; yield to it, we love Him all. Yet great reason there was, we shall see, Christ should so put it, being to infer the second. For at that there will be some sticking, which would not be if we were not defective in this former, of love. If our love were not light, His commandments would not be heavy. If love were as it should be, nothing is heavy to it. *Amor erubescit nomen difficultatis,* 'love endures not the name of difficulty,' but shames to confess any thing too hard for it. *De internis affirmare tutum,* saith the Heathen; 'it is safe affirming of any thing within us,' where no man can convince us, for none is privy to it but ourselves. How many shall we hear say, I have ever affected, wished you well, borne you good will, and never a word true. Forasmuch then as there be two loves, saith St. John, one in word and tongue, and that 1 Joh. 4. 20.
is feigned; and another in deed and truth, and that is right; and that Christ conditioneth not, if ye say ye love Me, but if ye love Me indeed; we must come to St. James' assay, *ostende mihi,* "shew me thy faith;" and as well, shew me Jas. 2. 18.
thy love by some ostensive sign. So did Christ to us. *Ecce* 1 Joh. 3. 1.
quantam charitatem ostendit! "Behold how great love"—not, He verbally protested, but really "shewed!" and so they to do the like, to shew it.

Why thus they shew it. He is gone away, and they be very sad for it; which sheweth they love Him, and would keep Him still. But that may be a sign they love themselves, in that they are to have some good by His stay with them.

2. Their keeping His commandments.

That may deceive you. But, will you have a sign infallible? Take this; His commandments, His word. He that keeps it, loves Him:—true in the affirmative. He that keeps it not, loves Him not:—true in the negative. This then is the second condition; If ye love Me (not, keep Me still, but) "keep My commandments." Let your heart be troubled, not, if ye keep not Me, but if you keep not them. Not, if not Me; Me, that is, My flesh: but, not Me; Me, that is, My word, whereof the commandments are an ab-

SERM. III. stract. The word is the better part of Me, better than My flesh; strive to keep that, be troubled for not keeping that, and then your love is past "if," true indeed.

And is this the other part of the condition? This somewhat troubleth us; for who can do this, keep the commandments? as good condition with us, to fly, or walk on the sea. We are even as well able to do the one as the other. So, upon the matter, all this promise falls out to prove nothing; the condition cannot be kept, and so the covenant void. No Holy Ghost or Comforter to be hoped for or had; we are but deluded.

Deluded? God forbid! Christ loves us too well to delude us: He will never do it. A *melius inquirendum* would be had, to look a little better into it, and not so lightly lose our interest in such a gift as the Holy Ghost. It stands us so in hand to get the condition made good: else we forfeit our estate in the promise.

If we be to be relieved, it is by the word *Mea,* that they be His. And some alteration there is plainly in them, by Him and His coming. It is not said for nought, and that by way of opposition, that "the law came by Moses, but
Joh. 1. 16, 17. grace came by Him," "and grace for grace;" that is, not only grace active which we receive, which relieveth us in the keeping them, but grace passive too which we find with Him, which relieves in abating the rigour, when we are called to account about them. You shall find an alteration in this very point. The Apostles would not press the Gentiles to be circumcised: being circumcised, St. Paul testifieth they
Gal. 5. 3. become "debtors to keep the whole Law;" "a yoke, saith
Acts 15. 10. St. Peter, that neither they," the Apostles, "nor their fathers were able to bear," it was so heavy. This, as they came by Moses. But after Christ with His grace came, and His grace with Him, when they came to be His, *mandata Ejus,* saith
1 Joh. 5. 3. St. John, *gravia non sunt,* "they are not heavy." And Himself That best knew the price of it, saith plainly of His
[Mat. 11. 30.] "yoke," that it "is easy," and it were hard to gainsay Him.

This qualifying then groweth two ways. 1. One, that the Law, at the very giving it by Angels, was, saith St. Paul,
Gal. 3. 19. *ordinata in manu Mediatoris,* "ordained to be in the Mediator's hand," that is, Christ's, Whose hands are not so

heavy as Moses' were. 2. The other, that *Pater omne judicium dedit Filio*, saith Himself, "His Father hath made Him [Joh.5.22.] Judge of the keeping or not keeping them." All judicial power and proceeding concerning them is committed over to Him.

By the first, that they are ordained to be in His hand, He may take them into His hands when He will; and having them in His hands, order them and ease them as pleaseth Him. *Lex in manu Mediatoris* is it we must hold by. If a bruise in the reed, Moses would break it quite. If the flax smoke and flame not out, he would quench it straight. So will not He; His hand will not break the one, nor His [Mat. 12. 20.] foot tread on the other. To Mary Magdalene He ordained, [Mar. 14. 8.] that, *fecit quod potuit* should serve, and He would require no [Mar. 9. 24.] more. *Credo, Domine, adjuva incredulitatem meam*, "I believe, Lord, help my unbelief:"—a belief mixed with unbelief, would never have endured Moses' assay; *in manu Mediatoris* it did well enough. Thus He ordained, he that neither doth them, nor prepared himself, *non fecit, neque præparavit*, he Lu. 12. 47. shall be punished; but if he prepare, stir up himself, have a care, a respect unto them, that it seemeth, *in manu Mediatoris*, will be taken. That if there be, saith the Apostle, 2 Cor. 8. 12. *prompta voluntas*, "a ready will," a man "shall be accepted according to that he hath, and not according to that he hath not." For the Mediator is man, and hath had experience Heb. 4. 15. of man's infirmities; He knoweth our metal and our mould, Heb. 5. 2. [Ps. 103. 14.] and what our condition will bear; He knoweth there is that conflict in us, "we cannot do what we would." And indeed, [Gal. 5.17.] why should concupiscence to evil be reputed sin on the worst part, and a like desire, *concupivi desiderare mandata Tua*, not Ps. 119. 40. be as well reckoned for as much on the better part, though it be not full out "according to the purification of the Sanctuary?" [2 Chron. 30. 19.] Thus, as in His hands ordained.

Then again, as in His court, to be judged. For the court may alter the matter much, as with us here it doth. *Sedens in solio justitiæ*, as to some, "in His tribunal seat of strict [Prov. 20. 8.] justice;" there sitting, sentence will proceed otherwise than *si adeamus thronum gratiæ*, if we have access to Him in His "throne of grace," where we may "obtain mercy and find Heb. 4. 16. grace." And St. James brings us good tidings, that *super-*

SERM. III. *exaltat, &c.* the throne of grace is the higher court; and so
Jas. 2. 13. an appeal lieth thither, to whom He will admit. "To cruel men, saith he, there shall be judgment without mercy;" which sheweth, judgment with mercy shall be to some other to whom He will vouchsafe it.

And thus, it must stand upon *Mea,* and *manu Mediatoris,* and the throne of grace, or else even those here, the Apostles, it will go wrong with them, they will hardly be relieved in their claim of a "Comforter." For within twenty-four hours and less, it came indeed to an "if," their love. They loved Him not so well, but they loved their own safety better; fell
Mat. 26. 69, &c. away, and fled away, and denied Him; even he that said he loved Him best.

And what, kept they His commandments? Sinned they
Jas. 3. 2. not? *In multis omnes,* saith St. James, "in many things all;" and "if they should say otherwise," saith St. John, "that they had no sin"—not, they were somewhat proud,
1 Joh. 1. 8, 9. and there were no humility, but—"they were very liars, and there were no truth in them." So that keeping the commandments and having of sin must stand together, or else they kept them not.

But this they kept, and so may we too: they were troubled, their hearts were troubled for not keeping them; and at the throne of grace that was accepted; and the not keeping not reckoned a breach of the commandment, if we be troubled for it.

Again, as well saith St. Augustine, amongst His commandments this is one, which we must not fail duly to keep; and that is, the commandment of daily praying, *dimitte nobis,* forgive us our not keeping, which helps all the rest. We
Mar. 9. 24. keep, Lord, help our not keeping, as well as "I believe, Lord, help my unbelief." A true endeavour with an humble repentance, for so he resolves, and then *omnia mandata facta deputantur, quando quod non sit ignoscitur;* 'all are accounted as kept, when what is not is pardoned out of His mercy;' and so the rest rewarded out of His bounty
Mat. 20. 6. That alloweth a day's wages for an hour's work, as to them that came at the eleventh hour to the vineyard, that is, at five of the clock after noon. Thus will it be with us in hope; thus was it with them. For the covenant held,

and the prayer went forward, and "the Comforter" came notwithstanding.

Now to Christ's part. *Rogabo Patrem et dabit*; that Christ will pray, and His Father give. And there is nothing more effectually sheweth they were short in their condition than these two words, 1. *rogabo*, and 2. *dabit*. The Father shall give. It is His free gift, not due debt, upon desert of the former. And *dabit roganti*, give it to Christ's prayer, rather for Rogation week's sake with Him, than for any work of supererogation with them. But it cometh from God's bounty, and Christ's entreaty, without which our love and commandment-keeping would not carry it; they are not sufficient to weigh it down *pondere meriti*; it must come *rogatu Christi*, or not at all. Then, not to lean on them; Christ it is, and His intercession, we take to. Not, you shall love, and keep My commandments, and then My Father shall be bound; but, and then Christ shall pray, and the Father will give if Christ pray, and not otherwise. II. The covenant.

But a doubt here ariseth: may we love Christ, or keep His commandments, before we have the Holy Ghost, without Whom first had it is certain we can do neither? How shall we love Christ or keep His commandments, that we may receive the Holy Ghost, when unless we first receive we can neither love Him nor keep them, nay, not so much as say, "Jesus is the Lord, but by the Holy Ghost?" Nay, not so much as think that, or any other thought that is good? How saith He then, Keep and I will give, when He must give or we cannot keep? 1 Cor. 12. 3. 1 Joh. 4. 2. 2 Cor. 3. 5.

This scruple will soon be removed by *habenti dabitur*. A promise may be made, *tam habenti quam non habenti*, 'as well to him that hath a thing already, as to him that hath it not at all.' To him that hath it already in a lower or less, may be promised to have it in a more ample measure or more high degree, than yet he hath; or to him that hath it in one kind, that he may have it in some other. To all, save Christ, the Spirit is given in measure. Where there is measure, there are degrees: where there be degrees of more and less, the more may well be promised to him that hath the less. To him that hath it in the degree of warm breath, it may well be promised in tongues of fire. To him Mat. 13. 12. Joh. 3. 34.

SERM. III. that hath it as the first fruits, which is but a handful, it may well be promised as in the whole sheaf, which filleth the bosom. But, that which is more agreeable to this text here,
1 Pet. 4. 10. we consider the Spirit, as St. Peter, *multiformem;* the Spirit in His graces, or the graces of the Spirit, as "of many kinds." "Of many kinds," for our wants and defects are many. Not to go out of the chapter: in the very next words, He is called
[Joh. 14. 17. 26.] "the Spirit of truth;" and that is one kind of grace, to cure us of error. In the twenty-sixth verse after, "the Spirit of holiness," which is His commŏn name, which serveth to reduce us from a moral honest life to a holy, and wherein the power of religion doth appear. And here He is termed "the Comforter," and that is against heaviness and trouble of mind. To him that hath Him as "the Spirit of truth," which is one grace, He may be promised as "the Spirit of holiness," or comfort, which is another. It is well known, many partake Him as "the Spirit of truth" in knowledge, Which may well be promised them, for sure yet they have Him not as the sanctifying Spirit. And both these ways may He be had of some who yet are subject to the Apostles' disease here, heavy and cast down, and no cheerful spirit within them. So they were not clean destitute of the Spirit at this promise making, but had Him; and so well might love Him, and in some sort keep His commandments, and yet remain capable of the promise of a Comforter for all that. So that Christ may proceed to His prayer, that His Father would send them the Comforter.

3. Christ's intercession. Where we begin with matter of faith. For we have here the article offered to us, and set down in the three Persons, 1. *Ego,* 2. *Ille,* and 3. *Alium;* 1. "I," 2. "He," and 3. "Another." 1. "I will pray the Father," that is, Christ the Son. 2. "And He shall give" it, that is, the Father—His Person is named. 3. *Alium,* "another" third Person besides, that is *Paracletum,* the Holy Ghost. 1. One praying; 2. the other prayed to; 3. the third prayed for. 1. *Filius orans;* 2. *Pater donans;* 3. *Spiritus consolans.* 'The Son praying; the Father granting; the Spirit comforting;'—a plain distinction.

And Christ's prayer sets us to seek His other nature. For here He entreats as inferior to His Father, in state of man;

but in the twenty-sixth verse as equal to His Father, in the nature of God, joins in giving with like authority. *Rogabo*, as man; *Dabo*, as God.

Finding the Father giving here, and the Son giving there, we have the proceeding of the Holy Ghost from both; *Quem mittet Pater*, "Whom the Father shall send," in the twenty-sixth of this; *Quem Ego mittam*, "Whom I will send," in the twenty-sixth of the next. Called therefore "the Spirit of the Father," and again called "the Spirit of the Son," the Spirit of both, as sent and proceeding from both. [John 14. 26; 15. 26.] Mat. 10. 20. Gal. 4. 6.

And last, the equality of the Holy Ghost. For sending and procuring, He must send and procure them one equal to Himself, as good every way, or else they had changed for the worse, and so pray Him to let His prayer alone; they were better as they were, they shall be at a loss.

4. His Father's giving.

Christ will pray; and if He pray, great likelihood there is He will speed. He that is sued to, is easy to entreat, He is a Father; and He That doth sue is gracious to prevail, He is a Son. *Pater a Filio rogatus*, great odds the suit is half obtained ere begun. Specially, His suit being not faint or cold, but earnest and instant, as it was. He sued by word, and it was *clamore valido*, "with strong crying" in a high key; *et lachrymis*, and He added "tears," saith the Apostle, and they have their voice. And yet stayed not there, but His blood speaks too; cries higher and "speaks better things than the blood of Abel." And the effect of His prayer was, not only *Pater condona*, "Father, forgive them;" but *Pater* dona, 'Father, give them' the Holy Spirit to teach, "sanctify," and comfort them. This was His prayer, and His prayer prevailed; as good as His word He was. His Father should send, He said; and His Father did send, and the Holy Ghost came;—witness this day. Heb. 5. 7. Heb. 12. 24. Lu. 23. 34. Joh. 17. 17.

5. Giving "the Comforter."

And came in that sort He undertook; even in that kind whereof they had most need; most welcome to them, as their case then stood, under the term of *Paracletus*, "Comforter." If we ask, why under that term? To shew the peculiar end for which He was sent, agreeable to the want of their private estate to whom He was sent.

If they had been perplexed, He would have prayed for

SERM. III. "the Spirit of truth." If in any pollution of sin, for "the sanctifying Spirit." But they were as orphans, cast down [Joh. 16. 6.] and comfortless, *tristitia implevit cor eorum,* "their hearts full of heaviness;" no time to teach them now, or frame their manners, they were now to be put in heart. "The Spirit of truth" or holiness would have done them small pleasure. It was comfort they wanted, a "Comforter" to them was worth all.

Many good blessings come to us by the Holy Ghost coming, and the Spirit in any form of truth or holiness, or what we will, by all means worthy to be received, even all His gifts; but a gift in season goes beyond all, carrieth away the name from all the rest. Every gift then in his time. When troubled with erroneous opinions, then "the Spirit of truth;" when assaulted with temptations, then "the Spirit of holiness;" but when oppressed with fear or sorrow, then is the time of "the Holy Ghost the Comforter." Sorrow doth chill, and make the spirits congeal: therefore He appeareth in fire, to give them warmth; and in a tongue, the instrument of comfort, by ministering a word in due season; and cloven, that it might meet with dismays of all sorts, and comfort them against all.

And so did it, and that apparently. For immediately upon the receiving it, they were thought to be "full of new wine." That was but an error, but so comforted they were as, before being exceeding fearful, they grew exceeding full of courage and spirit; so as even when they Acts 5. 41. were scourged piteously, *ibant gaudentes,* "they went away" —not patiently enduring, but even sensibly—"rejoicing," not as men evil entreated, but as persons dignified, having got a new dignity, "to be counted worthy to suffer for Christ's name."

6. "Another Comforter." A "Comforter" then; and two things are added: 1. *Alium,* and 2. *Qui manebit in æternum.* 1. "Another Comforter," and 2. "That shall abide with them for ever." Both which are verified of Him, even in regard of Christ; but much more in regard of other earthly, fleshly, worldly comforts, and comforters whatsoever. "Another;" which word presupposes one besides, so that two there be. 3. One they

have already; and now another they shall have, which is no evil news. For thus instead of a single, they find a double comfort. But both they needed.

This sets us on work to find the first, and we shall not need to seek far for Him. Speak to them of a "Comforter," and they understood it not but of Christ, all their comfort in Him; lose Him, and lose all. Indeed, Christ was one; was, and is still. And the very term of *Paracletus* is given Him
by St. John; and though it there be turned "an Advocate," 1 Joh. 2. 1.
upon good reason, yet the word is the same in both. Christ had been their "Comforter," while He was their "Bridegroom" and they "the children of the Bride-chamber." Mat. 9. 15.
But expedient it was He should go, for expedient it was they had one in Heaven; and expedient withal, they had one in earth, and so another in His stead.

For the first; even now absent, He is our "Comforter" 1.
still that way we named right now; that is, our "Advocate," to appear for us before God, there to answer the slanderous
allegations of him that is the accuser of us and our brethren. Rev. 12. 10.
And a comfort it is, and a great comfort, to have a good "Advocate" there, in our absence; for then we be sure our cause shall take no harm.

But secondly, if as an "Advocate" He cannot defend us, 2.
because the accusation oft falleth out to be true, if "Moses Joh. 5. 45.
accuse us" too; yet a second comfort there is, that as a
High "Priest for ever" He is entered into the holy places Heb. 7. 17.
"made without hands," there by His intercession to make Heb. 9. 11, 12.
atonement for them as sinners, whose innocency as an Advocate He cannot defend.

And to both these, He addeth a third at the beginning 3.
of this chapter, that His leaving them is but to take up Joh. 14. 2.
a place for them, to be seised of it in their names whom He will certainly come again and receive to it, there to be for ever with Him.

And in the mean time He will take order we shall have supply of "Another;" in absence of His body, the supply of His Spirit. That if we look up, we have a Comforter in Heaven, even Himself; and if we look down, we have a Comforter on earth, His Spirit; and so are at an anchor in both.

SERM. III. For as He doth in Heaven for us, so doth the Spirit on earth in us, frame our petitions and "make intercession for
Rom. 8. 26. us, with sighs that cannot be expressed." And as Christ is our witness in Heaven, so is the Spirit here on earth,
Rom. 8. 16. "witnessing with our spirits that we" pertain to the adoption and "are the children of God." Evermore, "in the
[Ps. 94. 19.] midst of the sorrows that are in our hearts, with His comforts refreshing our souls." Yet not filling them with false comforts, but as Christ's Advocate here on earth, soliciting us daily and calling upon us to look to His commandments, and keep them; wherein standeth much of our comfort, even
[2 Cor. 1. 12.] in "the testimony of a good conscience." And thus these two—this one, and this other; this second, and that first, yield plentiful supply to all our wants.

7. To "abide for ever." A second note of difference is in the tenure they shall have of this other, that He shall stay with them still; which of Christ they had not. For this is the grief, when we have one that is our comfort, that we cannot hold him; and this their fear, that when they have another, still they shall be changing, and never at any certainty. Christ, as man, they could not keep. Given He was by the Father, but given for term of years; that term expired, He was to return.
Joh. 1. 14. Therefore His abode is expressed by the word ἐσκήνωσε, the setting up of a tent or tabernacle, to be taken down again and removed within a short time; no dwelling of continuance. But "the Holy Ghost" shall continue with us
1 Cor. 3. 16. 1 Cor. 6. 19. still, and therefore He is allowed "a Temple," which is permanent and never to be taken down. We have in Him a state of perpetuity, to our endless comfort.

Howbeit, it may be well thought, *alium* and *manebit in æternum* are not put so much for Christ, to make a difference from Him, as for these same other *terrenæ consolatiunculæ*, 'petty poor comforts and solaces of the world,' which God hath given us and we may use; but we must look after *Paracletum alium*, "another" and another manner "Comforter," when all is done. For of these it may be, we shall feel some comfort, while we be in health and meetly good estate, and in case not much to need it. But let us come into their cases here, the heart troubled, the mind oppressed, the spirit wounded; and then, what earthly thing will there

be can minister any sound comfort to us? It will not be; we must needs seek for this *Paracletum alium* here at any hand. What speak I of the mind? If but ache come into a joint, we know, we have tried them and found them, they are not able to drive away the least pain from the least part. And how then, when sickness cometh, and sorrow, and the pangs of death, what comfort in these? Comfort? Nay, shall we not find discomfort in the bitter remembrance of our intemperate using them, and little regard of the true Comforter? Shall we not find them, as Job found his friends, like winter-brooks, full of rain in winter, when no need of it, Job 6. 15,
when it rains continually; but in summer, when need is, not 17.
a drop in them? So when our state of body and mind is, that we can sustain ourselves without it, then perhaps some they yield; but when sorrow seizeth on the heart, then none at all. In the end, we shall say to them as he did, "Mise- Job 16. 2.
rable comforters are ye all." Wherefore "another Comforter" we are to seek, That may give us ease in our disease of the mind, and in the midst of all our sorrows and sufferings make us *ire gaudentes*, 'go away rejoicing.' No other will do it but this; that, when we have Him, we need look no further.

The other is likewise a difference; of staying with us "for ever." "For ever?" The weak poor comfort we have by the creatures here, such as it is, we have no hold of it; it stays not, not "for ever," nay, not for any long time. There be two degrees in it: 1. *Non in æternum*, that is too plain; 2. Nay, not *manet nobiscum*, they stay not with us; *fugiunt a nobis*, 'they fly from us' many times in a moment, as Solomon's fire of thorns, a blaze, and out straight.

Nay, if they would tarry with us, would they not tire us? Even manna itself, did it not grow loathsome? Do we not Nu. 11. 6.
find that when we are ready to starve for hunger, and have meat to drive it away; if we use it any while, the meat is as irksome as the hunger was, and we are as hungry for hunger as ever we were for meat? That we may not be cloyed, we change them; and even those we change them for, within a while cloy us as fast. What shall we do? where shall we find comfort aright? Ever, *per quod fastidio occurritur, fastidium incurritur;* so that if they would tarry, we must

SERM. III. put them away; the not tarrying of them with us, that is, the change of them is it that makes us able to endure them.

Well then, comfort us they cannot when we need it, we must pray for *alium*. If they could, they cannot stay; not for any space, much less for ever. If they could, their very stay would prove fastidious, and yield us but discomfort. Seeing then we cannot entreat them to stay with us, and [Eph. 6. 13.] if we could, "in the evil day" they could not stead us, but then fail us soonest when our need is greatest; let us seek for "another," that through sickness, age, and death, may abide with us to all eternity, and make us abide with Him in endless joy and comfort.

The application to the Sacrament. Such is this here which Christ promised, and His Father sent this day; and which He will send, if Christ will ask; and Christ will ask if, now we know the covenant and see the condition, we will seal to the deed.

To a covenant there is nothing more requisite, than to put the seal. And we know the Sacrament is the seal of the new covenant, as it was of the old. Thus, by undertaking the duty He requireth, we are entitled to the comfort which Lu. 22. 19. here He promiseth. And "do this" He would have us, as is plain by His *hoc facite*.

And sure, of all the times in our life, when we settle ourselves to prepare thitherwards, we are in best terms of disposition to covenant with Him. For if ever we be in state of love toward Him, or toward one another, then it is. If ever troubled in spirit, that we have not kept His commandments better, then it is. If ever in a vowed purpose and preparation better to look to it, then it is. Then therefore of all times most likely to gain interest in the promise, when we are best in case, and come nearest to be able to plead the condition.

Besides, it was one special end why the Sacrament itself was ordained, our comfort; the Church so telleth us, we so [Exhortation at the time of the celebration of the Communion.] hear it read every time to us: *He hath ordained these mysteries, as pledges of His love and favour, to our great and endless comfort.* "The Father shall give you the Comforter." Why He giveth Him, we see; how He giveth Him, we see not. The means for which He giveth Him, is Christ; His entreaty by His word in prayer, by His flesh and blood in sacrifice, for His blood speaks, not His voice only. These Heb. 12. 24. the means for which, and the very same the means by which He giveth the Comforter; by Christ the Word, and by Christ's body and blood, both. In tongues It came, but the tongue is not the instrument of speech only but of taste, we all know. And even that note hath not escaped the ancient Divines; to shew there is not only comfort by hearing the word, but we may also "taste of His goodness, how gracious He is," and be "made drink of the Spirit." That not only by the letter we read, and the word we hear, but by the flesh we eat, and the blood we drink at His table, we be made partakers of His Spirit, and of the comfort of It. By no more kindly way passeth His Spirit than by His flesh and blood, which are *vehicula Spiritus*, 'the proper carriages to convey it.' *Corpus aptavit Sibi, ut Spiritum aptaret tibi;* Christ fitted our body to Him, that He might fit His Spirit to us. For so is the Spirit best fitted, made remeable, and best exhibited to us who consist of both.

Ps. 34. 8. 1 Cor. 12. 13.

This is sure: where His flesh and blood are, they are not *exanimes*, 'spiritless' they are not or without life, His Spirit is with them. Therefore was it ordained in those very elements, which have both of them a comfortable operation in the heart of man. One of them, bread, serving to strengthen it, or make it strong; and comfort cometh of *confortare*, which is 'to make strong.' And the other, wine, to make it cheerful or "glad;" and is therefore willed to Ps. 104. 15. be ministered to them that mourn, and are oppressed with [See Prov. 31. 6.] grief. And all this to shew that the same effect is wrought in the inward man by the holy mysteries, that is in the outward by the elements; that there the heart is "established [Heb. 13. 9.] by grace," and our soul endued with strength, and our conscience made light and cheerful, that it faint not, but evermore rejoice in His holy comfort.

To conclude: where shall we find it if not here, where under one we find "Christ our Passover offered for us," and [1 Cor. 5. 7.] the Spirit our Pentecost thus offered to us? Nothing remaineth but the Father Himself, and of Him we are sure too. *Filium in pretium dedit, Spiritum in solatium, Se servat in præmium,* 'His Son He gave to be our price, His Spirit to be our comfort, Himself He keepeth to be our everlasting reward.' Of which reward there, and comfort here, this day and ever may we be partakers, for Him That was the price of both, Jesus Christ!

A SERMON

PREACHED BEFORE

THE KING'S MAJESTY AT WINDSOR,

ON THE TWELFTH OF MAY, A.D. MDCXI., BEING WHIT-SUNDAY.

JOHN xvi. 7.

Yet I tell you the truth; it is expedient for you that I go away: for if I go not away, the Comforter will not come unto you; but if I depart, I will send Him unto you.

[*Sed Ego veritatem dico vobis; expedit vobis, ut Ego vadam: si enim non abiero, Paracletus non veniet ad vos; si autem abiero, mittam Eum ad vos.*]

[*Nevertheless I tell you the truth; it is expedient for you that I go away: for if I go not away, the Comforter will not come unto you; but if I depart, I will send Him unto you.* Engl. Trans.]

"BUT if I go, I will send Him to you." And He did go, and He did send Him, and this day He did send Him. So that between this text and this feast there is that mutual reference and reciprocation that is between *promissio missionis* and *missio promissionis*, 'the promise of the sending' and 'the sending of the promise;' the promise of the sending, the substance of the text, and the sending of the promise, the substance of the solemnity; it being the solemnity of *mittam* and *veniet*, both in the text, the sending and coming of the Holy Ghost.

Christ's words they be, and all is nothing else but a setting forth or demonstration of the *non veniet*—of *non veniet*, the not coming, and of *expedit*, the expediency of Christ's going, and consequently of this feast.

There seems to be a question here, whether best the Comforter come, or not come; that is, whether any Whitsuntide

SERM. IV. or no? The question of His coming grew out of another, of Christ's going; whether best Christ go or not go, that is, whether any Ascension-day or no. The Apostles were all mainly against His going, and so opposed hard against the Ascension. But Christ here resolveth the point thus: if they were against the Ascension, they lost *festum Paracleti*, a feast which they might not miss out of their calendar; and so with promising them this, persuades them to bear with that; to yield to the Ascension, in hope of Whitsuntide.

Which two feasts are both in the text, and the two main points of it. Here is an *abeam*, a going, and here is a *veniet*, a coming; Christ's going, that is the Ascension; the Holy Ghost's coming, that is Pentecost, the day which we now celebrate, as it were *ἀντιβαλλόμενα*, one to make amends for the other. And ye shall observe it is usual. Anon after Christmas-day, and the poor estate of Christ's birth, there cometh the Epiphany with a star, and great men's oblations, as by way of compensation. Presently after Good-Friday and the sorrow of His passion, Easter-day followeth straight, the day of His triumph, to revive us again. And even so here, upon His Ascension or going from us, there ensueth Whit-Sunday, the mends together withal. No *impedit* without an *expedit*, no *abeam* but a *mittam;* no going away to bring a loss, but a coming too to make a supply.

The truth is, Ascension-day, though to Him it were a day of glory, yet to them it could not be but a day of sorrow. It was a going to His Father, but it was a going from them. Going from them, they were to lose Him; and loss breeds sorrow; and a great loss, as this was, great sorrow. It did
Joh. 16. 6. so: the very next words before these are, "Your hearts are full of sorrow." And good reason. 1. To part with, to forego any friend, is a grief. Not without some grief doth
2 Tim. 4. 10. the Apostle recount, that even Demas was fallen off, and had forsaken him. 2. And if any friend, how much more of such a friend as Christ was to them? It was a festival
Mat. 9. 15. all the while, and they "the children of the Bride-chamber," so long as He was with them. To forego such an one, must fill up the measure a good way.

3. But to fill it full: if to part with such an one be grievous at any time, then to part with Him; then He to leave us

and we Him, when we have most need of Him, when troubles are at hand, is above measure grievous. And at hand they were, persecutions to rise, and they to be in that case, that they that cut their throats should "think they did God good service." If needs He would leave them, He would stay till fair weather. Now a tempest is toward, then to be left, is the worst time that may be. Joh. 15. 2.

Now join all these—1. of a friend, 2. of such a friend, 3. at such a time, to be deprived—and tell me if there were not great reason, *ut tristitia impleret cor eorum*, "their hearts should be full of sorrow" for His going. *Non expedit ut abeas.* This for them.

Now for Christ; we shall see, *quam incertæ providentiæ nostræ.* It falleth out many times men are grieved with that which is for their good, and earnestly are set on that which is not expedient for them. It was their case in desiring Christ might not go. All was out of mistaking. Therefore Christ begins: "But I tell you the truth;" as much to say, You are in an error all the while, "your hearts be full of sorrow" because your heads are full of error. You conceive of My stay as beneficial to you, but falsely: "I tell you true," it is so far from that as *impediet*, 'it will hinder you,' turn to your loss. You apprehend My going as an hindrance, but err. 1. "I tell you true," *expedit vobis*, "it will be your gain." 2. This gain and loss are set down both: 1. the loss, in the not coming; 2. the gain, in the coming of the Comforter, this day. 3. This coming, or not coming, depends upon Christ's going, or His stay. *Non veniet nisi*, 'if Christ go not He cometh not:' *veniet si*, 'if Christ go, He cometh.' Seeing then ye shall be losers by My stay, and gainers by My going, be not for My stay, My stay will deprive you of Him; *non veniet.* Be not against My going, My absence will procure you Him; *mittam.* I love you not so evil, as to stay with you for your hurt. Be not you grieved, be not against that which is for your good.

The manner of this answer is, 1. first, *retorquendo*—holden ever to be the best. You think it will hinder you; I say συμφέρει, "it will benefit you" that I go. 2. Then to prove it He proceeds, *abducendo ad absurdum.* For why, "if I go

SERM. IV. not," there will follow a main inconvenience, which by no means is to be admitted, and that is, *non veniet Paracletus.* The expedience of *veniet* we deduce out of the inconvenience of *non veniet.*

This inconvenience, if He go not. What, if He go? He will come certainly, for He will be sure to send Him. Now choose whether I shall go, and you have Him; or stay, and you want Him. The answer is clear: have Him ye must, want Him ye may not. So, if this be the case, if no Ascension, no Pentecost, we yield, *Ascendat Christus, ut descendat Paracletus.*

The division.

Where we have to consider of these. 1. Of the reason:

I. "It is expedient," "expedient for you I go."

II. Then of the two. 1. The inconvenience of *non veniet,* the Holy Ghost not coming; 2. and of the necessity of *si non abiero,* that Christ must go, that He may come.

III. And last, of *veniet* and *mittam,* His coming, and Christ's sending. Where we are to treat, 1. of *Paracletus,* His name and nature first; 2. and then of the time, and manner of His sending.

I. The reason. "It is expedient." [Coloss. 3. 12.]

There is no act of our Saviour Christ's, but ever at the first view there sheweth forth; no speech, but ever at the first hearing there soundeth some virtue in it. As here in this, that virtue which the Apostle calleth πρᾳότητα, His "mildness" and equity—the beams of that virtue brake forth in this. 1. Herein is equity: this very first, that He would yield to yield them a reason of His departure; not use His authority as well He might, come and go at His pleasure—who could ask Him why? but even condescends to render them, though far His inferiors, a reason of His going and coming; which sure He was no way bound to do.

2. And what reason? that is next. It is not *licet,* what is lawful for Him, but *expedit,* what is "expedient" or meet to do.

3. And thirdly, His *expedit* is not *expedit Mihi,* but *expedit vobis;* meet or "expedient," not for Himself, but for them to whom He renders it.

1. A reason given.

There was amongst the heathen, one[a] that would have his will stand for reason. And was there none such among the

[a] Conf. Juv. Sat. vi. 222.... Sit pro ratione voluntas.

people of God? Yes; we find one of whom it was said, Thus it must be, for Hophni will not have it so, but thus. 1Sam.2.16. His reason is, "for He will not;" and God grant none such be found among Christians!

2. Not *licet*; but *expedit*. 1 Cor. 6. 12. 1 Cor. 10. 23.

But among Christians, there were that stood with St. Paul upon *licet*: what they might do, this was lawful for them, and who shall abridge them of it? St. Paul may well seem to have had relation there to His Master's reason here, where He teacheth them a better rule, if they could hit of it, that *licet* is not it, *expedit* is Christ's, and is the true Christian's reason.

3. Not *expedit Mihi*, but *expedit vobis*.

And not *expedit* at large; for so we know not whom it refers to. It may be to Himself, *expedit Mihi*; as all the world's reasons tread inward. No; but *expedit vobis*, for them, their profit and benefit, rather than His own. We find one before in this Gospel, and he was the High Priest, Joh. 11. 50. that made his from *expedit*; but it was *expedit nobis*—so reasons Caiaphas there. But Christ our High Priest taketh it the other way. I do it because "it is expedient for you" that I do it. And the Apostle followeth Him in that too: use your rulers, your spiritual rulers, so as "they may do Heb.13.17, 18. their office with joy, not with grief;" ἀλυσιτελὲς, "for that is not good for you;" not for you, hear you, and let them go. Well, certainly herein is equity, herein is mildness, in these two first words. It was to His Father and to His glory He went: He would not do it, but acquaint them with the reason of it; and that reason was, He would not do it but that it was for their good. I have enough from these three, if we learn to avoid 1. Hophni's *non vult enim*, to make our *vult* our *enim*; and the 2. Corinthians' standing with him upon his *licet*; 3. and frame our rule by *expedit*; and that, not Caiaphas' *expedit nobis*, but Christ's *expedit vobis*: for you it is good, you the Disciples; and make that the rule of our going out and coming in. This for *expedit vobis*.

II. The inconvenience of *non veniet*.

If it be good, and good for them, they will not hinder it; *Nemo impedit quod expedit*; that lesson will soon be learned, to yield to that which is for our behoof. All the matter will be, to bring *expedit vobis* and *ut Ego abeam* together; to understand that good; how *Ego abeam* can be "expedient"

SERM. IV. for them. Indeed it is hard to conceive. This we can well conceive—*expedit vobis ut Ego veniam,* 'expedient it is, that
Rev. 22. 20. I come'—and say with the Apostle, *etiam veni,* "yea, come Lord," come quickly. And this we can also—*expedit vobis ut Ego maneam,* 'expedient it is, that I tarry'—and say with them, Luke the twenty-fourth, *mane nobiscum Domine;* yea,
Lu. 24. 29. "tarry with us, good Lord." It is more than expedient for Thee so to do. But *expedit vobis ut Ego abeam,* "expedient
[John 6. 60.] I go My way and leave you," *durus est hic sermo,* "it is a hard saying," and who can endure it, that it should be good for them or for any to have Christ go from them or forsake them?

And sure, the proposition is not so hard, but the reason that induceth it is as hard and more, if more may be: "The Comforter will not come." Be it so; let Him not come, stay you. *In Te satis nobis,* we are well enough, we desire no other Comforter. And the other moveth not neither, "unless I go:" why may He not stay, and He come notwithstanding? What hinders it but we may enjoy both together? Two difficulties which must be cleared, or we cannot proceed.

Non veniet, that may be answered with *ne veniat.* But He is "a Comforter." No comforter to Christ; no loss so great as to lose Him: if we may keep Him, we care not—*ne veniat.* Stay His ascension, we fear not Pentecost. But He is in earnest, and tells us for a truth it is altogether expedient the Holy Ghost come; so expedient, *ut expedit ut Ego abeam, potius quam Ille ne veniat;* 'better I go than He not come;' of the twain, better I spared than He. So it must be, else He saith nothing; else the balance hangs even, one as good as the other; they may take which they will, say they were well enough as they are. But weigh the feasts together, Ascension and Pentecost, the expedience of *Ego abeam,* and the expedience of *Ille veniet;* better Christ depart than the Holy Ghost stay from us. This sets before us and shews us the greatness of this day's benefit, consequently the highness of this feast; not only that it is equal to any of those precedent;—that the Holy Ghost is equal to Christ, else should we be at an after-deal, and change for our loss: no, St. Augustine prayeth well, *Domine da mihi alium Te, alioqui non dimittam Te,* 'Give us another as good as Yourself, or we will never leave that, or consent that You leave us;' —but that some inequality there is, else they might stand as they are, seeing they should be never the better; but sure as the case standeth, more for their behoof than Christ Himself.

We shall never see it in kind, the expedience of *veniet,* the absolute necessity of His coming, till we see the inconvenience of *non veniet,* that it by no means may be admitted, we cannot be without Him. First then, absolute necessity it is; in both the main principal works of the Deity all three Persons co-operate, and have their concurrence. As in the beginning of the creation, not only *dixit Deus* was required, which was the Word, but *ferebatur Spiritus,* the motion of the Spirit, to give the spirit of life, the life of nature. As in the Genesis, so in the Palingenesy of the world, a like necessity; not only the Word should take flesh, but flesh also receive the Spirit to give life, even the life of grace to the "new creature." It was the counsel of God that every Person in the Trinity should have His part in both, in one work no less than the other, and we therefore baptize into all Three.

1. The inconvenience of *non veniet.*

Gen. 1. 3. Gen. 1. 2. Joh. 1. 14. Gal. 6. 15.

But I add secondly; more than expedient it is the work of our salvation be not left half undone, but be brought to the full perfection, which with *non veniet* cannot be: if the Holy Ghost come not, Christ's coming can do us no good; when all is done, nothing is done. No? said not He *consummatum est?* Yes, and said it truly in respect of the work itself; but *quoad nos,* 'in regard of us' and making it ours, *non consummatum est,* if the Holy Ghost come not too. Shall I follow the Apostle, and *humanum dicere,* "speak after the manner of men, because of our infirmity?" God Himself hath so expressed it. A word is of no force though written, which we call a deed, till the seal be added: that maketh it authentical. God hath borrowed those very terms from us: Christ is the Word, the Holy Ghost the Seal *in Quo signati estis. Nisi veniat,* if the Seal come not too, nothing is done.

Joh. 19. 30. Rom. 6. 19. Eph. 4. 30.

2. Yea, the very will of a testator, when it is sealed, is still in suspense till administration be granted. Christ is

SERM. IV. the Testator "of the New Testament;" "the administration
Heb. 9. 15. is the Spirit's." If that come not, the Testament is to small
1 Cor. 12. 5, 11. purpose.

3. Take Christ as a purchaser. The purchase is made, the price is paid, yet is not the state perfect unless there be investiture, or, as we call it, livery and seisin: that maketh
2 Cor. 5. 5. it complete. *Perquisitio*, that very word is Christ's; but the investiture is by the Spirit. If He come not, we lack that; that we may not lack; and so, not lack Him. What will ye that I say? Unless we be joined to Him, as well as He to us; as He to us by our flesh, so we to Him by His Spirit; nothing is done. The exchange is not perfect, unless as He taketh our flesh, so He give us His Spirit; as He carrieth up that to Heaven, so He send this down into earth. Ye know it is the first question the Apostle asked,
Acts 19. 2. "Have ye received the Holy Ghost since ye believed?" If not, all else is to no purpose. Without it, we are still, as
Jude ver. 19. Jude calleth us, *animales, Spiritum non habentes*, "natural men, but without the Spirit." And this is a certain rule,
Rom. 8. 9. *Qui non habet*, "He that hath not His Spirit, is none of His," Christ profiteth him nothing.

Shall I let you see one inconvenience more of *non veniet?* As nothing is done for us, so nothing can be done by us, if He come not. No means on our part avail us aught.
[Joh. 3. 5.] 1. Not Baptism; for *nisi ex Spiritu*, if He come not, well may it wash soil from our skin, but no stain from our soul;
[Tit. 3. 5.] no "laver of regeneration" without "renewing of the Holy
2 Cor. 3. 6. Ghost." 2. No preaching neither; for that is but "a letter that killeth," except the Spirit come too and quicken it.
Joh. 6. 63. 3. No Sacrament; we have a plain text for it, "the flesh profiteth nothing," if the Lord and Giver of life, the Spirit, be away. 4. To conclude, no prayer; for *nisi*, 'unless' the
Rom. 8. 26. Spirit help our infirmity, and make intercession with us, we neither know how, nor what to pray. So the Spirit must come to all, and It goeth through; neither can aught be done for us, or by us without It. Away then with *ne veniat;* we cannot say it, we may not think it. We cannot spare this first. Another *veniat* there must be, a second Advent besides Christ's. Christ's Advent begins all, this ends all our solemnities. Come He must; and we must all agree

to say, *Veni Creator Spiritus;* the inconvenience of *non veniet* we cannot endure.

But then, there ariseth a new difficulty upon *si non abiero.* 2.
We see a necessity of His coming, but we see no necessity The necessity of *si*
of Christ's going. Why not Christ stay, and yet He come? *non abiero.*
Why may not Christ send for Him, as well as send Him? Or, if He go, come again with Him? Before it was, *Ne veniat Ille, mane Tu:* now it is, *Veniat Ille, et mane Tu.* Why not? Are they like two buckets? one cannot go down, unless the other go up? If it be so expedient He come, Christ I trust is not impedient, but He may come.

Christ sure and He are not ἀσύστατοι, 'incompatible;'
They may be, and abide together well enough. We believe [Mat.1.20.]
He was conceived by the Holy Ghost: then, no antipathy between Them. At His baptism He was known by this,
that "the Spirit rested and stayed upon Him:" why not Joh. 1. 32.
now, as well? We see not how this holdeth, "If I go not He will not come." It cannot be denied They two can stay together well enough; and the time shall come we shall enjoy Them both together, and the Father with Them. That time is not yet; now, it is otherwise. Not for any let in Themselves, that is not all; but for some further matter and considerations noted by the Fathers, for which it was expedient Christ should go, that the Holy Ghost might come.

First, for *veniet.* The Holy Ghost cannot come as He 1. On the
should. He should come as God. The stay of Christ would Holy Ghost's
have been a let of the manifestation of His Godhead. To part.
manifest His Godhead, being to shew great signs and work great wonders, if Christ had still remained and not gone His way, They would not well have been distinguished, and great odds have been ascribed to Christ. So the Holy Ghost had wanted the honour and estimation due to Him; an impeachment it would have been to His divinity. But Christ ascending, all such imaginations cease.

From *mittam Eum:* a little impeachment it would have
been, to Christ's equality with His Father. For, He not 2. On
going to send Him, but staying still here, the sending of Christ's.
the Spirit would have been ascribed to the Father alone, as His sole act. This would have been the most; that the

SERM. IV. Father for His sake had sent Him, but He as God had had no honour of the sending. Being ascended and glorified, *mittam* will straight be conceived—*Quem mittet Pater, et Quem mittam a Patre;* that with the Father He sends Him equally, and we alike beholden to Them both.

Joh. 14. 26. Joh. 15. 26.

3. On theirs, as their case was to be.

A third is in *vobis*, on their part also. As their case was to be, it was so meet, even in regard of them. They were to be sent abroad into all coasts, to be scattered all over the earth to preach the Gospel, and not to stay together still in one place. His corporal presence would have stood them in small stead, He could have been resident but in one place, to have comforted some one of them; St. James at Jerusalem: as for John at Ephesus, or Thomas in India, or Peter at Babylon, as good for them in Heaven as in earth,—all one. The Spirit That was to succeed, was much more fit for men dispersed. He could be, and was present with them all, and with every one, by Himself, as filling the compass of the whole world.

4. On theirs, as their case was then. 1. For His bodily presence.

This, as their case was to be. But the Fathers rather pitch upon their estate, as presently it was; *vobis*, that is, *vobis sic dispositis*, 'for you,' that is, 'you so disposed' as I find you are. So, it is *ad homines*, to them affected in such sort as then they were. Whereby he giveth us to understand, some are in that case as it is expedient Christ withdraw Himself from them. And is there any *vobis*, can any man be in that case it should be good for Christ to depart from him? It seemeth so. We see oftentime the case so standeth even in regard of this life, that from some it is good their meat be taken, and yet is meat the stay of their life; that from some it is good their blood be taken, yet blood is nature's treasure, and that holdeth us in life; that from some light be taken, in some disease of the eyes, yet is light the comfort of this life. All this we conceive: *expedit ut cibus, ut sanguis, ut lux abeat,* and all this better than *expedit ut Christus abeat;* we may spare them all better than Him.

Yet Christ it is That telleth it us, and telleth it us for a matter of great truth, these were—and whose case is better than these? But if these, some there are in that case it may be said to them truly, It is expedient I be gone.

And what case may that be? Even that case that maketh the mother many times withdraw herself from her young child, whom yet she loveth full tenderly, when the child groweth foolishly fond of her; which grew to be their case just. Christ's flesh, and His fleshly presence, that, and none but that. So strangely fond they grew of that as they could not endure He should go out of their sight; nothing but His carnal presence would quiet them. We know who said, "If Thou hadst been here, Lord;"—as if absent He had not been as able to do it by His Spirit, as present by His body. And "a tabernacle" they would needs build Him, to keep Him on earth still; and ever and anon they were still dreaming of an earthly kingdom, and of the chief seats there, as if their consummation should have been in the flesh. These fancies—indeed, errors they fell into, about the flesh; they had need have it taken from them. The Spirit was gone quite; they had more need to have Him sent. This was at no hand to be cherished in them, they were not to be held as children still, but to grow to man's estate, to perfect age and strength, and so consequently to be weaned from the corporal presence of His flesh; nor to hang all by sense, to which, it is too true, they were too much addicted. The corporal therefore to be removed, that the spiritual might take place; the visible, that the invisible; and they, not in sight or sense as hitherto, but in spirit and truth henceforth to cleave unto Him. To say with the Apostle, "If we have known Christ after the flesh, yet now henceforth we know Him so no more." This was for them, and we should have been no better, as now we are; the flesh will but hinder the spirit, even the best.

Joh. 11. 21. Mat. 17. 4. 2 Cor. 5. 16.

This, for His bodily presence. But the Fathers go yet further and enquire, whether this also be not true in His spiritual presence; and resolve that even in regard of that, it is no less true. To some *vobis*, it is expedient that, even after that manner also, Christ go from them. And who are they?

2. For His spiritual presence.

1. One *vobis*, when men grow faint in seeking, and careless in keeping Him, as in Canticles the third, "lie in bed, and seek Him." Gone He was, and meet He should so

As grown faint. Cant. 3. 1.

SERM. IV. be, to teach them to rise and seek, to watch and keep Him better.

As overweening. 2. Another *vobis*, when men grow high conceited and overweening of themselves, and their own strength; and

Ps. 30. 6. say, with David, *non movebor*, as if they had Christ pinned

Mat. 26. 33. to them; and with Peter, *etsi omnes non ego*. It is more than time Christ be gone from such, to teach them to see and know themselves better.

But if Christ leave us, if He withdraw His spiritual presence, we fall into sin; and that cannot be expedient

Ps. 119. 67, 71. for any. "Good, that I have been in trouble," for "before I was troubled, I went wrong;" but not good for any, to fall into sin. Yes indeed: *Audeo dicere*, saith St. Augustine, 'I dare avow it,' *expedit superbo ut incidat in pec-*

[Conf. S. August. Serm. 285. 3.] *catum*—there are the very terms—'it is expedient they fall into some notorious sin,' as David, as Peter did, that their faces may be filled with shame, and they by that confusion

2 Cor. 12. 7. learn to walk with more humility. "The messenger of Satan" that was sent the Apostle to buffet him, was of this nature, and to no other end sent, but to prevent this malady. In a word, Christ must withdraw—no remedy—that we may grow humble, and being humble, the Holy Ghost may come; for He cometh to none, rests on none,

Isa. 57. 15. 1 Pet. 5. 5. "giveth grace to" none, but "the humble." So we see, Christ may be and is, even according to His spiritual presence, withdrawn from some persons, and for their good, (*Christus abit, ut Paracletus veniat,*) and that many ways

Ps. 108. 5. meet it is, it so should be. This makes us say, Go, "Lord, set up Thyself above the heavens, and Thy glory over all the earth."

III. Of *Mittam Eum*. 1. *Eum* the Person. If He go not, the Holy Ghost will not come. But, if Christ go, will He come? shall we not be left to the wide world without both? will the Comforter come? He will; for Christ will not fail but send Him. If He take His body from our eyes, He will send His Spirit into our hearts. But sent He shall be: here is *mittam Eum*, and so He did. Christ sent Him, and He came; and in memory of this *veniet et mittam*, hold we this day. He did, to them; but will He also to us? He will. And shall we see "fiery tongues?" That is not Christ's promise, to send "fiery tongues;" but *Illum,* "Him," "the Comforter." And comfort it is we seek. It is not the "tongues," or "fire," we care for, or will do us good. We conceive, I trust, after two manners He came as this day: 1. one visible, "in tongues of fire that sat upon their heads;" 2. the other invisible, by inward graces whereby He possessed their hearts. The former was but for ceremony at first; the other is it, the real matter, *Illum,* "Him." And Him this day as well as that, this day and ever, He will not fail to send. Always we are to think His promise and His prayer were not for these only, but for all that should believe on Him, by their word, to the world's end.

Now this last point—these two, 1. *mittam,* 2. *Illum*—we are specially to look to. Christ is gone, once for all. We have no hold now but of this promise, "I will send Him." That we take heed we forego not Him, and lose our part in the promise too. A great part of the world is sure in this case: Christ is gone, and the Comforter is not sent. Not this; for I speak not of the world's comfort, the rich man's *qui habebat hîc consolationem,* "who had his comfort here," in good fare and bravery, and all manner delights of the flesh—flesh-comforts; but this here is *Paracletus Qui est Spiritus.*

1. *Illum,* that is, *Spiritus Sanctus.*

Lu. 16. 25.

And because all religions promise a spiritual comfort, it is said further, *Paracletus Qui est Spiritus veritatis;* no spirit of error, but "the Spirit of truth." And because all Christians, though counterfeit, claim an interest in *Spiritus veritatis,* yet further it is added, *Paracletus Qui est Spiritus sanctus.* He is no unclean Spirit, but one sanctifying, and leading us into an holy and clean life. This is the true Comforter, and none other, That Christ promiseth to send.

2. *Paracletum.*

[John 16. 13.]

Christ will send Him. But, that we mistake Him not, not unless we call for Him, and be ready to entertain Him, for *cletus* is in *Paracletus.* Of which let me tell you these three things; it is the chief word of the text, and chief thing of the Feast. It is translated "Comforter:" that translation is but *ad homines,* for their turn to whom He speaks; for as their case was, they needed that office of His most. But the true force of the word *paracletus* is

SERM. IV. *advocatus*—not the noun but the participle—"one called to," sent for, invited to come, upon what occasion, or for what end soever it be. For what end soever it be, the person sent for is *paracletus* properly, *pro eâ vice;* for that
[1 Cor. 2. 12.] time and turn, *advocatus*. But because "the spirit of the world" ruleth in this world, the worldly affairs come thickest, our affections in that kind so many and oft, it is come to pass that the lawyer hath carried away the name of *advocatus* from the rest, and they grown to be the *paracleti* of this world, called for even from the Prince to the Peasant, and consulted with, none so often. The Physician, he hath his time and turn of advocation, to be a *paracletus* too, but
Acts 4. 36. nothing so oft: as for Barnabas, which is interpreted "the
[Tit. 3. 13.] son of consolation," never till both "Zenas the Lawyer,"
[Col. 4. 14.] and "Luke the Physician" have given us over; never called for, but when it is too late.

1. Our duty, to call for Him for Comfort. But first, from *mittam Paracletum,* this we have. *Mittam,* Christ "will send;" but *Paracletum,* if you send for Him. *Veniet,* "come He will," but not come, unless called; nor sent, but sent for. If we call Him, *veniet,* "He will come;" if we send for Him, He will send Him. That is our duty, but what is our practice? We miss in this first, we call not for Him. We find no time for Him, He is fain to call for us, to ring a bell for us, to send about to get us, and then are we *advocati,* not He. When we send for Him, He is *Paracletus;* when He for us, then we are, and not He: if we be that, if we be *advocati,* and not rather *avocati,* every trifling occasion being enough to call us away. Thus we stumble at the very threshold; and do we yet marvel if Christ send Him not, nor He come?

2. For counsel. Men are sent for, for some end; and divers are the ends, thereafter as our need is. We send not for them only when we are in heaviness, to comfort us, but when we are in doubt, to resolve us; which is the second signification, and so *Para-*
1 Joh. 2. 1. *cletus* is turned "advocate," or "counsellor." And the Holy Ghost looketh to be sent for for both—for counsel, as well as for consolation. For both; He is good for both. Yea, many are His uses; and therefore He thinketh much to be sent for but for one, as if He were good for nothing else. If we be in doubt, He is able to resolve us; if per-

plexed, to advise and to guide; if we know not how, to frame our petition for us; if we know not, to teach; if we forget, to remember us; and not only one use, as we fancy, if we be out of heart, to comfort us.

And because His uses be many, His types are so. "Water" Joh. 3. 5.
sometimes, sometimes "fire." One while "wind," one while Acts 2. 3. Joh. 3. 8.
"ointment;" and according to our several wants we send to 1 Joh. 2. 20.
Him: for fire, to warm; for wind, to cool; for water, to cleanse us; for oil, to supply us. And as His types, so His
names: "the Spirit of truth," "the Spirit of counsel," the Joh. 15. 26.
"Spirit of holiness," "the Spirit of comfort." And ac- Isa. 11. 2. [John 14.
cording to His several faculties, we to invocate, or call for, 26.]
Him by that name that is most for our use or present occasion. For all these, He looks we should send for Him.

Our error is, as if He were only for one use or office—for comfort alone: so, in all others we let Him alone, and if never in heaviness, never look after Him, or care once to hear of Him. But He is for advice, and direction also. No less *Paracletus*, "a Counsellor," than *Paracletus*, "a Comforter;" He is not sent by Christ to comfort only. Ye may see by the very next words: the first thing He doth
when He cometh is, He shall "reprove," which is far from Joh. 16. 8.
comforting. But sent He is, as well to mediate with us for God, as with God for us. God's *Paracletus*, "His Solicitor," to call on us for our duty; as our *Paracletus*, or "Comforter," to minister us comfort in time of need.

Our manner is, we love to be left to ourselves, in our consultations to advise with flesh and blood, thence to take our direction, all our life; and when we must part, then send for Him for a little comfort, and there is all the use we have of Him. But he that will have comfort from Him, must also take counsel of Him; have use of Him as well against error and sinful life, as against heaviness of mind. If not, here is your doom: where you have had your counsel, there seek your comfort; he that hath been your counsellor all the time of your life, let him be your comforter at the hour of your death. And good reason: He will not be *Paracletus* at halves, to stand by at all else, and only to be sent for in our infirmity.

Base it is to send for Him never but when in extreme

SERM. IV. need; but even otherwise, *extra casum necessitatis*, for entertaining of acquaintance and to grow familiar, as we use to do those we delight in. The word παρὰ giveth as much. He should be near us, by us; one ordinary, not a stranger, to call or send for a great way off. It is so expedient, that He may know us thoroughly, and we Him; the best and nearest way to find sure comfort, when most we shall need it. For he that should minister it soundly indeed, had need be familiarly acquainted with the state of our souls, that he may be ready and ripe, then. To go to a lawyer's reading, and not hear it, serves us not for our worldly doubts; nor to hear the physic lecture, for the complaints of our bodies. No; we make them *paracletos*, we call them to us, we question with them in particular, we have private conference, about our estates. Only for our souls' affairs, it is enough to take our directions in open Churches, and there delivered in gross; private conference we endure not, a *paracletus* there we need not. One we must have, to know throughly the state of our lands or goods; one we must have, entirely acquainted with the state of our body: in our souls, it holdeth not. I say no more; it were good it did. We make Him a stranger all our life long; He is *Paraclitus*, as they were wont to pronounce Him; truly *Paraclitus*, 'One Whom we declined,' and looked over our shoulders at; and then in our extremity, suddenly He is *Paracletus*; we seek and send for Him, we would come a little acquainted with
Mat. 25. 12. Him. But take we heed of *nescio vos*. It is a true answer; we take too little a time to breed acquaintance in. *Nescio vos*, I fear, they find that so seek Him: *Paracletus*, they do not, *Paraclitus*, rather.

2. His sending: 1. The time. *Mittam*. This, of *Paracletus*. Now of *mittam*, the 1. time, and the 2. manner; both are to the purpose. The time, that when He sends we make ready for Him. The time of the year was this time, in the spring, the fairest and best part of it. The time of the month, the third day; (so they deduce from the fifteenth day, the day of the Passover, and so fifty days, it will so fall out by calculation:) that is the beginning of the month. The time of the day: it was before "the
Acts 2. 15. third hour," that is nine of the clock in the morning plainly. So it was still prime. These teach us, it would be in our

prime, the time of health and strength, when we lay the grounds of our comfort; not to tarry till the frost and snow of our life, "till the evil days come, and the years approach, whereof we shall say, we have no pleasure in them." He in the spring, we in the end of the year. He in the beginning of the month, we in the last quarter; nay, even *pridie calendas*. He before nine in the morning; we not till after nine at night. If we will keep time with Him, we know what His time is of sending. Eccl. 12. 1.

2. The manner. *Per paraclesin.* [Joh. 15. 26. 14. 26.] Ps. 119. 131.

The manner is best, and it is in the body of the word. As "the Spirit of truth" by preaching; as "the Holy Ghost" by prayer; the *Paracletus*, we know what He meaneth, *per paraclesin*, 'by invitation.' As the dove to baptism, the wind to prayer, (*aperui os et attraxi spiritum*,) the tongue to a sermon, the *Paracletus* to *paraclesis*, as it were a refreshing; —so friends meet, and nourish love and amity, one with another. And even *humanum dicere*, after natural men, when our spirits are spent and we wax faint, to recover them (or never) in the natural man, it is done no way more kindly than by nourishment; specially, such as is apt to breed them, as one kind is more apt than other. There is "a spiritual meat," and "a spiritual drink," saith the Apostle; in which kind there is none so apt to procreate the Spirit in us as that flesh and blood which was itself conceived and procreate by the Spirit, and therefore full of spirit and life to them that partake it. It is sure to invite and allure the Spirit to come, there is no more effectual way; none, whether Christ will send Him, or whether He will come more willingly, than to the presence of the most holy mysteries. And namely, at this feast, concerning which our Saviour Christ's voice is to sound in our ears, *Si quis sitiat, veniat ad Me;* "If any thirst, let him come to Me and drink, which He meant and spake," saith St. John, "of the Spirit," Which was to begin at that time especially, when He was newly glorified. *De Meo accipiet*, saith Christ of Him, and it is no where more truly fulfilled, that He shall take of Christ's and give it us, than it is done of that which is His most intrinsically. That was this very day, and no better opportunity, no fitter time, to receive the Spirit, than the day of the Spirit; the day of Christ's send- 1 Cor. 10. 3, 4. Joh. 7. 37. Joh. 16. 14.

SERM. IV.

ing, and of His coming. When shall He be sent or come, if then He do not? But keeping the time and observing the manner, we trust in His promise, and call upon Him, that so He will send Him; and upon the Holy Ghost, that so He will come. And as we be His *paracleti*, 'His guests,' so He will be ours, dwelling with us with His assistance, and being in us by His graces, to life eternal. Which Almighty God grant, &c.

A SERMON

PREACHED BEFORE

THE KING'S MAJESTY AT WHITEHALL,

ON THE THIRTY-FIRST OF MAY, A.D. MDCXII., BEING WHIT-SUNDAY.

Acts xix. 1—3.

And it came to pass, &c. that Paul came to Ephesus, and found there certain disciples,

And said unto them, Have ye received the Holy Ghost since ye believed? And they said unto Him, We have not so much as heard whether there be an Holy Ghost.

And he said unto them, Unto what were ye then baptized? And they said, Unto John's baptism.

[*Factum est autem, cum Apollo esset Corinthi, ut Paulus peragratis superioribus partibus veniret Ephesum, et inveniret quosdam discipulos,*

Dixitque ad eos, Si Spiritum Sanctum accepistis credentes? At illi dixerunt ad eum, Sed neque si Spiritus Sanctus est, audivimus.

Ille vero ait, In quo ergo baptizati estis? Qui dixerunt, In Joannis baptismate. Latin Vulg.]

[*And it came to pass, that while Apollos was at Corinth, Paul having passed through the upper coasts came to Ephesus; and finding certain disciples,*

He said unto them, Have ye received the Holy Ghost since ye believed? And they said unto him, We have not so much as heard whether there be any Holy Ghost.

And he said unto them, Unto what then were ye baptized? And they said, Unto John's baptism. Engl. Trans.]

Here is a question. "Have ye received the Holy Ghost?" And here is an answer to it: Nay, "not so much as heard, whether any Holy Ghost or no." There is no fitter time to ask and resolve this question of His receiving than this day,

SERM. V. the day He was received visibly; nor to amend this answer (not[1], whether any or no) than this day, on which He declared Himself to the world, when it was both heard and seen, that there was a Holy Ghost.

Acts 2. 33. [[1] so much as heard]

The part narrative. The first question. The narrative is thus briefly. St. Paul came to Ephesus, and there he found certain disciples. At the first meeting, the very first question he asks is, *si recepistis;* "whether they had received the Holy Ghost?" Mark it well. It is the first point he thinks meet to be enquired of, or to inform himself concerning.

The answer. The Apostle, no doubt, hoped for an answer affirmative from them, that they had "received Him." Theirs is a strange negative; that not only they had not received Him, *sed neque*, but were so far from that as they had not so much as heard whether there were any to receive, whether there were any at all. Whom they should have received, Him they had not heard of. This was a great rudeness. And yet disciples they were, and disciples that had believed, and believed a good while since. And they were twelve, it is said at the seventh verse, that is, a full jury; and yet put the Holy Ghost upon their verdict, that they return is an *ignoramus*.

The second question. The Apostle little looked for such rudeness at Ephesus, the most civil place of all Asia. This answer almost posed him, yet he gives them not over. Nay, he must not leave them thus. "Whether one or no:" this answer of force begets another question, to find where the error was. Disciples they were, and therefore baptized; baptized, and yet had not heard of the Holy Ghost? He muses how, or into what they had been baptized, and asks them that. They tell him, "into John's baptism," and further they had not gone. Of John's baptism I will not stand now to enlarge: this is certain, a baptism it was wherein, it seems, there was no mention, nor no hearing of the Holy Ghost.

The answer.

The error. Now, by this time, their rudeness that seemed strange at the first, is not now strange, when the reason of it is known. And it might seem in some sort to excuse them, in that they were but at John's baptism; and so it did. But yet to accuse them withal, that they were but at John's baptism, (for it was now more than twenty years since John was dead,) that all this while they were no further; that, as he saith to the Hebrews, "considering the time, whereas Heb. 5. 12. they might have been teachers, they had need to be catechised in the very rudiments of religion."

Yet quencheth he not this flax, though it did but smoke; The rectifying. bears with them, rates them not, but teacheth them; first, Mat. 12. 20. that as John was to Christ, so was John's baptism to Christ's baptism, in manner of a *parate viam*, or introduction, *in venturum*, 'to one That was to come,' and they no otherwise to conceive of it.

It was Apollos' case, in the chapter before, verse the twenty-fifth, he knew not but John's baptism neither, at the first. And these, it may well be, were his disciples. But as Aquila there taught him, so doth the Apostle these here, "the way of truth more exactly." And so being Acts 18. 26. taught, they were baptized with a baptism where they both heard of and received the Holy Ghost.

Thus doth end the narrative part. And therein he gives The Apostles' patience. us example in himself, of his own rule to Timothy. If we meet with such as these at Ephesus, raw and evil-catechised Christians, that we grow not abrupt, but exercise our office "in all long-suffering and doctrine;" not in doctrine alone, 2 Tim. 4. 2. but "in long-suffering and doctrine;" for without suffering, and suffering long otherwhiles, all our doctrine will do but little good.

Out of all this we gather these points. First, the neces- The part dispositive. sity of receiving the Holy Ghost, in that it is his first care, his first question he asks. Of the other Persons in the Godhead, it is enough we hear of them and believe in them: of the Holy Ghost it is not so. To hear of Him, or believe in Him, will not serve, but we are to receive Him too. To know, not only *quod sit*, 'that He is,' but to certify ourselves, *quod insit*, 'that He is in us;' "for He shall remain Joh. 14. 17. with you, and shall be in you"—it is Christ.

But then receive we cannot, unless first we hear; hear that there is one to receive, or ever we receive Him. First, notice of His being; and then, sense of His receiving. And indeed, the hearing of Him is a way to His receiving; for though not every one that hears receives, yet none receives but he hears first. So that ground must first be laid.

SERM. V. And to lay that ground, no better way than the Apostle here directs us to by his second question, get us to our baptism. Ask, into what we were baptized? There we shall not fail, but resolve ourselves that one there is, receive Him after as we may.

The right order. Now, but that the Apostle had a better conceit of these here than there was cause, and so erred of charity, supposing these disciples better scholars than they were, he would have begun with the latter, and first asked them, if ever they heard of Him; and then after, if they had received Him. For that is first in nature, *an sit*, then *an insit*.

There then let us begin. I am sorry and ashamed, that we shall need deal with *an sit*. Yet, I know not how, as these days of ours grow from evil to worse, and from worse to worst of all, it is no more than needs. Not that I doubt of any such who, as these here at Ephesus, "have not heard
Rom. 10.18. of the Holy Ghost," for no doubt long ere this, "His sound is gone out into all lands;" but rather, such other as St. Paul found at Ephesus too, I can tell them no better than he
1 Cor. 15.32. doth, "beasts" in the shape of men. That have heard, and yet take to themselves—a Christian liberty they call it, and that forsooth, humbly, simply, and modestly; but indeed—an unchristian licentiousness, proudly, lewdly, and malapertly, to call in question what they list; and to make queries of that which the Christian world hath long since resolved and ever since believed, concerning God, Christ, and the blessed Spirit;—no less matters.

The division. So then to these two parts we reduce all: I. The hearing
I. of Him first; then II. the receiving of Him. I. The hearing, and therein; 1. where we shall hear of Him, and 2. what we shall hear of Him. 1. Where we shall hear of Him at our baptism. 2. And what we shall hear of Him there; that one there is at least, and I trust somewhat else besides.

II. II. Then the receiving of Him. And in it three points: 1. first, that this question must be answered too, and so we bound to receive Him. And that, either *affirmative* or *negative*. We have, or we have not. 2. Then, have we received Him? How to know if we have. 3. Have we not received Him? How to procure, if we have not. In the former, of hearing, is matter of faith. In the latter, of receiving, matter of moral duty. Both meet to be entreated of at all times; but at no time so fit and so proper, as at this feast.

I. The hearing.

There is no receiving of him that is not. Therefore no talk of receiving, no place for the first question, "Have ye received?" till the latter be first resolved, Is there one to receive? For resolution whereof he might have sent them to the very beginning of Genesis, where they should have heard, "the Spirit of God moved on the face of the waters." Gen. 1. 2.
Or to the law, where the same Spirit came down upon the Num.11.25.
seventy elders. Or to the Psalms, where they should have heard David say of Him, *emitte Spiritum et creabuntur,* Ps. 104. 30.
"send forth Thy Spirit, and all shall be made." And *Spiritum Sanctum ne auferas,* "take not Thy Holy Spirit" from Ps. 51. 11.
me. Or to the Prophets—the Prophet Esay, Christ's first text, "The Spirit of God is upon me." The Prophet Joel, Isa. 61. 1. Lu. 4. 18.
St. Peter's text this day, "I will pour My Spirit upon all Joel 2. 28.
flesh."

Or if ever they had heard of our Saviour Christ, St. Paul might have sent them to His conception, where they should have heard the Angel say, *Spiritus Sanctus superveniet in te,* Lu. 1. 35.
to the Blessed Virgin. To Christ's baptism, where He came Lu. 3. 22.
upon Christ in a visible shape. To His promise so often Joh. 14. 26.
iterate, of sending them "the Holy Ghost." To His *caveat,* Joh. 15. 26. Joh. 16. 7.
"not to sin against the Holy Ghost" in any wise; it was a Mat. 12. 31. 32.
high and heinous offence, it could not be remitted.

Or if they had heard of the Apostles, of Christ's breathing on them, and willing them to "receive the Holy Ghost." Joh. 20. 22.
Or but of this day, and in what sort He was visibly sent down, like fiery tongues, upon each of them. Or of their Acts 2. 3.
solemn meeting and council at Jerusalem, and decrees there, the tenor whereof was, "it seemed good to the Holy Ghost Acts 15. 28.
and us." Or but of the strange end that happened to Ananias, they could not choose but have heard his offence told him by Saint Peter, "he had lied to the Holy Ghost;" Acts 5. 4.
and straight upon it, "he had not lied to man, but to God" directly.

2. At Baptism. 1. That one there is.

All this he might, yet this he did not, but takes a plain course, sends them to their baptism, still supposing it to be Christ's baptism they were baptized with, the only true baptism. And, seeing the Apostle upon good advice took that

SERM. V. for the best way, we cannot follow a better direction; and so, let us take it. We mean not, I trust, to renounce our baptism. By it we are that we are. And at it we shall not fail but hear, There is a Holy Ghost. Express mention of Him is directly given in charge in the set form of baptism prescribed by our Saviour, that all should be, as we all are,
Mat. 28. 19. baptized "in the Name of the Father, the Son, and the Holy Ghost."

Yea, I add further; he could no better refer them than to baptism. For a special prerogative hath the Holy Ghost
Tit. 3. 5. in our baptism, above the other two Persons. That "laver," is His "laver" properly; where, we are not only to be baptized into Him, as into the other Two, but also, even to be baptized with Him, which is proper to Him alone. For,
Joh. 3. 5. besides the water, we are there, to be "born anew of the Holy Ghost" also, else is there "no entering for us into the kingdom of God."

This for baptism. But let me also tell you a saying—it is St. Basil's, and well worth your remembering. He beginneth with, *In Hoc baptizamur,* and proceedeth three degrees further, all rising from thence naturally; they be but the train of baptism.

[De Spirit. Sanct. 27. ad fin.] 1. First. *Et quomodo baptizamur, ita et credimus,* 'as we are baptized, so we believe.' As is our baptism, so is our belief. And our belief is there, at our baptism, repeated from point to point. A point whereof is, "I believe in the Holy Ghost." And we desire to be baptized in that faith. There He is now again, at our baptism.

Yea, before we become so far, even, at Christ's conceiving, there we hear of Him first, "Who was conceived by the Holy Ghost." 2. So, three several times, we there hear of Him. 1. "Which was conceived by the Holy Ghost." 2. "I believe in the Holy Ghost," and 3, "in the name of the Holy Ghost." At our baptism, all three. And "in
2 Cor. 13. 1. the mouth of three witnesses is every point sufficiently established."

[Vid. S. Basil. de Spirit. Sanc. 29] 2. St. Basil proceeds. *Et quomodo credimus, ita et glorificamus.* As from baptism to belief, so from believing to giving glory. And there, he flatly avoweth—which all the Christian world knew to be true, nor was there ever heretic found so bold as to deny it—that the δοξολογία, as they call it, that is, the use of saying, "Glory be to the Father, the Son, and Holy Ghost," this form of concluding Psalms, and hymns, and thanksgivings, was ever received, and retained in the Church from the beginning, as with us still it is. So was baptism, so was thanks for the baptized party, the new member of the Church, so all concluded. So that way we hear of Him there again.

3. Yet once more, and it is his last. *Et quomodo glorificamus, sic et benedicimus.* 'As we glorify God, so we bless men;' as we give glory to Him, so we receive blessing from Him. How? the form is often heard, and well known, it is the Apostle's; "The grace of Christ our Lord," "the love of God" His Father; *communio,* and "the fellowship of the Holy Ghost, to be with us." So after baptism, so after sermon, so is the congregation ever dismissed. Then, there, we glorify Him. And in Him we there are blessed. And so we hear of Him once more, *quod sit,* that a Holy Ghost there is. 2 Cor.13.14.

Upon the matter, no baptism, no belief, God no glory, men no blessing, but still we hear of Him. So as if any but see baptism, hear but the creed, be at the daily service, hear the Church rendering glory to God, receiving blessing from the Bishop or Priest; by some of these, or all of these, they cannot choose but hear of the Holy Ghost. There is then no saying for us, *Sed neque audivimus.* Away with that, and say with St. Basil, *In Hoc baptizamur*—there we begin: *et quomodo* 1. *baptizamur, sic credimus;* 2. *et quomodo credimus, sic glorificamus;* 3. *et quomodo glorificamus, sic benedicimus.* So, 'we are baptized in Him; 2. and as we are baptized, so we believe; and 3. as we believe, so glorify we God; and 4. as we glorify God, so bless we men;' bless, and are blessed. These four, they are all here, and they are not far fetched, they have no curious speculation in them, they will serve for any honest or good-hearted Christian to rest in, and they need go no further than, *in Quo ergo baptizati estis.*

2. That He is God.

Thus we are referred, and we know where we are sure to hear of Him. But if we stay a little upon *in Quo baptizati,* and look better into it, this is not all, but we shall find further, not only that such an one there is, but take more

SERM. V. perfect notice of Him. And first, that He is God. And by no other, but by the same steps we went before.

1. God, first. For that we cannot be baptized into any name, but God's alone. The Apostle disputes it at large that it cannot be, that it is not lawful, to be baptized into St. Peter's name, or into his, or into any name else, but God's only. But in His name we are baptized, even in the name of the Holy Ghost: that proves Him God.

1 Cor. 1. 13, &c.

2. God, secondly. For we believe in Him. We there profess it. *Et nemini Christianorum unquam dubium fuit, nos in Deum, non in creaturam, credere,* saith Athanasius *ad Episcopos Afros.* 'Never any Christian doubted of this, that we believe not in any creature, but in God alone.' Believing then in Him, we acknowledge Him to be God.

[c. 11.]

3. God, thirdly. For we ascribe to Him glory. And glory is proper to God only; so proper, that He saith expressly, *Alteri non dabo,* He will not "part with it to any other." But we render Him glory, and "with the Father and the Son, *pariter,* together, He is worshipped and glorified." Therefore God with them, even in that respect.

Isa. 42. 8.

[Nicene Creed.]

4. Lastly, God, from blessing also, for that is one of God's peculiars. To bless in His name, by putting His name upon children, old and young, upon the congregation, to bless them. But with His name we bless, no less than with the rest. Therefore as they, so He, "God above all," as to bless, so to be "blessed for ever."

Num. 6. 22—27.

[Rom. 9. 5.]

And upon these four we rest. These four, 1. to be baptized into Him, 2. to believe in Him, 3. to ascribe glory to Him, 4. to bless by Him, or in His name, they are acts, such acts, as cannot be given to any, but to God only; and so evidently we there hear of Him, that He is God also. And such are the two acts in the Creed of Constantinople, To be Lord and Giver of life, and to speak by the Prophets. Such are many other attributes and works, that cannot agree to any but God, ascribed to the Holy Ghost, which might be, and which elsewhere have been alleged. But now we are to keep us to our baptism, and go no further.

3. God in unity.

And if we will stay yet but a little at our baptism, and hearken well; as we hear that He is God, so shall we that He is God in unity. For there we hear but, *In nomine,* but of one name. Now, as the Apostle reasoneth, *Abrahæ dictæ sunt promissiones, et Semini ejus. Non dicit seminibus, quasi in multis, sed tanquam in Uno, Semini ejus;* "To Abraham and his seed, were the promises made. He saith not, to the seeds, as of many; but to his Seed, as of one." So we are baptized, *non in nominibus, quasi multis, sed in nomine, quasi uno;* 'not in the names, as of many, but in the name, as of one.' One name and one nature, or essence. *Unum sumus,* saith Christ of two of them; *Unum sunt,* saith St. John of all three. This we hear there. Gal. 3. 16. Joh. 10. 30. 1 Joh. 5. 7.

4. Distinct.

Unum sunt, but not *unus.* For as from the name we deduce the unity, so from the number, Three, do we the Trinity—one in name and nature, yet distinct between themselves. Distinct in number, as in our baptism; "The Father, Son, Holy Ghost." And that number distinct to the sense, as at Christ's baptism; the Father in the voice, the Son in the flood, the Holy Ghost in the shape of a dove. And that shewed to be a distinction of persons, in Christ's promise. 1. *Ego,* the Person of Christ; *Patrem,* the Person of the Father; 3. and *Paracletum,* the Person of the Holy Ghost. The Holy Ghost, I say, distinct from the Father "The Lord and His Spirit hath sent Me." From the Son, *Paracletum alium,* by *alium*—the Son one, He another. And distinct, as a Person; for to omit other personal acts which properly agree to none but a reasonable nature determined, as to be "the Lord," to "speak," "teach," "reprove," "comfort," "be a witness," place Bishops, make decrees in council; that which we hear of at our baptism ascribed to Him, to conceive the human nature of Christ, is an act so personal, as in propriety of speech can agree to none, or be affirmed of none, but of an entire Person. This we hear. Joh. 14. 16. In Person. Isa. 48. 16. 2 Cor. 3. 17. Joh. 16. 13. Acts 11. 12. Acts 13. 2. Joh. 14. 26. Lu. 12. 12. Joh. 16. 7, 8. Rom. 8. 16. Acts 20. 28. Acts 15. 28.

5. Proceeding.

A Person, then, distinct by Himself, yet as a Person, not of or from Himself. And this we hear from the very term itself of *Spiritus.* For even as *filius alicujus,* so *spiritus alicujus est ab aliquo,* proceed from him, whose son or spirit they are. So the Son of God, and Spirit of God, do from God: God of God, either. *Eo ipso* then, that He is *Spiritus Domini,* He proceeds without more ado.

From the Father and the Son.

Proceeds, and from both. 1. From the Father, the Constantinopolitan Council, from the express words, "Who pro- Joh. 15. 26.

SERM. V. ceedeth from the Father;" 2. From the Son; the Council of Toledo, the eighth, from the visible sign, where the Son breathed on the Apostles, and willed them from Him to

Joh. 20. 22. "receive the Holy Ghost." And, *Non a Semet Ipso loque-*
Joh. 16. 13. 14. *tur, sed de Meo accipiet,* sheweth fully as much. Briefly;
Joh. 14. 26. Joh. 15. 26. sent by the Father, *Filioque,* 'and by the Son' too. And so,
Mat. 10. 20. Gal. 4. 6. "the Spirit of the Father," *Filiique,* "and of the Son" too.

6. Breath-wise. Proceeding from them, and not by way of generation—that is Christ's proper; He is often termed "the Only-
Ps. 104. 30. begotten," and so none but He—but by way of, *emitte Spiritum,* emission, sending it forth; that is, out of the very body of the word spirit, by spiration, or breathing. One breathing, yet from both; even as the breath, which carrieth the name and resemblance of it, is one yet from both the nostrils, in the body natural.

All these are expressed, or implied, in our baptism. And now lastly, to return home to our purpose, proceeds from Them to come to us; is breathed from them, to inspire us;
Rom. 5. 5. sent by Them, to be given us; *per Spiritum Sanctum Qui datus est nobis,* "by the Holy Ghost which is given us"—given to receive, and so to be received of us. Which openeth the way and maketh the passage over to the second question, *Si recepistis,* "have ye received?" And so, as we see, the two parts follow well and kindly, one upon the other. For this now is the last thing to be heard of Him, that it is not enough to hear of Him, but that we are to receive Him also, and to give account to St. Paul that we have so done.

So then, we have now cleared the first question, at our baptism, and have "heard," 1. that such a one there is; 2. and that He is God; 3. God, in unity of name; 4. yet in number distinct, and distinct as a Person by Himself; 5. a Person by Himself, yet not of Himself, but proceeding; 6. proceeding from both Persons, that stand before Him, the Father and the Son; 7. and that breath-wise. And so we have done with that. But yet we have not done though. For the other question must be answered too; no remedy,—it imports us. For as good not hear of Him at all, as hear and not receive Him.

II. The second part. Thither then I come. "*Si recepistis?*" "Have ye received the Holy Ghost?" Wherein these three points: 1. that we are liable to this question, and to the affirmative part of it, that we have, and so are bound to receive Him; for so *si* presupposeth; 2. if we so have, how to know it; 3. if we have not, how to compass it.

How much it importeth us to receive Him, we may esteem by this, that St. Paul makes it his article of *Imprimis*; begins with it at the first, as the most needful point. 1. The necessity.

Two things are in it. First, that receive we must. Secondly, that it must be the Holy Ghost we are to receive. 1. Of receiving.

Receive? What need we receive any spirit, or receive at all? May we not, out of ourselves, work that will serve our turns? No; for holy we must be, if ever we shall rest in His holy hill, for "without holiness none shall ever see God." But holy we cannot be by any habit, moral or acquisite. There is none such in all moral philosophy. As we have our faith by illumination, so have we our holiness by inspiration; receive both, both from without. Heb. 12. 14.

To a habit the philosophers came, and so Christians may; but that will not serve, they are to go farther. Our habits acquisite will lift us no farther than they did the heathen men; no farther than the place where they grow, that is, earth and nature. They cannot work beyond their kind—nothing can; nor rise higher than their spring. It is not therefore, *si habitum acquisistis*, but *si Spiritum recepistis*, we must go by.

But then, why *recepistis Spiritum Sanctum*, "the Holy Ghost?" No receiving will serve, but of Him? The reason is, it is nothing here below that we seek, but to heaven we aspire. Then, if to heaven we shall, something from heaven must thither exalt us. If "partakers of the Divine nature" we hope to be, as great and precious promises we have that we shall be, that can be no otherwise than by receiving One in Whom the Divine nature is. He being received imparts it to us, and so makes us *consortes Divinæ naturæ*; and that is the Holy Ghost. 2. Of receiving the Holy Ghost. 2 Pet. 1. 4.

For as an absolute necessity there is that we receive the spirit, else can we not live the life of nature, so no less absolute that we receive the Holy Spirit, else can we not live the life of grace, and so consequently never come to the life of

SERM. V. glory. *Recepistis spiritum*, gives the life natural. *Recepistis*
1 Cor. 15. 45. *Spiritum Sanctum*, gives the life spiritual.

1. There holdeth a correspondence between the natural and the spiritual. The same way the world was made in the beginning, by the Spirit moving upon the waters of the deep, the very same was the world new-made, the Christian world, or Church, by the same Spirit moving on the waters of baptism.

2. And look, how in the first Adam we come to this present life, by sending the breath of life into our bodies, so in the second come we to our hold in the other life, by sending the Holy Ghost into our souls.

3. By that Spirit which Christ was conceived by, by the same Spirit the Christian also must be. Not to be avoided, absolutely necessary all these, it cannot be otherwise.

2. Another necessity of His receiving. For the house will
Lu. 11. 24. not stand empty long. One spirit or other, holy or unholy,
will enter and take it up. We see the greatest part of the
Isa. 29. 10. world by far are entered upon and held, some by "the spirit
of slumber," that pass their time as it were in a sleep, with-
Isa. 19. 14. out any sense of God or religion at all. Others by the spirit
of giddiness, that reel to and fro, and every year are of
1 Tim. 4. 1. a new religion. Others by "the spirit of error," "given
[2 Thes. 2. 11.] over to believe lies through strong illusion." And they that
Lu. 11. 24. seem to know the truth, some with "the unclean spirit,"
Jam. 4. 5. some with "the spirit of envy," or some such, for they are
many, that a kind of necessity there is to entertain and re-
[1 Sam. 18. 10.] ceive the good Spirit, that some or other "evil spirit from
God" seize not upon us. From which God deliver us!

3. A third necessity there is we receive Him, for that with
Him we shall receive whatever we want, or need to receive,
for our soul's good. And here fall in all His offices.
Tit. 3. 5. By Him we are regenerate at the first in our baptism.
Heb. 6. 2. By Him after confirmed in the imposition of hands. By
[Ps. 51. 10. 104. 30.] Him after renewed to repentance, "when we fall away,"
1 Joh. 2. 27. by a second imposition of hands. By Him taught all our
Joh. 14. 26. life long that we know not, put in mind of what we forget,
2 Cor. 3. 6. stirred up in what we are dull, helped in our prayers, re-
Rom. 8. 26. lieved in "our infirmities," comforted in our heaviness;
Eph. 4. 30. in a word, "sealed to the day of our redemption," and

raised up again in the last day. Go all along, even from Rom. 8. 11.
our baptism to our very resurrection, and we cannot miss Him, but receive Him we must.

And on the other side, *si non recepistis,* without Him received, receive what we will, nothing will do us good.
Receive the word, it is but a killing letter; receive bap- 2 Cor. 3. 6.
tism, it is but John's baptism, but a barren element; re- Gal. 4. 9.
ceive His flesh, "it profiteth nothing;" receive Christ, it Joh. 6. 63.
will not do, for *qui non habet Spiritum Christi, hic non est* Rom. 8. 9.
Ejus, "he that hath not His Spirit, is none of His." So, Christ renounces him, He hath no part in him. To receive Christ, and not the Holy Ghost, is to no purpose. To conclude, if we receive not Him, we be but *animales, Spiritum* Jude 19.
non habentes, "only men of soul, having not the Spirit."
Et animalis homo, "the natural man," that never received 1 Cor. 2. 14.
the Spirit, neither perceiveth nor receiveth the things of God, hath nothing to do with them. So that *Spiritum non habentes* is enough, and there needs no more, but only that to condemn us. All this laid together, we see *recepistis Spiritum* is no more than needs; and it must needs have an answer.

2. If we have received, how to know it. 1. Whether received the Spirit.

The next point is, how to certify ourselves, whether we have received this Spirit, or no. I say, 1. whether the Spirit, first; 2. and then, whether that Spirit be the Holy Ghost, after.

Of the Spirit, the signs are familiar. For if It be in us—as the natural spirit doth—at the heart It will beat, at the mouth It will breathe, at the pulse It will be felt. Some one of these may, but all these will not, deceive us.

1 The heart.

At the heart we begin, for that is first; *Dabo vobis cor*
novum et spiritum novum. "A new heart and a new spirit" Ezek. 36. 26.
we shall find. We shall be "renewed in the spirit of our Eph. 4. 23.
mind." *Sane novum supervenisse spiritum, nova desideria* [Vid. S. Bernard. in Fest. Ascens. 3. 8.]
demonstrant, saith Bernard; 'that a new spirit is received, no better way to know, than by new thoughts and desires.' That he that watches well the current of his desires and thoughts, may know whether and what spirit it is he is led by, old or new. Therefore our Saviour Christ "breathed into them," when He first gave them the Holy Ghost, that they
might receive Him there within, even *in visceribus,* "in the Jer. 31. 33.

SERM. V. inward parts." *A timore Tuo, Domine, concepimus Spiri-*
Isa. 26. 18. *tum salutis;* we shall know 'the Spirit is conceived by the fear of God in our hearts,' it is as the *systole* or 'drawing in,' to refrain us from evil. And we shall know it by
Rom. 5. 5. *charitas Dei diffusa est in cordibus nostris,* "the love of God there shed abroad in our hearts." Which is as the *diastole* or 'dilating it out,' to all that good is.

2. The speech. But then, this every one may say—all is well within; and their word must be taken, we cannot gainsay them. For no man knows in so saying, whether they say true or no. Therefore we go yet further and say, *idem est vitæ et vocis organon,* 'the breath that serves us for life, or to live by, the same serves us also for the voice, or to speak by.' So that
[Ps. 135. 17.] way ye shall know it. For if *in ore ipsorum non est spiritus,* "no breath be to be perceived in their mouths;" if they
Ps. 115. 7. "speak not through their throats," they are but idols and no better. Will ye see it at the mouth? *Credidi, propter*
Ps. 116. 10. *quod locutus sum,* said he; and *habentes eumdem Spiritum,*
2 Cor. 4. 13. "if we have the same Spirit," saith the Apostle, we shall do no less. This we know for certain, that upon this day the Holy Ghost came in the shape of tongues, and they are for speech. And this likewise, that upon the receiving the Holy Ghost, these here in the text and generally all other speak, and that with new tongues, not such as they spake with before. The miracle is ceased, but the moral holdeth still: where the Holy Ghost is received there is ever a change in
Eph. 4. 29-31. the dialect, a change from cursed, unclean, "corrupt com-
Eph. 5. 3. munication," unto "such as becometh Saints."

3. The work. But then again, because even birds too may be, and are sometimes taught to speak, and that, holy phrases for a need, therefore further yet to the pulse we go, and touch it. To the hand, to the work, and enquire of that. The Holy
Joh. 20. 22. Ghost was first given and received by the "breath" inward,
Acts 2. 3. for the heart. Then, by "fiery tongues," for the speech. But ever after, and here in this place, the Holy Ghost, we
Acts 8. 17. know, was given and received by laying on of hands; and that, to admonish us, that by *imposita,* and by *admota manus,* by lifting up, and laying to our hands, we may know we have received Him; we have had laying on of hands, if we use laying or putting our hands to any good work.

As for what is in the heart, *quis cognoscit illud?* "who Jer. 17. 9.
knows it?" Not we ourselves; our own hearts oft deceive
us. And there is a *verbis confitentur,* "confess at the mouth," Tit. 1. 16.
with a *factis negant,* "deny with the deeds;" and that de-
ceives too. But there is *opus fidei,* "the work of faith," from 1 Thes. 1. 3.
fides quæ operatur, "faith that worketh"—that is St. Paul's Gal. 5. 6.
faith; that can shew itself by his working—that is St. James's Jas. 2. 18.
faith; and there may well be the Spirit. But without works,
there it may not be. For without works, St. James is flat, Jas. 2. 17.
it is but "a dead faith," the carcase of faith, and there is no
Spirit in it. No Spirit, if no work. For *usque adeo proprium
est operari Spiritui, ut nisi operetur nec sit;* 'so kindly it is
for the Spirit to be working, as if It work not It is not.'
There is none to work; *spectrum est, non Spiritus,* 'a flying
shadow it is, a Spirit it is not,' if work It do not.

And yet I cannot deny, works there may be and motion,
and yet no Spirit, as in artificial engines, watches, and jacks,
and such like. And a certain artificial thing there is in
religion, we call it hypocrisy, that by certain pins and gins
makes show of certain works and motions as if there were
Spirit, but surely Spirit there is none in them. Vain men
they are, that boast of the Spirit, without the work; hypocrites they are, that counterfeit the work, without the Spirit.
You shall easily discover these works, that they come not
from the Spirit, by the two signs in Psalm the fifty-first, Ps. 51. 10. 12.
נכוי, and נדיבה, 1. "constant," and 2. "free." They that
come from cunning, and not from the Spirit, ye shall know
them by this, they be every foot out; they are not "constant," they continue not uniform long, and when the barrel
is about, or the plummets down, they stay. But howsoever,
long they will not hold, but vanish like "the cloud," dry Hos. 6. 4.
away like "the dew" of the morning, לא נכוי, no constancy.

And ye shall know them again by the other note, נדיבה.
Which makes the difference between the creatures and the
Spirit. For the creatures are produced from without; the
Spirit doth *emanare,* proceed from within. So these, they
have *principium motus ab extra,* that that makes them go is
something, some engine without; they flow not freely, they
come not kindly, as from within, לא נדיבה, 'no natural motion'—ingenious but not ingenuous. Ingenuity and con-

SERM. V. stancy, the free proceeding, the constant continuing of them, will soon disclose whether they come from a spirit or no; will soon shew they come from the heart of hypocrisy, not from the spirit of true piety.

2. Whether received the Holy Ghost. And these will serve to know whether from a spirit. Now, whether that spirit be holy or no. For divers times Rom. 8. 15. doth the Apostle distinguish and say, "We have not re- 2 Tim. 1. 7. ceived this spirit" but that, as Romans the eighth chapter, and fifteenth verse, and the second of Timothy, the first 1 Cor. 2.12. chapter, and seventh verse; and namely, "that we have not received the spirit of the world, but the Holy Spirit Which is of God." This same spirit of the world, it is *sacer spiritus,* [Virg. Æn. 3. 57.] for there is no touching it, but not *Sanctus. Sacer,* as he called *sacra fames;* for *sancta fames* he could never have called it. That spirit of the world, be it from policy, or be it from philosophy, both are *res sacræ,* (and *sanctæ* also may be, as they may be used) but of themselves secular they are, and from men; holy, or from Heaven, they are not. But Acts 2. 2. this Spirit, this Wind, must blow from Heaven, not from our caves here beneath. And so you shall soon discern it. Do but mark the coasts, whence and whither it bloweth, the motive and the mark, and you shall distinguish it straight; for if from a secular reason, if to an end beneath, *virtus ab* Lu. 24. 49. *imo* it may be, *virtus ab alto* it is not.

For example, I do forbear to sin: what is my motive? Mic. 6. 16. Because, as Micah saith, it is against "Omri's statutes," some penal law; I shall incur such a penalty, be liable to such an action, if I do not. It is well; but all this is but the spirit of the world; *e Prætorio, non Sanctuario,* bloweth 'out of Westminster Hall, not out of the Sanctuary.'

I go further, to a better spirit. Though there were no penal law, I forbear to sin, because it is a brutish thing, and so against reason; and ignominious, and so against my credit and reputation. Nay then, further yet; because I shall thereby endanger my soul, for that it will bar me of Heaven, or be a means to bring me to hell, for the heathen men took notice of both these places. All this while this is no more than the spirit of the philosophy schools will teach, Acts 19. 9. no more than might be taught "in the school of Tyrannus," before St. Paul ever came in it. It bloweth, this wind, out of Aristotle's Gallery, not out of the Sanctuary yet; *e Lycæo, non Sanctuario.* But if with eye to God I forbear, because in so doing I shall offend Him and do evil against the rule of His justice, the reverence and majesty of His Presence, the awful regard of His Power, the kind respect of His Bounty and Goodness; this now cometh from the Sanctuary, this wind bloweth from Heaven, this is right *Sanctus* indeed.

This is the line. Again, look to the level. If it be Demetrius' end, here in the chapter, *Isthinc est acquisitio nobis,* "by this we have our advantage." If it be theirs, *paremus nobis nomen,* so I shall make my name famous upon earth, or any of that level, it is but of the world; *sacer spiritus,* not *sanctus.* But if of our well-doing God's will be the centre, and His glory the circumference; we do it, not that our will, but His be done; not our name, but His be hallowed; the act is holy, and the Spirit is of the same kind. Otherwise, philosophical, politic, moral it may be; theological, religious, holy, it is not. Our line and our level, or inducements or impediments to our doings, mark them what coast they come from, and whither they bend, ye shall easily conclude; as before, whether *recepistis Spiritum,* so here, whether *recepistis Sanctum* or no.

Acts 19. 25.
Gen. 11. 4.

And thus we know whether we have received. But, if we have not, how then? How may we, by the grace of God, so dispose ourselves as we may receive Him? And now we are come to the duty of the day, for this is the day of His receiving.

3. If we have not received, how to procure it.

The ways are two: 1. one, that we lay no bars to keep Him from us; 2. the other, that we use all good means to allure Him to us.

First, that we fall not into St. Stephen's challenge, that we "resist not the Holy Ghost," and His coming. And "resist" Him we do, if we lay any impediments in His way, nay, if we remove them not; as the manner is, as they do that draw the curtains, or open the casements, that would take in breath.

1. The removing impediments.
Acts 7. 51.

Of these, I find three of note: quit they must be all, or no receiving Him.

One, and a chief one, is pride. For the Holy Ghost will 1. Pride.

SERM. V. not rest but upon the lowly, saith Esay; nor God "give
Isa. 57. 15. grace, but to the humble," saith Solomon. That we there-
Prov. 3. 34. fore pray to Him That "giveth grace to the humble," to
give us the grace to be humble, that so we may be meet to
Mat. 3. 16. receive Him. For at His first coming He came "as a dove,"
Mat. 11. 29. and "did light upon Him" That was Himself "humble and
meek," like a dove, and willeth us to learn that lesson of
Him, as that which will make us meet to receive the dove
1 Pet. 3. 4. which He received, whose qualities are like His, of "a meek
and quiet spirit;" which howsoever the world reckon of it,
is with God a thing much set by.

[Gen. 1. 2.] In the beginning, "the Spirit moved on the waters," and
Joh. 7. 38, 39. at Baptism It doth so. And our Saviour Christ speaking
of the graces of the Spirit, doth it in terms of water; and
water, we know, will ever to the lowest place. Pride then is
a bar, and humility a disposing means, to the prime receiving
the Holy Ghost.

2. Carnality. Another impediment is carnality. For spiritual and carnal are flat opposite. *Quod sanctum est, mundum est,* ever; no holiness, without cleanness. So that, the unclean spirit must be cast out, ere the Holy Ghost received. A clean
1 Joh. 2. 27. box it must be that is to hold this "ointment." The dove
1 Cor. 6. 19. lights on no carrion. Into our bodies, as a "temple," He is
to come; as into stews, He will not. And that which we said right now of water, we here repeat again. The Spirit in the beginning moved there, and at Baptism came thither again, and His gifts are as streams of water; and water, we know, is a cleanser. To keep ourselves clean, is a means; to pour ourselves out into riot and excess, is a bar, keeps Him far away from us.

3. Malice. [Jas. 4. 5.] But the third is, *ex totâ substantiâ,* against the Holy Ghost; and that is "the spirit in us that," as St. James saith, "lusteth after envy;" after envy, or malice, or what-
Acts 8, 23. soever savoureth of "the gall of bitterness;" in which whosoever are, St. Peter saith plainly, they have no part, or fellowship, either in giving or receiving the Holy Ghost. The Holy Ghost, as in the body He is expressed by the breath, and in that form given by Christ; so in the soul, by mutual or reciprocal love, which is, as it were, the life's breath of the soul. So is His nature, and so is His sign.

The dove brought "an olive-branch," and that is the sign Gen. 8. 11.
of love and amity; and so is His office, "to shed abroad Rom. 5. 5.
love in our hearts; and how can that be received, if malice be not first of all voided out? They are as opposite as St. Luke's fire from Heaven, and St. James' "fire from hell:" Acts 2. 3. Jas. 3 6.
one must be quenched, or the other will not burn.

Now these being removed, 1. pride, 2. lust, and 3. malice, 2. The using the means.
and so a place made, we are to invite the Spirit by all good means He loveth, and as it were to gather wind as much as we can. To that end to get us to the place, and to visit it oft, where this air breatheth; and that is, as we find, "the Nu. 11. 16.
door of the Sanctuary." If any be stirring, if any be to be found, there it is. No place on earth which the Holy Spirit more frequenteth, hath duer commerce with, than the holy places where the remembrance of His Name is put; for thither He will come to us, and bless us, with His blessing.

Being there, it is but an easy lesson, yet David thinks 1. Prayer.
meet to teach it, as by his example,—*Os meum aperui, et* Ps. 119. 131.
Spiritum attraxi—to open our mouth and draw It in. And that opening is by prayer. Zachary calleth it *spiritum pre-* Zech. 12. 10.
cum, the spirit, that is, the active inspiration, or attraction of It, where we express our desire to draw Him in. Which very attraction or desire hath a promise, by the mouth of our Saviour Christ Himself, that His Heavenly Father will give the Holy Ghost, *αἰτοῦσιν Αὐτὸν*, "to them that will make Lu. 11. 13.
petition, seek and sue, open their mouth, and pray for It."

Then secondly, look how the breath and the voice *in natu-* 2. The word.
ralibus go together; even so do the Spirit and the word in the practice of religion. The Holy Ghost is "Christ's Spi- Rom. 8. 9.
rit," and Christ is "the Word." And of that Word, "the Joh. 1. 14.
word that is preached" to us is an abstract. There must 1 Pet. 1. 25.
then needs be a nearness and alliance between the one and the other. And indeed, but by our default, "the word and Isa. 59. 21.
the Spirit," saith Esay, shall never fail or ever part, but one be received when the other is. We have a plain example of it this day, in St. Peter's auditory; and another, in Corne- Acts 2. 37.
lius and his family; even in the sermon-time, "the Holy Acts 10. 44.
Ghost fell upon them," and they so received Him.

Yea, we may see it by this, that in the hearing of the

SERM. V. word where He is not received yet He maketh proffers, and worketh somewhat onward. Upon Felix, took him with a
Acts 24.25. shaking, and further would have gone, but that he put it over to "a convenient time," which convenient time never came. And upon Agrippa likewise, somewhat it did move him, and more it would, but that he was content to be a
Acts 26.28. Christian ἐν ὀλίγῳ, to take his religion by a little, as it were upon a knife's point, and was afraid to be a Christian *in multo,* 'too much' a Christian.

That we see not this effect, that with the word the Spirit s not received as It would be, the reason is It is no sooner gotten than It is lost. We should find this effect, if after we had heard the word, we could get us a little out of the noise about us, and withdraw ourselves some whither, where we might be by ourselves, that when we have heard Him speak
Ps. 85. 8. to us, we might hear what He would speak in us. When we have heard the voice before us, we might hear the other be-
Isa. 30. 21. hind us, *Hæc est via.* When the voice that soundeth, the
Job 4. 16. other of Job, *Vocem audivi in silentio;*—there hear Him reprove, teach, comfort us, within. Upon which texts are grounded the soliloquies, the communing with our own spirits, which are much praised by the ancients, to this pur-
Ps. 39. 3. pose: for *in meditatione exardescit ignis,* 'by a little musing or meditation, the fire would kindle' and be kept alive, which otherwise will die. And certain it is that many sparks kindled, for want of this, go out again straight, for as fast as it is written in our hearts, it is wiped out again; so fast as the seed is sown, it is picked up by the fowls again, and so our receiving is in vain, the word and the Spirit are severed, which else would keep together.

3. The Sacrament. Lastly, as the word and the Spirit, so the flesh and the Spirit go together. Not all flesh, but this flesh, the flesh that was conceived by the Holy Ghost, this is never without the Holy Ghost by Whom it was conceived; so that, receive one, and receive both. Ever with this blood there runneth still an artery, with plenty of Spirit in it, which maketh that we
1 Cor.10.3; 12. 13. eat there *escam spiritualem,* "a spiritual meat," and that in that cup we be "made drink of the Spirit." There is not only *impositio manuum,* but after it, *positio in manus;* 'putting on of the hands, but putting it into our hands.' *Impositio*

manuum, 'putting on of hands,' in *accepit panem et calicem;* and *positio in manus*, 'putting it into our hands,' in *accipite, edite, bibite.* And so, we in case to receive body, blood, Spirit and all, if ourselves be not in fault.

Now then, if we will invite the Spirit indeed, and if each of these, by itself in several, be thus effectual to procure It, put them all, and bind them all together. *Accipite verba,* "take to you words," Osee's words, words of earnest invocation. *Suscipite insitum verbum,* "receive," or take to you "the word," St. James' word, "grafted into you" by the office of preaching. *Accipite corpus, accipite sanguinem;* 'take the holy mysteries of His body and blood;' and the same, the holy arteries of His blessed Spirit. Take all these in one—the attractive of prayer; the word, which is "spirit and life;" the bread of life, and the cup of salvation;—and is there not great hope we shall answer St. Paul's question as he would have it answered, *affirmative?* "Have ye received?" Yes; we have received Him. Yes sure. Then, if ever; thus, if by any way. For on earth there is no surer way than to join all these; and He so to be received, if at all.

All together jointly.

Hos. 14. 2.

Jas. 1. 21.

[Joh. 6. 63.]

So, we began with hearing outward, and we end with receiving inward. We began with one Sacrament, Baptism; we end with the other, the Eucharist. We began with that, where we heard of Him; and we end with this other, where we may and shall, I trust, receive Him. And Almighty God grant we so may receive Him at this good time, as in His good time we may be received by Him thither, whence He this day came of purpose to bring us, even to the holy places made without hands, which is His heavenly kingdom, with God the Father Who prepared it, and God the Son Who purchased it for us! To Whom, three Persons, &c.

A SERMON

PREACHED BEFORE

THE KING'S MAJESTY, AT WHITEHALL,

ON THE TWENTY-THIRD OF MAY, A.D. MDCXIII., BEING WHIT-SUNDAY.

EPHESIANS iv. 30.

And grieve not (*or*, be not willing to grieve) *the Holy Spirit of God, by whom ye are sealed unto the day of redemption.*

Nolite contristari [*Spiritum Sanctum Dei, in Quo signati estis in diem redemptionis.* Latin Vulg.]

[*And grieve not the Holy Spirit of God, Whereby ye are sealed unto the day of redemption.* Engl. Trans.]

SERM. VI.

THIS request, or counsel, or caution, or precept, or what ye will call it, of the Apostle's, is sure very reasonable; "the Holy Ghost, by Whom we are sealed to the day of redemption, that we should not grieve Him."

Not "the Holy Ghost." He is the Spirit of the great and high God; and so, for His dignity's sake. Not Him again, as by Whose means we have our signature against the great "day of redemption;" and so, even for His benefits' sake. These two, 1. for his greatness, or 2. for His goodness—greatness in Himself, goodness to us; for either of these, or for both of these, we would be so respective of Him as "not to grieve Him."

"Not to grieve Him." He might well, and as one would think, should rather have said, yield Him all cause of joy and contentment; it had been but reason so. Now that He doth not move—only this; that we would not minister unto Him any cause of grievance. And what could He say less? To such a Person, and for such a benefit, it is but even a small pleasure. If not rejoice Him, yet "grieve

Him not." And it is so reasonable, I see not how well it can be denied Him.

Now then as we see it is but reasonable, this request, so is it exceeding fit for this time. It is for the Holy Ghost, and this is the Holy Ghost's feast. It mentioneth His sealing, for a reason; and this is, as I may call it, His first sealing-day. This the day on which the Spirit of God first set His seal upon the Fathers of our faith, the blessed Apostles. On which He then did, and on which He ever will, though not in like manner, yet in like effect, it being His own day, visit us from on high, if by some grievance or other we disappoint Him not, and so drive Him away.

So, what easier request than this, *Nolite contristari?* And what fitter time to move for the Holy Ghost, than upon His own feast and upon His sealing-day? And this is the sum.

The parts fall out evidently two: 1. the party, for whom The division.
this request is preferred; 2. and a duty, or (it is not worth making a duty) rather a common ordinary courtesy to be done Him. 1. the party, "the Holy Spirit of God, by Whom we are sealed to the day of redemption." 2. The duty, or what ye call it, *Nolite contristari.*

In the party, two motives there be: 1. His Person, and I.
2. His benefit. 1. His Person in these: "the Holy Spirit 1.
of God." 2. His benefit in these: "by Whom ye are sealed to the day of redemption." His Person set forth in the original with very great energy, such as our tougue is not able to express it fully enough. For it is not *Πνεῦμα ἅγιον Θεοῦ*, but with greater emphasis; but three words, and three articles, every word his several article by itself, *τὸ Πνεῦμα, τὸ ἅγιον, τοῦ Θεοῦ.* "The Spirit," not a Spirit; and not Holy but "the Holy;" nor of God, *Θεοῦ*, but of *ὁ Θεὸς*, "the God," the only, living, and true God. All "*thes*;" never an *a* among them.

Then, His bounty or benefit vouchsafed us: "by Whom 2.
we have our sealing to the day of redemption." Wherein these four points come to be weighed: 1. "of redemption," first, what and how it is. 2. Then, that it hath a day, "the day of our redemption." 3. That against that day we are to be "sealed." 4. That "the Holy Ghost" keepeth

SERM. VI. that seal, and His office it is to pass it to us. This is the benefit.

Now, either of these is a motive of itself. 1. His Person: "Grieve not the Holy Spirit of God"—and there stay, for that of itself is reason enough. 2. Or leave out His Person, set that by and say, but even, Him Who seals unto you so great a favour as to save you at the great day; Him, be He what He will, God or man, Spirit or flesh, Holy or common—"grieve Him not." This is reason enough too; grieve Him not for His own—if not for His own, yet not for His seal's sake.

II. The duty followeth. To this Person great, and of great bounty beside, to speak as Naaman's servants did to him, [See 2 Kings 5. 3.] *Si rem grandem dixisset Apostolus*, 'if the Apostle had enjoined us some great piece of service,' we ought not to have thought much of it. How much more then, when he saith but this, "Do not grieve Him," and there is all, which is no positive or actual piece of service, of pains or of peril, only a privative of disservice, as they call it, which is ever as little as can be required: *Non contristari.*

Non contristari; or at least, *Nolite contristari*, for there
1. 2. be two degrees: 1. that we do it not; 2. that willingly we do it not. That we have a will not to do it. Which reading [Jas. 4. 6.] "offers more grace." For much depends upon our willingness or not-willingness to it.

In both which, we have 1. first to weigh, whether we can grieve Him, or He be grieved; that so we may understand the phrase and take it right. 2. Then, how it is we do it, and what those grievances be; that so we may take notice of them, and be careful to avoid them.

3. 3. Last of all, the fitting it to the time and shewing it seasonable. For, by occasion of the Person, His feast; and by occasion of "the day of redemption," the day of sealing also will fall in, and the intended action with it. Which, as we shall shew, is itself a kind of signature. Do it not, this time do it not; it is His own feast now, it is His sealing-day, this; now then, *Nolite contristari.* Thus lie the parts. Of which, that what shall be spoken, &c.

I. "Grieve not." Two sorts of persons there be that, if we be well advised, we would be loath to grieve: 1. great persons, 2. and such as carry the reputation of being good. Not great, in regard of their power, they may do us a displeasure:—the motive of fear. Not good, in regard of their bounty. Others are, and we may be, the better for them:—the motive of hope. If he be great, though he seal us nothing, no wisdom to offend him. If he be to seal us a favour, though otherwise he be not great, for his favour's sake favour him so much as, Grieve him not. Either of these available; but where they meet, there is *vis unita.* Specially, if we add, *in quo vos,* that our parts be in it; and *signati estis,* that either he already hath, or is ready to do it for us;—the motive of love, and of the greatest love, the love of ourselves. Then it comes home indeed. These three meet all in this party. 1. He is τὸ Πνεῦμα τὸ ἅγιον τοῦ Θεοῦ. 2. *Sigillum habet.* 3. *In Quo vos.*

I begin with *quantus,* 'how great.' He is "the Spirit of God." And were it but the spirit of man, our own spirit, sins of the greater size would be forborne, as for other divers, so even for this reason, that they be *gravamina spiritus,* 'grievances against our own spirit,' which every one feels, whose conscience is not seared. And if the Apostle had said, Eschew them, for that they breed *singultum et scrupulum cordis,* "the upbraiding or vexing of the heart," as Abigail excellently termeth it; or, as Solomon, *vulnus spiritus,* "the wound or gall of the spirit;" or, as Esay, *compunctionem,* "the prick or sting of conscience;" or, as our Saviour Himself, "a worm which" once bred "never dies," nor never leaves gnawing; he had said enough. But this even the heathen could have said too.

I. "Not the Spirit of God."

1 Sam. 25. 31. Prov. 18. 14. Isa. 6. 9. Mark 9. 44. [See Rom. 11. 8. Vulg.]

The Apostle doth like an Apostle; tells us truly, there is a greater matter belongs to it than so. There is a far higher spirit than ours, than any in man—our spirit is nothing to it—"the Spirit of God:" they be grievances against It.

To speak then of the Spirit of God: "God is a Spirit," and God hath "a Spirit." Hath many, created in His power, and at His command; but hath one, one above all, uncreated, *intimum substantiæ,* 'of His own substance;' known ever, by the article τὸ, as St. Basil observeth, "the Spirit," the sovereign Spirit. Styled ever, with this addition, His

The Spirit of God. Joh. 4. 24. Isa. 48. 16.

SERM. VI. own Spirit; the Spirit not of any Saint, *in concreto* or *in abstracto*, but even of God Himself.

Joh. 3. 8. Our Saviour Christ teacheth us to take notice of Him, as we do of the wind, by His effect. For the wind, it is a body of air, but so thin and subtle as it is next neighbour to a spirit. We see foul rule here in the world sometimes, houses blown down, trees blown up by the roots. When we see this, we know straight, this cannot be done without some power. And that power, we are sure, cannot subsist of itself, it is an accident;—must, needs, have his inherence in some substance. That substance if it be visible, we call it a body; if invisible, a spirit. So our Saviour tells us, *spiritus est qui spirat*. It is the wind did this, blew all these down.

And even so of the Spirit of God, when as upon this day they that could scarce speak one tongue well on a sudden were able perfectly to speak to every nation under Heaven, every one in his own tongue, this we know could not come to pass but by some power. And sure we are, that power must have for his subject some substance; and not any visible or bodily. Then, some spirit it must be; and no spirit in the world could effect this; and so, the Spirit of God.

But the relation of these tongues depends upon St. Luke's credit. There was after a more strange and famous operation, which in all stories we find. The temples of idols blown down all the world over; yea, the world itself blown quite about, turned upside down, as it were, from Paganism, and the worship of heathen gods, to the truth of Christian religion. And that, maugre the spirit of the world, which blustered and bent itself against it, *totis viribus*. This we find; and for certain, this work and this power could not come from any other spirit but the Spirit of God only. Thus we take notice of Him by His effects; and of His greatness, by the greatness of His effects.

2 The Holy Spirit. "The Spirit of God," and "the Holy Spirit:" what needs this? To make Him great, as the world goes, what needed "Holy?" Or, if a title must be added to that end, there were other styles many, in the eye of flesh more magnificent and likely to shew Him for great, than this of holiness.

The spirit of principality, of courage, power, government; divers other. And all these are from Him too, He the Eph. 4. 11. fountain of all. So the Apostle tells us. And though the Spirit be all these, yet choice is made of none of all these, but only of this one, "Holy," from among them all, *τὸ ἅγιον*. And His title is not the High and Mighty; nor, the Great and Glorious; but only, "the Holy Spirit." Nor do the Seraphims and powers of Heaven cry, *Magnus*, or *Celsus*, or *Fortis*, thrice; but *Sanctus, Sanctus, Sanctus*, "Holy and Isa. 6. 3. thrice Holy," to God Himself; making choice, I doubt not, of His sovereign attribute, to laud and magnify His glorious Name by. Which teacheth us a lesson, if we would learn it; that it is the attribute in God, which of all other He doth, and which of all other we should most esteem of. And by virtue of this, if we kept right, places and times, and persons and things sacred, should be in regard accordingly. For this we may be sure of: were there in God's titles a title of higher account, the Spirit of God should have been styled by it. But in God, "Holy, Holy," is before "Lord of Hosts." His Holiness first, His Power after.

3. "The Holy Spirit of God."

Thus have we two reasons *de non gravando:* 1. first, were He but the Holy Spirit, for that He would be spared. For without all question, He is the more to be set by by reason of that attribute. It is God's chief, as ye may see, in the Ex. 28. 36, 37. High Priest's forehead; as ye may hear, out of the Angels' Isa. 6. 3. mouths.

2. Then again, that He is God's, and not a Spirit, but "the Spirit of God;" we will forbear Him somewhat, I trust, for His sake Whose He is. Put these two together.

And to these two for a surplusage join, that He is not only *Dei*, but *Deus*, "of God," but "God" also; and then we have our full weight for this part, for His greatness.

And this we shewed last feast. We are baptized into Him, we believe in Him, we yield Him equal glorifying, we bless by Him, or in His Name, no less than of the other two: so in the Deity He is. And a person He is; for to "seal," which He is said here to do—to "seal" is ever an act personal. Thither then I now come, even from His greatness to His goodness.

For He is not great, as the Great Chan, but He is good

SERM. VI. withal. And great and good withal, that carries it ever.
If *in Quo vos* come to it, that this goodness reach to us.

2. "The Holy Spirit of God, by Whom sealed." And sure, this Party, His greatness set apart, is to us the
author of many a benefit. No Person of the Three hath
so many, so diverse denominations as He; and they be all
to shew the manifold diversity of the gifts He bestoweth
Gen. 1. 2. on us. They count them. 1. His מרחפת, or "agitation,"
which maketh the vegetable power in the world. 2. His
Gen. 1. 20. נפש חיה, "spirit or soul of life," in the living creatures.
Gen. 2. 7. 3. His נשמת חיים, "heavenly spirit of a double life" in
Ex. 31. 3. mankind. 4. Then that in Bezaleel, that gave him excel-
Nu. 11. 16, 17. lency of art. 5. That in the seventy elders, that gave them
Nu. 24. 14, &c. excellency of wisdom to govern. 6. That in Balaam and
the Sibyls, that gave them the word of prophecy, to foretell
Acts 2. 5, 8. things contingent. 7. That of the Apostles, this day, that
gave them skill to speak all tongues. All these are from Him.
All these He might, but doth not reckon up any of them.
And that because, though they be from "the Holy Spirit of
God," yet not from Him as holy; but as the Spirit of God
only, without eye or reference to this attribute, "holy," at all.

But from the Holy Spirit, or the Spirit as He is holy,
cometh the *gratum faciens*, the gift of gifts, the gift of grace,
which He bestoweth on His Saints and servants, and maketh
them such by it. We waive all the former, all the *gratis
data*, and take ourselves only to this. And here again there
Joh 16. 8. come in upon us as many more. 1. The grace reproving
and checking them within, when they are ready to go astray;
Acts 16. 6, 7. *spiritus reflans*, 'the wind against them,' not suffering them
to go into Asia or Mysia, when they shall do no good there,
but making them even wind-bound as it were. 2. *Spiritus
Joh. 16. 13. afflans*, 'the wind with them,' "guiding them," and giving
Joh. 14. 26. them a good pass "into all truth." 3. The grace, teaching
them what they knew not, and calling to their minds that
they did know and have forgot. And so, *spiritus difflans*,
'blowing away and scattering,' as it were, the mist of error
2 Cor. 3. 6. and forgetfulness. 4. The grace, quickening them and stirring them up, when they grow dull, and even becalmed.
Rom. 8. 26. 5. The grace, inspiring and inditing their requests, when
they know not what or how to pray. 6. The Spirit breath-
Rom. 5. 5. ing, and "shedding abroad His love in their hearts;" which

makes them "go bound in the Spirit," and as it were with Acts 20. 22.
full sail to Jerusalem, when it is for His service. 7. And last, the Spirit "sealing" them an assurance of their estates 2 Cor. 1. 22.
to come; which is the most sovereign of all the seven, as that which doth sanctify, that is, sever and set us apart from the rest of the world, and *proprios dicare*, 'make us His own peculiar.'

Now this benefit we find here, woven and twisted with another, for two are mentioned, 1. redeeming, and 2. sealing. We must look to *suum cuique*. Both are not the Holy Ghost's; one belongs to Christ. His, the office to redeem, and that day, "the day of redemption," His. The other, to "the Holy Ghost." The seal is His, and His the day of sealing. We are to pass both these offices. To be redeemed, questionless; but take this withal, it is not enough that, to be redeemed, if by this seal also it be not passed to us.

Of these then briefly. 1. "Redemption" there is. 2. That hath "a day." 3. Against that day, we to be "sealed." 4. "The Holy Ghost" hath that "seal;" He is to do it, that office is His.

Christ's is first: we must then go a little from the Holy Ghost; we will come to Him again straight.

Oft we have heard, in redemption there is emption, a 1. Redemption.
buying, and re, that is back; a buying back of that, which formerly hath been lost or made away.

It is of two sorts; 1. real, and 2. personal. Redemption real, of our estates, lands, or goods; redemption personal, of our own selves, souls and bodies. This in the text seemeth to be personal: *in Quo vos*, "by whom you," you yourselves—there is not mention of any possessions. And ever of the twain this is the greater. You know who said "skin for Job 2. 4.
skin, all that a man hath" to redeem himself. But indeed upon the matter, this redemption is of both. For Christ's redemption is not of one half, but a total entire redemption both of persons and estates.

Now, men's persons come to need redeeming by captivity; and in that case, there must be a ransom. Men's estates come to need it, upon a sale outright; and in that there needs a new purchase.

SERM. VI. We were gone both ways. Both are in the seventh to the Romans. At the twenty-third verse, "there is a law
[Rom. 7. 23.] in our members leading us captive;" when either we are taken, and carried away by strong hand, with a temptation,
[Rom. 7. 14.] or overwrought by the sleights of the enemy. At the fourteenth verse there is a sale, "carnal and sold under sin;" when, for some consideration as we think, but many times scarce valuable, we make away our estates by our own voluntary act.

Christ redeems us from both. His "ransom" ye shall
Eph. 1. 14. find, ἀντίλυτρον. And His "purchase," *redemptionem περιποιήσεως*, that is "of purchase," plain. His purse went not
Nu. 35. 28. for either, but His Person. His death, as the high priest's, freed us from captivity; His blood, as the blood of the covenant, was the price that cleared our estates from all former bargains and sales.

2. "The day of redemption." This "redemption" hath "a day." But by this reckoning, that day should be past. The day of His Passion was the day of that payment, and that is past; how can we be sealed against it then? But, if ye mark it well, lightly there are more days than one go to a full redemption—two at least; and till the second come, the redemption is not complete.

In the real, there is one day of 1. paying the money; another, of 2. putting in possession, ever. That lightly is not the same day, but sometimes a good while after.

In the personal; 1. One day, when concerning a prisoner, a condemned man, it is graciously said by His Majesty, He shall not die. 2. Another, when this is put under seal, and brought to the prison for his release; and possibly, a good distance between these.

I know, all is counted as good as done, when the money is paid, or the word spoken; but the prisoner lieth by it still, and the possession is out of our hands till the second day cometh: to that is "the day of redemption" consummate.

And even so stands it with us. "The ransom" was paid down, the sentence reversed, the day of His Passion. The putting us in possession, the perfect setting us free, that hath another day not yet come. For out of possession we are as yet, and in a kind of prison we are still. The first day, the pay-day is past; we hold a memory of it, of all days, on Good-Friday. But Himself tells us of another day after that, the day of His second appearing; and when that comes, then He bids us "lift up our heads" and look up cheerfully, for then "our redemption draws nigh," is even hard at hand; that is our full, perfect, plenary redemption indeed. And till that come, for all "the firstfruits of the Spirit," we "groan" still, as subject to vanity and corruption; our prison-irons as it were, and all the creatures together with us do the like. Thus far redemption, and the day of it; and thus far Christ's office.

Lu. 21. 28.

Rom. 8. 22. 23.

3. "Ye are sealed" against that day.

Now between these two redemption days, the first and the second, cometh in the seal. And, against that second day come, which is in truth the very day of full redemption, it will stand us in hand to provide we be sealed, and have this mark of separation. It is exceeding material. No claim of redemption without it. In vain shall we say we are redeemed, unless we then have this seal to shew. Therefore, not to rest upon redemption with a blank, or the conceit of that, but know there is a further matter still, even *obsignati estis*, and look to that. For when that day comes, all will go by it. In very deed, upon the point, the day itself goes by it: for if sealed, then a day of redemption; if otherwise, then no day of redemption, but a day of utter desolation.

Ezek. 9. 2-7.

Ye have a type of this in the Old Testament. Six fellows came forth with axes, to make havoc and destroy. There goes one before, and makes a Tau in the foreheads of some certain persons. They, and none but they, spared; the rest hewed in pieces, every mother's son.

Rev. 7. 1-3.

The like again, in the New Testament. The four Angels hold the four winds, ready to destroy the earth. But first goeth one with a seal, and a proclamation there is to make stay, "till we have sealed" some; and that done, as for the rest, destroy them and spare not. As much to say: these with the seal are they to whom the redemption shall be applied, and for whom only it is available. Pass over these; these are Mine, I see My seal upon them. The rest, *nescio eos;* I find not My mark, "I know them not;" do with them what ye will.

[Mat. 25. 12.]

And, because I spake of passing over, in the Passover it

SERM. VI. was so; both acts there. The Lamb slain—there is re-
Ex. 12. 6, 7. demption; the posts stricken with hyssop dipped in the blood—there is the signature. Answerable to these two, with us: redemption by the Son of God at Easter; and the sealing by the Holy Ghost at Whitsuntide.

But further yet. These with the seal, not only save them,
Heb. 4. 5, 11. destroy them not; but let them also "enter into My rest,"
Mat. 25. 21. My glory, "My joy." I did not only ransom their persons, but I redeemed also their estates; purchased an estate of
Mat. 25. 34. bliss for them, and in their names. This was "prepared" by the Father, redeemed by the Son, and now, the conveyance of it sealed by the Holy Ghost:—let them possess it.

And by this ye see how great matters, both personal and real, depend upon this seal; how much it importeth us not to miss it. What reckoning we now make of it, how light, it skills not. The day will come, if we had the whole world to give we would, to be found with seal upon us.

4. "By whom ye are sealed."

This seal, which makes up all, and without which nothing is authentical, is in the dispensing and disposing of the Holy Ghost. We are therefore of necessity to pass His office also; that so all the Trinity may co-operate, and every Person have a hand in the work of our salvation. Remember, I have told you heretofore, that Christ without the Holy Ghost is as a deed without a seal, as a testator without an executor. It is so. For all He hath done, redemption or no redemption goeth by this seal; all that Christ hath wrought for us, by that the Holy Spirit doth work in us. And the Apostle as he saith here, He the party "by Whom ye are sealed to the day of redemption," so he might have added, And without Whom ye are left blank for the day of destruction. For by and from Him we have it, and by and from any other we have it not.

And if it be not to be had from any other, we may well think it excludeth ourselves, and our own spirit. There were, I wot well, in the heathen, and may be in the Christian, other good moral virtues; but they will not serve to seal us against the day here specified. One may have them all, and be never the nearer at "the day of redemption." That which is then to stand us in stead—let us not deceive ourselves—we spin it not out of ourselves, as the spider doth her web; it is of the nature of an aspiration, or of an impression. It is from without, as breathing and as sealing is. And it is the breath of this Spirit, the Spirit of God, and the print of His seal must do this. From without it cometh, from the Spirit of God, not our own spirit. That we fancy not we may have it, some other way, from our own selves. "It is He That hath made us, and not we ourselves"—God the Father. "It is He That hath redeemed us, and not we ourselves"—God the Son. And it is He That hath sealed us, and not we ourselves—God the Holy Ghost. That the whole glory may redound to the blessed Trinity, and he that rejoiceth may rejoice in the Lord. [Ps. 100. 3.] [See 2 Cor. 10. 17.]

Then to end this point. 1. There is "a day" in coming. 2. "A day of redemption" to some it is, and may prove so to us. 3. To us it may, if we be found "sealed." 4. Found "sealed" we cannot be but by the Holy Ghost's means, we must be beholden to Him; He keeps the seal, He sets it to. 5. To Him we shall be beholden, and He will set it to if we "grieve Him not." Why then, this brings us directly to the duty, *nolite contristari*, "grieve Him not."

II The duty. 1. "Grieve not."

This Party, Whose favour may thus much stead us, and that against a time we shall so much stand in need of it, what can we say or do worthy of Him? We no doubt will rise straight in our magnifical lofty style, and say, What? Why work Him all possible joy and jubilee; and all too little. Sure it were so to be wished. But hear you, *interim*, I would, saith the Apostle, we would but do thus much for Him, as not "grieve" Him. Even as in another place touching God's name, we in our rising vein would say, God's name? What but glorify it, make it famous, renowned every where? Ye say well, saith he; in the mean time, I would His Name might not be evil spoken of by your means; let your *lætificat* and *glorificat* alone, and but even *nolite contristari*. The Apostle pleads but for that, that will content him; and I would He might not fail of that till the other come. Rom. 2. 24.

And that, I trust, He shall not fail of, *non contristari*. We will never stand with Him for this. It is but a small matter this, but even *rationabile obsequium*, a request of great modesty; rather a courtesy than a duty, not to "grieve." Rom. 12. 1.

1. Not any man. Prov. 3. 29.

Not to "grieve?" Why reason would, saith Solomon, we

SERM. VI.

should not grieve any of our neighbours, seeing they dwell by us and do us no hurt. But, as I said, not the great, if there be any wisdom, nor the good, if there be either grace or good-nature in us.

2. Not God.

Well, howsoever we deal with men here, high or low, good or otherwise, in any wise take heed of offering it to God.
Isa. 7. 13. Why, saith Esay, "is it not enough for you to grieve men, but will ye grieve my God also?" "Provoke we Him,"
[1 Cor. 10. 22.] saith the Apostle, "Are we stronger than He?" As if he should say, That were extreme folly.

3. Not "the Spirit of God."

But yet one step farther. I say, and Christ saith as much; if God, yet not "the Holy Spirit of God" though, not that Person. Sins and grievances against the other two may and
Mat. 12. 32. shall; sin against Him "shall never be forgiven." "Grieve not" Him then at any hand.

1. Whether we can "grieve."

But I ask, can we "grieve the Spirit of God," that is, God? Can He be grieved? Indeed they be two questions: 1. can we? and 2. can He? I should answer somewhat strangely but truly to say, we can, and He cannot. For we may, on our parts, "grieve," that is, do what in us lieth to "grieve" Him. And with Him the endeavour is all, and to do what we can *habetur pro facto*, though the effect follow not. This we can, so badly demean ourselves as, if it were possible by any means in the world that grief could be made to fall into the Divine Essence, let Him look to it, we would do that should provoke it in Him, that should even draw it from Him. Let Him thank the high supereminent perfection of His nature that is not capable of it: if it were, or any way could be, we would put Him to it.

Mat. 5. 28. Now I find in the Gospel, from our Saviour's own mouth, "He that looketh on a woman with lust after her, hath" on his part "committed adultery with her," the woman in the meanwhile remaining chaste, as never once thinking of any such matter. Then if the one party may be an adulterer, and the other, as I may say, not adultered; why not, in like sort, one grieve, and yet the other not grieved? Always this use we may make of it, *ad exaggerandam peccati malitiam*, to aggravate some sins, and shew the heinousness of some sinners, that do on their part all they can to do it, and that is all one as if they did it. This is Tertullian.

Contra Marcion. l. 2. [16-29.]

But God forbid it should lie in the power of flesh to work any grief in God; or that we should once admit this conceit, the Deity to be subject to this or the like perturbations that we be. And yet both this passion of grief and divers other, as anger, repentance, jealousy, we read them ascribed to God in Scripture; and as ascribed in one place, so denied as flatly in another. One where it is said "it repented God He had made Saul king:" in the same place by and by after, "the Strength of Israel is not a man, that He can repent." One where, "God was touched with grief of heart;" another, "there is with Him the fulness of all joy for ever," which excludeth all grief quite.

How to understand this phrase.

1 Sam. 15. 11, 29.

Gen. 6. 6.

Ps. 16. 11.

How is it then? How are we to understand this? Thus; that when they are denied, that is to set out unto us the perfect steadiness of the Nature Divine, no ways obnoxious to these our imperfections. And that is the true sound Divinity.

But when they are ascribed, it is for no other end but even *humanum dicere,* for our "infirmity," to speak to us our own language, and in our own terms, so to work with us the better. Lightly, men do nothing so seriously as when they do it in passion; nor indeed any thing thoroughly at all, or, as we say, home, unless it be edged with some kind of affection. Consequently, such is our dull capacity, we never sufficiently take impression, God will do this or that to purpose, except He be so represented unto us as we use ourselves to be when we go through with a matter. In punishing, we pay not home unless we be angry: when God then is to punish, He is presented unto us as angry, to note to us He will proceed as effectually as if He were so indeed. We are not careful enough, we think, of that we love, unless there be with our love some mixture of jealousy: when God then would shew how chary He is of the entireness of our love towards Him, He is said to be "a jealous God." We alter not what once we have set down, but when we repent: when God then changeth His course formerly held, He is made as if He did repent—though so to do, were ever His purpose. And so here, we withdraw not ourselves from whom we have conversed with before, but upon some grievance: when the Spirit of God then withdraweth Himself for

Rom. 6. 19. [S. Aug. Quæst. in Genes. 39. Vid. etiam de Gen. ad liter. l. 4. c. 9. 18.]

[Ex. 20. 5.]

SERM. VI.

a time and leaves us, He is brought in as grieved; for that, if it were otherwise delivered, it would not so affect us, nor make in us the impression that this way it doth. So that, "Grieve Him not," that is in direct terms, Give Him not cause to do that which in grief men use to do, to withdraw Himself and to forsake you. If ye do, believe this, He will as certainly give you over as if He were grieved in earnest. This is from Saint Augustine.

How to have use of this phrase.

By this time we know how to conceive of this phrase aright. Now, how to have use of it. And of this *humanum dicit,* this use we may have. First, upon these places where we thus find affections attributed to God, our rule is ever to reflect the same affection upon ourselves which is put upon Him; to be jealous over ourselves, to be angry or grieved with ourselves for that, which is said to anger or to grieve God. And that upon this soliloquy with ourselves, that how light soever we seem to make of sin, yet in that it is said thus to "grieve God's Holy Spirit," it must needs be some grievous matter certainly. And yet, methinks, it toucheth not the Spirit of God though; He shall lose nothing by it. He needs not to grieve at it. Of the twain, it should rather seem to concern us; we may come short of our redemption by the means, and, a worse matter than that, be cast into eternal perdition. The loss is like to be ours. And is this said "to grieve the Holy Spirit of God," and shall it not grieve us, whom it more nearly concerneth? Shall we be said to grieve Him with it, and not ourselves be grieved for it? This or some to like effect.

Then it teacheth us, this phrase, withal, what in this case we are to do when it happeneth. Sure, even that which we would do to one grieved by us, whom we make special account of, and would be right loath to lose his favour; never to leave, but to seek by all means to recover him, by shewing ourselves sorry and grieved for grieving of him, by vowing never to do the like more, by undertaking any thing that may win him again. The only way to remedy it, is to take us to the same affection; as here, that it grieve us to do any thing may turn Him to grief; or, if we have done it, never cease to be grieved with ourselves till we have recovered Him, His favour, and His grace again.

Now then, were it not well to take notice of these grievances, that we might avoid, not offer them; and so fulfil the Apostle's *nolite contristari?* Divers there be. But one of them we cannot but take notice of, this verse is so hemmed in with it on both sides. Our verse begins with "And," which couples it to the former. And the very same that is in the former, is repeated over again in the next after. And this it is; to set a seal upon our lips from foul language, bitterness, cursing, swearing without any sense at all. That these come not out of our mouths. That we leave these in any case: and then follows our verse, "And grieve not the Holy Spirit;" as if He pointed us to these and said, These are such whereby we "grieve the Spirit of God," and all good men that hear them. And that is one special way to "grieve the Spirit," to grieve good men, in whom It is. His very coming, this day, in shape of tongues, sheweth He would have the print of His seal upon that part, upon the tongue; and His fire from Heaven, breath, not this "fire" from "hell," thus sparkle from it. St. James makes short work: "If any would be holden for religious, and refrain not his tongue from these, that man's religion is to be prized as little worth." This from "And," the first word, the copulative to the bordering verse, which I could not avoid.

2. How we do "grieve" Him.

"And grieve not."

[Eph. 4. 29, 31.]

[Vid. S. August. de Gen. ad liter. l. 4. c. 9. 18.]

Jas. 1. 26.

But I choose rather to hold myself to the point of sealing, within the text, and the grievances against it, which I reduce to these two: 1. either before, when we are not yet sealed, but are to be, when He offers to do it; 2. or after, when we are already past His hand and His seal upon us. There are grievances both ways.

How in the act of sealing.

First, the Spirit of God doth come and offer to seal us: our part were to invite Him to come if He did not, but if He come to be glad of it; but in any wise to be willing withal. Otherwise, *Ipsum nolle, contristari est.* For if we be not willing, but refuse, and shift Him off still, is it not *justum gravamen?* But even as there were that, when Christ set His foot on land, and offered to come to them, "entreated Him He would be gone again;" so when the Holy Ghost makes the like proffer, He hath His Gergesenes too, that can spare Him and His seal both. Men are, I know not how, even loath, and as it were afraid; think it a dis-

1. Before it. 1.

Mat. 8. 34.

SERM. VI. grace to them, many—and that would be called men of spirit—that any seal or mark of holiness should be set or seen upon them. Content with a label without any seal to it, all their life long. And of those label-Christians we have meetly good store. As the Spirit of God, they like Him well enough, to have their breath and life and moving from Him, yea hearts and tongues too if He will; but as the Holy Spirit, not once to be acquainted with Him. And what is
Isa. 30. 11. this plain, but their speech, "Cause the Holy One to cease from us?" But yet I do not say, not at all; for if He will come and seal them some quarter of an hour before they die, for that they will not stand with Him. But they desire to wear the signature of the flesh or of the world, of pride or of lust, as long as they are able to stand on their legs.
Jude 19. *Animales*, all their life; and *Spiritum habentes*, at the hour of their death. *Clinici Christiani*, 'beddered Christians,' as the Primitive Church calleth them; when the flesh leaves them, let the Spirit take them and seal them; then the seal, and ye will, but not before. But this is an indignity, and cannot be well taken. He will not endure thus to be trifled with and shifted off when He would; and if then He seals us not, when we would, we have our mends in our own hands.

2. But secondly, say we be willing He come; is it not our part against He comes to dispose ourselves, and be ready wrought to receive the figure of His seal? Then, if either He find us so indurate in malice and desire of revenge, or sins of that sort, that as good offer Him a flint to seal, which will take no print; or, on the other side, find us so dissolved as it were, and even molten in the sins of the flesh, that as good offer Him a dish of water to seal, that will hold no figure;—both come to one: 1. not to suffer Him to do it, and 2. not to be in case to receive it; 1. not disposed to it, or 2. indisposed for it. And can He choose but reckon this as a second *gravamen*, and go His way, and leave us as He found us?

After it. These two, before we be; two more, when we be sealed.
1. For when we have well and orderly received, then doth it behove us carefully to keep the signature from defacing or bruising. If we do not, but carry it so loosely as if we

cared not what became of it, and, where we are *signati* to be close and fast, suffer every trifling occasion to break us up, have our souls lie so open as all manner of thoughts may pass and repass through them; is not this a third? When one shall see a poor countryman, how solicitous he is, if it be but a bond of no great value, to keep the seal fair and whole; but if it be of higher nature, as a patent, then to have his box, and leaves, and wool, and all care used it take not the least hurt: and on the other side, on our parts, how light reckoning we make of the Holy Ghost's seal, vouchsafe it not that care, do not so much for it as he for his bond of five nobles, the matter being of such consequence; this contempt, must it not amount to a grievance? Yes, and that to a *grave gravamen*, 'a grievous one.' For this is even *margaritas porcis* right. [Mat 7. 6.]

2. But yet further. If having received this seal upon us, we so far forget ourselves as we be brought to let His *æmulus*, the fiend, the evil spirit, whom He can by no means endure, even to *super-sigillare*, 'set his mark over it,' seal upon seal; put his print, with his image and superscription, above and upon the Holy Ghost's; this is so foul a disgrace as He can never brook it. And shall we once conceive but, upon so bad usage as this, He will do what men grieved used to do, say presently, *Migremus hinc*, Away, here is no place to stay, and so leave us with our new image upon us.

And if so, a worse matter than all yet. For He no sooner gone, but in His place another will come, and, as he hath sealed us, so seize on us; and not alone neither, but company with him, "seven more worse than himself, and the end of that man worse than his beginning," a thousandfold. These they be then, these four; not to offer these is *non contristari*. Lu. 11. 26.

2. *Nolite contristari.*

But then, if our hap be so evil as we do, yet that we remember *nolite*, do it not willingly, have a will not to do it. If we fall into any of the former four; 1. neglect to receive Him when He cometh, 2. dispose not ourselves as we should against He cometh, happen to 3. bruise or mar our seal, yea 4. admit a sealing upon it, of the world upon God, the flesh upon the Spirit, profane upon holy; yet let not

SERM. VI. our will be to it, at least not our whole will, not our full consents. Let it but happen *per accidens*, as we say, either surprised with the violence, or wearied with the importunity of the temptation, or circumvented with the sleights of the serpent: but ever carry *voluntatem,* if it may be; or else, as in the schools they call it, *velleitatem de non contristando*. A great matter depends on this; for wilfully to do it, that

Heb. 10. 29. is indeed to grieve, if it be not more, even "to work despite to the Spirit of Grace."

Application to the time.

Now to draw to an end. This request never comes so fit as on this day. For there is in the text a day of redeeming; and there is by like analogy, a day of sealing. As that Christ's, so this the Holy Ghost's day. Now, if the sealing-day be the Holy Ghost's, then, *reciproce,* the Holy Ghost's day, that is the day of sealing. And this is the Holy Ghost's day. And not only for that originally so it was, but for that it is to be intended ever, He will do His own chief work upon His own chief feast; and *opus diei,* 'the day's work,' upon the day itself. So that now we are come about to our first grievance, not to refuse Him, not at any time, but not at His own time; not then, when He sits in His office, and offers to set His seal on us.

Application to the Sacraments.

And that He now doth. For when we turn ourselves every way, we find not, in the office of the Church, what this seal should be but the Sacrament; or what the print of it, but the grace there received, a means to make us,

2 Cor. 5. 5. and a pledge or "earnest" to assure us that we are His.

The outward seal should be a thing visible, to be shewed; and the Sacrament is the only visible part of religion, and nothing subject to that sense but it. This I find, that the Schoolmen, when they numbered seven, those seven were the seven seals; so for seals they have been ever reputed. But what doubt we? One of them is by the Apostle named

Rom. 4. 11. a seal in express terms, "The seal of righteousness." And if one, then the other; both are of like nature. Only this difference between them, for which we have great cause highly to magnify the goodness of God; that where the one seal, the seal of baptism, can be set to but once, and never repeated more, this other should supply the defect thereof, as whereby, if we have not preserved the former figure entire and whole, we might be, as it were, new signed over again. And that not once alone and no more, but that it should be iterable; whereby it cometh to pass, that of this sealing there be many days, many days to seal us well, and make us sure against that one day, "the day of redemption:" God therein providing for our frailness; as indeed without it a great many of us, I know not how we should have done.

This then is the seal. I add further, that it may be rightly called the seal of our redemption, as whereby the means of our redemption is applied unto us; the body and the blood, one broken, the other shed, of Him Whom God "sealed" to that end, even to redeem us.

A seal of redemption.

Joh. 6. 27.

And by, and with these, there is grace imparted to us; which grace is the very breath of this Holy Spirit, the true and express character of His seal, to the renewing in us the image of God whereunto we are created. And with grace, which serveth properly *pro totâ substantiâ,* to and for the whole substance of the soul, the two streams of it, one into the understanding part, the other into the seat of the affections. Into the understanding part, the assurance of faith and hope, into the part affective, the renewing of charity, the ostensive part of this seal, *in quo cognoscent omnes,* "by which all men may know," and *sine quo cognoscet nemo,* without it no man, that we are sealed aright and are truly His. This grace we are thus to receive there; only, that we "receive it not in vain;" "be not wanting to it" after, "neglect it not," "quench it not;" "fall not from it;" but "stand fast," and "continue in" it; be careful to "stir it up;" yea, "to grow" and increase in it, more and more, even to the consummation of it, which is glory—glory being nothing else but grace consummate, the figure of this stamp in his full perfection.

The print of this seal.

Joh. 13. 35.

2 Cor. 6. 1.
Heb. 12. 15.
1 Tim. 4. 15.
1 Thes. 5. 19.
Gal. 5. 4.
Rom. 5. 2.
Acts 13. 43.
2 Tim. 1. 6.
2 Pet. 3. 18.

Resolve then not to send Him away, on His own day, and nothing done, but to receive His seal, and to dispose ourselves, as pliable and fit to receive it. And that shall we but evil do, nay not at all, unless it please Him to take us in hand and to work us ready for it. To pray Him then so to do, to give us hearts of wax that will receive this impression; and having received it to give us careful minds withal well to look to it, that it take as little harm as our infirmity will permit. That so we may keep ourselves from this unkind sin of grieving Him That hath been, and is, so good to us. Which the God of mercy grant us, for His Son, and by His Spirit, to Whom, &c.

A SERMON

PREACHED BEFORE

THE KING'S MAJESTY, AT GREENWICH,

ON THE TWELFTH OF JUNE, A.D. MDCXIV., BEING WHIT-SUNDAY.

Psalm lxviii. 18.

Thou art gone up on high, Thou hast led captivity captive, and received gifts for men; yea, even the rebellious hast Thou led, *that the Lord God might dwell there.* Or, *for thine enemies.* Or, *among men.*

[*Ascendisti in altum, cepisti captivitatem, accepisti dona in hominibus; etenim non credentes, inhabitare Dominum Deum.* Latin Vulg.]

[*Thou hast ascended on high, Thou hast led captivity captive, Thou hast received gifts for men; yea, for the rebellious also, that the Lord God might dwell among them.* Engl. Trans.]

This is Christ the Prophet here speaketh to. That He it is, the Apostle is our warrant, Ephesians the fourth chapter, and eighth verse. There he applies it to Christ: "Thou art gone up," saith the Prophet here, in the second person; "He is gone up," saith the Apostle there of Him in the third. Eph. 4. 8.

To Christ then, and to Christ "gone up," or "ascended;" and therefore "ascended," they be the last words of this verse, "that God might dwell among us." Which cannot be applied to Christ Himself in person, for then He was not to go "up on high" from us, but to stay here still below with us. Therefore God here is God the Holy Ghost, Who this day came down after Christ was "gone up," to be not only among us, but even "in us," saith our Saviour; "to be in us and abide with us for ever." So the text begins with Joh. 14. 17, 16.

SERM. VII. the ascending of Christ, and ends with the descending of the Holy Ghost. And that was upon this day; and so we are
Lu. 4. 21. come to Christ's *hodie impleta est,* "This day is this Scripture fulfilled," the best application of every text.

The sum. Our books tell us, the Scripture will bear four senses; all four be in this, and a kind of ascent there is in them.

1. First, after the letter and in due consequence to the word immediately next before this, the last word of the verse, which is Sinai. It is a report of Moses' ascending thither. For he, from the bottom of the Red Sea, went up to the top of Sinai, leading with him the people of Israel that long had been captive to Pharaoh; and there "received gifts," the Law, the Priesthood, but above all, the "Ark of the covenant," to be the pledge of God's presence among them. This is the literal.

2. This of Moses, by analogy doth King David apply to himself; to his going up to mount Sion, and carrying the ark
2 Sam. 6. 1-19. up thither. For all agree, this Psalm was set upon that occasion. The very beginning of it, "Let God arise," &c. sheweth as much;—the acclamation ever to be used, at the
[Num. 10. 35.] ark's removing, as is plain by the tenth of Numbers, verse thirty-five. Now this was done immediately upon his con-
2 Sam. 5. 6, 7. quest of the Jebusites; whom a little before he had taken captives and made tributaries there. What time also, for
2 Sam. 6. 19. honour of the solemnity, *dona dedit,* he dealt "bread" and
1 Chron. 16. 3. "wine to all the people," gift-wise, as we find, the first of Chronicles, sixteenth chapter and the third verse. This is the analogical; as Moses to Sinai, so David to Sion.

3. From these two we arise to the moral sense, thus. That, as whensoever God's people are carried captive and made thrall to their enemies; as when God seemeth to be put down, and lie foiled for a time, that one may well say, *Exsurgat Deus,* to Him: so when He takes their cause in hand and works their deliverance, it may well be said, *Ascendit in altum,* "He is gone up," as it were, to His high throne or judgment-seat, there to give sentence for them. Ever the Church's depressing is, as it were, God's own humiliation; and their deliverance, after a sort, His exaltation. For then He hath the upper hand. And this is the moral.

Now from this we ascend to the Prophetical sense, "to 4.
the testimony of Jesus, which is the spirit of all prophecy." Rev. 19. 10.
For if in any captivity, as of Egypt, of Babylon, God be said to be down; and in any strange deliverance, such as those were, to be got up on high; in this of Christ, of all other, it is most pregnantly verified. That the highest up-going, higher than Sion or Sinai far; that the most gracious triumph that ever was. When the principalities and powers that had carried, not Israel but mankind, all mankind into captivity; they as captives were led before His chariot, attended, as it is in the next verse before, with "twenty Ps. 68. 17.
thousands of Angels." What time also the gifts and graces of the Holy Ghost were shed forth plenteously upon men, which was this very day; and God, not by a wooden ark but by His own Spirit, came to dwell among them.

And in this sense, the true prophetical meaning of it, doth the Apostle deliver it to us, and we to you. That God Which ever and at all times doth, then and at that time did most specially shew the valour of His victory, and the bounty of His triumph, when "He went up on high," &c.

To put that in other order, which is itself well-ordered The division.
already, were but to confound it. The order as it stands is very exact. I. Christ's ascending first; II. then the I.
manner; III. and last the end of it. 1. The ascending II. III.
in these; "Thou art gone up," &c. 2. The manner is triumph-wise, and that two ways: 1. leading His captives before Him; 2. scattering His gifts about Him; 3. and then thirdly, all to the end that God by His Spirit, the true Ark of His presence indeed, "might rest with us for ever." Or you may, if you please, of these four make two moieties, and give the two former to Christ's ascending, the two latter to the Holy Ghost's descending, in *dona dedit hominibus*, the peculiar of this day.

"Thou art gone up,"—a motion; and "on high,"— I. Christ's ascending: The motion.
a place. Christ in His ascendant going up, Christ "on high" is a good sight. A better sight to see Him so, *tanquam aquila in nubibus* than *tanquam vermis in pulvere*, 'an eagle in the clouds than a worm in the dust,' as a great while we did. To see "a cloud to receive Him" Acts 1. 9.
than a gravestone to cover Him. Better "leading captivity"

SERM. VII. than Himself led captive. Better "receiving gifts for men" than receiving wrong from them. Yet it is strange, St. Paul commenting upon this verse, (Ephesians the fourth, ver. 8,) whereto we shall often have recourse as we are looking at

1. From whence. Eph. 4. 9. "His going up on high," pulls us back and tells us of His being here down below: "In that He ascended," what is it, saith he, but that He descended first? A note out of season one would think. But he best knew what was proper and pertinent, and that is, that Christ's going up is *ascensus post descensum.*

And this, as it is for His glory—for when one hath been down, then to get up is twice to get up—far more for His glory, than if He never had been down. And the lower He hath been down, the more glorious is His getting up. *Bis vincit qui victus vincit;* 'being overcome to overcome is twice to overcome,' for so he overcomes his overcomers, and that is a double victory. As for His glory, so for our good. For His being above before He was below, is nothing to us. But being below first, and then that He went up, that is it we hold by. As the Son of God He came down, as the Son of man He went up. If as the Son of man, there is hope that the sons of men may do the like.

But always remember there must be a descent before. *Ascendit Angelus et factus est diabolus.* Why? He never descended first, and therefore is now in the bottom of hell. But He That first descended, and ascended after, is now in the top of Heaven. To teach us this high top must have a deep root. He that is thus high now, was once low enough. We to be as He was, before we be as He is. Descending by humility, condescending by charity. For he that so descends with Him, he it is and none other that shall ascend up after Him. This is St. Paul upon *ascendisti,* His motion.

1. The place whither. "On high." 2 Kings 2. 16. Now, will you hear him upon *in altum,* "on high," the pitch of his motion? "On high" is somewhat a doubtful term: if it be but to some high mountain, as they thought of Elias, it is "on high," that. How high then? The Apostle takes the true altitude for us. Neither to Sion, nor to Sinai:—set one upon the other, and Pelion upon Ossa

Acts 1. 9. too, it is higher yet. So high, saith St. Luke, "till a cloud

came and took Him out of their sight." And what became of Him then? That the Apostle supplies. He came ὑπε- Eph. 4. 10.
ράνω—ὑπὲρ 'above,' ἄνω 'aloft;' ὑπὲρ οὐρανῶν, ὑπὲρ πάντων τῶν οὐρανῶν, "above all the heavens," even the very highest of them.

Keeping just correspondence between his High and His low. That was *ad ima terræ*, to the "lowest parts of the [Eph. 4. 9.]
earth," than which none lower, none beneath them. This was *ad summa cœli*, 'the highest top of the heavens,' than which none higher, none above them.

So, *exsurgat Deus*, the first verse, is not enough; that was but from the lower parts of the earth to the upper parts of it. *Ascendat in altum*, 'Let Him go up on high;' "Set up Ps. 57. 5.
Thyself, O Lord, above the heavens"—there is His right place. And so now He is where He should be. This for *in altum*.

But we must not stand taking altitudes; this is but the gaze of the Ascension. The Angels blamed the Apostles; Acts 1. 11.
that blame will fall upon us, if we make but a gaze of it. What is there in it *hominibus*, "for us men?"

First, is He "gone up on high?" We may be sure then all is done and despatched here below. He would not hence *re infectâ*, till His errand were done He came for. All is despatched—for look to the text; He went not up till the battle fought, and the victory gotten. For the next point is, "Captivity is led captive." So no more for Him here to Joh. 19. 30.
do; *consummatum est*. And after it was *consummatum est* Lu. 13. 32.
for us, no reason but it should be *consummatus sum* with Him also.

But though all be done here, all is not there; there above, 2.
whither He is gone. There is somewhat still to be done for us. We have our cause there to be handled, and to be handled against a false and slanderous adversary—so Job Job 1. 10.
found him. By means of His being there "on high," *habe-* Job 2. 4. 1 Joh. 2. 1.
mus Advocatum, saith St. John, "we have an Advocate" will see it take no harm. And what were such an one worth in place there!

But as our case is, for the most part, we rather stand in 3.
need of a good High Priest to make intercession, than of a ready Advocate to put in a plea for us. And He is there

SERM. VII. likewise to that end; "on high" within the *sanctum sanctorum*, as "a faithful High Priest" for ever to appear, and
Heb. 2. 17. to make an atonement with God for our transgressions. Thus there all is well.

4. But how shall we do here, if He be gone up "on high" [Deut. 33. 26.] from us? Not a whit worse: *Ascensor cœli auxiliator*, saith Moses, Deuteronomy the thirty-third, ver. 26. By being there He is the better able to help us, to help us against our enemies. For in that He is "on high," He hath the vantage of the high ground; and so able to annoy them, to
Acts 9. 4. strike them down, and lay them flat—St. Paul found it;
Ps. 11. 6. yea to "rain down fire and brimstone, storm and tempest, upon them."

5. To help us against our wants. Wants both temporal, for
Ps. 68. 9. from "on high" He can "send down a gracious rain upon His inheritance," to refresh it; and spiritual, for from "on high" He did send down the gifts and graces of the Spirit, the *dona dedit* of this feast, and of this text both. Look to the text. He is so gone up that our enemies are His captives: we shall not need to fear, they can go no farther than their chain. And though He be gone, *dona dedit*, He is ready to supply us upon our need with all gifts requisite. We shall not need to want; for no good thing will He with-
Ps. 84. 5. [See Vulg.] hold from them that have *ascensiones in corde*, that have their hearts upon Him and upon His ascension; that lift up their hearts to Him there.

6. There is yet one, and I keep that, for it shall be the last. In that He is ascended into Heaven, Heaven is to be as-
Heb. 10. 20. cended to; "by the new and living way that is prepared through the veil of His flesh," a passage there lieth thither. They talk of discoveries, and much ado is made of a new passage found out to this or that place: what say you to
Ps. 27. 13. this discovery *in altum*, this passage into the "land of the living?" Sure it passes all. And this discovery is here, and upon this discovery there is begun a commerce, or trade of intercourse, between Heaven and us. The commodities whereof are these gifts, we shall after deal with them—and a kind of agency; Christ being there for us, and the Spirit here for God; either, agent for other. It is the happiest news this, that ever came to mankind. For *hominibus*, "for

mankind" it is He is gone up; for that is to be repeated to all three, and every of them ἀπὸ κοινοῦ. 1. "He is gone up on high," for *men;* 2. "led captivity captive," for *men;* 3. as well as "received gifts for *men.*"

His going up then is not all for Himself; some part, and that no small part, "for us." For thither He is gone, *ut Præcursor noster,* as our "Forerunner" or Harbinger; *pandens iter ante nos,* saith the Prophet Micah, "to make way before us," "to prepare a place" and to hold possession of it in our names, saith He Himself. Till, say the Angels, "as He was seen to go up, so shall He likewise be to come down again." Once more to descend, (it is His last,) and upon it, His last ascending into His high tribunal-seat, there as our favourable Judge to give us the *Ite benedicti,* the immediate warrant for our ascensions. And so He shall take our persons thither, where He now is in our persons, that "where He is we may be there also." And thus much for His "going up on high."

Heb. 6. 20. Mic. 2. 13. [See Vulg.] [Joh. 14. 2.] Acts 1. 14. Mat. 25. 34. [Joh. 14. 3.]

II. The manner of His ascending. In jubilee. Ps. 47. 5.

Now the manner, how He went. *Ascendit Dominus in jubilo,* saith the forty-seventh Psalm, a proper and peculiar Psalm for this day. For this is the fiftieth day, and fifty is the number of the jubilee; we must look for a jubilee ever at Pentecost. He went up *in jubilo.* Now to a jubilee there go two acts: 1. the releasing of prisoners, one; 2. and the new giving or granting estates *gratis, dona dedit,* the other. And both are here.

In triumph.

He went up in triumph, as a Roman victor up to the Capitol; as David, after his conquest, up to Sion: so He to the Capitol in Heaven, to the Sion that is above, the high and holy places made without hands. Now, two *actus triumphales* there were: 1. one, captives led bound before the chariot; 2. the other, casting abroad of new coin, or as they called them, *missilia,* among the multitude. And these two are in this. This the manner of His going up, like the Jews' jubilee, like the Heathens' triumph. 1. First then of His valour, in His victory, leading His captivity. 2. Then of His bounty in His triumph, dispersing His gifts.

I. Leading "captivity captive."

Of the first. Here is a captivity led in triumph. A triumph is not but after a victory, nor a victory but upon a battle; and ever a battle presupposeth hostility, and that

SERM. VII. some quarrel whereupon it grew. His ascension is His triumph, His resurrection His victory, His death His battle, His quarrel is about *hominibus*, about us "men," for another captivity of ours that had happened before this.

I ask then, what was this captivity here? Of whom? when taken? when led? For taken it must be, before it can be led in triumph. Some interpret it by Satan, say it [Lu. 22. 53.] was by him and "the power of darkness." Some other, that it was Adam and all his progeny; and so we are in it too. And both say well; they and we were taken together. For when they were taken captives, we that then were in their hand and power as captives to them, were taken together with them. So both were taken, and by Christ both; but not both alike. Both were taken, but not both led. They were taken and led; we are taken, and let go. And not let go barely, but rewarded with gifts, as it is in the verse. Both these are within the compass of this Psalm.

To begin with this of the verse; we find it more particularly set down, Colossians the second. There, of the "principalities and powers of hell" it is said, Christ "spoiled them, made a show of them, triumphed over them in His own person." (Col. 2. 15.)

With these He had battle at His death, and then He seemed to lose the field. But up again He got at His resurrection; and then got the day, carried the victory clear. 1 Cor. 15. 54. For lo, as with a trumpet, the Apostle soundeth the victory, *Absorpta est mors in victoriâ*, "death is swallowed up in victory."

But what was the quarrel? That began about us, *hominibus*; in every branch we must take in that word. For no other quarrel had He, but that these whom He leads away captive here, had led us captive away before.

And the quarrel was just; for we were His, twice His. Ps. 138. 8. Isa. 64. 8. 1 Cor. 6. 20. 1 Pet. 1. 19. 1. His once by creation, "the work of His hands." 2. His again now, by redemption, "the price of His blood." He had no reason to lose that was His quite. It stood not with His honour to see them carried away without all recovery.

But how came we captives? Look to Genesis the third. Gen. 3. 6. Rom. 7. 23. 1 Pet. 2. 11. There ye find *lex membrorum*, as St. Paul calleth it; "fleshly lusts," as St. Peter, a garrison that lieth in us, even in our

loins, and "fighteth against our souls." They surprised
Adam, and of whom one is overcome, his captive he is. So
was he led away captive, and in him all mankind. The
effect whereof ye see at Christ's coming. The spirit of error
had, in a manner, seized on all the world. And if error had
taken his thousand, sin had his ten thousand, we may be
sure; and this was the first captivity under the power of
Satan. For sin and error are but leaders under him, take
to his use; and so all mankind held captive of him at his
pleasure. And oh, the thraldom and misery the poor soul
is in, that is thus held and hurried under the servitude of
sin and Satan! The Heathens' *pistrinum*, the Turkey galleys are nothing to it. If any have felt it he can understand me, and from the deep of his heart will cry, "Turn Ps. 126. 4.
our captivity, O Lord."

Will ye then see this "captivity" turned away, and those
that took us taken themselves? Look to His resurrection. Rev. 5. 12.
Agnus occisus est is true, like a lamb He died; but that was,
respect had to His Father. To Him He was a lamb in all
meekness, to satisfy His justice, and to pay Him the ransom
for us and for our enlargement, Whose prisoners justly we
were. That paid, and justice satisfied, the "hand-writing of Col. 2. 14.
the law that was against us" was delivered Him, and He cancelled it. Then had He good right to us. But death, and
"he that had the power of death, the devil," for all that Heb. 2. 14.
would not let Him go, but detained Him still wrongfully.
With them, the lamb would do no good; so He took the
lion. Died a lamb, but rose a lion, and took on like a lion
indeed; "broke up the gates of death," and made the gates
of brass fly in sunder; trod on the serpent's head and all to[1] [[1] *i. e.* entirely.]
bruised it; "came upon him, took from him his armour Lu. 11. 22.
wherein he trusted, and divided his spoils." So it is in the
Gospel, so in this Psalm. Till He had right, He had no
might, was a lamb. But He had no sooner right, but He
made His might appear, was a lion; *et vicit Leo de tribu* Rev. 5. 5.
Juda. His right was seen in His death, His might in His
resurrection.

Ye see them taken: now, will ye see them led? Of this
victory, this here is the triumph. And if ye will see it more
at large, ye may in the Prophet Osee; and out of him in the Hos. 13. 14.

SERM. VII. Apostle, the first of Corinthians, the fifteenth chapter: death led captive without His sting; hell led as one that had lost
1 Cor. 15. 55, 56. the victory; "the strength of sin," the law, rent and fastened to His cross, ensign-wise; the serpent's head bruised, borne
[1 Sam. 17. 54.] before Him in triumph, as was Goliath's head by David returning from the victory. And this was His triumph.

So then, upon the matter here is a double captivity, a first, and a second. 1. A first, and in it *captivans* they, and *captivata* we. 2. A second, and in it *captivans* He, and *captivata* they. They took us and He took them. And this is the jubilee, that He That was overcome did overcome; and they that had overcome were overcome themselves. That *captivans* is become *captivata,* and *captivata* is brought out of captivity and set at liberty. For the leading of this captivity was the turning away of ours.

Gen. 14. 1—16. The "five kings" took Sodom and carried Lot away prisoner. Comes me Abraham upon them, takes the five kings and Lot in their hands: so Lot and they both became Abra-
1 Sam. 30. 1—20. ham's captives. The Amalekites took Ziklag, David's town, his wives, children, and all his people. David makes after them, takes Amalek, and with them his own flock too; and so became master of both. So did the Son of Abraham, and the Son of David, in this captivity here.

For all the world as an English ship takes a Turkish galley, wherein are held many Christian captives at the oar. Both are taken, Turks and Christians; both become prisoners to the English ship. The poor souls in the galley, when they see the English ship hath the upper hand are glad, I dare say, so to be taken; they know it will turn to their good, and in the end to their letting go. So was it with us, we were the children of this captivity. They to whom we were captives, were taken captives themselves, and we with them. So both came into Christ's hands; they and we His prisoners both. But with a great difference. For they are carried in triumph to their confusion, as we see, and after condemned to perpetual prison and torments. And we, by this new cap-
Rom. 8. 21. tivity, rid of our old, and restored to the "liberty of the sons of God." So that in very deed this captivity fell out to prove our felicity; we had been quite undone, utterly perished, if we had not had the good hap thus to become Christ's prisoners.

It is not good simply to be taken captive; but thus it is. For *felix captivitas capi in bonum;* 'he is taken in a good hour that is taken for so great a good.' A happy captivity then may we say; indeed so happy as no man can be happy if he be not thus taken prisoner by Christ. It is the only way to enjoy true liberty. And this for this great "captivity" here led.

Other inferior captivities there be in this life, and those not lightly to be regarded neither. But this of mankind is the main; the rest all derived from this, and but pledges of it. We have lived to see, that *Ascensor Cœli* was *Auxiliator noster,* and *Ductor captivitatis nostræ* even this way.

In the year 1588, the Invincible navy had swallowed us up quick, and made full account to have led us all into captivity. We saw them led like a sort of poor captives round about this isle, sunk and cast away the most part of them, and the rest sent home again with shame. Eight years since they that had vowed the ruin of us all, and if that had been, the thraldom of this whole land; they were led captives in the literal sense, (we saw them) and brought to a wretched end before our eyes. So He That here did, still can, and still doth "lead captivity captive" for the good of His. Take these as remembrances here below, but look up beyond these to our great *captivam duxisti* here; and make this use of both, that we both these ways "being delivered out of the hands of our enemies," and from the slavery of Satan, "might serve Him" Whose service is perfect freedom, "in righteousness and holiness before Him all the days of our life."

[A.D. 1588. the year of the defeat of the Spanish Armada.]

Lu. 1. 74, 75.

And this for the first point of *ascendit in jubilo*—a principal part whereof was the releasing of captives—and so much for the triumph of His victory. Nor for the bounty of His triumph. In that, His valour, valour in leading captivity; in this His magnificence, magnificence in distributing His gifts.

Accepit dona. All this while, there hath been nothing but going up. Here now, there is something coming down, even love with his handful of gifts, to bestow them on us—which is the second part; even His largess or bounty, as it were the running of the conduits with wine, or the casting abroad

Scattering His gifts.

SERM. VII. of His new coin among the lookers on, on this, the great and last day of the feast, the conclusion or shutting up of His triumph. This is the day of *dona dedit* in kind, and *dona dedit* the high honour of this feast. Always the height of His place, the glory of His triumph, makes Him not forget us, we see by this. He sends these for a token that He is still mindful of us.

Four points there be in it. 1. "Received," first; 2. then, "gifts;" 3. thirdly, "for men;" 4. and last, an enlargement of this last word men; for such men as of all men seemed least likely to get any of them, "even for His enemies."

Accepit, dedit. "Received." The Prophet here saith, *dona accepit;* the Eph. 4. 8. Apostle, he saith, *dona dedit,* and both true. *Accepit et dedit,* for *accepit ut daret;* 'He did give what He received,' for 'He received to give.' So, what He received with one hand, He gave with the other. For He received not for Himself, but for others; not to keep, but to part with them again. And part with them He did—witness this day, the day of the giving.

"Received" from whom? Whosoever the party was He received them from, He seems to stand well affected to us. Joh. 20. 17. It is the Father. And we see He said true of Him, "I go up to My Father, and to your Father," that is, yours as well as Mine. Which appeareth in His fatherly goodness, ready to part with them to us. Yet not immediately to us, but by Him to us; that seeing by Whose hands they come, we might know, know and acknowledge both, for Whose sake both He giveth and we receive them. We of Him, He of his Father; but for us, and for our use.

2. *Dona.* "Received gifts." Alas! poor captives never think of any; *Tantum libera nos,* is all they say. 'Free us only,' and we desire no more. This one gift is enough, will richly content them, even the gift of liberty we even now spake of. Enough Jas. 4. 6. for them, but not enough for Him; "the Scripture offereth greater grace." He will let them go, but not let them go away empty; send them away rewarded, and not with one gift, but plurally, *dona,* with many. So many, as in the next verse He saith, they be even laden with them. And not give them again their former estate freely—the jubilee of the law; but a far better than that was, even in Heaven, which

is far beyond the laws, and is indeed the jubilee of the Gospel.

To speak of these gifts in particular, one hour-glass will not serve, they be so many. To recapitulate *dona in dono*, all in one: it is the gift of gifts, the gift of the Holy Ghost, the proper gift or *missile* of this day. *O si scires donum Dei*, Joh. 4. 10.
saith our Saviour of it, if we but knew this gift! And God grant we may know it, that is, that we may receive it, for then we shall, but otherwise we shall never know it; for *nemo scit nisi qui acceperit*, "but he that receiveth it, no Rev. 2. 17.
man knoweth it."

But God it is, this gift. The text is direct; this giving is to the end "God may dwell with us." That cannot be, if He that is given were not God. So then man He carried up to Heaven, God He sent down to earth; our flesh is there with God, His Spirit here with us. *Felix captivitas* we said before, *felix cambium* may we now say: 'a happy captivity' that, 'a blessed exchange' for us this.

This is but one; it is expressed plurally—*dona*, many; there be many in it. It is as the ark of the covenant; the ark was not empty, no more is this. The two tables that teach the heart, the hidden manna that feedeth the soul, the censer that perfumeth all our prayers, the rod which makes us do as itself did, of withered and dead to revive and flourish again. Great variety of gifts there are in it, and all are feathers of the dove mentioned in this Psalm, verse thir- [Ps. 68. 13.]
teen; either the silver feathers of her wing, or the golden of her neck, for all are from her. They are reduced all to two; 1. "The gifts," 2. "the fruits." "The gifts," known 1 Cor. 12. 4.
by the term *gratis data*; "the fruits," pertaining to *gratum* Gal. 5. 22.
faciens. But the *gratum faciens* being to every man for himself, the *gratis data* for the benefit of the Church in common; these latter are ever reckoned the proper, and most principal, *dona dedit* of this day. And indeed they are all in all. For by them are the scions planted, on which the other, the fruits, do grow.

And so it is. For what were the true and proper "gifts" this day sent down? were they not a few tongues? And Acts 2. 3.
those tongues had heads, and those heads belonged to men, and those men were the Apostles. Upon the point, these

SERM. VII. "gifts" in the end will fall out to prove men; the gift ever leading us to the office, and the office to the persons by whom it is borne.

Eph. 4. 8. In the place where the Apostle comments upon this verse, and upon this word "gifts," ask him what the "gifts" be? He will tell us, *Ipse dedit quosdam Apostolos,* "He gave some Apostles, some Prophets, some Evangelists;" these were of the gifts. These three now are gone, their date is out. But in the same period, he puts pastors and doctors too; and them we have still, and they are all the remains that are now left of the *dona dedit* of this day. A point I wish to be well thought on; that for these gifts this feast is holden, that for these we keep this high holy-day.

What, and are these such goodly gifts? Yea "the Apostles, Prophets, Evangelists," we grant, for we love to build sepulchres as well as the Pharisees; they must be dead, ere we esteem them. Oh, if we had lived in the Apostles' days, we would have made othergates[1] account of them, that we would. [*i. e.* another manner.] We know how our fathers then did; we would even have done the same. For those we have left, it is daily heard and seen how poor a rate we set on them. This we find: the Apostles themselves were fain to magnify their own apostleship and to say, Well, they hoped the day would come when their people's faith were as it should be, that they also should be esteemed according to their "measure," that is, better than they were. (2 Cor. 10. 14.) So that they were undervalued. I will not say the same of these, which are all that are now left of this *dona dedit:* that of these holy-day gifts there is but a working-day account. Yet these are they that daily do rescue men and women laden with sins, and so captives to Satan, from Satan's captivity, and take them prisoners to Christ. These they, by whose means and ministry are wrought in us those impressions of grace, which we call "the fruits of the Spirit," the price whereof is above all worldly gifts whatsoever. And if "God dwell among us," these be they by whose doctrine and exhortation we are edified, that is, framed and reared up a meet building for Him.

Truly, if we did but seriously think of *Ipse dedit,* Who gave; of *Spiritus Sanctus posuit,* Who placed them; (Acts 20. 28.) nay if but of the feast itself we hold, it would be better than it is;

if not for theirs, for the very feast's sake. For why keep we it? For these *dona dedit,* plain. And how prize we them? I list not tell how meanly. This I say then: either esteem them otherwise, or what do we keeping it? Put down the feast, wipe the day of Pentecost out of the calendar, keep it no more hardly. Never keep so high a feast for so low a matter. But if we will keep it, make better reckoning of *dona dedit hominibus* than hitherto we have, or presently we do.

Now the parties for whom all these: *Hominibus. Ascendit,* 3.
duxit, dedit, all for *hominibus,* "for men!" "For men" He *Hominibus.*
"ascended up on high;" "for men" He "led captivity;" "for men" He "received" these "gifts." They the cistern, into which all these three streams do flow. As God of God He received them, that as man to man He might deal them. I will tell you St. Paul's note upon this word, and indeed it is the only cause for which he there bringeth in this verse; the number—that it is *hominibus,* not *homini.* "To men," among them; to every one some, not to any one all. For no one man is *hominibus,* and *hominibus* it is He deals them to. None so complete but he wants some; none so bare left that he wants all. A note, if well digested, which would cause this fastidious disdain to cease, we have one of another.
"The spoils are divided to them of the household," come not Ps. 68. 12.
all to one man's hand; they be μερισμοὶ by proportion and Heb. 2. 4.
measure, part and part. So that any man, though he want this gift or that, have not all, if he have but some to do good and do good with that some, need not be dismayed. He is within the verge of Christ's bounty, of *dona dedit hominibus.*

The last is the enlargement of His largess of this clause in 4.
the grant. "For men?" yea, for some men, some special *Etiam inimicis.*
men, may some say, such as Abraham and David, God's friends; but not for His enemies nor for such as I. Yes; אך מורדים "even for His enemies," even for "His rebels," so is the nature of the word, even to them this day is He willing to part with His gifts. "His enemies?" why the devils themselves are no more but so, but His enemies; what, for them? No; it is *hominibus, etiam inimicis,* it is not *dæmonibus;* so they are out clear. But for men, though His enemies, there is hope in this clause. And O the bountifulness of God,

SERM. VII. that there is hope even for them, that He so far enlargeth the gifts of His feast!

Will ye but hear His commission given about this point? Lu. 24. 47. This it is; that "remission of sins," the chief gift of all, "in His Name be proclaimed to all nations." And all nations then, in a manner, were within the Apostle's *cum inimici essemus.* But that is not it, but the last words that follow; that this proclamation should be made, "beginning at Jerusalem." At Jerusalem? why there all the injuries were done Him, all the indignities offered Him that could possibly be offered Him, that could possibly be offered by one enemy to another. Begin there? why the stones were yet moist with His blood so lately shed, so few days before as scarce dry at the proclamation time. Well yet, there begin: this is *etiam inimicis* indeed. Enough to shew He would have His enemies should be the better for this day; *festum charitatis* this right.

And will ye now see this put in execution? This very day, so soon as ever these gifts were come, St. Peter thus [Acts 7. 52.] proclaims, that Holy and "Just One, ye have been the betrayers and murderers" of Him—that is *inimicis*, trow I, in [Acts 2. 38.] the highest degree. Well yet, "repent and be baptized, and your sins," yea even that sin also, "shall be done away, and ye shall receive the gift of the Holy Ghost." They that had laid Him full low, past ever ascending as they thought, even they have their parts in His ascension. They that bound Him as prisoner, He looses their captivity. They that did *damna dare* to Him, He doth *dona dare* to them. All to shew, *etiam inimicis* is no more than the truth; and what would we more? Then let no man despair of his part in these gifts, or say, I am shut out of the grant, I have so lived, so behaved myself, never dwell with God, I. Why, what art thou? A captive? Nay, art thou an enemy? Why, if *de hominibus, etiam inimicis;* if a man, though an enemy; this Scripture will reach him, if he put it not from him. The words are so plain; "for men, yea though His very enemies."

See then what difference is between the two feasts: the Resurrection, the first verse of the Psalm, "Let God arise, and let His enemies be scattered;" that is, *inimici dæmones,* Ps. 68. 1. or men that put Him from them. But now at this, "Let God arise, and let His enemies," that were, and would not be, be gathered; and let "those that hate Him," and now hate themselves for it, fly unto Him. It is the feast of Pentecost to-day. This is the day for *etiam inimicis;* to-day He hath "gifts" even for them too. And thus much for the latter part, and so for the whole triumph.

III. The end, "that God might dwell among" men.

The end now why all this. *Hominibus,* "for men, that God may dwell among men." God, that is the whole Trinity by this Person of it. Why? dwelt He not among men before? He did. I know not well whether it may be called dwelling, but sure never so did before as since these gifts came from Him.

1. Dwell, not visit.

Did not "dwell" (they call it visiting) then; went and came, and that was all. But since He came to settle Himself, to take His residence, not to visit any longer, but even to "dwell among them."

2. Among men, at large.

Nor "among men" before, but among some men. He was cooped up, as it were, *notus in Judæâ Deus,* and there was all. Since the "fulness of the Gentiles" is come in, Japhet into Shem's tents; all nations His neighbours are interested in Him and His gifts alike. St. Paul upon this verse, "He ascended," *ut impleret omnia. Impleret* His, *omnia* ours. Filled with His gifts He, full all; that is, all the compass of the earth full of His fulness.

Ps. 76. 1. Gen. 9. 27. [Rom. 11. 25.] Eph. 4. 10.

It is for love, even *φιλανθρωπία,* for His "love of men" that makes Him desire thus to "dwell" with us. This is evident by this *captivitas soluta,* and these *dona distributa,* by this "captivity led," that is, by His fighting for it; by these "gifts given," that is, by His bidding for it; that all this He doth and all this He gave, and all for no other end but this. So as, *quid requirit Dominus?* on His part, *quid retribuam Domino?* on ours; all is but this, *ut habitet nobiscum Deus,* that the true Ark of His Presence, His Holy Spirit, may find a place of rest with us. [Tit. 3. 4.] [Mic. 6. 8.] [Ps. 116. 12.]

Our duty.

What shall we do then? shall we not yield to Him thus much, or rather thus little? If He have a mind to dwell in us, shall we refuse Him? It will be for our benefit; we shall find a good neighbour of Him. Shall we not then say, as they did to the Ark, "Arise, O Lord, into Thy resting-place?" 2 Chron. 6. 41.

To prepare him a place.

But first, two things would be done. 1. The place would

SERM. VII. be meet; 2. and the usage or entertainment according. For the place, never look about for a soil where; the place are we ourselves. He must dwell in us if ever He dwell among us. *In* us I say, not beside us; שכינה is the word, and so it signifieth; *sic inter nos, ut in nobis.*

And if so, then *locus* and *locatum* would be suitable. A dove He is: He will not come but *ad tecta candida,* to no foul or sooty place. Ointment He is: poured He will not be but into a clean and sweet, not into a stinking or loathsome phial. To hold us to the word; God He is, and Holy is His title; so would His place be a holy place; and, for God, a
1 Cor. 3. 16. Temple. You know who saith, *Templum Dei estis vos,* "Know ye not ye are the Temples of God, if He dwell in you?"

2. To entertain Him. But it is not the place, though never so commodious, makes one so willing to dwell, as doth the good usage or respect of those, in the midst of whom it is. Here will I dwell, for I
Ps. 68. 16. have a delight, saith He. It would be such as to delight Him, if it might be; but such as at no hand to grieve Him. For then He is gone again; *migremus hinc* straight, and we force Him to it. For who would dwell where he cannot dwell but with continual grief?

And what is there will sooner grieve Him and make Him to quit us, than discord or disunion? Among divided men or minds He will not dwell. Not but where unity and love is. In vain we talk of the Spirit without these. Aaron's ointmen and the dew of Hermon—both types of Him—ye know
Ps. 133. 1. what Psalm they belong to; it begins with *habitare fratres in*
Ps. 68. 6. *unum.* It is in this Psalm before, "where men are of one mind in a house"—there He delights to be. This very day, they that received Him were ὁμοθυμαδὸν, "with one accord in one place." That ὁμοθυμαδὸν is the adverb of the feast. And the Apostle in his comment on this verse—no better
Eph. 4. 3. way, saith he, to preserve the "unity of the Spirit," or the Spirit of unity, choose you whether, than in the "bond of
Ps. 120. 5. peace." To say truth, who would be hired "to dwell in Mesech" where nothing is but continual jars and quarrels? Such places, such men, are even as *torrida zona,* not habitable by the Spirit, by this Spirit. But for the other spirit, the spirit of division, they are; *ut habitet dæmon inter eos,* a fit place for the devil, to dwell among such. Think of this

seriously, and set it down, that "at Salem is His Taberna- Ps. 76. 2.
cle," and Salem is "peace," and so the Fathers read it, *in* [Heb. 7. 2.]
pace factus est locus Ejus. Make Him that place and He will say, Here is my rest, "here will I dwell, for I have delight therein."

We said even now: to "dwell among us," He must dwell *in* us; and in us He will "dwell," if the fruits of His Spirit [Gal. 5. 22.] be found in us. And of His fruits the very first is love. And the fruit is as the tree is. For He Himself is love, the essential love, and love-knot of the undivided Trinity.

Now to work love, the undoubted both sign and means of By the Sacrament. His dwelling, what better way, or how sooner wrought, than by the sacrament of love, at the feast of love, upon the feast-day of love; when Love descended with both His hands full of gifts, for very love, to take up His dwelling with us?

You shall observe: there ever was and will be a near alliance between His *dona dedit hominibus,* and His *dona reliquit hominibus,* "the gifts He sent" and 'the gifts He left us.' He left us the gifts of His body and blood. His body broken, and full of the characters of love all over. His blood shed, every drop whereof is a great drop of love. To those which were sent, these which were left, love, joy, peace, have a special connatural reference, to breed and to maintain each other. His body the Spirit of strength, His blood the Spirit of comfort; both, the Spirit of love.

This Spirit, we said, we are to procure, that It may abide with us and be in us. And what is more intrinsical in us, abideth surer, groweth faster to us, than what we eat and drink? Then, if we could get "a spiritual meat," or get 1 Cor. 10. 3, 4.
"to drink of the Spirit," there were no way to that. And behold here they be. For here is "spiritual meat," that is breeding the Spirit; and here we are all made "drink of 1 Cor. 12. 13.
one Spirit," that there may be but one Spirit in us. And we are all made "one bread and one body," kneaded together and pressed together into one—as the symbols are, the bread, and the wine—so many as are partakers of one bread and one cup, "the bread of life," and "the cup of blessing," the Joh. 6. 35.
communion of the Body and Blood of Christ. And in figure 1 Cor. 10. 16.
of this, even King David dealt these two, "bread" and 1 Chron. 16. 3.
"wine," in a kind of resemblance to ours, when the Ark was

SERM. VII. to be brought home and seated among them—the Ark in type. And we to do the same this day when the Ark in truth did come, and will come to take up His rest in us.

Will ye now hear the end of all? By this means God shall "dwell with us"—the perfection of this life; and He dwelling with us, we shall dwell with Him—the last and highest perfection of the life to come. For with whom God dwelleth here, they shall dwell with Him there, certainly. Grace He doth give, that He may "dwell with us;" and glory He will give, that we may dwell with Him. So may He dwell, He with us: so may we dwell, we with Him, eternally. So the text comes about round. It began with an ascension, and it ends with one; began with Christ's, ends with ours. He ascended, that God might dwell with us; that, God dwelling with us, we might in the end ascend and dwell with God. He went up "on high," that the Spirit might come down to us below; and, that coming down, make us go the same way, and come to the same place that He is. Sent Him down to us, to bring us up to Him.

Where we shall no less truly than joyfully say; This is our rest for ever. To which rest, *Ascensor cœli, Ductor captivitatis, Largitor donorum,* 'He that is gone up to Heaven, the Leader of captivity, the Great Receiver and Giver of these gifts,' vouchsafe to bring us; that as this feast is the period of all the feasts of the year, so this text, and the end of it, to dwell with God, may be the end of us all; of our desires here, of our fruition there! Which, &c.

A SERMON

PREACHED BEFORE

THE KING'S MAJESTY AT GREENWICH,

ON THE TWENTY-NINTH OF MAY, A.D. MDCXV. BEING WHIT-SUNDAY.

LUKE iii. 21, 22.

Now it came to pass, when all the people were baptized, and that Jesus also was baptized, and did pray, the heaven was opened,

And the Holy Ghost came down upon Him in a bodily shape like a dove, and there was a voice from Heaven, saying, Thou art My beloved Son, in Whom I am well pleased.

[*Factum est autem cum baptizaretur omnis populus, et Jesu baptizato, et orante, apertum est cœlum,*

Et descendit Spiritus Sanctus corporali specie sicut columba in Ipsum, et vox de cœlo facta est, Tu es filius Meus dilectus, in Te complacui Mihi. Latin Vulg.]

[*Now when all the people were baptized, it came to pass, that Jesus also being baptized, and praying, the Heaven was opened,*

And the Holy Ghost descended in a bodily shape like a dove upon Him, and a voice came from Heaven, which said, Thou art My beloved Son; in Thee I am well pleased. Engl. Trans.]

THIS is the feast of the Holy Ghost. And here have we in the text, a visible descending of the Holy Ghost. The feast of the Holy Ghost.

Another there was, besides this; but this hath the vantage of it, three ways: 1. the worthiness of the Person. Here, It descends upon Christ, Who alone is more worth than all those there. 2. The priority of time; this here was first, and that other, the Holy Ghost but at the second hand. 3. The generality of the good: that other was proper but to one calling, of the Apostles only. All are not Apostles; all are Acts 2. 1-4. The coming down of the Holy Ghost upon Christ. *Dignius. Antiquius. Communius.*

SERM. VIII.

Christians. This of Christ's concerns all Christians; and so the more general by far.

The feast of baptism. The baptism-day of the first Christians. Acts 2. 41.

That it is of baptism, is no whit impertinent neither; for this is the feast of baptism. There were "three thousand" this day baptized by the Apostles, the first Christians that ever were. In memory of that baptism, the Church ever after held a solemn custom of baptizing at this feast. And many, all the year, reserved themselves till then; those except, whom necessity did cause to make more haste.

The baptism-day of the Apostles. Acts 2. 3, 41.

But, upon the point, both baptisms fell upon this day. That wherewith the Apostles themselves were baptized, of fire. And that wherewith they baptized the people, of water. So that, even this way, it is pertinent also.

Christ's baptism a high mystery. The presence of the whole Trinity. 1. At the creation.

To look into the text, there is no man but at the first blush will conceive there is some great matter in hand. 1. First, by the opening of Heaven; for that opens not for a small purpose: 2. then, by the solemn presence of so great Estates at it; for here is the whole Trinity in person. The Son in the water, the Holy Ghost in the dove, the Father in the voice. This was never so before, but once; never but twice in all, in all the Bible. Once in the Old Testament, and once in the New. In the Old, at the creation, the beginning of Genesis. There find we God, and the Word with God creating, and "the Spirit of God moving upon the face of the waters." And now here again, at Christ's christening in the New.

Gen. 1. 1-3.

2. At Christ's Christening.

Ex. 37. 7-9. That, a new creation. 2 Cor. 5. 17.

The faces of the Cherubims are one toward the other; that is, there is a mutual correspondence between these two. That was at the creation; this, a creation too: "if any be in Christ, he is a new creature" of this new creation. That was the *genesis*, that is, "the generation" of the world; this, the παλιγγενεσία—the Apostle's word—that is, "the regeneration," or spiritual new birth, whereby we be born again the sons of God. And better not born at all, than not so born again.

That, a new generation. Tit. 3. 5.

This then, being every way as great, (indeed, the greater of the twain,) meet it was, they all should present themselves at this, no less than at that; and every one have his part in it, as we see they have. All, I say, seeing the commission for baptism was to run in all their names, and itself ever to be ministered accordingly.

The commission for us, Mat. 28. 19. The execution of it.

To lay forth the members of the division. A double baptism we have here; double for the parties, and double for the parts.

The division. 1. Christ's. 2. The people's.

For the parties; we have here two parties. First the people. Then Christ.

Christ's and the people's. In water. In the Holy Ghost.

For the parts; we have here two parts. For this first, both of Christ and the people, was but John's baptism, was but *baptismus fluminis*, as they call it, 'water-baptism.' But there is another part besides to be had, even *baptismus Flaminis*, 'the baptism of the Holy Ghost.'

That second part is set down in a sequel of four:

1. For first, after John's baptism, Christ prays. 2. Then, after His prayer, Heaven opens. 3. After Heaven open, the Holy Ghost descends. 4. Lastly, after His descent, comes the voice. And these four make up the other part, and both together a full baptism.

Of these then in order. I. Of the people's baptism. II. Of Christ's baptism. Christ's 1. by water, and then 2. by the Holy Ghost. In which, the four: 1. Christ's prayer, 2. Heaven open, 3. the Dove, and 4. the voice.

I. II.

1. The people's baptism.

"It came to pass, that when," &c. Two baptisms we have here: 1. the people's first. 2. Then Christ's. How it should come to pass the people should be baptized, we see good reason; but not how it should come to pass that Christ also. The people, they came "confessing their sins," and so needed "the baptism of repentance:"—so was John's baptism. For the people not being βαπτιζόμενοι, "baptized," but, to use the Apostle's word, βυθιζόμενοι, "even soused over head and ears" in their sins, in "many foolish and noisome lusts, which drown men in perdition," *tanquam sus a volutabro*, they had need to be washed from the wallow of their sin they had long lain in.

Mat. 3. 6. For their sins. Acts 19. 4. 1 Tim. 6. 9. 2 Pet. 2. 22.

And not only for their sin: even their righteousness, take it at the best, even that was not so clean but it needs come to baptism; *utpote stillantes quotidie super telam justitiæ saniem concupiscentiæ*—they be Pope Adrian's own words: 'as dropping every other while upon the web of those few good works we do, such stuff,' the Prophet resembles it to so homely a thing as I list not to tell you what it is; but it is *pannus menstruatus*, English it who will. Reason then, for the people;

For their very righteousness. *In quarum sentent.* Isa. 64. 6

SERM. VIII. and not only for *fæx populi*, but even *flos populi*, to be baptized. It might well "come to pass," that.

The people's children's baptism. 1 Pet. 2. 2. Job 14. 4. Ps. 51. 5. Ezek. 16. 6. Yea reason, that even they who of all the rest seem least to need it, the people's children, ἀρτιγέννητα βρέφη, the poor "new-born babes." For being "conceived of unclean seed,"—Job; and warmed in a sinful womb—David; at their birth, "polluted" no less in sin, than "in their blood"—Ezekiel; there is not *infans unius diei super terram*, as the Seventy read it, "not a child a day old" but needs *baptismus lavacri*, if it be but for *baptismus uteri;* 'the baptism of the Church, if it be but for the baptism it had in the womb.' Let the people then be baptized in God's name; good and bad, men and children and all.

II. Christ's baptism. It may seem Christ was not to be baptized. [S. Bern. in Circum. Dom. Nos. Serm. 3. 3.] 1 Pet. 1. 19. 1 Pet. 2. 22. 2 Cor. 5. 21. Acts 19 4. *Sed quid facitis baptizantes Jesum?* as Bernard asks at His circumcision, *Quid facitis circumcidentes Puerum hunc?* 'What do you circumcising Him,' in Whom nothing superfluous? So here, What do you baptizing Him, in Whom nothing unclean? What should He do being baptized? How comes that to pass? Go wash your spotted lambs, and spare not; this Lamb is "immaculate," hath not the least spot upon Him. *Qui non fecit peccatum*—it is Peter; *Qui non novit peccatum*—it is Paul; "neither did, nor knew sin," He hath none to repent of: what should He do at the "baptism of repentance?"

Mat. 3. 14. One might well ask, Why did not the Baptist repel Him finally? Not say, "I have need to be baptized of Thee," that is, Thou hast no need to be baptized of me—that was too faint, that was not enough; but, Thou hast no need to be baptized at all. Yea, one might well ask the water, with Ps. 114. 5. the Psalmist, "Why it fled not, and Jordan, why it was not driven back," at this baptism?

Yet Christ was baptized. Yet the verse is plain; that with the people, Christ also was baptized.

How came this to pass? Why baptized? Why with the people?

It may seem of very humility. Was it this? though He needed it not, yet for *exemplum dedi vobis* He would condescend to it, to give all a good example of humility; as He did at His Maundy [1], when He washed His Disciples' feet?

Indeed, I must needs say, great humility there was in it;

[[1] See Sparrow's Rationale, p. 125. new ed.]

as at His circumcision, to take on Him the brand of a malefactor, so here to submit Himself to the washing proper to sinners only. 2. Then again, not to take it alone, but to take it at the hands of one so far inferior to Him, as he reckoned not himself worthy to stoop and "unloose His shoe-latchet." 3. Again, that not baptized only, but baptized with the people. Not, St. John come and baptize Him at home; but with the multitude, the meanest of them—they and He together. And when? not upon a day by Himself, but when they. And where? not in a basin by Himself, but even in the common river, with the rest of the many. When and where they, then and there He.

Lu. 3. 16.

Not of humility, but of justice.

This sure was great humility, and to it we well might, and gladly we would ascribe it, but that Himself will not let us so do. For when the Baptist strained courtesy at it, He bade let be, "Thus it behoved" *implere omnem justitiam. Justitiam*—mark that, no courtesy, but "justice;" He makes a matter of justice of it, as if justice should not have been done, at least not "all justice," if He had not been baptized.

Mat. 3. 15

The justice in Christ, two ways considered.

Why, what justice had been broken? what piece of it, if He had not? To shew you how this comes to pass, we are to consider Christ as having two capacities, as they term them. So are we to consider Him—the second Adam; for so do we the first Adam, as a person of himself, and as the author of a race, or head of a society. And even so do we Christ; either as *totum integrale*, 'a person entire'—they call it a body natural, or as *pars communitatis*, which they call a body politic, in conjunction and with reference to others; which others are His Church, which "Church is His body." They His body, and He their head—so told us often by the Apostle. And as by Himself considered He is *Unigenitus*, "the Only-begotten," hath never a brother; so as together with the people, He is *Primogenitus inter multos*, "the First-begotten among many brethren."

1 Cor. 15. 22.

Eph. 1. 22, 23.

Joh. 3. 16.

Rom. 8. 29.

Not, as by Himself, from us.

To apply this to our purpose. Take Christ by Himself, as severed from us, and no reason in the world to baptize Him. He needed it not. Needed it not? Nay, take Him so, Jordan had more need come to Him, than He to Jordan, to be cleansed. *Lavit aquas Ipse, non aquæ Ipsum*, 'the waters

SERM. VIII. were baptized by Him, they baptized Him not;' He went into them *ut aquæ nos purgaturæ prius per Ipsum purgarentur* —it is Epiphanius—'that they which should cleanse us, might by Him first be cleansed.' It is certain; so He received no cleanness, no virtue, but virtue He gave to Jordan, to the waters, to the Sacrament itself.

In anchorato. [Anaceph. 7. ad fin.]

But as part of one body with us.

But then, take Him the other way as in conjunction *cum populo,* they and He one body, and the case is altered. For if He be so *cum populo,* with them, as He be one of them, as He be a part of a body with them, a principal part I grant, yet part though, reason would He do as they do, part and
Heb. 2. 14. part alike. "Inasmuch," saith the Apostle, "as the children were partakers of flesh and blood, He also took part with them." And so, inasmuch as they baptized, He also took such part as they, both went to baptism together. For, *ut pars toti congrua,* a kind of justice there is in it they should so do.

Not only as part with us, but as for us also.

But if we look a little farther, then shall we find greater reason yet. A part He is, and parts there be that in some case undertake for the whole; as the arm, to be let blood for all the body. And "it came to pass," that such a part He was; He undertook for us. For in His baptism He put
Gal. 3. 27. us on, as we "put Him on," in ours. Take Him then, not only as *cum populo,* but as *pro populo;* not only as *nobiscum,*
Isa. 53. 6. but as *pro nobis;* put Him in the case the Prophet doth, *Posuit super Ipsum iniquitates omnium nostrûm,* "put upon Him the transgressions of us all;" put Him as the Apostle
2 Cor. 5. 21. puts Him, *Factus est peccatum pro nobis,* "make Him sin for us," put all our sins upon Him; and then it will come to pass, He will need baptizing, He will need that for me and thee that for Himself He needed not, and baptism in that case may well be ministered unto Him.

To wash off our sins.

Nay then, as in another case the Prophet saith, that all Lebanon was little enough to find wood for a sacrifice; so
Isa. 40. 16. may we in this, that all Jordan is little enough to find water to His baptism. A whole river too little, in that case. For being first baptized, as I may say, in so many millions of sins of so many millions of sinners, in so foul a puddle; well might He then be baptized, if it were but to wash away that His former foul baptism. Well might it come to pass then.

One only scruple remains, how Jordan or any water could What bap-
do this, wash away sin. To clear it shortly; the truth is, it tism wash-
could not. It is no water-work, without somewhat put to it, eth sins off.
to help it scour. But nothing on earth; not, if you put to Not water Job 9. 30.
it "nitre," "much soap," "fullers'-earth," "the herb borith," Jer. 2. 22. [See
say the Prophets, all will not do, it will not off so. There- Vulg.]
fore, this of His in Jordan did not, could not do the feat,
otherwise than in the virtue of another to follow. For, after
this was past, He spake of another "baptism He was to be Lu. 12. 50.
baptized with." And that was it indeed; that, "the foun- Zech. 13. 1.
tain that was opened to the house of Israel, for sin and for
uncleanness;" that was *baptismus sanguinis*. "For without Heb. 9. 22.
blood," without the mixture of that, "there is no doing
away sin."

And so was He baptized. And He had *trinam mersionem*; But the
1. one in "Gethsemane," 2. one in "Gabbatha," 3. and a baptism of blood.
third in "Golgotha." In "Gethsemane," in His sweat of Mat. 26. 36. Joh. 19. 13.
blood. In "Gabbatha," in the blood that came from the
scourges and thorns; and in "Golgotha," that which came Mark 15. 22.
from the nails and the spear. Specially, the spear. There,
met the two streams of "water and blood," the true Jordan, Joh. 19. 34.
the bath or laver, wherein we are purged "from all our sins." 1 John 1. 7.
No sin of so deep a dye but this will command it, and fetch
it out. This in Jordan, here now, was but an undertaking of
that then; and in virtue of that, doth all our water-baptism
work. And therefore are we baptized into it: not into His
water-baptism, but into His cross-baptism; not into His baptism, but into His death. "So many as are baptized, are Rom. 6. 3.
baptized into His death"—it is the Apostle.

To take our leave of this point. This may be said: if it Our duty
be justice, that Christ come to baptism, much more that the out of Christ's
people. And how then comes it to pass that there is such baptism.
sacrilegious pride in some of the people, that, as if no such
thing were, set so light by it as they do? and that not John's,
as this was, but Christ's own baptism? Be sure of this, if
Christ thus did, to countenance and credit John's baptism Lu. 7. 30.
because it was the ordinance of God, much more His mind
is to give countenance, and to have countenance given, to
His own, which is God's ordinance, of a far higher nature.

And if the Lord thought not much to come to the bap-

SERM. VIII. tism of His servant, He will think much if the servant come not to the baptism of his Lord. This of His then is but a lesson to us, to invite us thereto; and we take it as the voice that spake to St. Paul, *Et nunc quid moraris? Surge, ablue peccata tua;* "And now why stay you?" why protract you the time? "Up, wash away your sins," with all the speed you may. For, if when the people was baptized, Christ was so, much more strongly it holds, when Christ Himself is so, that then the people should and ought to be baptized.

Acts 22. 16.

The second part of Christ's baptism.

Now Christ is baptized. And no sooner is He so, but He falls to His prayer. *Indigentia mater orationis,* we say, 'want begets prayer.' Therefore, yet there wants somewhat. A part, and that a chief part of baptism, is still behind.

1. Christ's prayer for somewhat yet wanting. 1 Joh. 5. 6. For the baptism of the Holy Ghost. 1 Joh. 5. 7, 8 Deu. 19. 15.

There goes more to baptism, if it be as it should be, than *baptismus fluminis;* yea, I may boldly say, there goes more to it, if it be as it should, than *baptismus sanguinis.* Christ "came in water and blood, not in water only, but in water and blood"—that is not enough, except "the Spirit also bear witness." So *baptismus Flaminis* is to come too. There is to be a Trinity beneath, 1. water, 2. blood, and 3. the Spirit, to answer to That above; but the Spirit's baptism coming too, in the mouth of all three all is made sure, all established throughly. This is it He prays for as man.

The baptism of blood we are quit of.

For the baptism of blood that was due to every one of us, and each of us to have been baptized in his own blood, to have had three such immersions; that hath Christ quit us of. When He was asked by the Prophet, "how His robes came so red?" He says, "He had been in the winepress." But there He had been, and that He had trod, alone; *et vir de gentibus non fuit Mecum,* "and not one of the people with Him," none but He there, in that; spares us in that.

Isa. 63. 2, 3.

But not either of water or of the Holy Ghost. Joh. 3. 5. 1 Cor. 10. 2.

But the other two parts He sets down precisely to Nicodemus, and in him to us all: 1. water, 2. and the Holy Ghost. Now the Holy Ghost we yet lack. So doth St. Paul—"baptized in the sea and the cloud;" by "the sea" meaning the elementary part, by "the cloud" the celestial part of baptism. Now that of the cloud we have not yet. So doth St. Peter—"the doing away the soil of the flesh," that Jordan can do; but that wherewith the conscience, or soul, should be presented before God, that is still wanting. And the baptism

1 Pet. 3. 21.

of the body, is but the body of baptism; the soul of baptism, is the baptism of the soul. Of the soul, with the blood of Christ, by the hand of the Holy Ghost, as of the body with water, by the hand of the Baptist; without which it is but a naked, a poor, and a dead element. Gal. 4. 9.

St. Paul tells us, that besides the circumcision that was the *manufacture*, there was another "made without hands." There is so, in baptism, besides the hand seen that casts on the water; the virtue of the Holy Ghost is there, working "without hands" what here was wrought. Col. 2. 11.

Christ's prayer for the Holy Ghost.

And for this Christ prays; that then it might, might then, and might ever, be joined to that of the water. Not in His baptism only, but in the people's; and as He afterwards enlarges His prayer, in all others' that "should ever after believe in His name." That what in His here was, in all theirs might be; what in this first, in all following; what in Christ's, in all Christians': Heaven might open, the Holy Ghost come down, the Father be pleased to say over the same words, *toties quoties*, so oft as any Christian man's child is brought to his baptism. Christ hath prayed now. Joh. 17. 20.

2. The opening of Heaven.

See the force of His prayer. Before it, Heaven was mured up, no dove to be seen, no voice to be heard—*altum silentium*. But straight upon it, as if they had but waited the last word of His prayer, all of them follow immediately.

For the bringing down the waters above the Heavens.

Heaven opens first. For if when the lower heaven was shut three years, Elias was able with his prayer to open it—it is our Saviour, in the next chapter following—and bring down rain; the prayer of Christ, Who is more of might than many such as Elias, shall it not be much more of force, to enter the Heaven of heavens, the highest of them all, and to bring down thence the waters above the heavens, even the heavenly graces of the Holy Spirit? Lu. 4. 25. Jas. 5. 17, 18.

For so, when our Saviour cried, "If any be athirst let him come unto Me, and I will give him of the waters of life," "This," saith St. John, "He spake of the Spirit." For the Spirit and His graces are very super-celestial waters; one drop whereof, issued into the waters of Jordan, will give them an admirable power to pierce even into the innermost parts of the soul, and to baptize it; that is, not only take out the stains of it and make it clean, but further, give it tincture, lustre, or gloss: for so is baptism properly, of βάπτω, taken Joh. 7. 37–9. Rev. 7. 14.

SERM. VIII. from the dyer's fat, and is a dyeing or giving a fresh colour,
and not a bare washing only.

2. To shew baptism is from Heaven. Always, the opening of Heaven opens unto us, that no
baptism without Heaven open; and so that baptism is *de cœlo,*
Lu. 20. 4. *non ab hominibus,* "from Heaven, not of men." So was it
By a door open. here, so it is to be holden for ever. 2. And "from Heaven;"
not *clanculum,* as Prometheus is said to get his fire, but
ἀνεῳχθῆναι, orderly, by a fair door set open, in the view of
much people; for all that were present saw the impression in
Rev. 4. 1. the sky. Which door was not mured up again; for we find
Mat. 16. 19. it still open, and we find that the keys were made and given
To shew our right to enter Heaven. of it, after this. 3. And all this, that there might not only
be a passage for these down, but for us up. For Heaven-gate,
ab hoc exemplo, doth ever open at baptism; in sign, he that
new cometh from the font, hath then right of entrance
in thither. Then, I say, when by baptism he is cleansed;
Rev. 21. 27. for before, *nihil inquinatum,* "nothing defiled can enter
there."

3. Out of Heaven open, what. Out of Heaven now open somewhat is seen, and somewhat
heard. 1. Seen: a dove descend—the apparition. 2. Heard:
Tu es Filius Meus—the voice. Under one, the testimony *visûs*
Ps. 48. 8. *et vocis,* 'of hearing and sight' both: that *sicut audivimus sic*
et vidimus, that "as we see we hear;" and back again, as we
hear, see; which is as much as can be to make full faith.

The apparition. 1. "The Holy Ghost." 1. The apparition. Wherein the points are six: 1. "The
Holy Ghost." First, that Person; for the Person by Whom
Christ was conceived, by the same it was most convenient
Christians should also be. But to go higher: the Person
That was author of *genesis* "the generation," meetest to be
Author likewise of "regeneration." The same Person, and in
the same element—the element whereof all were made, and
2 Pet. 3. 5, 6. wherewith all were destroyed after; that with the same all
should be saved again, the water itself now becoming the
1 Pet. 3. 20, 21. Ark—the drowning water, the saving ark, as St. Peter noteth.
That as then by His moving on the waters He put into them
Joh. 3. 5. a life and heat to bring forth, so now by His coming down
Tit. 3. 5. upon them, He should impregnate them to a better birth.
Symbol. Nicen. That as His title is, the Lord and Giver of life, He might be
the Giver of true life, that is, eternal life, whereto this life of
ours is but a passage of entry, and not otherwise to be accounted of.

2. "The Holy Ghost came down;" that is to say, in His 2. "Came down."
sign or symbol, the dove. Otherwise, the Spirit of God neither goes up nor comes down, It is every where, beneath as Ps. 139. 7.
well as above; but by a familiar phrase in Scripture, what
the dove did that represented Him, that is He said to do.

3. "Came down upon Him;" which is a decree yet further 3. "Upon Him."
than in Genesis. There He did but "move or flutter over Gen. 1. 2.
the waters"—enough for that effect then: here He cometh
nearer, lights and abides upon Him; which argues a greater Joh. 1. 33.
work in hand. And which argues too, a greater familiarity
to grow between the Spirit and our nature; for a bird, we
know, is familiar, when it doth so light upon one, and stay
too. But all this He doth, not to make Him to be aught, but
to shew Him only to be. Upon us when He comes, it is to
confer something. Not so upon Him: from the first minute
of His Conception, He had the Spirit without measure. To Joh. 3. 34.
confer nothing; only to declare that this was He That to
John's water-baptism should have power to add the Holy
Ghost, and so make it His own for ever after.

4. "Upon Him in a bodily shape." For His coming being 4. "In a bodily shape."
to bear witness to John and to all, that this was He; convenient it was He should appear, and so have "a bodily shape," Lu. 3. 22.
to come into the face of the court, and there to be seen and
taken notice of, as witnesses use to be. And one end it was,
why His baptism was set at the time when all the people's
was; that so all the people might see, and so take notice of
the Holy Ghost, and indeed of the whole Trinity.

5. What shape then? of what creature? All things quick 5. In the shape of a fowl.
in motion, as angels, as the wind, whereto He is elsewhere
compared, are set forth with "wings"—"the wings of the Ex. 25. 20. Isa. 6. 2.
wind." Of one with wings then, as most apt to express the Joh. 3. 8. Ps. 18. 10.
swiftness of His operation in all His works; but specially
in this. None of the other kind of creatures, though never
so light of foot, can sufficiently set forth the quickness of His
working. He goes not, He flies, He; *nescit tarda molimina:*
that He doth, He is not long in doing; therefore, *in specie*
volatilis, 'in the shape of a thing flying.'

6. And among those of that kind, in the shape of "a 6. "In the shape of a dove."
dove," as fittest for the purpose in hand. Not so much for
that it is noted to love the "waters," well, specially clear Cant. 5. 12.

SERM. VIII. waters, as these now be after Christ hath purified them. That is not all; but indeed special choice is made of it, to set forth to us the nature and properties of the Holy Ghost, which have many ways resemblance with those of this creature.

1. Noah's dove, for the olive-branch. Gen. 8. 11. And I will not go to Pliny for them, nor to any heathen writer of them all. For the word of God, the word of God hath sufficient. To that we will hold us.

There, the first dove we find, is Noah's dove with the olive-branch in her bill, a sign of peace—"peace," which is

Rom. 8. 23. Gal. 5. 22. the very "first fruits of the Spirit." It is Tertullian's note this; that as after the deluge, the world's baptism as it were, the first messenger of peace was the dove, so is it here again just: after Christ's baptism, the deluge or drowning of that which indeed drowned the world, that is, of sin, the very same apparition of the dove, and with another manner of peace than that; but with peace in both.

2. David's dove for the colour. Ps. 68. 13. Jer. 12. 9. 2. Next have you David's dove, for the colour, *pennæ columbæ deargentatæ*, with "feathers silver-white," to note *candor columbinus*, white as a dove, not "speckled" as a bird

Solomon's, for the eye. Cant. 1. 15; 4. 1, 5, 12. of divers colours. And to the same effect, Solomon's spouse for the eye; three several times there said to have *oculus columbarum*, "eyes single and direct as a dove," not leering as a fox, and looking divers ways. *Oculos columbinos*, not *vulpinos*.

3. Esay's dove, for the voice. Isa. 38. 14. 3. Then Esay's dove, for the voice, *gemebat ut columba;* in patience mourning, not in impatience murmuring or repining; for *carmen amatorium*, her voice. And no other voice to be heard from the first Church. Now they are ashamed of that voice; it is not *gemebant ut columbæ*, but

Isa. 59. 11. *rugiebant ut ursi;* to groan they begin like bears, but not mourn any more like doves. No such voice to be heard now, that put to silence.

4. Christ's dove, for bill and claw. Mat. 10. 16. 4. And last, our Saviour Christ's own, that is, innocent as doves; "harmless," both for bill and claw, not bloody or mischievous. Who ever heard of a dove that drew blood, or did any mischief to any?

The properties of the Spirit, like. Acts 2. 1. Now, *qualis species, talis Spiritus*, 'such as the shape was, such is the Spirit;' and these all four properties of it in the Holy Ghost. 1. He a Spirit That loves ὁμοθυμαδὸν, men "of

one accord"—as was seen this day. 2. *Et Qui fugit fictum,* Wis. 1. 5.
cannot abide these new tricks, mere fictions indeed, feigned by feigned Christians; party propositions, half in the mouth and half in the mind. 3. And when He speaketh, "speak- Rom. 8. 26.
eth for us with sighs not to be expressed,"—such is His love, and so earnest. 4. And hurts none, not when He is a dove, as here; no, not when He was fire, but *innoxius* Acts 2. 3.
ignis even then.

2. And as these in the Spirit That came down, so the very same in Christ, upon Whom He came down. The Spirit a dove, and Christ "a lamb"—like natured both: what the one in the kind of beasts, the other in the kind of fowls; that we may see the Holy Ghost lighted right. *Super quem?* "Upon whom shall My Spirit rest?" saith God, in Esay; and He answers, *super humilem,* "on the humble and meek." "Humble and meek?" Why, *discite a Me,* "learn" both those "of Me," saith Christ, for I am both, and a Master professed in them both. 2. The Spirit of the olive-branch, that is peace, on Him. For *Ipse est pax nostra,* "He is our peace." 3. The Spirit That loves *omni fictione carentes,* that is, all that hate equivocations, on Him; for "never was there guile found in His mouth." 4. And lastly, the harmless Spirit on Him; for He was so too, would "not break a bruised reed," He, "nor quench flax, though it did but smoke." Do no hurt at all.

The like properties were in Christ. Joh. 1. 29. Isa. 57. 15. Isa. 66. 2. Mat. 11. 29 Eph. 2. 14. 1 Pet. 2. 22. Mat. 12. 20.

3. Thirdly, what He is in Himself; and what He is, on Whom He descended, that, the very same, such for all the world, doth He make His Church, *homogenea cum homogeneis,* like nature, like properties, *per omnia.* And it is not so much, all this, to shew His nature, as to shew His operation; nor what He found in Christ, as what He works in Christians; *quâ animâ animet, quos spiritus spiret,* 'what soul He puts into them, what manner spirit He makes them of,' that He even endues them with these qualities of the bird whose shape He made choice of to present Himself in. *Quâ specie* in Him; shews *quo spiritu* in us. To wit, it makes them peaceable, to love singleness in meaning, speaking and dealing, to suffer harm, but to do none.

The like properties to be in Christians.

Peace, sincerity, patience, and innocency, these be the Ps. 68. 13.
"silver feathers" of this Dove; they be virtues, and which is

SERM. VIII. more, *virtutes baptismales*, 'the very virtues of our baptism,' no Christian to be without them; to be found in all, where *humidum radicale* of baptism is not clean dried up.

Christ's Church a dove. Cant. 2. 14; 5. 2, 12; 6. 9. The Holy Ghost is a Dove, and He makes Christ's Spouse, the Church, a Dove; a term so oft iterate in the Canticles, and so much stood on by Saint Augustine and the Fathers, as they make no question, No Dove, no Church. Yea, let me add this: St. Peter, when the keys were promised, never but then, but then I know not how, he is called by a new Mat. 16. 17. name, and never but there, "Bar-jona," that is, *Filius columbæ*. But so he must be, if ever he will have them. And his successors, if they claim by any other fowl, painted keys they may have, true keys they have none. For sure I am, *extra Columbam*, out of that Church, that is, such and so Joh. 20. 22, 23. qualified, *non est Columba*, there is no Holy Ghost, and so no remission of sins. For they go together, "Receive the Holy Ghost, whose sins ye remit, they are remitted."

They that make the Church no dove. And what shall we say then to them that will be Christians, that they will, and yet have *nihil columbæ*, nothing in them of the dove; quit these qualities quite, neither bill, nor eye, nor voice, nor colour; what shall we say? This, that Jesuits they may be, but Christians, sure, they are none. No dove's eye, fox-eyed they; not silver-white feathers, but party-coloured; no *gemitus columbæ*, but *rugitus ursi;* not the bill or foot of a dove, but the beak and claws of a vulture; no Judg. 9. 15. spirit of the olive-branch, but the spirit of the bramble, from whose root went out fire to set all the forest on a flame.

A chasing away of this dove. Ye may see what they are, they even seek and do all that in them lies to chase away this Dove, the Holy Ghost. The Dove, they tell us, that was for the baby-Church, for them to be humble and meek, suffer and mourn like a dove. Now, as if with Montanus they had yet *Paracletum alium*, 'another Holy Ghost' to look for, in another shape, of another fashion quite, with other qualities, they hold these be no qualities for Christians now. Were indeed, they grant, for Acts 2. 41, 46. the baby-Christians, for the "three thousand" first Christians, this day; poor men they did all *in simplicitate cordis*. And so too in Pliny's time: harmless people they were, the Christians, as he writes, did nobody hurt. And so to Tertullian's, who tells plainly what hurt they could have done, and yet would do none. And so all along the primitive Churches, even down to Gregory, who in any wise would have no hand in any man's blood. But the date of these meek and patient Christians is worn out, long since expired; and now we must have Christians of a new edition, of another, a new-fashioned Holy Ghost's making; Gregory the Seventh, St. Gregory the Seventh forsooth, who indeed was the first that, instead of the Dove, hatched this new misshapen Holy Ghost, and sent him into the world.

For do they not begin to tell us in good earnest, and speak it in such assemblies and places as we must take it for their tenet, that they are simple men that think Christians were to continue so still; they were to be so but for a time, till their beaks and talons were grown, till their strength was come to them, and they able to make their party good; and then this dove here might take her wings, fly whither she would, "and take her ease;" then a new Holy Ghost to come down upon Ps. 55. 6.
them that would not take it as the other did, but take arms, depose, deprive, blow up; instead of an olive-branch, have a match-light in her beak or a bloody knife.

A calling into question of this shape of a dove.

Methinks, if this world go on, it will grow a question problematic, in what shape it was most convenient for the Holy Ghost to have come down? Whether as He did, in the meek shape of a dove? or whether, it had not been much better He had come in some other shape, in the shape of the Roman eagle, or of some other fierce fowl *de vulturino genere?*

Sure, one of the two they must do; either call us down a new-fashioned Holy Ghost, and institute a new baptism—and if both these new, I see not why not a new Christ too—or else, make a strange metamorphosis of the old; clap Him on a crooked beak, and stick Him full of eagle's feathers, and force Him to do contrary to that He was wont, and to that His nature is.

But lying men may change—may, and do; but the Holy Ghost is *unus idemque Spiritus,* saith the Apostle, changes 1 Cor. 12. 4.
not, casts not His bill, moults not His feathers. His qualities at the first do last still, and still shall last to the end, and no other notes of a true Christian, but they.

It is rather like to prove true that Samuel long since said,

SERM. VIII. "Rebellion is as the sin of witchcraft;" for witches, they say, begin, are initiated, with renouncing of their baptism. And
A renouncing of this baptism. sure, these prick prettily towards it; for, say what they will, they be in the way to it, when they plainly disclaim and
1 Sam. 15. 23. renounce His qualities That was the author of it. For these baptismal virtues, they that take them away do what in them lieth to take away Holy Ghost, and baptism, and all.

I know they will fly to the fire of this day and say, He came in another shape. True, but for another purpose. It was to make Apostles, that; not Christians, as this here. Christians are made in a cooler element; and we have no Apostles to make now. God send us to make good Christians, to yield no worse souls to God than this dove here did so many hundred years together, till new Jesuits came up, and old Jesuits went down.

But, give them their fire, it will do them small pleasure, it will not light them a match, nor give fire to their train.
Acts 2. 3. When it came, that, it did no hurt; "it sat upon them all," but not so much as singed any one of them. Let them shew this fire ever blew up any. True, it gave them courage—they needed it, they were to undertake the whole world—but
Acts 5. 29. within the bounds of modesty, still "we ought to obey God rather than man;" not in saucy and traitorous terms, of
Isa. 59. 11. *old hats or rotten figs. Non est vox columbæ hæc—rugitus ursi*, rather.

In a word, this was none of Elias' fire; and you remember,
Lu. 9. 54, 55. they that harped upon that string, Who said to them, "You know not what spirit you are of;" not, what shape appeared
Gen. 8. 7. at your baptism; not Noah's "raven," that delights in dead carcases, but his dove. That shape came down upon Christ; the same comes down upon all that are baptized with His baptism, and are inspired with the same Spirit That He was. This for the apparition.

4. The voice. Now to the voice. *Accedit verbum ad elementum.* The dove was but a dumb show, and shews what was done in us; the voice, that speaks plainly, and declares what is done for us in our baptism. The dove, what the Spirit makes us the voice, from whom the Father takes us.

We saw Christ's humility before, in yielding to be baptized. This heavenly oracle here pronounced of Him, is in a sort a reward for His former Humility. There He was among a rabble of sinners, even in the midst of them. One, that had seen Him so, would have taken Him for none other. This dove, and this voice from Heaven, testifying so great things of Him—no sinner, no servant, but the very Son of God, His love, His joy, the *in Quo,* for Whom we all fare the better—this so honourable an elogy makes full amends for that. He lost nothing by His humility. No more did the Baptist, by his *non sum dignus* neither. That hand which he held not worthy to touch His shoe, was dignified to touch His head, and to pour water on it. Thus they both of them fulfilled righteousness, and both of them had a glorious reward for it.

1. First the Holy Ghost's coming, then the voice.

But first mark. Till the Spirit is come, the voice comes not: all depends on this day's work, the Holy Ghost's coming. He is the *medius terminus,* between Christ in Jordan and the Father in Heaven. He it is That makes the Father speak. the *Tu,* that is, *Tu super Quem Spiritus, Tu es Filius.* "Thou," that is, "Thou, on Whom the Spirit in this shape comes [Joh.1.33.] down, Thou art My Son:" that to go before. So was it in Genesis. "The Spirit moved upon the face of the waters," Gen. 1.2, 3 and then *et Dixit Deus;* but no *dixit Deus* before the Spirit be there first.

2. This voice, not for Christ, but for us. Joh. 12. 30.

Then, that *non propter Me vox ista,* as Christ elsewhere saith, "This voice came not for Him," but for us. Spoken to Him indeed, but to Him, not in His own, but sustaining our persons. It were fond to imagine otherwise, that this voice, or any of the rest, He needed for Himself. Either to have Heaven opened to Him;—it was no time shut. Or the Holy Ghost come down to Him: as God, the Holy Ghost proceeded from Him; as man, He proceeded from the Holy Ghost, they never parted company. Least of all the voice, *Tu es Filius;* who knew not that? It was said and sung long before, in the Psalm, "Thou art My Son." Ps. 2. 7. So all were for us, voice and all. Indeed, His whole baptism is not so much His as ours.

The meaning of "Thou art my Son." Gal. 3. 27.

The meaning is, "Thou," Christ, in their persons, art this. "Thou art;" and for Thy sake, all that are in Thee, all that by baptism have put Thee on, all and every of them are to Me, as Thou Thyself art; *filii, dilecti, complacentes.*

Will ye see what is in them? In *filii* first.

SERM. VIII. 1. "Enemies" we were. Now are we no enemies, but in league with Him, "in the new" league or "covenant," never to be altered as the former was. 2. So may we be, and yet "strangers" still. Nay 2. no "strangers," but naturalized now, and of "the commonwealth of Israel." 3. And that may we be too, and yet foreigners though, and no citizens, without the franchise. Yes, 3. now enfranchised also, and "citizens with the Saints." 4. Well, though of the city, not of the family though. Yes, 4. *domestici Dei*, "of His very household," now. 5. Of His household? so we may, and yet be but servants there. Nay, 5. no "servants" now, but "sons," by virtue of this *Tu es Filius*. So many degrees do we pass, ere we come to this *Filius*. Go forward now. 6. All sons are not beloved—Ham was not. Sons and beloved sons, a new degree, a sixth. 7. And yet again, all we love we take not pleasure in. Even beloved sons offend sometime, and so please not. The father, in the fifteenth chapter after, loved his wild riotous son but too well; yet small pleasure took he in him or his courses. But *complacitum est*, the seventh, that makes up all; a son, a beloved son, his father's delight and joy, there is no degree higher. And such are we by baptism made to God in Christ, through "the renewing of the Holy Ghost."

Rom. 5. 10. Heb. 8. 9. Eph. 2. 12, 19. Joh. 8. 35. Gal. 4. 7. Gen. 9. 25. Lu. 15. 20. [Tit. 3. 5.]

The change of the style from *servus*. Ex. 20. 2.

Filii. This is a new tenour now, the old style is altered. The voice that came last from Heaven before, ran thus; *Ego sum Dominus*, and that infers *Tu es servus*—that is the best that can be made of it. But here now it is *Tu es Filius*, and that necessarily infers *Ego sum Pater*; for *hæc vox patrem sonat*, 'this is a father's voice' to his child. A great change; even from the state of servants, as by creation and generation we were, and so still under the law, into the state of "sons," as now we are, being "new creatures" in Christ, regenerate and translated into the state of "grace wherein we stand."

Gal. 4. 5. 2 Cor. 5. 17. Rom. 5. 2.

The rise from a sinner to an heir.

And not only a great change, but a great rise also. At the first, we were but washed from our sins, there was all; but here, from a baptized sinner to an adopted son is a great ascent. He came not down so low, but we go up as high for it. For "if sons, then heirs," saith the Apostle—so goes the tenour in Heaven; "heirs," and "joint heirs" of Heaven, "with Christ," that is, for the possession and fruit of it, full

Rom. 8. 17.

every way as Himself; and this He brings us to, before He leaves us.

We speak much "of adoption:" would you know when it was, where, and by what words? Why now, here it is; these the very adopting words, by them the act of adoption actually executed. This, the very feast of adoption. A feast therefore, to be held in high account with us, as high as we hold this, to be the adopted children of God. Rom. 8. 15. Gal. 4. 5.

But we must remember, not only what we are, but *in Quo* all this; to whom we owe it all, that is, to Christ, the true natural Son. In Him it is, and out of Him it proceeds to come to us. "In Whom I am well pleased."

The Fathers do ponder this, *in Quo,* to good purpose; that it is not, *Qui placet,* Who pleases me well, or, which is all one, with Whom I am well pleased—yet so He might have said—but "in Whom." And that is more than both. Who pleases Me, or with Whom I am well pleased, goeth no further than Himself, His own person; but, "in Whom," that is, for Whose sake, with others. To Whom I bear such favour, as not only Himself pleaseth Me; but in Him, and for Him, others please me also. "In Whom" more than with Whom.

Again; if it had been *Qui,* it had shewed but what by nature He is, but this *in Quo* sheweth to what end He was sent—to be the *in Quo,* to bring all this about; even that in Him, the Son beloved, and well pleasing, we that neither were sons, but servants and those but bad ones neither; nor beloved, but full unlovely; and in whom no pleasure at all, displeasure rather; that in Him we might be received to grace, and made by adoption what He Himself is. Who, or with Whom. "In Whom" His nature. His end.

The *in Quo,* what we are in Him, we shall best conceive by the *sine Quo,* what we are without Him. For *sine Quo,* but that He with the people, none of all these had come to them. Heaven shut still, no dove seen, no *Tu es Filius* ever heard. We had "rotted" away in our sins without baptism, "the evil spirit" had seized on us instead of the Holy Ghost; no sons, but "cast out, with the evil servant, into utter darkness." "In Whom" best seen by without Whom. Joel 1. 17. 1 Sam. 16. 14. Mat. 25. 30.

But *in Quo,* God so highly well pleased with Him as at the very contemplation of Him, but turning to Him, and beholding Him, He lays down all His displeasure, and is pleased to Ps. 84. 9.

SERM. VIII.

accept us, and our poor and weak obedience; and further, to be so pleased with it as even to reward it also; *in Quo complacitum est.*

A turning from baptism to the Eucharist.

Complacitum est; and here baptism leaves us, and would God there we might hold us, and it might never be, but *complacitum est.* But when we fall into sin, specially some kind of sin, we put it in hazard; for He is not, He cannot then be well pleased with us. How then? His favour we may not finally lose, and to baptism we may not come again. To keep this text in life, *complacitum est,* "it hath pleased" the Holy Ghost, as He applied Christ's blood to us in baptism one way, so out of it to apply it to us another way, as it were in supplement of baptism. In one verse they be both

1 Cor. 12. 13. set down by the Apostle; 1. *in uno Spiritu baptizati,* 2. *in uno Spiritu potati.* And whom He receiveth so to His table to eat and to drink with Him, and every one that is well prepared He so receiveth, with them He is well pleased again certainly. On this day of the Spirit, every benefit of the Spirit is set forth and offered us, and we shall please Him well in making benefit of all. Specially of this, the only means to renew His complacency, and to restore us thither, where our baptism left us.

The same voice the second time for us also.

I end—only this: this voice, it came once more. Two several times it came. 1. Once here at His baptism, 2. and again, after, at His transfiguration in the mount; where He was not only said to be, but then and there shewed to be, in

Mat. 17. 2. glory, as the Son of God indeed—"His face like the sun, His raiment like the lightning." And both of these pertain to us likewise. The first is spoken of us, when by baptism we are received into Him, for the possibility and hope we have of it thereby. But time will come when this second shall be

Phil. 3. 21. spoken, and verified of us likewise. What time "He shall change our vile bodies and make them like to His glorious body," as then it was, and as now it is; the Heaven shall open, and He receive both them and us to eternal bliss, where we in Him, and He in us, shall have a perfect complacency for ever, &c.

A SERMON

PREACHED BEFORE

THE KING'S MAJESTY AT GREENWICH,

ON THE NINETEENTH OF MAY, A.D. MDCXVI., BEING WHIT-SUNDAY.

JOHN xx. 22.

And when He had said that, He breathed on them, and said unto them, Receive the Holy Ghost.

Hæc cum dixisset, insufflavit, et dixit eis, Accipite Spiritum Sanctum.

[*And when He had said this, He breathed on them, and saith unto them, Receive ye the Holy Ghost.* Engl. Trans.]

EVER, as upon this day, somewhat we are to speak of the Holy Ghost and of His coming. And this also, here, is a coming of the Holy Ghost. And not a coming only, but a coming in a type or form, by the sense to be perceived; and so suits well with the coming of this day. For so this day He came.

Three such comings there were in all. Once did our Saviour receive the Holy Ghost, and twice did He give It. Give It on earth in the text; and after, from Heaven on the day[1]. So three in all. At Christ's baptism, "It came upon Him in the shape of a dove." At this feast It came upon His Apostles in the likeness of "tongues of fire." And here now, in this comes breath-wise, having breath for the *symbolum* to represent it. The tongues have been heard speak, the dove hath had his flight, and now this third of breath falleth to be treated of.

Luke 3. 22.

[1 of Pentecost.]

Acts 2. 3.

It is the middle, this, of the three. That of baptism went before it; that serves to make Christians. This of breath comes after it; this serves to make them, as I may say, Christian-makers; such, whose ministry Christ would use to

SERM. IX. make Christians; make them, and keep them; make them so by baptism, and keep them so by the power of the keys here Joh. 20. 23. given them in the next words, for the remission of sins.

And as it follows well after that of baptism, so it goes well before the other of tongues. For first, there must be breath, before there be tongues wherewith the speech is to be framed. The tongues but fashion the breath into certain sounds, which without breath they cannot; and when that fails, their office is at an end. So, first breath; then, tongues. And another Joh. 7. 39. reason yet. It is said in the seventh chapter, "the Spirit was not to be given them till Christ was glorified;" and "glorified" He was in part, at His Resurrection. Then therefore given in part, as here we see. But much more glorious after, by His Ascension; given therefore then, in fuller measure. Here but a breath, there a mighty wind. Here but *afflatus*, 'breathed in;' there *effusus*, 'poured out'—the Spirit proceeding gradually. For by degrees they were brought on, went through them all, all three. Baptized, and so made Christians; breathed into, and so made what we are; had the tongues sit on them, and so many Apostles properly so called.

But three things may be said of this here; 1. that of all the three comings, first, it is the most proper. For most kindly it is for the Spirit to be inspired, to come *per modum spirationis*, in manner of breath; inasmuch as It hath the name *aspirando*, and is indeed Itself *Flamen*, the very breath, as it were, proceeding *a Patre Filioque*. So one breath by another.

2. Then the most effectual It is. For in both the other, the dove, and the tongues, the Spirit did but come, but light upon them. In this It comes, not upon them, but even into them, intrinsically. It is *insufflavit*, It went into their inward parts; and so made them indeed θεοπνεύστους, 'men inspired by God,' and that within.

3. And last it is of the greatest use. Both the other were but for once: baptism but once for every one; the tongues but once for all. This is *toties quoties;* so oft as we sin, and that is oft enough, we need it. Look how oft that, so oft have we use of this breath here breathed, as the next verse sheweth, for *peccata remiseritis*, the remission of sins.

The sum. Now what is here to do, what business is in hand, we cannot but know, if ever we have been at the giving of Holy Orders. For by these words are they given, "Receive the Holy Ghost; whose sins ye remit, &c." Were to them, and are to us, even to this day, by these and by no other words; which words had not the Church of Rome retained in their ordinations, it might well have been doubted, for all their *Accipe potestatem sacrificandi pro vivis et mortuis,* whether they had any Priests at all, or no. But as God would, they retained them, and so saved themselves. For these are the very operative words for the conferring this power, for the performing this act.

Which act is here performed somewhat after the manner of a Sacrament. For here is an outward ceremony, of breathing, *instar elementi;* and here is a word coming to it, "Receive ye the Holy Ghost." That some have therefore yielded to give that name or title to Holy Orders. As indeed the word Sacrament hath been sometime drawn out wider, and so Orders taken in; and othersome plucked in narrower, and so they left out, as it hath pleased both the old and the later writers. And if the grace here given had been *gratum faciens,* as in a Sacrament it should, and not, as it is, *gratis data,* but in office or function: and again, if the outward ceremony of breathing had not been changed, as it hath plainly, it had been somewhat. But being changed after into laying on of hands, it may be well questioned. For we all agree there is no Sacrament but of Christ's own institution; and that neither matter nor form He hath instituted, may be changed.

Yet two parts there be evidently: 1. *insufflavit,* and in it 2. *dixit;* 1. "He breathed," and 2. "He said." Of these two then, first jointly, and then severally. From them jointly, two points. Of the Godhead of our Saviour first; and then of the proceeding of the Holy Ghost from Him. The division. I.

Then severally. First *insufflavit,* and in it three points; II.
1. Of the breath, and the symbolizing of it with the Holy Ghost. 2. Secondly, of the parties: He that breathed, Christ; they that breathed into, the Apostles. 3. And last of the act itself; *sufflavit,* "breathing," *insufflavit,* "breathing into" them. After of *dixit,* "the word said," 1. *Accipite,* "of the receiving." 2. Then of the thing received, which is *Spiritum,* "the Spirit." And not every, or any Spirit, but *Sanc-*

SERM. VI. *tum,* "the Holy Ghost." And because that may be received many ways, which way of them It is here received.

I. Of the two parts jointly.

We proceed first jointly out of both, and begin with matter of faith. Two articles of it; 1. The Godhead of Christ, 2. The proceeding of the Holy Ghost from the second Person.

1. The Godhead of Christ: *Dixit.*

The first, rising out of the two main parts; for as *insufflavit* argues His manhood, so *dixit* doth His Godhead—His saying, "Receive the Holy Ghost;" for *hæc vox hominem non sonat,* no man of himself can so say. *Verus homo qui spirare,* true man, by His breathing. *Verus Deus Qui Spiritum donare,* 'true God, by His bidding them take, and so giving them the Holy Ghost.' To give that gift, to breathe such a breath, is beyond the power of men or Angels, is more than any can do save God only.

For that we say them also in our Ordering, the case is far different. We say them not as in our own, but as in His Person. We bid them from Him receive it, not from ourselves. This point will again fall in afterwards.

2. The proceeding of the Holy Ghost.

Next we argue for the Holy Ghost's proceeding from Him; and that evidently. For as He gave of His breath, so did He of the Spirit. The breath from His humanity, the Spirit from His Deity. The breath into their bodies, the Spirit into their souls. The outward act teaches visibly without, what is invisibly done within.

Thrice was the Holy Ghost sent, and in three forms. 1. Of "a dove;" 2. Of breath; 3. Of "cloven tongues." From the Father as a "dove;" from the Son as breath; from both as "cloven tongues"—the very cleft shewing they came from
Lu. 3. 22. two. At Christ's baptism the Father sent Him from Heaven, "in shape of a dove." So from the Father He proceedeth. After, at His rising here, Christ by "a breath" sends Him into the Apostles. So, from the Son He proceedeth. After, being received up into the glory of His Father, He together with the Father—the Father and He both sent Him
Acts 2. 3. this day down, "in tongues of fire." So, from both He pro-
Joh. 15. 26. ceedeth. "Proceeding from the Father," *totidem verbis,* and proceeding here from the Son, *ad oculum,* 'really.' Not in words only; we may believe our eyes, we see Him so to proceed. Enough to clear the point, *a Patre Filioque.*

This proceeding, as it holds each other-where, so specially

in this of *quorum remiseritis*, the remission of sins, for which it is here given. For in that, of all other, the Holy Ghost proceeds from Christ most properly. For inasmuch as the remission of sins came from and by Christ, very meet it was He should have the dispensing of His own benefit, and the Remitter of sins proceed from Him also. One by the blood out of His veins, the other by the Spirit out of His arteries; and He, as bleed the one, so breathe the other. He That should seal the acquittance, from Him That laid down the money. That howsoever in other respects, in this sure from Him, and none but Him, the Holy Ghost to proceed. With reference to *quorum remiseritis.*

Proceed; and proceed by way of breath, rather than any other way; that to be the ceremony or *symbolum* of it.

I proceed now to the second combination, of "breath," and the Holy Ghost. It is required in a sign, that choice be made of such a one, as near as may be, as may best suit and serve to express that is conferred by it. Now, no earthly thing comes so near, hath such alliance, is so like, so proper for it, as the breath—I make two stands of it: 1. breath and the Spirit; 2. Christ's "breath," and the Holy Spirit. II. Of the parts severally. 1. Of *insufflavit:* The breath.

First, breath is air; and air, the most subtile and, as I may say, the most bodiless body that is, approaching nearest to the nature of a spirit, which is quite devoid of all corporeity. So in that it suits well. 1. The symbolizing of breath with the Spirit.

But we waive all, save only the two particulars of the Holy Ghost, set down in the Nicene creed. 1. One, "The Lord and giver of life;" 2. the other, "Who spake by the Prophets."

For first, the Spirit giveth life; and breath is the immediate next means subordinate to the Spirit, for the giving it —for the giving it, and for the keeping it, both. Giving: at the first, "God breathed into Adam" *spiraculum vitæ*, and straight *factus est in animum viventem*, "he became a living soul." Keeping; for if the breath go away, away goes the life too; both come, both go together. Gen. 2. 7.

And as the Spirit it is That quickeneth, so it is the Spirit That speaketh, evidently. Dead men be dumb, all. And the same breath that is *organum vitæ*, is *organum vocis*, too. That we live by, we speak by also. For what is the voice, but 2. Of Christ's breath with the Holy Ghost.

SERM. IX. *verbum spiritu vestitum,* 'the inward word, or conceit, clothed with breath of air,' and so presented to the sense of hearing? So *vehiculum Spiritûs* it is, in both.

And, as the breath, and the spirit, so Christ's breath, and the Holy Spirit. *Accipite spiritum,* gives to man the life of nature; *Accipite Spiritum Sanctum,* to the Christian man, the life of grace.

And the speech of grace too. For this breath of Christ was it by which the "cloven tongues," after, had their utterance. He spake by the Prophets; and the Apostles, they were but as trumpets, or pneumatical wind-instruments; they were to be winded. Without breath they could not;
Rom. 10. 18. no breath on earth able so to wind, that their "sound might go into all lands, be heard to the uttermost parts of the earth." None but Christ's so far—so that was to be given them. This breath hath in it, you see, to make a good symbol for the Spirit; and Christ's breath, for the Holy Spirit.

It may be, at large, all this; but how for the purpose it is here given for, remission of sins? What hath breath to do with sin? not nothing. For if you be advised, *per afflatum spiritûs nequam* it came, 'by an evil breath;' and *per afflatum Spiritûs Sancti* it must be had away. The breathing, the pestilent breath of the serpent, that blew upon our first parents, infected, poisoned them at the first: Christ's breath entering, cures it; and, as ever His manner is, by the same way it was taken, cures it—breath, by breath.

For the better conceiving of the manner how, ye may call to mind that the Scriptures speak of sin sometime, as of a
Isa. 44. 22. frost; otherwhile, as of a mist, or fog, that men are lost in, to be dissolved, and so blown away. For as there be two proceedings in the wind, and according to them two powers
Job 37. 9. observed by Elihu; forth of the south, a wind to melt and dissolve; out of the north, a wind to dispel and drive away: and as in the wind of our breath there is *flatus,* 'a blast,' which is cooler, and which blows away; and *halitus,* 'a breath,' that is warm, and by the temperate, moist, heat, dissolves; answerable to these, there is in this breath of Christ a double power conferred, and both for the remission of sins; and that, in two senses, set down by St. John. 1. The one of *ne peccetis,* astringent, to keep men from sin,

and so *remissio peccandi;* 2. the other, *siquis autem peccaverit,* "but if any do sin," to loose men from it, and so remissio peccati. Shewing them the way, and aiding them with the means to clear their conscience of it, being done; remitting that is past, making that more remiss that is to come; as it were to resolve the frost first, and turn it into a vapour; and after it is so, then to blow it away. 1 Joh. 2. 1.

And other reasons there be assigned, why thus in breath, apt and good: 1. one, to shew the absolute necessity, the great need we have of this power, how evil we may be without it. As evil as we can be without our breath, so evil can we be without a means for remission of our sins; *οὐ μᾶλλον πνέομεν τὸν ἀέρα*—it is St. Basil. The Christian man, he lives not by the air that he breathes, more than he doth by it. Our own breath not more needful, than this breath of Christ's; "His loving-kindness" in it "better than the life itself," and we no longer to draw our breath, than to give Him thanks for it. This for the necessity. 1. Ps. 63. 3.

A second, to shew the quality, which is mild, of the same temper the breath is. No *spiritus procellæ,* which some would think perhaps more meet, to carry all before it. They know not the Holy Ghost, that so think; they remember not the dove. Violence in His work He could never skill of, His course hath ever been otherwise. And not His only, but Theirs, Whom He proceeds from. 2.

Let them but go to Elias' vision, and inform themselves of this point. There came first "a boisterous whirlwind," such an one as they wish for—but no God there. After it, a rattling "earthquake;" and after it, crackling flashes of fire:—God was in none of them all. Then came a soft still voice:—there comes God. God was in it, and by it you may know where to find Him. 1 Kings 19. 11, 12.

And as God, so Christ. How comes He? "He shall come down like the dew in a fleece of wool," and that is scarce to be heard. "He, He shall not roar nor cry, nor His voice be heard out into the street." How unlike them and their novices, that will needs bear His name! Ps. 72. 6. Isa. 42. 2.

And how the Holy Ghost comes here, we see. None of all the Three Persons, but in gentle mild manner.

It is against them, this, that take delight in these bluster-

SERM. IX. ing spirits, and think them the only men, cannot skill of any other. No river they, but the great Euphrates, that
Isa. 8. 6. runs with a huge noise. The waters of Shiloh run too soft for them. Well, the waters of Shiloh though the Prophets commend to us; and to them Christ sends us, and it is
Ps. 46. 4. they, when all is done, whose "streams shall make glad the City of God." This is sure, no spiritual grace is ever so truly wrought by these spirits, that take so on, till they be out of breath. The air indeed they beat, the heart they pierce not. The quiet calm breath shall do it to better pur-
Eccl. 7. 6. pose than these, that crackle like "thorns under a pot." This breath will thither, to the heart directly; and sin never
Job 4. 16. so kindly dissolved, as by *audivi vocem in silentio*—that way.
[Acts 2. 2.] Tell me not of the "mighty wind," and the "fire;" that was for Apostles. We are none; three degrees lower. And that wind they used very seldom though—once or twice perhaps; but this they used continually. I report me to their Acts, and to their Epistles. For the wind comes but at times, but the breath is continually at all times. And this is sure, when the "mighty wind" and the "fire" came, it may be St. Peter used it once or twice, and St. Paul as oft; but this of the breath they used more, nay most of all, and by it did more good than by the other.

For as for this, let it not trouble you that it is but breath, and breath but air, and so, one would think, too feeble; as indeed, what feebler thing is there in man than it? the more feeble, the more fit to manifest His strength by. For, as weak in appearance as it is, by it were great things brought to pass. By this puff of breath, was the world blown round about. About came the philosophers, the orators, the emperors. Away went the mists of error, down went the idols and their temples before it.

2. Of the party. 1. From Whom: Christ.

Which gives us a good passage from the breath to the Breather, Him That is the nominative case to *insufflavit*.

For we are not to look to the breath altogether, but somewhat too, from whose mouth it comes, whose breath it is. And Christ's it is. He it is That gives the vigour and virtue to it. The touch of His finger, the breath of His mouth, virtue goes from it, sin cannot stand before it, it sends it going, blows it away like a little dust.

Take this with you too. It is not Christ's breath, any breath of His, but His breath now after His rising, and so His immortal breath. A mortal He had, which He breathed out, *quando emisit Spiritum,* when "He gave up the Ghost" upon the cross. All the while He was mortal, He held His breath. Till it was more than so, He breathed it not, till it had in it the vigour and power of immortality; which neither sin can endure, but scatters straight, nor "the man of sin," for he also shall be "consumed with the breath of His mouth." Otherwise, unless it be this of Christ's, there is nothing in our breath to work this effect; not in any man's, to thaw a frost, or to scatter a mist. The soil of sin is so baked on men, they so hard frozen in the dregs of it, our wind cannot dissolve it. Hear the Prophet, after he had been long blowing at the sins of the people. "The bellows," saith he, "are burnt, the iron of them consumed, the founder melts in vain; for all his blowing, the dross will not away." But I, saith God, let Me take it in hand, let Me but blow with My wind, and "I scatter thy transgressions as a mist, and make thy sins like a morning cloud to vanish away." Turn we then to Him, Whose divine power, Whose immortal breath can do it; do it by Himself, and if by Himself, by others also into whom He will inspire it; whom in that regard the Prophet calleth God's "mouth," to "separate the precious from the vile."

Christ after His resurrection. Mat. 27. 50. [2 Thes. 2. 3.] 2 Thes. 2. 8. Jer. 6. 29. [Isa. 44. 22.] Jer. 15. 19.

Which being of His breath immortal, doth further shew, both that there is nothing in this power but pertains rather to another life than to this mortal of ours, even to that which is the life of the world to come; and that it shall never die, this power, but hold as long as there is any sin to be forgiven. Had it been His mortal breath, we might have feared the failing; now shall it never fail, so long as there is any to open his mouth to receive it. It is His immortal breath.

This for the Party from Whom. Now for *in eos,* those 'into whom' it came. Much bound we are to our Blessed Saviour for thus sending, and to the Holy Ghost for being thus sent, for seeing us furnished with a power we so much stand in need of. For sinning as we do, and even running ourselves out of breath in it, and the "wages" of that being eternal "death," what case were we in but for this breath!

2. The parties to whom. Rom. 6. 23.

SERM. IX. I see not how we should do without it. To say, therefore,
with them in the Gospel, *Benedictus Deus Qui dedit talem*
Mat. 9. 8. *potestatem*, "Blessed be God for sending such a power," for
sending it at all.

1. To men. But then secondly, *Qui dedit talem potestatem hominibus*, that "He gave it to men." For, as the Son of Man, He gave it; and as Man, to men He gave it—to the Sons of men upon earth, that we need not send up and down, and
Rom. 10. 6. cast "who shall go up to Heaven for us and fetch it thence." That if an Angel should come to us, as to Cornelius there did, he hath not this power to impart, he can but bid us
Acts 10. 32. "send to Joppa for Peter." He hath it, men have it, Angels have it not.

2. *In eos*, to simple men. *In eos*, is more yet; to men, and to such men, such simple men, for so they were, God wot, a full unfit and indisposed
Acts 4. 13. matter to receive it. "Idiots," it is St. Luke's word, "men utterly unlearned." And of no spirit or courage at all—the breath but of a damsel quailed the best of them. *Probatur Deus per Apostolos*, say the Schoolmen; if there were nothing else, 'His very Apostles were enough to prove Him to be
Ps. 8. 1, 2. God.' For "O Lord our Saviour, how excellent is Thy Name in all the world! Thou That out of the mouths of those that were little better than babes hast ordained Thy praise, and stilled Thine enemies," and put them all to silence.

3. To sinful men. But there is a worse matter than that. Not only "simple," but, which is farther off yet, "sinful men" they were.
Lu. 5. 8. Take their own confessions. St. Peter's:—"Go forth from
1 Tim. 1. 15. me, O Lord, for I am a sinful man." St. Paul's:—"Sin-
Jas. 3. 2. ners, whereof I am the chiefest." St. James':—"In many things we offend all," puts himself in the number of them
1 Joh. 1. 8. that offend many times. St. John's:—"If we (I for one) say we have no sin," what then? we are proud, there is no humility? No; but "we are liars, and there is no truth in us." Even to such, to sinners, this power given to forgive sins; to them that for sin were in fear themselves to be condemned.

Nay, which is not lightly to be passed by, all this done even at the very time when they were scarce crept out of their sin but three days before committed, in so wretchedly forsaking Him; and some more than so, and after would scarce believe He was risen, when they saw Him;—that even then did He thus breathe on them, and made them that He did. Now blessed be God, That at all gave such power to men, to such men, such simple men, such sinful men, *insufflavit in eos;* to secure us, be the men what they will that have received it, no sin of man shall make the power of God of none effect. This for *in eos.*

To the act now. It is first *sufflavit,* "breathed," and that 3.
was to keep correspondence with His Father at the first. By Of the act. *Sufflavit.*
breathing into Adam, the Father gave the soul, the Author of the life natural. *Ad idem exemplum,* the Son here by breathing gives the Holy Ghost, the Author of the life spiritual; the same passage, and the same ceremony held by both.

But *insufflavit* is more, "breathed it in," "into them." *Insufflavit.*
This *in* shews it pertains within, to the inward parts, to the very conscience, this act. His breath goeth, saith Solomon, *ad interiora ventris,* and His word with it, saith the Apostle, Prov. 18. 8.
"through, to the division of the soul and spirit." Thither Heb. 4. 12.
goeth this breath, and thither is farther than man can go. For howsoever the acts and exercises of outward jurisdiction may be disposable, and are disposed by human authority, yet this not so of *forum internum.* Somewhat there is still that comes from Christ, and none but Christ; somewhat that as it comes higher, so it goes deeper, than any earthly power whatsoever. This inward inspiring brings us to Christ's Deity again. The kings of the nations, send they can, and give power they can, but inspire they cannot. Array whom [Esth. 6. 8—11.]
they will, as Ahasuerus, with rich attire, arm them at all points, *induere,* in that sense; but not endue the soul with gifts and graces within, not arm their minds with valour and virtue; at leastwise, not with *virtus ex alto.* Only God, [Lu. 24. 49.]
whom He calls, He gives the inward talents to; and Christ, whom He sends, He sends His Spirit into. This argueth God plainly, and so Christ to be God.

Always this *insufflavit* shews, as wherewith He would do it, the Spirit, so what it is He would work, work upon, and renew. For if we be "renewed in the spirit of our minds," Eph. 4. 23.
the whole man will be so, straight upon it. There is no indication to that; for the change of the whole man is a certain sign the Spirit is come into us. As of Saul it is

SERM. IX. written, when the Spirit came into him he was "changed into quite another man," no more the same Saul he was [1 Sam. 10. 6, 9—11.] before; a new, another Saul then. Which holds not only in particular men, but even in the whole world. For when this breath came into it, *in interiora,* it was cast in a new mould presently, and did even wonder at itself, how it was become Christian. For the outward rigorous means of fire, imprisonment, of the whip, of the terror of the magistrate's Joh. 19. 10. sword; Pilate's, "Have not I power to crucify Thee, and power to loose Thee?" These daunt men, make them astonished, make *metum peccati,* 'fear to commit the outward act of sin.' But *odium oportet peccandi, non metum facias,* 'if sin shall ever truly be left, it must come of hatred, not of fear.' So it goes away indeed. And there it is, sin must be met with: if ever it shall rightly be put away, the spirit to be searched, and inward hearty compunction wrought there. And that is by this breath of Christ piercing thither, or not at all. So much for the *in.*

Et dixit. And now to *et dixit.* The words be three, the points according, three too. 1. *Accipite,* it is to be received; 2. *Spiritum,* a Spirit it is, that is to be received; 3. *Sanctum,* and that Spirit is the Holy Ghost. 4. Whereto we add, the Holy Ghost after what manner, for there be more than one.

1. *Accipite.* *Accipite* agrees well with breath. For that is received, we open our mouths and draw it in; our *systole* to meet with His *diastole.*

For this *accipite,* it is certain that at the breathing of this breath the Spirit was given. He gave them what He bade them take, He mocked them not. They received the Holy Ghost then, and, if ye will, really. Yet was not the substance of His breath transubstantiate into that of the Holy Ghost—none hath ever imagined that—yet said He truly, *Accipite Spiritum;* and no less truly in another place, *Accipite corpus.* Truly said by Him, and received by them in both. And no more need the bread should be changed into His body in that, than His breath into the Holy Ghost in this. No, though it be a Sacrament, (for with them both are so,) yet as all confess, both truly said, truly given, and truly received, and in the same sense without any difference at all. This for them.

For us, *accipite* sheweth first, it comes from without, it grows not within us; a breath inspired, not a vapour ascending; not *educta e*, but *inducta in*. It is not *meditati sumus sicut aranea*, "we spin it not out of ourselves, as the spider doth her web." It is not *concipite*, but *accipite*; "receive it" we do, 'conceive it' we do not. It were too fond to conceive, seeing our breath is made of air, and that is without us, that the Spirit should be made of any thing that is within us.

1. *Accipite*, not *concipite*.

Ps. 90. 9. [Vulg.]

We say again; it is *accipite*, not *assumite*. *Assumit, qui nemine dante accipit*, 'He assumes, that takes that is not given.' But *nemo assumit honorem hunc*, "this honour no man takes unto him, or upon him, till it be given him." As *quod accipitur non habetur* in the last, so *quod accipitur datur* in this. And both these are against the voluntaries of our age, with their taken-on callings. That have no *mitto vos*; unsent, set out of themselves. No *accipite*, no receiving; take it up of their own accords, make themselves what they are; sprinkle their own heads with water, lay their own hands on their own heads, and so take that to them which none ever gave them. They be *hypostles*—so doth St. Paul well term them, as it were the mock-apostles—and the term comes home to them, for υἱοὶ ὑποστολῆς they be, *filii subtractionis* right; work all to subtraction, to withdraw poor souls, to make them forsake the fellowship, as even then the manner was. This brand hath the Apostle set on them, that we might know them and avoid them.

2. *Accipite*, not *assumite*.

Heb. 5. 4.

Heb. 10. 39.

We may be sure, Christ could have given the Spirit without any ceremony; held His breath, and yet sent the Spirit into them without any more ado. He would not; an outward ceremony He would have, for an outward calling He would have. For if nothing outward had been in His, we should have had nothing but enthusiasts—as them we have notwithstanding; but then we should have had no rule with them; all by divine revelation: into that they resolve. For sending, breathing, laying on of hands, have they none. But if they be of Christ, some must say, *Mitto vos*; sent by some, not run of their own heads. Some say, *Accipite*: receive it from some, not find it about themselves; have an outward calling, and an outward *accipite*, a testimony of it. This for *accipite*.

SERM. IX. *Spiritum.* A spirit it is that is to be received, and much is said in this word spirit, it stands as opposed to many.
Spiritum. "The Spirit." Joh. 6. 63. 1. "The spirit" and "flesh"—Christ. 2. "The spirit" and "the letter"—St. Paul. 3. "The Spirit" and "the soul"—
2 Cor. 3. 6. St. Jude. 4. "The spirit" and "the mind." 5. "The spirit"
Jude 19. Eph. 4. 23. and a habit. 6. The Spirit and a sprite, *Spiritus* and *spectrum.* 7. The Spirit and Hero's *pneumatica,* that is some artificial motion or piece of work with gins within it. To all these.

1. Not "the flesh." 1. Not "the flesh," saith our Saviour; and if not the flesh, not any humour, for they are of the flesh. Neither they, nor their revelations, profit ought to this work.

2. Not "the letter." Jer. 23. 28. 2. Not the letter, saith St. Paul, not the husk or chaff; we have too much of them every day. *Quid paleæ ad triticum?* they rather take away life than give it; a handful of good grain were better than ten load of such stuff.

3. Not the soul. 3. Nor *animales Spiritum non habentes,* saith Jude, "men that have souls only;" and they serve them but as salt to keep them, that they rot not. They too have no part or fellowship in this business; "mere natural men, no spirit in them at all." Somewhat there is to be in us, more than a natural soul. *Φύσις* is one thing, *φύσησις* is another. Some inspiring needs, somewhat of *accipite.*

4. Not the mind. [Eph. 4. 23.] 4. Nay, saith St. Paul, "be ye renewed in the spirit of your minds." For the mind is not all, nor men to think so; if they once have got true positions, true maxims in their mind, then all is well. If the spirit be not also renewed, it is nothing.

5. Not a habit. 5. The spirit, not a habit gotten with practice, and lost again with disuse, as are the arts and moral virtues, against
[Lu. 24. 49.] the Philosophers. For though this be virtue, yet is it not *virtus ex alto,* this. No habitual, but a spiritual virtue, this.

6. Not a sprite. 6. *Spiritus, non spectrum;* for that is a flying shadow void of action—doth nothing. But the Spirit, the first thing we
Gen. 1. 2. read of It, It did hover and hatch and make fruitful the waters, and fit to bring forth something of substance.

7. Not Hero's *pneumatica.* 7. And last, which is by writers thought to be chiefly intended, Christ's Spirit, not Herò's *pneumatica;* not with some spring or device, though within, yet from without; artificial, not natural; but the very *principium motûs* to be within. Of ourselves to move; not wrought to it by any

gin or vice, or screw made by art. Else we shall move but while we are wound up, for a certain time, till the plummets be at the ground, and then our motion will cease straight. All which, but these last specially, are against the *automata*, the *spectra*, the puppets of religion, hypocrites. With some spring within, their eyes are made to roll, and their lips to wag, and their breast to give a sob: all is but Hero's *pneumatica*, a vizor, not a very face; "an outward show 2 Tim. 3. 5.
of godliness, but no inward power of it at all." It is not *accipite Spiritum.*

Thirdly, I say it would be known further, what Spirit; *Spiritum Sanctum.* for *accipite* it may be, somewhat they may have taken, it may be a Spirit. But whatsoever it is, it is not yet home, unless *Sanctum* come too. *Sanctum* it would be, if it be right. To be a man of spirit, as we call them that be active and stirring in the world, will not serve here, if that be all. I have formerly told you, there is a *Spiritum* without *Sanctum;* Spirit and Holy are two things. Two other spirits there be besides; and they well accepted of, and in great request. 1. One which St. Peter calls the "private" 2 Pet. 1. 20.
spirit; 2. the other, that St. Paul calls "the spirit of the 1 Cor. 2. 12.
world." Which two will consort well together for their own turns, and for some worldly end, but neither of them with this; for they are opposed to the Holy Ghost, both.

1. Not *spiritum suum.* The "private" spirit first. And are there not in the world somewhere, some such as will receive none, admit of at no hand no other Holy Ghost but their own ghost, and the idol of their own conceit, the vision of their own heads, the motions of their own spirits, and if you hit not on that that is there in their hearts, reject it, be it what it will; that make their breasts the sanctuary; that in effect say with the old Donatist, *Quod volumus Sanctum est,* 'that they will have Holy is Holy,' and nothing else? Men, as the Apostle speaks of them, causeless "puffed up with their fleshly Col. 2. 18.
mind?" His word is to be marked: φυσίωσις there, φύσησις here; *inflati* they, *afflati* these. They puffed up, these inspired. If it make to swell, then it is but wind, the Spirit doth it not; *inspirat, non inflat.* The word is *insufflavit;* there is in *sufflavit* a *sub* that beareth downward, and carries not up. So *Spiritum Sanctum* is not *spiritum suum.*

SERM. IX.

2. Nor *spiritum mundi.*

Nor *spiritus mundi* is not *Spiritus Christi.* Else doth St. Paul wrong to oppose them. It is too sure such a spirit there is as "the spirit of the world," and that the greatest part of the world live and breathe and move by it; and that it doth well sometimes, but without any reference to God, or Christ, or Holy Ghost. For even the acts they do of religion, are out of worldly reasons and respects. Herod's reason—*videns quia placeret populo,* saw the world would that way. Demetrius' reason—*periclitatur portio nostra,* it may prove dangerous to their worldly estate. The Shechemites—Oh set forward that point of divinity, for then "all they have is ours." See we not whence this wind blows, from what spirit this breath comes? From *spiritus mundi* plainly. And I know not how, but as if Christ's mouth were stopped and His breath like to fail Him, the world begins to fare as if they had got a new mouth to draw breath from; to govern the Church as if *spiritus Prætorii* would do things better than *Spiritus Sanctuarii,* and man's law become the best means to teach the fear of God, and to guide religion by. In vain then is all this act of Christ's; He might have kept His breath to Himself. But it will not so be. When all is done, the Spirit must come from the Word, and the Holy Ghost from Christ's mouth, That must do this, govern the Church. Thither we must for *Sanctum,* even to the Sanctuary, and to no other place.

[1 Cor. 2. 12.] Acts 12. 3. Acts 19. 27. Gen. 34. 23.

And a certain note it is, this, to discern the Holy Spirit of God from the spirit of what you will. From Christ It comes, if It be true; He breathes It. It cannot but be true, if It come from Him, for He is "the Truth." And as the Truth, so the "Wisdom" of God; that, if It savour of falsehood or folly, It came not from Him, He breathed It not. But His breath shall not fail, shall ever be able to serve His Church, without all the ἰδία ἐπίλυσις of the private spirit, and without all the additaments of *spiritus mundi.* And if we gape after them, we make this *accipite* more than needs; and if we do so, I know not what shall become of us.

Joh. 14. 6. 1 Cor. 1. 30. [2 Pet. 1. 20.]

Which way It is received.

But the Holy Ghost may be received more ways than one. He hath many *spiramina;* πολυτρόπως "in many manners" He comes; and *multiformis gratia* He comes with. He and

[Heb. 1. 1.] 1 Pet. 4. 10.

they carry the name of their cause; and to receive them, is to receive the Spirit. There is a *gratum faciens*, the saving grace of the Spirit, for one to save himself by, received by each without respect to others; and there is *gratis data*, whatever become of us, serving to save others by, without respect to ourselves. And there is *χάρις διακονίας*, "the grace of a holy calling;" for it is a grace, to be a conduit of grace any way. All these, and all from one and the same Spirit. 2 Cor. 8. 4.

That was here conferred, was not the saving grace of inward sanctimony; they were not breathed on to that end. The Church to this day gives this still in her ordinations, but the saving grace the Church cannot give; none but God can give that. Nor, the *gratis data* it is not. That came by the tongues, both the gift of speaking divers languages, and the gift of ἀποφθέγγεσθαι, speaking wisely, and to the purpose; and, we know, none is either the holier, or the learneder, by his ordination. [Acts 2. 4.]

Yet a grace it is; for the very office itself is a grace. *Mihi data est hæc gratia*, saith the Apostle in more places than one, and speaks of his office and nothing else. The Apostleship was a grace, yet no saving grace. Else, should Judas have been saved. Clearly then, it is the grace of their calling, this, whereby they were sacred, and made persons public, and their acts authentical; and they enabled to do somewhat about the remission of sins, that is not of like avail done by others, though perhaps more learned and virtuous than they, in that they have not the like *mitto vos*, nor the same *accipite* that these have. To speak with the least: as the act of one that is a public notary is of more validity than of another that is none, though it may be he writes a much fairer hand. And this, lo, was the grace here, by breathing conferred to them: of *Spiritum*, a spiritual; of *Sanctum*, a holy calling; and derived from them to us, and from us to others, to the world's end. Eph. 3. 8, &c. [Gal. 1. 15,16; 2. 9.]

But take heed we suck no error out of this word "holy," no more than we do out of the word "anointed." When time was, it was shewed, the anointing was no inward holiness, or ability to govern by, but the right of ruling only. So here, it is no internal quality infused, but the grace only of their spiritual and sacred function. Good it were, and much to be wished, they were holy and learned all; but if they be not, their office holds good though. He that is a sinner himself, may remit sins for all that, and save others he may, though himself be not saved; for it was not *propter se* he received this power, to absolve himself, but, as the next word is, *quorumcunque*, any others whosoever.

Some ado we have to pluck this out, but out it must. For an error it is, an old worn error of the Donatists; and but new dressed over by some fanatical spirits in our days, that teach in corners; one that is not himself inwardly holy, cannot be the means of holiness to another. And where they dare too, that: One that is not in state of grace, can have no right to any possession or place. For they of right belong to none, but to the true children of God; that is, to none but to themselves.

Fond, ignorant men! for hath not the Church long since defined it positively, that the baptism Peter gave was no better than that which Judas; and exemplified it, that a seal of iron will give as perfect a stamp, as one of gold? That as the carpenters that built the ark wherein Noah was saved, were themselves drowned in the flood; that as the water of baptism that sends the child to Heaven, is itself cast down the kennel; semblably is it with these: and they that by the word, the Sacraments, the keys, are unto other the conduits of grace, to make them fructify in all good works, may well so be, though themselves remain unfruitful, as do the pipes of wood or lead, that by transmitting the water make the garden to bear both herbs and flowers, though themselves never bear any. And let that content us, that what is here received, for us it is received; that what is given them, is given them for us, and is given us by them. Sever the office from the men; leave the men to God to whom they stand or fall; let the ordinance of God stand fast. This breath, though not into them for themselves, yet goeth into and through every act of their office or ministry, and by them conveyeth His saving grace into us all.

But, lest we grow discontent, that some do receive it, and that we all do not so—for this being the feast of the Holy Ghost, and of receiving it, it may grieve any of us to go his way, and not receive it—I will shew it is not so. For though as this breath we cannot all, and as the fiery tongues much less—these are but for some set persons; yet I will shew you a way, how to say *accipite Spiritum* to all, and how all may receive It.

And that is by *accipite corpus Meum.* For *accipite corpus,* Mat. 26. 26.
upon the matter, is *accipite Spiritum,* inasmuch as they two never part, not possible to sever them one minute. Thus, when or to whom we say *accipite corpus,* we may safely say with the same breath *accipite Spiritum;* and as truly every way. For that body is never without this Spirit: he that receives the one, receives the other; he that the body, together with it the Spirit also.

And receiving it thus, it is to better purpose than here in the text it is. Better, I say, for us. For in the text it is received for the good of others, whereas here we shall receive it for our own good. Now whether is the better, remission of sins, to be able to remit to others, or to have our own remitted? To have our own, no doubt. And that is here to be had. To the stablishing of our hearts with grace, to the cleansing and quieting our consciences. Which spiritual grace we receive in this spiritual food, and are
made to drink (I will not say of "the spiritual rock," but) 1 Cor. 10. 4.
of the spiritual "vine" that followeth us, which "vine" is Joh. 15. 5.
Christ. To that then let us apply ourselves. Both are received, both are holy, both co-operate to the "remission of
sins." The "body"—Matthew the twenty-sixth. The Spirit, Mat. 26. 28.
here evidently. And there is no better way of celebrating [Mat. 26. 26.]
the feast of the receiving the Holy Ghost than so to do, with receiving the same body that came of It at His birth, and that came from It now at His rising again.

And so receiving it, He That breathed, and He That was breathed, both of Them vouchsafe to breathe into those holy mysteries a Divine power and virtue, and make them to us the bread of life, and the cup of salvation; God the Father also sending His blessing upon them, that they may be His blessed means of this thrice-blessed effect! To Whom all, three Persons, &c.

A SERMON

PREACHED BEFORE

THE KING'S MAJESTY AT HOLYROOD-HOUSE, IN EDINBURGH,

ON THE EIGHTH OF JUNE, A.D. MDCXVII. BEING WHIT-SUNDAY.

LUKE iv. 18, 19.

The Spirit of the Lord is upon Me, because He hath anointed Me, that I should preach the Gospel to the poor; He hath sent Me, that I should heal the broken-hearted, that I should preach deliverance to the captives, and recovering of sight to the blind, and that I should set at liberty them that are bruised,

And that I should preach the acceptable year of the Lord.

[*Spiritus Domini super Me, propter quod unxit Me; evangelizare pauperibus misit Me, sanare contritos corde,*

Prædicare captivis remissionem, et cæcis visum, dimittere confractos in remissionem, prædicare annum Domini acceptum, et diem retributionis. Latin Vulg.]

[*The Spirit of the Lord is upon Me, because He hath anointed Me to preach the Gospel to the poor; He hath sent Me to heal the broken-hearted, to preach deliverance to the captives, and recovering of sight to the blind, to set at liberty them that are bruised,*

To preach the acceptable year of the Lord. Engl. Trans.]

SERM. X.

WE are fallen here upon Christ's first sermon, preached at Nazareth; and upon His very text. This I have read you was His text, taken out of the Prophet Esay, the sixty-first chapter, and first verse. There was no fear Christ would have ranged far from His matter, if He had taken none; yet He took a text, to teach us thereby to do the like. To keep us within; not to fly out, or preach much, either without, or besides the book.

And He took His text for the day, as is plain by His ap- Lu. 4. 21.
plication, "This day is this Scripture fulfilled in your ears." "This day this Scripture." Our Master's Scripture was for the day; so would ours be.

For the day; and for the present occasion. For among the writers it is generally received, that when our Saviour made this sermon, that year it was with the Jews the year of jubilee. And that therefore He told them, it was fulfilled in their ears, they might hear the trumpets sound to it. If it were so, this text of "the acceptable year" was as apposite as could be chosen. That, it seems, He turned the book purposely to find it; out of it to speak to them of the true jubilee.

And if it were so, the year of jubilee, it was the last that ever they held. For before fifty years came about again, they were swept away—Temple, sacrifice, jubilee, people and all. The jubilees of the Law then failing, being come to their period, comes Christ with His; with a new jubilee of the Gospel, the true one, as whereof those of theirs were but shadows only, which jubilee of the Gospel was "the acceptable year" which Esay here meant.

Will ye then give me leave now to say of this text of our The sum.
Saviour's, This Scripture suits well with this day, is fulfilled in it three ways? In the 1. coming of the Spirit; 2. the end for which, to send to proclaim; 3. the matter which, to proclaim a jubilee; 4. and a fourth I will add, of a present occasion, as fit every way.

First, it is of the coming of the Spirit. And this day the 1.
Spirit came. And the coming of the Spirit, in the text here upon Christ, was the cause of the coming of the Spirit, this day, upon the Apostles. From this coming upon Him, came the coming upon them; *super Petrum, super Jacobum, super* all the rest; upon them, and upon us all, from this *super Me.* All our anointing are but drops from His anointing; all our missions and commissions, but quills, as we say, out of this commission here, *misit Me. Sicut misit Me, Ego mitto vos.* He Joh. 20. 21.
sent Me, "as He sent Me, I send you." By that, and by no other commission, did they, or do we, or shall ever any come.

SERM. X. That first, and this second; the *misit* and the *ad.* Why came the Spirit on Christ? To send Him. Send Him to

2. what? *Ad evangelizandum.* And why came the Spirit on the Twelve this day, but for the very same end? And it came therefore for the purpose, in the shape of tongues. It is the office of the tongue to be a trumpet, to proclaim. It serves for no other end.

3. To proclaim what? "The acceptable year of the Lord," that is, the jubilee. Now fifty is the number of the jubilee; which number agreeth well with this feast, the feast of Pentecost. What the one in years, the other in days. So that this is the jubilee, as it were, of the year, or the yearly memory of the year of jubilee. That, the Pentecost of years; this, the jubilee of days. These three for the day.

4. And may we not add a fourth from the present occasion? I take it we may; and that not unfit neither, as peculiar to this very year, rather than to any other. There falleth out, lightly, but one jubilee in a man's age. 1. And this present year is yet the jubilee year of your Majesty's life and reign. 2. And this day is the jubilee day of that year. 3. And yet further, if we take not jubilee for the time, but for the joy—for the word jubilee is taken, as for the time of the joy, so for the joy of the time—and so refer it to the late great joy and jubilee, at your Majesty's receiving hither to your Nazareth, the country where you were brought up, which then was fulfilled in your ears; our ears, I am sure, were filled full with it. So that, first and last, the text suits with the day, and both suit well with the present occasion.

To return to our Saviour, Who standing now with His loins girt, ready to go about the errand He came for, as the manner is, He was first to read His commission. This it is, the words I have read, drawn and ready penned for Him long before by the Prophet Esay here, who had the honour to be the registrar of this, and divers other instruments, touching Christ's natures, Person, and offices. And, upon the reading of this, He entered in His office.

II. You may plainly know, it was His inauguration, this, or first entering on His office, by the proclamation following, of opening the gaol, and letting the prisoners go free. So is ever the fashion of princes, to make the joy general, of their coming to their kingdoms: to release those that stand committed; to grant free and general pardons to all that will sue for them; to be at the charge of *missilia,* certain new pieces of coin, to be cast abroad among the people.

Accordingly, were there this day of the Spirit's coming, by one sermon of St. Peter's, three thousand set at liberty that had been captives before under Satan. A largess of new tongues, as it were *missilia,* cast down from Heaven. A general pardon proclaimed, even for them that had been Acts 7. 52.
"the betrayers and murderers" of the Son of God, if they would come in. That it was, indeed, a right day of jubilee. And this is the sum of all.

I. The parts as they lie, are these: 1. First, of the Spirit's The division. I.
being on Christ; 2. anointing Him; 3. sending Him. These three.

II. Then, whereto He was so anointed and sent; to preach II.
the Gospel, or glad tidings, (glad tidings, or Gospel, both are one,) and that even to the poor.

III. Thirdly, whereof the tidings is; of an excellent phy- III
sician, a physician of the heart, one that can cure a broken heart.

IV. Of these hearts. 1. How they came broken first, and IV.
there are three ways here set down. 1. By being captives; 2. by being in a dark dungeon, where their sight was even taken from them; 3. by being there in irons so as they were even bruised with them. Three, able, I think, to break any man's heart alive.

2. Then, how they came cured. And that is by good news. Two proclamations, for κήρυξαι "to proclaim," is twice repeated: 1. One, containing a particular remedy of those three several maladies; 1. of a party, one with a ransom, or redemption for the captives; 2. with an engine, or tool, to knock off their irons; 3. with the keys of the prison, to let them out. And this to begin with. 2. Then, to conclude, with a second proclamation, that makes up all —of a year of jubilee; and so of restitution of them to their former forfeited estates, by God's accepting them to favour, this acceptable time.

This is the sum of Christ's commission here read; and indeed, a brief of His offices, all three. 1. In preaching the

SERM. X. glad news of the Gospel—of His prophecy. 2. In granting pardon, and enlarging prisoners—of His kingdom. 3. In proclaiming a jubilee—of His Priesthood, for that the peculiar of the Priest's office. So all are in, that pertain to Christ. And all, that to Jesus too, Who sheweth Himself Jesus in nothing so much, as in being the physician of a broken contrite heart.

I. Of the Spirit's being on Christ.

We cannot better begin, than with the Blessed Trinity. In the three first words, the three Persons reasonable clear. 1. The Spirit: 2. He, Whose the Spirit—*Domini:* 3. He, on Whom the Spirit, *super Me.*

"The Spirit," that is, the Holy Ghost. He Whose the Spirit, God the Father. He on Whom the Spirit, our Saviour Christ. He, the *super Quem* here.

These three distinct: 1. the Spirit, from the 2. Lord, Whose the Spirit is; 1. the Spirit That was upon, 3. from Him It was upon. Yet all three in one joint concurrence to one and the same work, the jubilee of the Gospel.

"Upon Me," is Christ's Person. But His Person only, according to one of His natures, His human. The Spirit was not upon Him, but as He was man. These three; 1. to be sent, 2. to be anointed, 3. to have a *super Eum,* savour of inferiority, all, to the Sender, Anointer, Superior. And so indeed for us, He became lower than in Himself He was.
Rom. 8. 3. "In the similitude of sinful flesh," had a Spirit to anoint
Phil. 2. 7. Him; *in formâ servi,* had a Lord to send Him about the message here.

But, that Christ suffer not in His honour, we supply; that the Spirit Who is here said to be *Spiritus Domini,* is else-
Rom. 8. 9. where said to be *Spiritus Christi*—"the Spirit of the Father,"
Mat. 10. 20. Gal. 4. 6. and "the Spirit of the Son," both. The Spirit That sent
Joh. 15. 26. Him here, sent by Him elsewhere, "Whom I will send." This sets Him upright again. As the one shews Him to be Man, so the other, to be God. And as God He hath no superior; no Lord to own Him, no Spirit to anoint Him.

And, if I mistake not, a kind of inkling of thus much is even in the very words. The word "Lord" in Esay, is plural; and so more Persons than one, Whose the Spirit is, and from Whom He proceeds. And if you would know how many, in Esay the words be two: so, not a single proceeding from one, but a double from two, as the word is double. St. Basil saith it short, 'Ὡς Θεὸς χορηγεῖ, ὡς ἄνθρωπος δέχεται, 'As God He sends It, as man He receives It.' Upon Him, as man; from Him, as God.

Of Him then, as man, three things here are said: "the Spirit" 1. was "upon" Him; 2. "anointed" Him; 3. "sent" Him. But it is said; "The Spirit is upon Me, because He hath anointed Me;" so as the anointing is set, as the ἕνεκεν οὗ, or cause, why He was upon Him. And then that, His anointing, as the cause, is first in nature. But it cannot be conceived but the Spirit must be also upon Him, to anoint Him; the Spirit is the *Unction:* the Spirit then was upon Him, two several times, for two several ends. 1. To anoint Him; 2. and after He was anointed, to send Him; the second. Of this anointing we are to touch, 1. when it was; 2. with what it was; 3. and how it comes to be termed anointing. 2. His anointing.

When was He thus "anointed?" Not now, or here, first, but long before; even from the very time of His conceiving. When "the Word became flesh," the flesh with the Word, and by means of it with the whole Deity, was "anointed" all over, and by virtue thereof filled with the fulness of all grace. For this we are to hold; that Christ was ever Christ, that is, ever "anointed," from the very first instant of all; He was never un-anointed, not one moment. 1. When was it. Joh. 1. 14.

"Anointed" with what? I have already told you, with the Deity, by virtue of the Personal union of the second Person of the Deity. Why then is the Holy Ghost called the Unction? Why is Christ expressly said to be anointed with the Holy Ghost? why not with the Father as well? 2. With what.

Why not? to retain to each Person His own peculiar, His proper act, in this common work of them all; or, as the Hebrews speak, to keep every word upon his right wheel.

Father, is a term of nature. So to the Father we ascribe what the Son hath by nature. For that He is the Son, is of nature, not of grace.

But that the manhood is taken into God, that was not of nature, but of grace. And what is of grace, is ever properly ascribed to the Spirit. "There are diversities of graces," 1 Cor. 12. 4.

SERM. X. all from the "same Spirit." And the proceeding of grace from it, not as by nature, but *ubi vult*, "blows where it lists"
Joh. 3. 8. freely. All then, of grace, proceeding from the Spirit: accordingly, the conception of Christ's flesh, and the sending it with the fulness of grace, or anointing it, is ascribed to the Spirit.

3. How called anointing. But this enduing with grace, how comes it to be called anointing? for nothing, but for the resemblance it hath with an ointment. An ointment is a composition we know; the ingredients of it, oil and sweet odours. By virtue of the oil
Ps. 109. 18. it soaks even into the bones, saith the Psalm; but it works upon the joints and sinews sensibly, makes them supple and lithe, and so the more fresh and active to bestir themselves. By virtue of the sweet odours mixed with it, it works upon
Ps. 45. 8. the spirits and senses; cheers him and makes him "glad," that is anointed with it. And not him alone, but all that are
Cant. 1. 3. about and near him, *qui in odore unguentorum*, that take delight in his company, to go and to run with him, and all for the fragrant sweet scent they feel to come from him.

Of which two, the oil represents the virtue of the power of the Spirit, piercing through, but gently, like oil. The odours, the sweet comfort of the graces that proceed from the Holy Ghost. Nothing more like. And this for His anointing.

His sending. Now the same Spirit That was thus upon Him at His conception to anoint Him, was even now upon Him again, to manifest, and to send Him. When? at His baptism, a little before. Not secretly, as then at His conception, but in a visible shape upon Him, before a great concourse of
Lu. 3. 22. people, (to shew there ought to be an outward calling) what time the dove laid that, which in it is answerable to our hands, upon Him.

Not to endue Him with aught—that was done before long—but to manifest to all, this was He; this, the party before anointed, and now sent, that they might take heed to Him. It was the Holy Ghost's first Epiphany this, He was never seen before; but Christ's second Epiphany. The other at His birth, or coming into the world; this now at His calling, or sending into the world. That first, to enable Him to His office; this, to design Him to it. By that, furnished for it; by this, sent, severed, and set about the work He came for.

But before we come to the work, let us first reflect a little upon these; they serve our turn, are for our direction. These both were done to Christ, to the end He might teach the Church, that the same were to be on them who in Christ's stead are employed in the same business, *ad evangelizandum.* The Holy Ghost, to be upon them; upon them, to anoint them, and to send them, both; but first to anoint, then to send them. To be, and in this order to be. Unless they be first "anointed," not to be sent; and though never so "anointed," not to start out of themselves, but to stay till they be sent.

The Spirit to be upon them; the same That upon Christ, though not in the same, but in a broad and a large difference, or degree, of being. Upon Him without measure; not so, on us; but on some less—the measure of the hin; on some more—the measure of the ephah; but every one, his homer at least. Some feathers of the dove, as it were, though not the dove itself; not the whole Spirit entire, as upon Him.

On His head the whole box of ointment was broken, which from Him ran down upon the Apostles, somewhat more fresh and full; and ever, the further, the thinner, as the nature of things liquid is; but some small streams trickle down even to us, and to our times still.

This on-being shews itself first, in that which stands first—the anointing.

I shall not need tell you, the Spirit comes not upon us now at our conception in the womb, to anoint us there. No; we behove to light our lamps oft, and to spend much oil at our studies, ere we can attain it. This way come we to our anointing now, by books; this book chiefly, but in a good part also, by the books of the ancient Fathers and lights of the Church, in whom the scent of this ointment was fresh, and the temper true; on whose writings it lieth thick, and we thence strike it off, and gather it safely.

You will mark, the anointing is set for the cause; "The Spirit is upon Me, because He hath anointed Me." Then *sublatâ causâ,* and *a sensu contrario,* the Spirit is not upon

SERM. X. Me, because He hath not anointed Me. Again, "because He hath anointed Me, He hath sent Me." And then it follows, because He hath not anointed me, He hath not sent Me. No speaking of the Spirit's on-being; no talk of sent by Him, without it. Where be they then that say, The less anointing, the more of the Spirit? Indeed, the more blind, the more bold; and so the fitter to go on some other errand perhaps, but not this.

No, no; the Spirit makes none of these dry missions, sends none of these same *inuncti*, such as have never a feather of the Dove's wing, nor any spark of the fire of this day, not so much as a drop of this ointment. You shall smell them straight that have it; "the myrrh, aloes, and
Ps. 45. 8. cassia will make you glad." And you shall even as soon find the others. Either they want odour:—anointed I cannot say, but besmeared with some unctuous stuff (go to, be it oil) that gives a glibness to the tongue to talk much and long, but no more scent in it than in a dry stick; no odours in it at all. Either odours they want, I say, or their odours are not laid in oil. For if in oil, you shall not smell them so for a few set sermons; if they be anointed, not perfumed or washed, for such Divines we have. If it be but some sweet water, out of a casting-bottle, the scent will away soon; water-colours, or water-odours, will not last. But if laid in oil throughly, they will; fear them not. To them that are stuffed, I know all is one; they that have their senses about them, will soon put a difference.

But what? If he be "anointed," then turn him off hardly with no more ado, without stay for any sending at all? Nay, we see here, only anointing served not Christ Himself. He was "sent," and outwardly "sent" besides. Messias He was, in regard of His anointing; Shiloh He was too, in regard of His sending. If you love your eyes, wash them in
Joh. 9. 7. the water of Shiloh, that is by interpretation "sent." Or, to speak in the style of the text, as He was Christ for His
Heb. 3. 1. anointing, so was He an Apostle for His sending. So is He called "the Apostle of our profession," with plain reference to ἀπέσταλκε here, the word in the text.

Unction then is to go before, but not to go alone, mission is to follow; and no man, though never so *peruntus, eo ipso*

to stir, *nisi qui vocatus erit sicut Aaron,* "unless he be called, Heb. 5. 4.
as was Aaron;" unless he be sent, as Christ here was; for
fear of *currebant et non mittebam eos,* in the Prophet; or Jer. 23. 21.
of "How shall they preach unless they be sent? in the Rom. 10. 15.
Apostle. For his life he knew not, if neither Aaron nor Christ, how any might step up without calling, sending, ordaining, laying on of hands: all are one.

And mark well this, that the Holy Ghost came upon Christ alike for both, that there is the Holy Ghost no less in this sending than in the anointing. The very calling
itself is a "grace," expressly so called, Romans the twelfth, Rom. 12. 3.
and Ephesians the third, and in divers places else. Every Eph. 3. 7.
grace is of the Holy Ghost; and goeth ever, and is termed by the name of the Holy Ghost usually. And in this sense the Holy Ghost is given and received in Holy Orders, and we do well avow that we say, "Receive the Holy Ghost."

But we have not all, when we have both these; for shall we so dwell upon anointing and sending, as we pass by the *super Me,* the first of all the three, and sure not the last to be looked after? A plain note it is but not without use, this situation of the Spirit, that He is *super.* For if He be *super,* we be *sub.* That we be careful then to preserve Him in His *super,* to keep Him in His due place, that is, "above." In sign whereof the dove hovered aloft over Christ, and "came down upon Him;" and in sign thereof we submit our heads in anointing to have the oil poured upon, we submit our heads in ordaining to have hands laid upon them. So submit we do, in sign that submit we must; that not only mission, but submission is a sign of one truly called to this business. Somewhat of the dove there must be, needs; meekness, humbleness of mind.

But lightly you shall find it, that those that be *neque uncti neque loti,* 'neither anointed nor scarce well washed;' the less ointment, the worse sending, the farther from this submissive, humble, mind. That above? Nay, any above? Nay, they inferior to none. That above, and they under? Nay, under no Spirit; no *super,* they. Of all prepositions they endure not that, not *super;* all equal, all even at least. Their spirit not subject to the spirit of the Prophets, nor of the Apostles neither, if they were now alive; but bear themselves so high,

SERM. X. do *tam altum spirare,* as if this Spirit were their underling, and their ghost above the Holy Ghost. There may be a sprite in them, there is no Spirit upon them that endure no *super,* none above them. So now we have all we should; unction out of *unxit,* mission out of *misit,* submission out of *super Me.*

II. The end whereto. Forward now. "Upon Me." How know we that? "Because He hath anointed Me." "Anointed," to what end? "To send." "Send" whereto? That follows now. 1. "To bring good tidings." Both whereto and whom to. 1. Whereto? "To bring good tidings." 2. Whom to? "To the poor."

1. Whereto? If the Spirit send Christ, He will send Him with the best sending; and the best sending is to be sent with a message of good news; the best, and the best welcome. We all strive to bear them, we all love to have them brought; the Gospel is nothing else but a message of good tidings. And Christ, as in regard of His sending, an Apostle, the Arch-Apostle, so in regard of that He is sent with, an Evangelist, the Arch-Evangelist. Christ is to anoint: this is a kind of anointing; and no ointment so precious, no oil so supple, no odour so pleasing, as the knowledge of it; 2 Cor. 2.16. called therefore by the Apostle *odor vitæ,* "the savour of life unto life," in them that receive it.

2. "To the poor." 2. Send with this, and to whom? "To the poor." You may know it is the Spirit of God by this. That Spirit it is; and they that "anointed" with It, take care of the poor. The spirit of the world, and they that anointed with it take little keep to evangelize any such, any poor souls. But in the tidings of the Gospel they are not left out; taken in by name, we see: in sending those tidings there is none Acts 10. 34. excluded. "No respect of persons with God." None of nations; to every nation, Gentile and Jew: none of conditions; to every condition, poor and rich. To them that of all other are the least likely. They are not troubled with much worldly good news; seldom come there any posts to them with such. But the good news of the Gospel reacheth even to the meanest. And reaching to them it must needs be general, this news. If to them that of all other least likely, then certainly to all. *Etiam pauperibus* is, as if He had said, even to poor and all, by way of extent, *ampliando.*

But no ways to engross it, or appropriate it to them only. The tidings of the Gospel are as well for "Lydia the purple seller" as for "Simon the tanner;" for "the Areopagite," the judge at Athens, as for "the jailor" at Philippi; for "the elect lady," as for widow "Dorcas;" for the "Lord Treasurer of Ethiopia," as for "the beggar at the beautiful gate of the temple;" for "the household of Cæsar," as for "the household of Stephanas;" yea and, if he will, for "king Agrippa" too.

Acts 16. 14. Acts 10. 6. Acts 17. 34. Acts 16. 30. 2 John 1. Acts 9. 36. Acts 8. 27. Acts 3. 2. Phil. 4. 22. 1 Cor. 1. 16. Acts 26. 27.

But if you will have *pauperibus* a restringent, you may; but then you must take it for "poor in spirit," with whom our Saviour begins His beatitudes in the mount;—the poverty to be found in all. As indeed I know none so rich but needs these tidings; all to feel the want of them in their spirits; no *dicis quia dives sum;* as few sparks of a Pharisee as may be, in them that will be interested in it.

Mat. 5. 3. Rev. 3. 17.

III. The tidings of a Physician for broken hearts.

Well, we see to whom: what may these news be? News of a new physician, *Καρδίατρος, Medicus cordis,* one that can give physic to heal a broken heart. And news of such an one is good news indeed. They that can cure parts less principal, broken arms or legs, or limbs out of joint, are much made of, and sent for far and near. What say you to one that is good at a broken heart? make that whole, set that in joint again, if it happen to be out? So they understood it plainly by their speech to Him after, *Medice cura Teipsum.*

Lu. 4. 23.

The heart, sure, is the part of all other we would most gladly have well. "Give me any grief to the grief of the heart," saith one that knew what he said. *Omni custodiâ custodi cor,* saith Solomon, "keep thy heart above all:" if that be down, all is down; look to that in any wise. Now it is most proper for the Spirit to deal with that part; it is the fountain of the spirits of life, and whither indeed none can come but the Spirit, to do any cure to purpose; that if Christ, if the Spirit take it not in hand, all cures else are but palliative; they may drive it away for a while, it will come again worse than ever. Now then to *medice cura,* as Christ after saith, to this new cure.

Ecclus. 25. 13. Prov. 4. 23.

Of the hearts. 1. How they came broken.

In every cure, our rule is first to look to *de causis morborum,* how the heart can be broken; then after, *de methodo medendi,* the way here to help it.

SERM. X.

How comes the heart broken? The common hammer that breaks them is some bodily or worldly cross, such as we commonly call heart-breakings. There be here in the text three strokes of this hammer, able I think to break any heart in the world.

1 By being captives.

1. Captivity. They be captives first; and captives and caitiffs, in our speech, sound much upon one. It is sure

Ps. 137.1,2.

a condition able to make any man "hang up his harp," and "sit weeping by the waters of Babylon." There is one stroke.

2. In a dark dungeon.

2. There follows another, worse yet. For in Babylon, though they were captives, yet went they abroad, had their liberty. These here are in prison; and in some blind hole there, as it might be in the dungeon, where they see nothing. That, I take it, is meant by "blind" here in the text; blind for want of light, not for want of sight, though those two both come to one, are convertible. They that be blind, say they are dark; and they that be in the dark, for the time are deprived of sight, have no manner use of it at all, no more than a blind man. Now they that row in the galleys yet this comfort they have, they see the light; and if a man

Eccl. 11. 7.

see nothing else, the light of itself is comfortable. And a great stroke of the hammer it is, not to have so much as that poor comfort left them.

3. And "bruised" with irons there.

3. But yet are not we at the worst; one stroke more. For one may be in the dungeon and yet have his limbs at large, his hands and feet at liberty. But so have not those in the text, but are in irons; and those so heavy and so pinching, as they are even τεθραυσμένοι, "bruised" and hurt with them. See now their case. 1. Captives; and not only that, but 2. in prison. In prison; not above, but in the dungeon, the deepest, darkest, blindest hole there; no light, no sight at all. 3. And in the hole, with as many irons upon them, that they are even "bruised" and sore with them. And tell me now, if these three together be not enough to break Manasses', or any man's heart, and to make him have *cor contritum* indeed.

They be; but what is this to us? This is no man's case here. No more was it any of theirs that were at Christ's sermon; yet Christ spake to the purpose, we may be sure.

We may not then take it literally, as meant by the body: Christ meant no such captivity, dungeon, or irons. That He meant not such, is plain. He saith, He was sent to free captives, to open prisons; but He never set any captive free in His life, nor opened any gaol, in that sense, to let any prisoner forth. Another sense then we are to seek. Remember ye not, we began with the Spirit? the business the Spirit comes about is spiritual, not secular. So all these spiritually to be understood. As indeed they are all three applicable to the case of the Spirit, and a plain description of all our states out of Christ, and before He take us in hand.

1. There is captivity there, wherein men are held in slavery under sin and Satan, worse than that we now speak of. St. Paul knew it, speaks of it, and when he hath so, crieth out, "Wretched man that I am, who shall rid me of it?" Rom. 7. 24. Verily, there is no Turk so hurries men, puts them to so base services, as sin doth her captives. Give me one that hath been in her captivity, and is got out of it, *et scit quod dico*, 'he can tell it is true I say.'

2. There is a prison too; not Manasses' prison. But ask David, who never came in any gaol, what he meant when he said, "I am so fast in prison, as I know not how to get Ps. 88. 8. out." And that you may know what prison that was, he cries, "O bring my soul out of prison!" A prison there is Ps. 142. 7. then of the soul, no less than of the body. In which prison were some of those that Christ preached here too; St. Mat- Mat. 4. 16. thew saith, "they sat in darkness and in the shadow of death," even as men in the dungeon do.

3. There are chains too;—that also is the sinner's case, he is even "tied with chains of his own sins," saith Solomon, Prov. 5. 22. with "the bonds of iniquity," St. Peter; which "bonds" are Acts 8. 23. they, David thanks God for breaking in sunder. There need Ps. 116. 16. no other bonds we will say, if once we come to feel them. The galls that sin makes in the conscience, are "the entering Ps. 105. 18. of the iron into our soul."

But you will say, We feel not these neither, no more than the former. No do[1]? Take this for a rule: if Christ heal them that be broken-hearted, broken-hearted we behove to be ere He can heal us. He is *Medicus cordis* indeed; but it

[[1] Not do so?]

SERM. X. is *cordis contriti*. It is a condition ever annexed, this, to make us the more capable; and likewise a disposition it is, to make us the more curable. That same *pauperibus* before, and this *contritis* now, they limit Christ's cure, His cure and His commission both; and unless they be, or until they be, this Scripture is not, nor cannot be fulfilled in us. In our ears it may be, but in our hearts never.

That, as such as come to be healed by His Majesty are first searched, and after either put by or admitted as cause is; so there would be a scrutiny of such as make toward Christ. What, are you poor? Poor in spirit?—for the purse
[Rev.3.17.] it skills not. No, but *dicis quia dives*, "in good case:"
Christ is not for you then, He is sent to the poor. What,
Ps. 119. 70. is your heart broken? No, but heart-whole, "a heart as
brawn:"—then are you not for this cure. In all Christ's dispensatory, there is not a medicine for such a heart, "a heart like brawn," that is hard and unyielding.

Christ Himself seems to give this item, when He applies
Lu. 4. 25, 27. it after. "Many widows," "many lepers," saith He, and so
many sinners. "Elias sent to none but the poor widow of Sarepta;" "Eliseus healed none, but only Naaman," after his spirit came down, was broken. No more doth Christ, but such as are of a contrite heart.

Verily, the case as before we set it down, is the sinner's case, feel he it, feel he it not. But if any be so benumbed, as he is not sensible of this; so blind as, dungeon or no dungeon, all is one to him; if any have this same *scirrhum cordis*, that makes him past feeling, it is no good sign; but it may be, our hour is not yet come, our cure is yet behind. But if it should so continue, and never be otherwise, then were it a very evil sign. For what is such a one's case but,
Prov. 7. 22. as Solomon saith, "as the ox that is led to the slaughter"
without any sense, "or the fool" that goes laughing when he is carried to be well whipped? What case more pitiful?

You will say; we have no hammer, no worldly cross to break our hearts. It may be. That is Manasses' hammer, the common hammer indeed, but that is not King David's hammer, which I rather commend to you; the right hammer to do the feat, to work contrition in kind. The right is the sight of our own sins. And I will say this for it; that I never in my life saw any man brought so low with any worldly calamity, as I have with this sight. And these I speak of were not of the common sort, but men of spirit and valour, that durst have looked death in the face. Yet when God opened their eyes to see this sight, their hearts were broken, yea even ground to powder with it; contrite indeed.

And this is sure; if a man be not humbled with the sight of his sins, it is not all the crosses or losses in the world will humble him aright.

This is the right. And without any worldly cross this we might have, if we loved not so to absent ourselves from ourselves, to be even *fugitivi cordis*, to run away from our own hearts, be ever abroad, never within; if we would but some- Isa. 46. 8.
times *redire ad cor*, return home thither and descend into ourselves; sadly and seriously to bethink us of them, and the danger we are in by them; this might be had, and this would be had if it might be. If not, in default of this (no remedy) the common hammer must come; and God send us Manasses' hammer to break it; some bodily sickness, some worldly affliction, to send us home into ourselves! But sure the Angel must come down and the water be stirred; else Joh. 5. 4.
we may preach long enough to uncontrite hearts, but no good will be done till then.

I have been too long in the cause; but the knowledge of the cause, in every disease, we reckon half the cure. To the healing now.

The word for heal in Esay, where this text is, signifies to bind up. The cure begins with ligature, the most proper cure for fractures, or aught that is broken. Nay, in wounds and all, as appeareth by the Samaritan. The flux is so stayed, Lu. 10. 34.
which, if it continue running on us still, in vain talk we of any healing. It is not begun till that stay and run no longer. The sin that Christ cures He binds up, He stays—to begin with. If He cover sin, it is with a plaister. He covers and cures together, both under one.

This word "broken-hearted" the Hebrews take not as we do: we, broken for sin; they, broken off, or from sin. And we have the same phrase with us; to break one of the evil fashions or inclinations he hath been given to. So to break the heart. And so must it be broken, or ever it be whole.

SERM. X. Both senses: either of them doth well, but both together best of all.

2. How they are cured. [Æschyl. Prom. V. 378. Ed. Cant. 1809.] Acts 10. 6. 32. By good tidings.

This done, now to the healing part. The heathen observed long since: Ψυχῆς νοσούσης εἰσὶν ἰατροὶ λόγοι, 'the soul's cure is by words;' and the Angel saith to Cornelius, of St. Peter, "He shall speak to thee words" by which thou and thy household shall be saved.

And by no words sooner, than by the sound of good tidings. Good news is good physic sure, such the disease may be, and a good message a good medicine. There is power in it both ways. Good news hath healed, evil news hath killed many. The good news of Joseph's welfare, we

Gen. 45.27. see how it even "revived" old Jacob. And the evil of "the

1 Sam. 4. 18. Ark of God taken," it cost Eli his life. Nothing works upon the heart more forcibly either way.

Proclaimed. What are these news, and first how come they? By κηρύξαι they come; no secret-whispered news, from man to man in a corner; no flying news. They be proclaimed, these: so authentical. Proclaimed; and so they had need. For if our sins once appear in their right form, there is evil news certainly; let the devil alone with that, to proclaim them, to preach damnation to us. *Contraria curantur contrariis*, we had need have some good proclaimed, to cure those of his.

Two proclamations here are, one in the neck of another. Of which the former, in the three branches of it, applieth in particular a remedy to the three former maladies, is the topic medicine, as it were; the latter is the panacea, makes them all perfectly whole and sound.

1. The first proclamation. The first proclamation. To the captive first, that there is one at hand with ransom to redeem him. This will make him a whole man.

2. To them in the dungeon; of one to draw them forth thence and make them ἀναβλέψαι, see the light again.

3. To them in chains; of one to strike off their bolts and loose them, to open the prison door and let them go; ἀποστεῖλαι, to make Apostles of them, and send them abroad into the wide world. It is the fruit of Christ's ἀπέσταλκε, this ἀποστεῖλαι, Christ's Apostleship was, and is, to make such Apostles.

Now this is nothing but the very sum of the Gospel: 1. of one coming with a ransom in one hand, to lay down for us the price of our redemption from Satan's captivity. 2. And with "the keys of hell and death" in the other. Keys of two sorts: 1. one to undo their fetters and loose them; 2. the other to open the dungeon and prison-door—both the dungeon of despair, and the prison of the law, and let them out of both. There can be no better news, nor kindlier physic in the world, 1. than word of redemption to captives; 2. than to see the light again, to them in the limbo; 3. than of enlargement to them in bands; but specially, than of a dismission from prison, dungeon, irons and all. And this is proclaimed here, and published by Christ in His Sermon at Nazareth; and was after performed and accomplished by Him, at His Passion in Jerusalem.

Rev. 1. 18.

2. The second proclamation

This is good news indeed, but here comes better. It is seconded with another proclamation, that makes up all. For in very deed, they that by the first proclamation were so released; for all that, and after all that, what were they but a sort of poor snakes turned out of the gaol, but have nothing to take to? Coming thither, they were turned out of all that ever they had. That their case, though it be less miserable, yet is miserable still; the *languor morbi* still hangs upon them.

We lack some restorative for that. Here comes now physic to cure that and make them perfectly well, a second *κηρύξαι*, that they shall be restored to all that ever they had. How so? For hark, here is "the acceptable year," that is, a jubilee proclaimed. And then even of course they are, by force of the jubilee, so to be. The nature of the jubilee was so, you know. Then not only all bond set free, all prisons for debt set open; but beside, all were restored then to their former mortgaged, forfeited, or any ways aliened estates, in as ample manner as ever they had or held them at any time before.

A restitution *in integrum*, a re-investing them in what they were born to, or were any ways possessed of; that if they had sold themselves out of all, and lay in execution for huge sums, as it might be ten thousand talents, then all was quit, they come to all again, in as good case as ever

SERM. X. they were in all their lives. There can be no more joyful news, no more cordial physic, than this. The year of jubilee? why that time so acceptable, so joyful, as it hath even given a denomination to joy itself. The height of joy is jubilee, the highest term to express it is *jubilate;* that goes beyond all the words of joy whatsoever.

And this comes well now; for the jubilee of the Law drawing to an end, and this very year being now the last, Christ's jubilee, the jubilee of the Gospel, came fitly to succeed. Wherein the primitive estate we had in Paradise, we are re-seized of anew. Not the same *in specie,* but as good, nay better. For if for the terrestrial Paradise by the flood destroyed we have a celestial, we have our own again, I trow, with advantage.

"A year" it is called, to keep the term still on foot that formerly it went by. Only this difference: the year there was a definite time, but here a definite is put for an indefinite. This year is more than twelve months. In this "acceptable year" the Zodiack goes never about. On this day of salvation the sun never goes down. For in this the jubilee of the Gospel passeth that of the Law: that held but for a year, and no longer; but this is continual, lasts still. Which is plain, in that divers years after this of
2 Cor. 6. 2. Christ's the Apostle speaks of it as still in *esse;* even then makes this proclamation still, "Behold this is the day, behold now is the acceptable time." Whereby we are given to understand that Christ's jubilee, though it began when
Rev. 14. 6. Christ first preached this sermon, yet it ended not with the end of that year as did Aaron's, but was *Evangelium æternum;* as also *perpetui jubilæi,* everlasting good news of a perpetual jubilee, that doth last and shall last as long as
Acts 3. 21. the Gospel shall be preached by Himself, or others sent by Him, to the end of the world, "the time of restoring all things."

It is called "acceptable," by the term of the benefit that happened on it, which was our acceptation. For then we and all mankind were made, not δεκτέοι, that is, 'acceptable,' but as the word is, δεκτοὶ, that is, actually "accepted," or received by God, out of Whose presence we were before cast. And being by Him so received, we did ourselves re-

ceive again, "the earnest of our inheritance," from which Eph. 1. 14.
by means of the transgression we were before fallen.

There is much in this term, "accepting." For when is one said to be accepted? Not when his ransom is paid, or the prison set open; not when he is pardoned his fault, or reconciled, or become friends; but when he is received with arms spread, as was the lost child in the Gospel, *ad stolam* Lu. 15. 20, 22.
primam—as the term is, out of that place. Three degrees there are in it: 1. Accepted to pardon—that is *συγγνώμη*. 2. Accepted to reconciliation—that is *καταλλαγή*. And further, 3. accepted to repropitiation, that is *ἱλασμὸς*, to as good grace and favour as ever, even in the very fulness of it. They shew it by three distinct degrees in Absalom's receiving. 1. Pardoned he was, while he was yet in Geshur; 2 Sam. 13. 39.
2. reconciled, when he had leave to come home to his own, 2 Sam. 14. 23 33.
house; 3. repropitiate, when he was admitted to the king's presence, and kissed him. That made up all, then he had all again. And that is our very case.

Nay indeed, that is not all. It is more than so: *δεκτὸς* here is in the text of Esay, רצון; and that imports more. For that word is ever turned by *εὐδοκία*, and that is Christ's own acceptation, "In Whom I am well pleased," and the Mat. 17. 5.
very term of it. And he that is so accepted, I know not what he would have more.

This is the benefit that fell at this time; and for this that fell on the time, the time itself it fell on is, and cannot be but, acceptable; even *eo nomine*, that at such a time such a benefit happened to us. And in this respect, it ever hath and ever shall be an acceptable welcome time, this, and holden as a high feast; like as the benefit is high, that befel us on it. *Festum*, 'a feast,' for the pardon; *festum duplex*, for the reconciliation; *festum magis duplex*, for the being perfectly accepted to the favour of God, and by it re-accepting again our prime estate.

Nay last, it is called not only *annus acceptus*, but *annus Domini acceptus*, or *acceptus Domino*: not only, "the acceptable year," but "of the Lord," or "to the Lord;"—for so the Hebrew reads it, with the sign of the dative, as if to God Himself it were so. And to Him so it is, and to His holy Angels in Heaven so it is. For if the receiving any

SERM. X. one contrite sinner, by repentance, be matter of joy to the whole court of Heaven—if the receiving of but one; what
Lu. 15. 10. shall we think of the general receiving of the whole mass, which this day was effected?

Now if to Heaven, if to God Himself it be so; to earth, to us, shall it not be much more, whom much more it concerneth, I am sure? God getteth nothing by it; we do: He is not the better for it; we are: ever the receiver, than the giver. The giver more glory, but the receiver more joy. That if it be the joy of Heaven, it cannot be but the jubilee
Ps. 66. 1. of the earth, even of the whole earth: *Jubilate Deo omnis terra.*

Lev. 25. 9. The jubilee, ever it began with no other sound, but even
Josh. 6. 4. of a cornet, made of the horns of a ram. Of which horns they give no other reason but that it was so in reference to
Gen. 22. 13. the horns of that "ram that in the thicket was caught by the horns," and sacrificed in Isaac's stead, even as Christ was in ours. To shew that all our jubilee hath relation to that special sacrifice, so plainly prefiguring that of Christ's. Which feast of jubilee began ever after the High-Priest had offered his sacrifice, and had been in the *Sancta sanctorum.* As this jubilee of Christ also took place, from His entering
Heb. 9. 11. into the holy places "made without hands," after His propitiatory sacrifice offered up for the quick and the dead, and for all yet unborn, at Easter. And it was the tenth day that; and this now is the tenth day since.

The memorial or mystery of which sacrifice of Christ in our stead is ever *caput lætitiæ*, 'the top of our mirth,' and the
Ps. 116. 13. initiation of the joy of our jubilee. Like as *accipiam calicem salutaris*, our taking "the cup of salvation," is the memorial of our being accepted or received, and taken again to salvation. Wherewith let us also crown this jubilee of ours. That so all the benefits of it may take hold of us; specially the redintegration of the favour of God, and the assurance or pledge of our restitution to those joys, and that jubilee, that only can give content to all our desires, when the time shall
[Acts 3. 21.] come of "the restoring of all things."

A SERMON

PREACHED BEFORE

THE KING'S MAJESTY, AT GREENWICH,

ON THE TWENTY-FOURTH OF MAY, A.D. MDCXVIII., BEING WHIT-SUNDAY.

Acts ii. 16—21.

But this is that which was spoken by the Prophet Joel;
And it shall be in the last days, saith God, I will pour out of My Spirit upon all flesh: and your sons and your daughters shall prophesy, and your young men shall see visions, and your old men shall dream dreams:
And on My servants and on Mine handmaids I will pour out of My Spirit; and they shall prophesy:
And I will shew wonders in Heaven above, and tokens in the earth beneath; blood and fire, and the vapour of smoke:
The sun shall be turned into darkness, and the moon into blood, before that great and notable day of the Lord come:
And it shall be, that whosoever shall call on the name of the Lord, shall be saved.

[*Sed hoc est quod dictum est per Prophetam Joel;*
Et erit in novissimis diebus, dicit Dominus, effundam de Spiritu Meo super omnem carnem: et prophetabunt filii vestri et filiæ vestræ, et juvenes vestri visiones videbunt, et seniores vestri somnia somniabunt:
Et quidem super servos Meos, et super ancillas Meas in diebus illis effundam de Spiritu Meo, et prophetabunt:
Et dabo prodigia in cælo sursum, et signa in terrâ deorsum, sanguinem, et ignem, et vaporem fumi:
Sol convertetur in tenebras, et luna in sanguinem, antequam veniat dies Domini magnus et manifestus:
Et erit; omnis, quicumque invocaverit nomen Domini, salvus erit. Latin Vulg.]

[*But this is that which was spoken by the Prophet Joel;*
And it shall come to pass in the last days, saith God, I will pour out

SERM. XI.

of My Spirit upon all flesh: and your sons and your daughters shall prophesy, and your young men shall see visions, and your old men shall dream dreams:

And on My servants and on My handmaidens I will pour out, in those days, of My Spirit; and they shall prophesy:

And I will shew wonders in Heaven above, and signs in the earth beneath; blood, and fire, and vapour of smoke;

The sun shall be turned into darkness, and the moon into blood, before that great and notable day of the Lord come:

And it shall come to pass, that whosoever shall call on the name of the Lord shall be saved. Engl. Trans.]

These words may well serve for a sermon this day; they were a part of a sermon preached as this day. The first Whitsun-Sermon that ever was; the first Whit-Sunday that ever was. St. Peter preached it. And this was his text, out of the second chapter of the Prophet Joel. As Christ the last year out of Esay, so Peter this out of Joel. Both took texts; both for the day, and for the present occasion.

The occasion of this here was a lewd surmise given out by some, touching the gift of tongues, this day sent from Heaven.

It shall be my first note. That look, how soon God from Heaven had sent His fiery tongues upon His Apostles, the devil from hell presently sent for his fiery tongues, and put them in the mouths of his apostles, to disgrace and scoff at those of God's sending.

Ye may hear them speak, at the thirteenth verse: Well fare this same good new wine! These good fellows have been at it, and now they can speak nothing but outlandish. Some little broken Greek or Latin they had, and now out it comes.

Thus that which was indeed *grande miraculum*, they turned into *grande ludibrium*. Of the great mystery of this
Mat. 3. 11. day, they made a mere mockery. Those that were "baptized with the Holy Ghost" they traduced, as if they had soused themselves in "new wine." Here is the Holy Ghost's welcome into the world. This use doth the devil make of some men's wits and tongues, to pour contempt on that which God
Heb. 10. 29. poureth forth, all that ever they can; even "to work despite to the Spirit of grace."

The sum. Being to make an apology for himself and the rest, and indeed for the Holy Ghost, St. Peter first prays audience, at the fourteenth verse; then tells them soberly, they miss the matter quite, at the fifteenth. It was too early day to fasten any such suspicion upon any such men, as they were, to be gone before nine in the morning. But this he stands not on, as not worth the answering.

Here, at this verse, he tells them it was no liquor, this specially, no such as they surmised. If it were any, if they would needs have it one, it was the Prophet Joel's, and none other. Something poured on, nothing poured in. Nothing but the effusion of the Holy Ghost. "This is it that was spoken by the Prophet Joel."

So, *habemus firmiorem sermonem propheticum;* and this 2 Pet. 1. 19. which seemed to happen thus on the sudden, it was long since foretold; and he alleges for it this text of the Prophet, that such a thing "there should come to pass," an "effusion of the Spirit," and that a strange one. And this they would find it to be, this prophecy of the Spirit poured, this day fulfilled in their ears.

Of which text the special points be two: 1. of the Spirit's The division. pouring: 2. of the end whereto.

The first I reduce to these four. 1. The thing; 2. the act; I. 3. the party by whom; 4. the parties upon whom. 1. *De Spiritu Meo* is the thing. 2. *Effundam* the act. 3. *Dicit Dominus,* the Party by Whom. 4. *Super omnem carnem,* the parties upon whom it is poured.

Then the end whereto. And in that four more. The last II. end of all in the last word of all, *salvabitur.* That is the very end, and a blessed end, if by any means we may attain to it. Then are there three other conducting to this; two main ones, and one accessory, but yet as necessary as the other. 2. Close to it, in the end, there is calling on the Name of the Lord: "He that calleth on the Name of the Lord, shall be saved." 3. And farthest from it at the beginning, there is *prophetabunt,* to call upon us to that end: "And My servants shall prophesy." 4. And between both these there is a memorandum of the "great day of the Lord." Which is not from the matter neither, nor more than needs. For then, at that day, we shall stand most in need of saving; if we perish then, we perish for ever. And

SERM. XI. the mention and memory of that day will make us not despise prophesying, nor forget invocation; but be both more attentive in hearing of prophecy, and more devout in "calling on the name of the Lord." So it may well go for a third conducting means to our salvation.

Now to bring this to the day. This, it is said, shall be
Heb. 1. 1. "in the last days." Which with St. Peter here, and with St. Paul, Hebrews the first; yea, and with the Rabbins themselves, are the days of the Messiah. So, of our Messiah Christ, to us, and of none other. Of Whose days this is the very last. For having done His errand, He was to go up again, and to send His Spirit down, to do His another while; which is the work of this day. As His first then, the taking of our flesh, so His last, the giving of His Spirit; the giving It abundantly, which is the *effundam* here.

It remaineth that we pray to Him, Who thus of His Spirit poured forth this day, that He would vouchsafe on the same day to pour of It on us here; that we may so hold this feast, the memory of It, and so hear the words of this prophecy, as may be to His good acceptance, and our own saving in the great day, "the day of the Lord."

I. Of the Spirit's pouring.

Of the thing poured, first. *De Spiritu Meo,* the Spirit of God. First of Him, to give Him the honour of His own day.

De Spiritu.

The Spirit is of Himself Author of life; and here is brought in, as Author of prophecy. They both are in the Nicene Creed; 1. "The Lord and Giver of life," 2. and, "Who spake by the Prophets." Life and speech have but one instrument, the spirit or breath both. Of it these four.

1. Prophecy can come from no nature but rational; the Spirit then is *natura rationalis.* And determinate it is, distinct plainly here two ways; 1. the Spirit, from Him Whose the Spirit is, Him That says, *de Spiritu Meo.* 2. That Which is poured, from Him That poureth It; *Fusus a Fusore.* Being then *natura rationalis determinata,* He is a Person, for a person is so defined.

2. Secondly, effusion is a plain proceeding of that which is poured; as spiration is so too, in the very body of the word spirit. So, a Person proceeding.

3. Thirdly, being a Person, and yet being poured out, He

behoves to be God. No person, Angel, or Spirit, can be poured out, can be so participate. Not at all; but not "upon all flesh"—not dilated so far. God only can be that. So the Person, the proceeding, the Deity of the Holy Ghost, all in these words. And not a word of all this mine; but thus deduced by St. Ambrose, and before him by Didymus Alexandrinus, St. Hierome's master. [Didym. de Sp. S. lib. 1. circ. med. ap. S. Hieron.]

4. But fourthly, you will mark; it is not 'My Spirit,' but "of My Spirit." The whole Spirit, flesh could not hold—not "all flesh." And parts It hath none. 1. Understand then, "of My Spirit," that is of the gifts and graces of the Spirit—beams of this light, streams of this pouring. Otherwhere others, here the gift of prophecy and tongues. [S. Ambr. de Sp. S. lib. 1. c. 8.] *al.* 7.

2. Which *de Spiritu* is also said, to keep the difference between Christ and us. Upon Him the Spirit was; "the Spirit of God upon Me," last year. Upon us, not the Spirit; but *de Spiritu,* "of My Spirit" only, this year. Lu. 4. 18. The text of the last year.

2. The act, *effundam.*

The next is the act, *effundam;* in it four more. 1. The quality, in that it is compared to a thing liquid, *fusile,* 'poured out.' This seems not proper. Pouring is as it had been water, He came in fire. It would have been kindled rather than poured. True, but St. Peter in proper terms makes his answer refer to their slander; and that was, that it was nothing but "new wine," a liquor. Their objection being in a thing liquid, his answer behoved to be accordingly. And well it might so, Christ had so expressed it, both lately in His promise, "Ye shall be baptized with the Holy Ghost within few days;" and formerly, under the terms of "waters of life," where St. John's exposition is, "This He spake of the Spirit." Not then given, but to be given, straight upon Christ's glorifying, which is now, this very day. The Holy Ghost then is not all fire. [Acts 2. 13.] Acts 1. 5. Joh. 7. 39.

And this quality falls well within the two graces, of 1. prophecy, and 2. invocation, here given. 1. Prophecy: Moses the great Prophet likened it to the "dew falling upon the herbs," or "the rain poured on the grass." And that likening is so usual as מורה, *moreh,* the word in Hebrew for rain, is so for a preacher too, that it poseth the translators which way to turn it; and even in that very chapter of Joel, whence this text is taken. Deu. 32. 2.

SERM. XI.

Acts 2. 33.

2. And invocation is so too; a pouring out of prayer, and of the very heart in prayer.

3. And the third, of the latter day, may be taken in too. Then there shall be a pouring forth also of all the phials of the wrath of God.

2. The quality then first; the quantity no less. For pouring is a sign of plenty; *effundam* not *aspergam*, the first prerogative of this day. For the Spirit had been given before this time, but never with such a largess; sprinkled, but not poured. Never till now, in that bounty that now. This was reserved for Christ. For when there was *copiosa sanguinis effusio* on His part, there was likewise to be *copiosa Flaminis effusio* on the Holy Ghost's. He as liberal of His grace, as Christ of His blood. That there might be to us
Ps. 130. 7. *copiosa redemptio* between Them both, it is *effundam copiose* in both.

Effundam tells us farther, the Spirit came not of Himself, not till He was thus poured out. It is no *effluet*, but *effundam*.
Lu. 22. 37. *Sic oportet implere,* that so order might be kept in Him, in the very Spirit, and we by Him taught to keep it. Not to start out till we be sent, nor to go on our own heads, but to stay till we be called. Not to leak out or to run over, but to stay till we be poured out in like sort. Seeing Christ would not go unsent, *misit Me,* last year; nor the Holy Ghost run unpoured this year; it may well become us to keep in till we be poured and sent, any year. And yet the Spirit is no less ready to run than God is to pour It. One of these is
Isa. 6. 8. no bar to the other. *Ecce ego, mitte me. Ecce ego,* "Behold I am ready," saith Esay, and yet *mitte me,* "send me," for all that. Effluence and effusion, influence and infusion, will stand together well enough.

4. Lastly, *effundam* is not as the running of a spout. To pour is the voluntary act of a voluntary agent, who hath the vessel in his hand, and may pour little or much; and may choose whether he will pour out any at all, or no. As shut the heaven from raining, so refrain the Spirit from falling on us.

2. And when He pours, He strikes not out the head of the vessel and lets all go; but moderates His pouring, and dispenses His gifts. Pours not all upon every one; nay,

not upon any one, all; but upon some in this manner, upon 1 Cor. 12. 4—11.
some in that; not to each the same. And to whom the same, not in the same measure though; but to some "five," to some "two," to some but "one" talent. The text is plain Mat. 25. 15.
for this. There are divers assignations in it: 1. To divers parties; "sons," "servants," "old men," and "young men." 2. Of divers gifts; "prophecies," "visions," and "dreams." 3. And then of divers degrees; one clearer than the other, the "vision" than the "dream." *Singulis prout vult*, at the 1 Cor. 12. 11.
Pourer's discretion, to each as pleaseth Him best.

3. The Party pouring: *dixit Dominus.*

The Party pouring is, *dixit Dominus*, "the Lord That said." But *dixit Dominus Domino meo*, "The Lord said to my Lord;" Which of these? The latter *Domino meo*, "my Lord," David's Lord and ours, *Dominum nostrum*, in our Ps. 110. 1.
Creed, that is, Christ. How appears that? Directly at the thirty-third verse after, "He being now exalted by the right hand of God, and having received the promise of the Holy Ghost from the Father, He hath poured out this that ye now see and hear." Christ then. And not the Father? Yes, He too; for of Him Christ is said to receive it. Not only *dixit Dominus Domino meo*, but *dedit Dominus Domino meo*. And so, as in the nineteenth of Genesis, *Pluit Domi-* Gen. 19. 24.
nus a Domino, "from the Lord the Lord poured it." And but one *effundam*, with but one effusion Both, as with one spiration He came from Both. Both with one effusion pour Him; Both with one spiration breathe Him. It is expressly so set down, Revelations, chapter twenty-two, "The foun- Rev. 22. 1.
tain of the water of life issued from the seat of God and of the Lamb." So have you here the whole Trinity: 1. *Quis*, 2. *Quid*, 3. *a Quo;* the Father by the Son, or the Son from the Father, pouring out the Holy Ghost.

2. And may we not also find the two natures of Christ here? *Effundam* is *fundam ex.* "I will pour out;" out of what? what the cistern into which It first comes, and out of which It is after derived to us? That is the flesh or human nature of Christ, on which It was poured at His conception, fully to endow it, for "in Him the fulness of the Godhead Col. 2. 9.
dwelleth bodily;"—mark that "bodily." And It was given to Him without measure, and "of His fulness we all receive." Joh. 1. 16.
From this cistern this day issued the Spirit by so many

SERM. XI. quills or pipes, as it were, as there are several divisions of the graces of the Holy Ghost. And so now we have both *a Quo* and *ex Quo*. The divinity into this humanity pouring the Spirit, Which from His flesh was poured down this day *super omnem carnem*, "upon all flesh." Which fitly brings in the next, *super omnem carnem*.

4. The parties upon whom. *Super omnem carnem.* On whom this pouring is, which is the last point; *super omnem carnem*. In which there are three points, as the words are three: 1. *Carnem* first, that is, men. "For doth God take care for oxen," saith the Apostle, or for any flesh
1 Cor. 9. 9. but ours? No, not for any flesh, but the "flesh" which "the
Joh. 1. 14. Word" did take. And for that He doth.

But we are spirit too, as well as flesh; and in reason, spirit on spirit were more kindly. There is nearer alliance between them.

Yet you shall find the other part, flesh, is still chosen.

1. *Super carnem.* 1. First, to magnify His mercy the more, that part is singled out that seemeth farther removed; nay, that is indeed quite opposite to the Spirit of God here poured out.
Isa. 40. 6. For what is flesh? It is proclaimed, in the fortieth of Esay, "it is grass." And not *gramen*, but *fœnum*, that is, grass withering and fit for the scythe. Is that the worst? I
[Rom. 8. 3.] would it were; but *caro peccati*, "sinful flesh" it sets forth yet. Upon "sinful flesh" He should have poured somewhat else than His Spirit.

So two oppositions: 1. flesh and Spirit absolutely in themselves; 2. then, "sinful flesh" and the Holy Spirit. All which commends His love the more, thus to combine things so much opposite. This first.

And withal, that which right now I touched, to shew the introduction to this conjunction of these so far in opposition either to other, even *Verbum caro factum*, that made this sym-
Hos. 2. 15. bolism. By which "a gate of hope" was opened to us by His incarnation, *in spem* of our inspiration, which this day
Acts 2. 33. came *in rem*. For His flesh exalted to the right hand of God remembered us that were flesh of His flesh, and derived down this fountain of living water to it, *saliens in vitam æternam;* springing, and raising us with it whence it came, for
Joh. 4. 14. water will ever rise as high as the place from whence it came, that is, up to Heaven, up to eternal life.

2. *Super*, "upon" it; "upon" it is without, on the outside of it. Had not *fundam in* been better than *fundam super;* 'into' them than "upon" them? Not a whit. 2. *Super.*

Indeed, both ways I find the Spirit given. At Christ's baptism the dove came "upon Him." At His resurrection, Lu. 3. 22.
insufflavit, "He breathed into" them. And so hath He parted Joh. 20. 22.
His Sacraments: baptism is *effundam super*, upon us, from without; the Holy Eucharist, that is *comedite*, that goeth in. Upon the matter, both come to one. If It be poured on, It soaks in, pierces to the very centre of the soul, as in baptism sin is washed thence by It. If It be breathed in, It is no sooner at the heart but It works forth, out It comes again; out at the nostrils in breath, out at the wrist in the beating of the pulse. So both in effect are one.

1. But it is *super* here, for these reasons; first that we may know the graces of the Spirit, they are ἔξωθεν, 'from without.' In us, that is, in our flesh, they grow not; neither they, nor any good thing else. And not only ἔξωθεν, 'from without;' but St. James' ἄνωθεν too, "from above, from the Jas. 1. 17.
Father of lights." Both these are in *super;* and but for these, we might fall into a phantasy they grew within us, and sprung from us; which, God knoweth, they do not.

2. Another reason is, for that "upon" is the preposition proper to initiation into any new office. So is the manner, by some such outward ceremony "upon," to initiate. By anointing or pouring oil "upon." By induing, *induemini*, putting some robe or other ensign "upon." By imposition, or laying hands "upon." All "upon." Baptism, which is the Sacrament of our initiation, is therefore so done. So the dove came "upon" Christ. The "tongues," here "upon" Acts 2. 3.
these, to enter them, either, into their new offices.

A third, last but not least, to inure them to this preposition *super*, which many can but evil brook. No *super*, no superiority they; all even, all equal; fellows and fellows. "The right hands of fellowship," if you will; but not so Gal. 2. 9.
much as imposition of hands, *super*. For if *super*, then *sub* follows; if "upon," then we 'under;' if above, then we beneath. But no *sub* with some; submit neither head nor spirit to any. Yet *super Me*, said Christ, last year, and it may become any that became Him; it may well become *super*

SERM. XI. *carnem.* *Super* then must stand, and be stood upon; confusion will come if it be not.

2. *Super omnem carnem.* *Super carnem, super omnem carnem.* "Upon flesh," and "upon all flesh." Not some one, not Jews' flesh alone; in regard of whom this *omnem* is here specially put in, for they
Ps. 147. 20. had in a manner engrossed the Spirit before, by a *non taliter omni.* And yet upon them too, for upon their "sons" and their "daughters," as it followeth; but upon them now no more, than upon any other. This is a second prerogative of this day. The first *effundam* that is. 1. Before, sparingly sprinkled; now, plentifully poured. 2. Now again, *super omnem:* before, upon but some; now indifferently, upon all.

For so when we say "all," we mean none is excluded, but
Acts 15. 9. now may have it. "He hath put no difference between them
Rom. 10. 12. and us," saith St. Peter. *Non est distinctio,* saith St. Paul.
Eph. 2. 14. The "partition is thrown down" now. Go but to the letter of the text, "all flesh." 1. No sex barred—upon "sons and daughters;" so either sex. 2. No age—upon "young men" and upon "old." The one, "visions;" the other, "dreams." 3. No condition—on "servants" as well as "sons," on "handmaids" no less than "daughters." 4. No nation—for, if ye mark, the Spirit is poured twice; upon their "sons" in this,
Acts 2. 18. and again upon His "servants" in the next verse. His "servants," whether they be their sons or not, whose sons soever they be, though the sons of them that are perhaps strangers to the first covenant; and yet even then God had ever His "servants," as well out of that nation as in it.

Now in sign that thus, "upon all flesh," they heard them
Acts 2. 5. speak the tongues of "all flesh," even of "every nation under
Ps. 76. 1. Heaven." That where before a few "in Jewry," now many all the world over. No longer now, *notus in Judæâ Deus,*
Ps. 67. 2. "His way should be known upon earth, His saving health among all nations."

Yet not *promiscuè* though, without all manner limitation. No; the text limits it. I must again put you in mind of the two pourings mentioned in it. One, the *super omnem carnem,* in this the fifteenth verse; the other, the second, *super servos Meos* in the next, the eighteenth. And *super servos Meos* is the qualifying of *super omnem carnem.* "Upon all flesh," that is, all such as will be "My servants;" as will give in their names to that end, as "will call upon Me." *Quicunque invocaverit*—so concludes Joel. "As will believe and be baptized"—so concludes St. Peter here his sermon. This gives them the capacity, makes them vessels meet to receive this effusion. By which all Turks, Jews, Infidels, are out of the *omnem;* and counterfeit Christians too, that profess to serve Him, but all the world sees whom they serve. And by this, much flesh is cut off from *omnem carnem.* But so with this qualifying, "upon all;" for any other I know not. And this for the pouring.

II. The end whereto. *Salvabitur.* [Mark 14.4.]

And now, *Utquid effusio hæc?* 'To what end all this?' For it is not to be imagined this pouring was casual, as the turning over of a tub, nor that the Spirit did run waste; then it were, *Utquid perditio hæc?* An end it had. And that follows now; "and your sons," &c. The Spirit is given to many ends, many middle, but one last, and that last is in the last word, *salvabitur;* the end then of this pouring is the salvation of mankind. Mankind was upon the point to perish, and the Spirit was poured, as a precious balm or water, to recover and to save it. So the end of all is—and mark it well! that the Spirit may save the flesh, by the spiritualizing it; not, the flesh destroy the Spirit, by carnalizing It; not, the flesh weigh down the Spirit to earth hither, but the Spirit lift up the flesh thither to Heaven, whence It came.

Means to that end. 1. Prophecy. 2. Prayer.

To this last here are three, middle, concluding ends more. 1. Prophecy first; 2. Invocation last; both of which are well here represented, three ways. 1. In the "tongues," the symbol of the Holy Ghost this day: the one, prophecy, being God's tongue to us; the other, invocation, being our tongue to God. 2. In the Spirit—both being acts of the Spirit or breath: prophecy breathes It into us, prayer breathes It out again. 3. In the pouring—both pourings after a sort; that which prophecy doth infuse, pour in at the ear, invocation doth *refundere*, or 'pour forth back again,' in prayer out of the heart.

And beside these two a third there is, which is wedged in between them both, as stirring us, first and last, both to hear prophecy more attentively, and to practise invocation more

SERM. XI. devoutly, which I wish may never depart out of our minds—the memory of the latter day.

3. Memory of the latter day. Thus they stand subordinate. That men may be saved, they are to "call upon the name of the Lord:"—that at least. That they may so call to purpose, they are to be called on to it, and directed in it, by *et prophetabunt.* And that they might perform this to "all flesh," they were to speak with the "tongues" of all flesh; which was the gift here of this day, without just cause scoffed at. But tongues are but as the cask, wherein prophecy, as the liquor, is contained: I will set by the empty cask and deal with *prophetabunt,* the liquor in it only.

1. *Prophetabunt.* Prov. 29. 18. Isa. 32. 14, 15. Prophecy stands first in the text, "without which," saith Solomon, "the people must needs perish." That saying of Esay is much used by the Fathers, *Tenebræ et palpatio, donec effundatur super nos Spiritus de excelso.* "All is dark; men do but grope till the Spirit be poured on us from above," to give us light, by this gift of prophecy.

This term is kept by Joel, as well when he speaks of God's "servants," that is of us, as when of them and their "sons." And ever after, in the New Testament, it is retained still as a usual term by the Apostle to the Corinthians, Ephesians, Thessalonians, all his Epistles through.

[Acts 21. 9, 10.] But not in the sense of foretelling things to come. For so can it be verified only upon Agabus, St. Philip's daughters, and upon St. John; which are too few for so great an effusion as this. That indeed was the chief sense of it in the Old Testament; and well, while Christ was yet to come. Christ, He was the stop of all prophetical predictions. Then it had his place, that. But now, and ever since Christ is come, it hath in a manner left that sense, at least in a great part, and is not so taken in the New.

The sense it is there taken in—to expound this place of Peter by another of Paul, citing this very same text of the Prophet—is *et prophetabunt* here, by *quomodo prædicabunt* there, prophesying, that is, preaching. Whereby, after a new manner, we do prophesy, as it were, the meaning of ancient prophecies; not make any new, but interpret the old well, take off the "veil of Moses' face." Find Christ, find the mysteries of the Gospel, under the types of the

Rom. 10. 13, 15.

Ex. 34. 33. 2 Cor. 3. 13.

law; apply the old prophecies so as it may appear "the spirit of prophecy is the testimony of Jesus." And he the best prophet now, that can do this best. Rev. 19. 10.

This sense we prove by these in the text. "The Spirit was poured on them, and they did prophesy." What did they? How prophesied St. Peter? He foretold nothing; all he did was, he applied this place of the Prophet to this feast. And a little beneath, the passage of the sixteenth Psalm, to Christ's resurrection. And after that, the place of another Psalm, to His ascension. Acts 2. 31 Ps. 16. 10. Acts 2. 34. Ps. 110. 1.

And the rest, on whom It was poured too, how prophesied they? All, we read, they did was, *loquebantur magnalia Dei,* they "uttered forth the wonderful things of God," but foretold not any thing that we find. So as to prophesy now, is to search out and disclose the hidden things of "the oracles of God," and not to tell beforehand what shall after come to pass. Acts 2. 11. [Rom. 3. 2.]

But what say you to "visions" and "dreams" here? Little; they pertain not to us. The text saith it not. You remember the two pourings. 1. One upon their "sons;" 2. the other upon His "servants." This latter is it by which we come in. We are not of their "sons," we claim not by that; God made us His "servants," for by that word we hold.

Now in this latter pouring on His "servants," which only concerns us, "visions" and "dreams" are left out quite. If any pretend them now, we say with Jeremiah, "Let a dream go for a dream," and "let My word," saith the Lord, "be spoken as My word:" *Quid paleæ ad triticum?* What, mingle you chaff and wheat? We are to lay no point of religion upon them now; prophecy, preaching is it, we to hold ourselves unto now. As for "visions" and "dreams," *transeant,* 'let them go.' Jer. 23. 28.

But then, for prophecy in this sense of opening or interpreting Scriptures, is the Spirit poured upon all flesh so? Is this of Joel a proclamation for liberty of preaching, that all, young and old, men-servants and maid-servants may fall to it? Nay, the she sex, St. Paul took order for that betimes, cut them off with his *nolo mulieres.* But what for the rest? may they? For to this sense hath this Scripture been 1 Cor. 14. 34.

SERM. XI. wrested by the enthusiasts of former ages, and still is, by the anabaptists now. And by mistaking of it, way given to a foul error, as if all were let loose, all might claim and take upon them, forsooth, to prophesy.

Nothing else this but a malicious device of the devil, to pour contempt upon this gift. For, indeed, bring it to this once, and what was this day falsely surmised will then be justly affirmed—*musto pleni*, or *cerebro vacui*, whether you will: but *musto pleni*, "drunken" Prophets then indeed;
Isa. 51. 21. howbeit "not with wine," as Esay saith, but with another as heady a humour, and that doth intoxicate the brain as much as any must or new wine; even of self-conceited ignorance, whereof the world grows too full. But it was no part of Joel's meaning, nor St. Peter's neither, to give way to this phrensy.

No? Is it not plain? The Spirit is poured "upon all flesh." True, but not upon all to prophesy though. The text warrants no such thing. In the one place it is, "And your sons shall:" in the other, "And My servants shall." But neither is it, All their "sons;" nor, All His "servants" shall. Neither, indeed, can it be. There must be some "sons," and some "servants," to prophesy to, to whom these Prophets may be sent, to whom this prophecy may come. "All flesh" may not be cut out into tongues; some left for ears,
'Ακούει οὐδεὶς οὐδὲν οὐδένος. some auditors needs. Else a Cyclopian Church will grow upon us, where all were speakers, nobody heard another.

How then, shall the Spirit be poured "upon all flesh?" Well enough. The Spirit of Prophecy is not all God's Spirit, He hath more beside. If the spirit or grace of
Zech. 12. 10. prophecy upon some, "the spirit of grace and prayer," in Zachary, upon the rest. So between them both, the Spirit will be "upon all flesh," and the proposition hold true: *prophetabunt* must not make us forget *invocaverit*. All the Spirit goes not away in prophesying, some left for that too; and there is the *quicunque* (*quicunque invocaverit*) and no where else.

But if St. Peter will not serve, St. Paul shall; he is
1 Cor. 14. 31. plain. "Ye may all prophesy one by one:"—what, the skippers of Holland and all? I trow not. But "all" there,
[1 Cor. 14. 29.] is plain. "All," that is, "all" that be "Prophets." And I
Nu. 11. 29. wish with all my heart, as did Moses, that "all God's people

were Prophets;" but, till they be so, I wish they may not
prophesy: no more would Moses neither. Now in the same
Epistle, St. Paul holds it for a great absurdity, to hold
"all" are Prophets. With a kind of indignation he asks it,
"What, are all Prophets?" No more than "all Apostles"— 1 Cor. 12. 29.
as much the one as the other. Then, if "all" be not "Prophets," all may not prophesy, sure. For, with the Apostle
in the same place, "the operation," that is, the act of pro- [1 Cor. 12. 4—6.]
phesying, "the administration," that is, the office or calling,
and "the grace," that is, the enabling gift, these three are
ever to go together. No act in the Church lawfully done,
without them all. Then the Apostle's "You all may" is,
All you may that have the gift.

And not you that have it neither, "the gift," unless you
have the calling too; for as God sent gifts, so He gave men
also, "some Apostles, some Prophets." Men for gifts, as 1 Cor. 12. 28.
well as "gifts for men." *Misit* in Christ, as well as *unxit*, [Ps. 68. 18.]
last year. And in His servants, *vocavit*, as well as *talenta* Mat. 25. 14.
dedit. Not to be parted, these.

I conclude then. *Et prophetabunt;* but such as have been
at the door of the Tabernacle, as have been the sons of the
Prophets, men set apart for that end. And yet even they
also, so as they take not themselves at liberty to prophesy
whatsoever takes them in the tongue, the dreams of their
own heads, or the visions of their own hearts; but remember their *super*, and know there be Spirits also to whom
"their spirits be subject." So much for the seventeenth 1 Cor. 14. 32.
and eighteenth verses.

But how now come we thus suddenly to the signs of the 2. The mean between both. The latter day.
latter day, and to the day itself? For they follow close, you
see. It is somewhat strange that from *et prophetabunt*, He
is straight at doomsday without more ado.

The reasons which I find the Fathers render of it are
these: First, the close joining of them is to meet with
another dream that hath troubled the Church much. And
that is, that it may be there will be another pouring yet
after this, and more Prophets rise still. Every otherwhile,
some such upstart spirits there are, would fain make us so
believe. Here is a discharge for them.

No, saith Joel, look for no more such days as this after

SERM. XI. this. Therefore to this day He joins immediately, from this day He goes presently to, the latter day, as if He said, You have all you shall have. When this pouring hath run so far as it will, then cometh the end; when this is done, the world is done; no new spirit, no new effusion, this is the last. From Christ's departure till His return again; from this day of Pentecost, a "great day and a notable," till the last "great and notable day" of all; between these two days, no more such day. Therefore, in the beginning of the text, He called them "the last days," because no days to come after them. No pouring to be looked for from this first day of those last. No other but this, till *dies novissimus novissimorum*, 'the very last day of all;' till He pour down fire to consume "all flesh" that, by the fire this day kindled by these fiery tongues, shall not be brought to know Him, and call upon His name.

A second is, being to speak by and by of *salvabitur*, that we should be saved, He would let us see what it is we should be saved from. That helpeth much to make us esteem of our saving. Saved then from what? "from blood, and fire, and the smoulder of smoke;" that is, from the heavy signs here, and from that which is after these, and beyond all these far, "the great and terrible day of the Lord." This sight of *unde*, 'from whence,' will make us apprize our saving at a higher rate, and think it worth our care then, in that day to be saved.

And last, it is set here, *per modum stimuli*, 'to quicken us,'
2 Cor. 5. 11. *ut scientes terrorem hunc*, saith St. Paul, that entering into a sad and sober consideration of it, and "the terror" of it, we might stir up ourselves by it, to prepare for it. And set it is between both, to dispose us the better to both. To that which is past, *et prophetabunt*, to awake our attention to that; and to that which follows, *invocaverit*, to kindle our devotion in that, and so by both to make sure our salvation.

"The day of the Lord," the Prophet calls it *dies Domini*; as it were opposing it to *dies servi*, to our days here. As if he said, These are your days, and you use them indeed, as if they were your own. You pour out yourselves into all riot, and know no other pouring out but that; you see not any great use of prophesying, think it might well enough be spared; you speak your pleasures of it and say, *musto pleni*, or to like effect, when you list. These are your days. But know this, when yours are done, God hath His day too, and His day will come at last, and it will come terribly when it comes.

When that day comes, how then? "*Quid fiet in novissimo?*" the Prophet's ordinary question, "What will ye do at the last?" how will you be saved, *in die illo*, "in that day?" Jer. 5. 31.

We speak sometime of great days here;—alas! small in respect of this. There is matter of fear sometime in these of ours; nothing to the terror of this. "Great" it is, and "notable," as much for the fear, as for any thing else in it. This a "terrible" one indeed, *et quis potest sustinere*, "Who can abide it?" saith Joel in this very chapter. Look to it then. On whom He poureth not His Spirit here, on them He will pour somewhat else there, even the phials of His wrath: possibly before, some; but then all, certainly. [Joel 2. 11.]

And that you may not only hear of this day, but see somewhat to put you in mind of it, *Ecce signa*. Terrible signs shall come upon earth, sword and "fire:" from the sword, pouring out of "blood;" from "fire," a choking "vapour of smoke," or as the Hebrew is, "a pillar of smoke;" which then doth *palmizare*, 'goeth up straight like a pillar or a palm-tree,' when the fire increaseth more and more; for when it abateth, it boweth the head and decayeth, which this shall never do. [Judg. 20. 40.]

Nay further, "wonders in Heaven." For these tongues of Heaven thus despised, Heaven shall shew itself displeased too; the lights of Heaven, as it were, for a time put out, for contempt of the heavenly light this day kindled. "The sun dark," as if he hid his face; "the moon red as blood," as if she blushed at our great want of regard in this, a point so nearly concerning us.

For indeed, these eclipses, though they have their causes in nature, as the rainbow also hath; yet what hinders but as the rainbow, so they may be signs too, and have their meaning in Scripture assigned; and even this meaning here? This I see, that all flesh are smitten with a kind of horror and heaviness when they happen to fall out, as if they portended

SERM. XI. somewhat, as if that they portended were not good; for *dies atri* they have been, and are reckoned, all the world over.

Mat. 24. 8. But these "are but the beginnings of evils," scarce the dawning of that day; but when the day itself cometh, "the [Joel 2. 11.] great day," then it will pour down, "and who," saith Joel, "may abide it?" A fair item for them that despise prophecies, and so doing make void the counsel of God, against their own souls.

I have much marvelled why on this Sunday, Whit-Sunday as we call it, the day of the white sun, the Prophet should present the black sun thus unto us. But the Prophet did nothing but as inspired by the Holy Ghost, which makes me think he thought the fire of that day would make the fire of this burn the clearer, and that pouring down make this pouring pass the readier; that he thought that day a good meditation for this—and for such I commend it to you, and so leave it; and come to *invocaverit,* the only means left us now to escape it.

3. *Quicunque invocaverit.* I dare not end with *prophetabunt,* or with this; I dare not omit, but join *invocaverit* to them. For what? From *prophetabunt* come we to *salvabitur* straight, without any medium between? No, we must take *invocaverit* in our way, no passing to salvation but by and through it. For what? is the pouring of the Spirit to end in preaching? and preaching to end in itself, as it doth with us? a circle of preaching, and in effect nothing else,—but pour in prophesying enough, and then all is safe? No; there is another yet as needful, nay, more needful to be called on, as the current of our age runs, and that is, "calling on the Name of the Lord."

This, it grieveth me to see how light it is set; nay, to see how busy the devil has been, to pour contempt on it, to bring it in disgrace with disgraceful terms; to make nothing of Divine service, as if it might be well spared, and *invocaverit* here be stricken out.

But mark this text well, and this invocation we make so slight account of sticks close, is so locked fast to *salvabitur,* closer and faster than we are aware of.

Two errors there be, and I wish them reformed: one, as if prophesying were all we had to do, we might dispense with invocation, let it go, leave it to the choir. That is an error.

Prophesying is not all, *invocaverit* is to come in too; we to join them, and jointly to observe them, to make a conscience of both. It is the oratory of prayer poured out of our hearts shall save us, no less than the oratory of preaching poured in at our ears.

The other is, of them that do not wholly reject it, yet so 2.
depress it, as if in comparison of prophesying it were little worth. Yet, we see, by the frame of this text, it is the higher end; the calling on us by prophecy, is but that we should call on the Name of the Lord. All prophesying, all preaching, is but to this end. And indeed prophecy is but *gratia gratis data;* and ever *gratis data* is for *gratum faciens,* a part and a special part whereof is invocation. There is then, as a conscience to be made of both, so a like conscience to be made of both; not to set up the one and magnify it, and to turn our back on the other and vilify it. For howsoever we give good words of invocation, yet what our conceit is our deeds shew.

I love not to dash one religious duty against another, or, as it were, to send challenges between them. But as much as the text saith, so much may I say; and that is, that it hath three special prerogatives, by this verse of the Prophet.

1. First, it is *effundam,* ours, properly; and *effundam Spiritum Meum,* the pouring out of our Spirit, to answer that of God's Spirit in the text. *Prophetabunt* is not ours, none of our act, but the act of another. The stream of our times tends all to this. To make religion nothing but an auricular profession, a matter of ease, a mere sedentary thing, and ourselves merely passive in it; sit still, and hear a Sermon and two Anthems, and be saved; as if by the act of the choir, or of the preacher, we should so be, (for these be their acts,) and we do nothing ourselves, but sit and suffer; without so much as any thing done by us, any *effundam* on our parts at all; not so much as this, of calling on the Name of the Lord.

2. The second: this hath the *quicunque.* We would fain have it, *Quicunque prophetiam audiverit,* he that hears so many sermons a-week cannot choose but be saved; but it will not be. No; here stand we preaching, and hearing sermons; and neither they that hear prophesying, nay nor they that prophesy themselves, can make a *quicunque* of either. Wit-

SERM. XI. ness *Domine, in nomine Tuo prophetavimus*, and, "Lord, Thou hast preached in our streets," and yet it would do them no

Mat. 7. 22. Lu. 13. 26. good; *Nescio vos*, was their answer for all that.

And yet how fain would some be a prophesying! It would not save them, though they were; and is it not a preposterous desire? we love to meddle with that pertains not to us, and will do us no good: that which is our duty and would do us good, that care we not for.

Tongues were given for prophecy. True; but no *quicunque* there, for all that; but to whom none are given to prophesy, to them yet are there given to invocate. And there comes it in, the *quicunque* lies there. *De Spiritu Meo super omnem carnem*—here it comes in; at invocation, not at the other. Let it suffice; it is not *quicunque prophetaverit* here, *quicunque invocaverit* it is. The Prophet saith it, the Apostles

Rom. 10. 13. say it both, πᾶς ὃς ἄν. Peter here; Paul, Romans, tenth chapter, and thirteenth verse.

Last, this is sure, *invocaverit* is ἐχόμενον σωτηρίας, 'it stands nearest, it joins closest to *salvabitur*.' Both one breath, one sentence; the words touch, there is nothing between them. *Salvabitur* is not joined hard to *prophetabunt*, it is removed farther off. To *invocaverit* it is a degree nearer at least. Nay the very next of all.

The text shews this, in a sort, but the thing itself more; for when all comes to all, when we are even at last cast, *salvabitur* or no *salvabitur*, then, as if there were some special virtue in *invocaverit*, we are called upon to use a few words or signs to this end, and so sent out of the world with *invocaverit* in our mouths. Dying, we call upon men for it; living, we suffer them to neglect it. It was not for nothing it stands so close, it even touches salvation; it is, we see, the very immediate act next before it.

And yet I would not leave you in any error concerning it. To end this point; shall *invocaverit* serve then? needs there nothing but it? no faith, no life? St. Paul answers this home;

Rom. 10. 14. he is direct, Romans the tenth; "How can they call upon Him, unless they believe?" So invocation presupposeth faith.

2 Tim. 2. 19. And as peremptory he is, "Let every one that calleth on," nay, that but "nameth the Name of the Lord, depart from

Ps. 66. 18. iniquity:"—so it presupposeth life too. For "if we incline to wickedness in our hearts, God will not hear us." No invocation that, not truly so called; a provocation rather. But put these two, faith and *recedat ab iniquitate* to it, and so whoso calleth upon Him, I will put him in good sureties, one Prophet, and two Apostles, both to assure him he shall be saved.

And that is it we all desire, to be "saved." "Saved," indefinitely. Apply it to any dangers, not in the day of the Lord only, but even in this our day; for some terrible days we have even here. I will tell you of one; the signs here set down bring it to my mind. A day we were saved from, the day of the Powder-treason, which may seem here in a sort to be described—"blood and fire, and the vapour of smoke;" a "terrible" day sure, but nothing to "the Day of the Lord." 4. *Salvabitur.*

From that we were saved; but we all stand in danger, we all need saving, from this. When this day comes, another manner of fire, another manner of smoke. That fire never burnt, that smoke never rose; but this "fire" shall burn and never be "quenched," this "smoke" shall not vanish, but "ascend for ever." I say no more, but in that, in this, in all, *qui invocaverit, salvus erit;* invocation rightly used is the way to be safe. [Mark 9. 43, 4, 5, 6. 8.] Rev. 19. 3.

This then I commend to you. And of all invocations, that which King David doth commend most, and betake himself to, as the most effectual and surest of all; and that is, *Accipiam calicem salutaris, et nomen Domini invocabo;* to call on His Name, with "the cup of salvation" taken in our hands. No invocation to that. That I may be bold to add, which is all that can be added, *Quicunque calicem salutaris accipiens nomen Domini invocaverit, salvus erit.* Another *effundam* yet, this. Ps. 116. 13.

Why, what virtue is there in the taking it, to help invocation? A double. For whether we respect our sins, they have a voice, a cry, an ascending cry, in Scripture assigned them. They invocate too, they call for somewhat, even for some fearful judgment to be poured down on us; and I doubt our own voices are not strong enough, to be heard above theirs. 1.

But blood, that also hath "a voice," specially innocent blood, the blood of Abel, that cries loud in God's ears, but [Gen. 4. 10.]

SERM. XI. nothing so loud as the blood whereof this "cup of blessing" is "the communion;" the voice of it will be heard above all, [1 Cor. 10. 16.] the cry of it will drown any cry else. And as it cries higher, so it differs in this, that it cries in a far other key, for far Heb. 12. 24. "better things than that of Abel:" not for revenge, but for [Mat. 26. 28.] "remission of sins;" for that, whereof it is itself the price [Joel 2. 31.] and purchase, for our salvation in that "great and terrible day of the Lord," when nothing else will save us, and when it will most import us; when if we had the whole world to give, we would give it for these four syllables, *salvabitur*, "shall be saved."

2. But it was not so much for sin David took this cup, as to [Ps. 116. 12.] yield God thanks for all His "benefits." In that case also, there is special use of it; and both fit us. As the former, of drowning of our sins' cry, so this also. For to this end are we here now met, to render publicly and in solemn manner our thanksgiving for His great favour this day vouchsafed us, in pouring out His Spirit; and with It His saving health upon all flesh, all that call upon Him; then to take place, [Acts 2. 20.] when we shall have special use of it, in the "great" day, the "day of the Lord." And very agreeable it is, *per hunc sanguinem pro hoc Spiritu*, 'for the pouring out of this His Spirit, to render Him thanks with the blood that was poured out to procure it;' (and this is our last *effundam*, and a real *effundam* too) for this effusion of both, the one and the other, and for the hope of our salvation, the work both of the one and of the other.

To the final attainment whereof, by His holy word of prophecy, by calling on His Name, by this Sacrament of His blood poured out, and of His Spirit poured out with it, He bring us, &c.

A SERMON

PREACHED BEFORE

THE KING'S MAJESTY AT GREENWICH,

ON THE SIXTEENTH OF MAY, A.D. MDCXIX., BEING WHIT-SUNDAY.

Acts x. 34, 35.

Then Peter opened his mouth, and said, Of a truth I perceive that God is no accepter of persons:
But in every nation he that feareth Him, and worketh righteousness, is accepted with Him.

Aperiens autem Petrus os suum, dixit, In veritate comperi, quia non est personarum acceptor Deus:
Sed in omni gente qui timet Eum, et operatur justitiam, acceptus est Illi.

[*Then Peter opened his mouth, and said, Of a truth I perceive that God is no respecter of persons:*
But in every nation he that feareth Him, and worketh righteousness, is accepted with Him. Engl. Trans.]

I forget not that we celebrate, to-day, the coming of the Holy Ghost; and I go not from it. You shall find in the next chapter, at the fifteenth verse, that to this text belongeth a coming of the Holy Ghost.

For at the uttering of these very words, as "St. Peter [Acts 10. 44.] began to speak to them, the Holy Ghost fell upon all that heard them." It is indeed the second solemn coming of the Holy Ghost. That in the second chapter was the first, and this the second that ever was.

Of which twain, this is the coming that comes home to us, and that two ways: 1. one, in respect of the parties on whom; 2. the other, in respect of the time when. The

SERM. XII. parties. For those whom the Holy Ghost came on before,
were Gentiles indeed, but yet proselytes, that is, half Jews:
Acts 2. 5. "out of every nation under Heaven;" but, "that came to
Acts 8. 27. Jerusalem to worship." And the same was the case of the
eunuch in the eighth chapter, and not a right Gentile among
them all. But here now are a sort of very Gentiles indeed, *in puris naturalibus*, such as we and our fathers were; no proselytes ever. This centurion, the *antesignanus*, 'the standard-bearer' to us, and to all that were mere heathen men indeed; and this coming, our coming properly. Never in kind, never to very Gentiles indeed till now.

[Acts 2.10.] It is well sorted, you see. On the Jews and Proselytes, at
Acts 10. 1. Jerusalem, their city; on the Gentiles, at Cæsarea, Cæsar's
city, and of the cities in Palestine, fitting the Gentiles best.

1. Well observed it is, about the calling of the Gentiles, that
Jonah 1. 3. that in the Old, and this in the New Testament, they came
Acts 10. 5. both from one place, from Joppa both. Thence loosed Jonas
to Nineveh, thence set out Peter to Cæsarea.

2. Secondly; that Cæsarea is the Nineveh, as it were, of the
Isa. 36. 13. New Testament. Nineveh was the city "of the great King"
of the Gentiles at that time; Cæsarea, Cæsar's city, as great
Lu. 2. 1. a King over the Gentiles at this, from whom went "a commandment that the whole world should be taxed."

3. Thirdly, that was performed by Jonas, this by "Bar-
Mat. 16. 16, 17. jonas:" so is St. Peter called by our Saviour, when he made
Mat. 16. 13. his confession, that "Christ was the Son of God;" and that
was at Cæsarea. Where, what he confessed then, he comes to preach now. That of Jonas an omen, as it were, of this here of St. Peter. Jonas, and Bar-jonas, from Joppa they went both; both from one place; both to one end; both to
Acts 11. 18. convert the Gentiles, to shew that "God had given them
also repentance to life."

Alway, this the better. For Jonas at Nineveh, he ends
Jonah 3. 4. with "Nineveh shall be destroyed." Bar-jonas at Cæsarea,
with *acceptus est Illi;* that the end of the text. Or, if you
Acts 10. 43. will go to the end of the sermon, the end is, "shall obtain
remission of sins," as good as it every way.

2. So the parties fit well; the time as well. The Holy Ghost here came upon them as they were at a sermon, even as we now are. "Peter opened his mouth;" they stood attentive;

the Holy Ghost came down. That to be here, is a disposition to receive the Holy Ghost. And it may please God, the like may befall us, being occupied now as they then were.

Of that sermon, these are the first words. Of which words, what can be said more to their praise, than that which the Angel saith of them the next chapter at the fourteenth verse; that Peter being sent for should, at his coming, "speak words to Cornelius, by which both he and his household should be saved." Those words the Angel there spake of, that Peter should speak, are these I have read: God of His goodness send them the same effect!

The sum.

Acts 11. 14.

In veritate comperi, shews they are a *compertum est;* and that is authentical with a test. So is this, *teste Cornelio et totá familiá,* 'witness he and his whole family and friends.' Such are most praised, for they are *animata exemplo,* 'have a soul put into them by an example.' Specially, when they be so reduced to a singular, as that singular afterwards is reduced to a general; both which are in this. Best preaching of a text, when the commentary stands before it, as here; for what is in the text propounded was fulfilled in the auditory, ere they went.

As fulfilled in them in particular, so extended to all in general, for it hath an *omni gente* put to it; that nothing was done to him there, but the same shall be done to any other. Any of any nation, that shall be found in like sort disposed, as we find he was; that is, whose "prayers and alms shall come up into remembrance before God." God shall not be wanting to them, but provide them of further means requisite to their salvation.

It is a thing well befitting the providence of God; all His creatures, when He hath made them, to see them provided of such things as are needful for them. As He doth, saith the Psalm, for "the young ravens;" saith the Gospel, for the poor "sparrows" valued, two of them at a farthing: *naturas rerum minimarum non destituit Deus,* 'the smallest things that be, He leaves them not destitute.'

Ps. 147. 9.

Mat. 10. 29.

If not them, His half-farthing creatures, much less men, as He is pleased to speak with the least, "more worth than many sparrows." So God argues with Jonas: if he made such ado for his gourd, which "sprung up in one night and withered

[Mat. 10. 31.]

Jonah 4. 10, 11.

SERM. XII. in another, should not God spare Nineveh, wherein there were so many thousands that knew not their right hand from their left," Gentiles though they were?

Mat. 5. 45. And if His care extend to all men, and He make "His rain to fall and His sun to shine upon the evil and unkind,"
Deu. 32. 2. shall He not bring the "rain of His word," as Moses calls it,
Mal. 4. 2. to fall on them, and make His "Sun of righteousness," as Malachi calls it, to "arise upon them that fear Him?" A view whereof we may take, in this family here, even of the Sun of righteousness, the white Sun, rising upon one that feared God with all his household, gave much alms and prayed to God daily.

Written by him, this; but not written for him only, that it was Whit-Sunday with him; but for us also, to whom it shall likewise be, if we be *de gente Corneliâ* express and follow him in that which was accepted of in him.

The division. Two points we have to proceed on. 1. The first here is a point newly perceived by St. Peter. 2. The second, what that was. A point newly perceived in these, 1. *In veritate comperi*, "Of a truth I perceive." 2. What the point was in these, "that in every nation, &c."

I. In that St. Peter saith, "Truly I now perceive," as if before he had not, as indeed he had not; for he was in the mind before that but *in unâ gente*, but now he perceives that *in omni gente* is the truer tenet; that even to St. Peter there were some things *incomperta*, something not perceived at first, that came to be perceived after.

II. Then an instance. What that was. And it was about God's accepting. Both ways: *privative*, what God accepts not; *positive*, what He accepts. Accepts not "persons"—that is once; but accepts of such as "fear Him and work righteousness, of what nation soever"—be he an Italian; of what condition soever—be he a centurion; all is one.

Of which two the one, fear, is an affection within, of the heart. The other, "worketh righteousness," is an action without, of the hand. Cornelius' heart and Cornelius' hand, these they be. Whence we shall learn three points more. 1. One, how we may be accepted to God, if we be as Cornelius here was; and I would we so were! 2. The other, that when all is done, all is but accepting though. *Except* He could to our fear and works both, and so is not bound; but *accept* He will though, of His grace and goodness, and as it follows immediately the next verse, for His word's sake which He sent, "preaching peace by Jesus Who is Lord over all."

The last, whereunto accepted; and that, as appeareth in III.
the forty-seventh verse, was to the Sacrament, and by it to the remission of sins, and to the receiving the Holy Ghost in a more ample measure. *Opus diei*, 'the proper of this day.'

"Of a truth I perceive." He that saith "Of a truth I per- I.
ceive now," in effect, as it were, saith before he did not so. A point newly per-
For "I perceive now," is the speech of one that is come to ceived. *Comperi.*
perceiving of that which before he perceived not.

On this we pitch first. That so great an Apostle, for all *Tu es Petrus*, and *Rogavi pro te*, and *Pasce oves Meas*, doth Mat. 16. 18.
ingenuously confess that now he had found that which till Lu. 22. 32. Joh. 21. 16.
now he had not; for, since the beginning of the chapter, he had not. So that all his *comperis* were not yet come in. By like his chair was not yet made, or he had not yet taken handsel of it. But how it comes to pass after, at Rome, I know not; at Cæsarea we see it was not so. And they that, Acts 11. 2.
in the next chapter, called him *coram*, to answer this sermon, sure they seem as then not to have been fully persuaded that St. Peter could perceive all things, and not miss in any.

Job, though in misery, yet in scorn saith to some in his time, "Indeed you, you are the only men, you perceive all." Job 12. 2.
Moses did not so. There was a case wherein he was *nesciens* Nu. 15. 34.
quid de eo facere deberet, Moses "knew not what he should do." There was a case whereof Elisha was fain to say, *Et* 2 Kings 4.
Dominus non nunciavit mihi, "God hath not shewed it him." 27.
But when God did, might not Moses and he both have said, as Peter doth here, "Of a truth" before I did not, "but now I do perceive?" Yea, but this is Old Testament.

And was it not in the New? There Caiaphas, he saith, "Tush, you perceive nothing,"—he perceived all. But Ce- Joh. 11. 49.
phas, he saith, he perceived not all. For here he now saith he perceiveth something, and all his *comperis* came not at once. So saith Peter, and so Paul, "all our knowledge is 1 Cor. 13. 9.
in part," and so is all "our prophesying" too, and puts himself in the number.

Of a truth then we perceive St. Peter comes nothing near

SERM. XII. his successor—that would be. He perceives all that is to be perceived at once; can have nothing added to his knowledge from the first instant he is set down *in cathedrâ;* can have no new *comperi,* his *comperis* come in all together; gets Caiaphas' knowledge by sitting in Cephas' chair.

They begin to scorn this themselves now, and pray him to get a good general council about him, and he shall perceive things never the worse.

But it is not this only they differ in, in something beside.
Acts 10. 26. For Peter took "Cornelius up from the ground;" his successor let Cornelius' lord and master lie still hardly; not a captain of Cæsarea he, but even Cæsar himself. Of a truth we may perceive nothing like Cephas in this neither.

Joh. 4. 25. The woman at the well-side said, "The Messias, when He comes He will tell us all." Yet when He came, He told them
Joh. 13. 7. not all at once. Even to *Tu es Petrus* He said, *Tu nescis modo scies autem post hæc;* and of those *post hæc*s this here
Joh. 16. 12. was one. As they should be able to "bear," for all they were not then able. And as it should be for them; for "it was
Acts 1. 7. not for them to know all, not the times and seasons," and such other things as "the Father had put into His own power."

I speak it for this, that even some that are far enough from Rome, yet with their new perspective they think they perceive all God's secret decrees, the number and order of them clearly; are indeed too bold and too busy with them. Luther said well that every one of us hath by nature a Pope in his belly, and thinks he perceives great matters. Even they that believe it not of Rome, are easily brought to believe it of themselves. And out they come with their *comperis,* with their great confidence propound them. But *comperi* is one thing; *in veritate comperi,* another: *comperi,* they may say, and that may be doubted of, but *in veritate comperi,* that is it.

We may take up the text a point further. *In veritate comperi* will bear two senses. 1. One, I perceive that, I did not before; 2. the other, I perceive that, the contrary whereof I did conceive before. Not to perceive is but to be ignorant; but St. Peter, in this, had not only been ignorant, but had positively held the quite contrary, *ad oppositum, Quod non ex omni gente* at any hand. At the fourteenth verse before, for the Jewish meats, we see, he contests with God: Not I, Lord, no heathenish meat, I never eat any. And at the twenty-eighth, no less unlawful to eat with heathen men.

Ignorance is but *privative;* this is *positive,* and so an error. An error in the great "mystery of godliness," a part whereof [1 Tim. 3. 16.]
was "preached unto the Gentiles;" that they also had their part in Christ. And this is not his error alone; the Apostles and brethren seem to have been in the same; they convented him for his new *comperi,* and he was fain to answer for it. That for the time, general it was, this error; and for aught we know St. Stephen, that was stoned before this, departed the world in the opinion of *in unâ,* not *omni gente;* for then sure this truth was not perceived, not received publicly.

Then is not every error repugnant to God's election. Why every error, more than every sin? God is able to pardon and not to impute error in opinion, as well as error in practice; and *nonne errant omnes qui operantur malum,* saith Solomon, "Do not all err that do evil?" Yes sure. Did not the High- Prov. 14. 22.
Priest offer, as well for the errors, as for the transgressions Lev. 5. 15.
of the people? And is not Christ made to us, by God, "wisdom" against the one, as well as "righteousness" against 1 Cor. 1. 30.
the other? It was St. Peter's case here.

This only we are to look to, that with St. Peter we be not wilful, if there come a clear *comperi;* but as ready to relent in the one, as to repent of the other. That when we be shewed our error, we open our eyes to perceive it; and when we perceive it with St. Peter here, we open our mouths to confess it. And that we do it with an open mouth, and not between the teeth, but acknowledge it plainly, it was otherwise than we thought. "I verily thought," saith St. Paul, Acts 26. 9.
"I ought to do" that which now all the world should not make me to do. This is St. Paul's. I now "comprehend," or rather "am comprehended," for καταλαμβάνομαι will bear Phil. 3. 12.
both, of which before I could not. This is St. Peter's retraction. Conclude then, if we happen to be in "some points [Phil. 3. 15.]
otherwise minded, God will bring us to the knowledge even of them." "Only in those whereto we are come, and whereof we are agreed on all sides, that we proceed by one rule," make a conscience of the practice of such truths as we agree

SERM. XII. of, "and those we do not shall soon be revealed unto us," and we shall say even of them, *in veritate comperi.*

II. What that point is, *privative.* 1. God is no accepter of persons. What is meant by persons.

What was this that St. Peter formerly had not, but now did perceive? That "God is no accepter of persons." Let us take with us, what is meant by "persons." For he that feareth God is a person; Cornelius was a person; so were all the persons in his household. The word in all the three tongues is taken as we take it, when we set personal against real, oppose the cause to the person; under it comprehending whatsoever is beside the matter or cause. The Greek and Hebrew properly signify the face; that we know shews itself first, and if it shew itself well, is *muta commendatio,* carries us, though it say never a word; as in Eliab, the goodliness
1 Sam. 16. 6. of his person moved even Samuel. Under the face then we understand, as I may say, and as we use to call it in apparel, the facing; under the person, all by-respects that do personate, attire, or mask any, to make him personable; such as are the country, condition, birth, riches, honour, and the like. And this person thus taken, of a truth we daily perceive that *in omni gente* men accept of this, and in a manner of nothing else but this; all goes by it. Well, with God it is otherwise, and with men it should be; God accepts them not, nor of any men, for them. This is the *comperi.*

And is this it? Why this was no news. Was Peter ignorant of this? It is not possible, I will never believe, but he had read the five books of Moses: why there it is
Deu. 10. 17. expressly set down, *totidem verbis.* Why, by the very light
Job 34. 19. of nature Elihu saw it, and set it down too. "No not the
1 Sam. 16. 7. person of princes." In Samuel's choice of David, there it is.
2 Chron. 19. 7. And King Jehoshaphat gave it in his charge, the second of Chronicles, the nineteenth chapter, and in other places beside; and how could he but know this?

You will say, St. Peter knew it before, but not with a *comperi,* as now he doth. And indeed many things we know by book, by speculation, as we say, and in gross, which when we come to the particular experience of, we use to say, Yea now I know it indeed, as if we had not known it, at least not so known it before. The experimental knowledge is the true *comperi in veritate,* when all is done. Was this it?

No; for had he not experience of this, and lay away his

book? Have not all experience daily? that God, in dealing His gifts of nature; outward—beauty, stature, strength, activeness; inward—wit to apprehend, memory to retain, judgment to discern, speech to deliver; that He puts no difference, but without all respect of "persons," bestows them on the child of the mean, as soon as of the mighty? So is it in wealth and worldly preferment," "He lifts the Ps. 113. 7.
poor out of the dust;"—nay, you will bear with it, it is the Holy Ghost's own term—"the dunghill, to set him with princes." So is it in His judgments; which light as heavy, yea more heavy otherwhile on the great than on the small; and shew that that way and every way, there is with Him no "respect of persons." And no man had better experience of this than he that spake it, than Peter himself, that without any respect, of a poor fisherman, was accepted to be an Apostle, the chief of the Apostles. St. Paul saith Gal. 2. 2.
well; "What they were in times past, it makes no matter, Gal. 2. 6.
God accepts no man's person," this they are now.

What shall we say then? that though he could not but know the general truth of this, yet was he once of the mind, that this general truth might admit of some exceptions;—one at the least. Not of persons? true. But nations are not persons, it held not in them. Of one nation God accepted before others, and that nation was the Jews. "You Amos 3. 2.
only have I known of all the nations of the earth," saith God in Amos. And *non taliter fecit omni nationi;* which *non* Ps. 147. 20.
taliter they took to be of the nature of an entail to Abraham's seed; that God was tied to them, and so to accept of *in unâ gente,* before and more than of all the rest.

This had run in St. Peter's head, and more than his. But now, here comes a new *comperi;* he perceives he was wrong. And if you ask how he perceived it? By relation of Cornelius' vision of the Angel, and by conferring it with his own. He saw his vision was now come to pass; Moses' unclean birds and beasts are become clean all, all to be eaten now; and the Gentiles, whom he held for no less unclean, to be eaten with, and to be gone in unto. All in one great sheet; *omni gente* and all. That the nation also comes to be understood under the word "person," no less than the rest; and none to be respected or accepted of God, for being in one

SERM. XII. corner of the sheet, that is, of one country more than of another; that in Christ neither Jew nor Gentile, all is one:
Acts 8. 27. Acts 10. 1. Acts 17. 34. and the black "Ethiopian," or the white "Italian;" the "Areopagite" in his long robe, or the centurion in his short mantle, or military habit; all conditions, all nations, are in
Rom. 11. 32. all "persons." "God hath shut up all in unbelief, that He might have mercy upon all." And good reason for it, if it
Gal. 3. 17. be but that of the Apostle's own framing, "If the law which came four hundred years after could not disannul the covenant made with Abraham so long before," by the same, nay by a better consequence, neither could the covenant with Abraham make the promise of God of none effect; the promise that was made in Paradise more than four times four hundred years before that of Abraham's, to the woman and to her whole seed.

The vision St. Peter saw, was at Joppa; he was gone as far from Jewry as there was any land; hard to the sea-side, to the very parting place, where they loosed usually, when they went to the lands of the Gentiles. Jonas loosed thence. And in a tanner's house it was, that as to "Simon the tanner" it was all one, he made leather indifferently of the badger as well as of the sheep's skin; as the skins were to "Simon the tanner," so the meat should be to Simon the Apostle. And it was a linen sheet, which very linen shewed they were all clean; for in linen the Jews wrapped the first-born of their clean beasts, if any happened to die before they came to be offered, and so buried it; but at no hand, any unclean beasts ever in linen. But now, in linen all; that if one clean, all; and so no person, calling, country excepted to, or accepted of, more than another.

2. *Positive:* Whom God accepteth: "In every nation he that feareth," &c.

Well then, no person. But we like not this destructive Divinity, that tells us what He doth not, and tells us not what He doth accept. If not the person, nor the person's nation,—what? accepts He of nothing? Yes; "in every nation," if any person there be "that feareth God and worketh righteousness"—he that brings these with him, is to God a person acceptable; such He will not let lie, but take them up, and lay them up, wherever He finds them.

Solomon in effect said as much long before, at the end of his long sermon, the Book of the Preacher. "Will ye, saith he, hear the sum of all sermons?" "Fear God"—there is "he that fears Him"—"and keep His commandments"—that is, "he that works righteousness,"—*hoc est totum hominis* read some, "there is all man hath that God will accept of;" or, *hoc est omnis homo* read other, and infer, *Si hoc est omnis homo, manifestum quod sine hoc nihil est omnis homo,* this is man, all that he is, for whatsoever besides this he is, is as if it were not; this is all things, for without this, with all his person and personableness, he is nothing in God's sight. This preached Solomon at Jerusalem to the Jew, and this Peter at Cæsarea to the Gentiles; *Hoc est omnis homo,* "This is for all men," saith Solomon; *Omni gente,* for "every nation," saith Peter. Eccl. 12. 13.

"Feareth" and "worketh" jointly.

"That feareth God, and worketh righteousness." Both these, and not the one without the other. Neither fear, which is dull and works not, for of such He accepts not; nor works, if they come not from within, from our hearts, from His true fear in our hearts, but be personate only, as were those of the Pharisee. We begin then there, within; for any thing that is personate in religion, and proceeds not from thence—*μόρφωσις,* St. Paul's "mask or vizor of godliness," St. Peter's *ἐπικάλυμμα,* "cloke" of Christian liberty—God plucks them off; He is so far from accepting them, as He casts them from Him, He cannot abide them. 2 Tim. 3. 5. 1 Pet. 2. 16.

I forgot to tell you, why not the person. God Himself tells Samuel, that He "looks not as man looks;" man looks upon the outside, the face and the facing, God looks to that which is farthest from the person; to that which is within, at the centre, that is, the heart. The inwards were God's part in every sacrifice, reserved ever to Him alone. By reserving them He shews what it is He chiefly accepts of. We must then look to that first. He first looks at the heart, and in the heart to the affection, for the heart is the seat of affections; and of all affections, that of fear; and of all fears, to the fear of God. 1 Sam. 16. 7.

Of God? why, how comes God to be feared? Fear is not but of some evil; and evil in God there is none. Not for any evil in Him; but for some evil we may expect from Him, if we fear not to offend Him, by doing that which is evil in His sight. Which punishment yet is not evil of itself, for

SERM. XII. punishment is the work of justice; but we call it as we feel it, *malum pœnæ*. And it we fear, and Him for it, or any that can inflict it.

Power and justice are, of themselves, fearful; power to all men, justice to evil men. But justice armed with power, that keeps all in awe. Now in God there is power: God's power is manifest even to heathen men. It is a part of the

Rom. 1. 19. γνωστὸν τοῦ Θεοῦ, "that which may be known of God, His power;" and go no farther but to the work of creation, saith the Apostle. Every man fears the mighty: for what he will do, we know not; what he can do, we know, and that ever presents itself first.

Rom. 13. 4. And in God there is justice, and the voice of justice, "If thou do evil, fear." Which justice of God is manifest like-

Rom. 2. 15. wise without Scriptures, by "the Law written in our hearts," the hearts even of the Heathen themselves, saith the same Apostle, whereby they are either "a law to themselves," (the better sort of them, Cornelius here,) or, if not, "their own thoughts accuse them for it, and their consciences bear witness against them," and at a sessions holden in their hearts, they condemn themselves. Which sessions is a forerunner of the great general sessions that is to ensue.

2 Cor. 5. 11. *Scientes igitur terrorem hunc*, saith St. Paul still, "knowing then this fearful judgment, we persuade men," and men are persuaded either to eschew evil yet undone, or to leave it if it be done, that it be not found in our hands, not taken about us.

This fear to suffer evil for sin, *malum pœnæ*, makes men fear to do the evil of sin, *malum culpæ;* what they fear to suffer for, they fear to do. Keeps them from doing evil at all, makes them avoid it; or keeps them from doing evil

[Job 1. 1.] still, makes them forsake it. It prevailed not only with Job

Jonah 3. 5. in the Old, but with the Ninevites. It prevailed not only

[Acts 10. 2.] with Cornelius in the New, but even with Felix; made him

Acts 24. 25. "tremble," though it had not his full work, for he was not so happy as to hear Paul out, but put it off till another time, which time never came.

1. First fear. [Ps. 111. 10.] First fear; and why fear first? Because it is first. It is called, and truly, for so truly it is, "the beginning of our wisdom," when we begin to be truly wise. In Adam it was so.

The first passion we read of, that was raised in him, that "He that feareth Him." Gen.
wrought upon him after his fall, was, "I heard Thy voice
in the garden, and I was afraid." There began his wisdom, in his fear; there began he to play the wise man,
and to forethink him of his folly committed. Fear is φιμὸς
φύσεως, as it is well called, 'of the nature of a bridle to our
nature,' to hold us in to refrain from evil, if it may be; if
not, to check us and turn us about, and make us turn from
it. Therefore "fear God, and depart from evil," lightly go Prov. 3. 7.
together, as the cause and the effect; you shall seldom find
them parted. So then, because it is first, it is to stand first,
and first to be regarded.

Another reason is, because it is most general. For it goes
through all, heathen and all. It goes to *omni gente;* for in
omni gente there is *qui timet.* For that they have so much
faith as to fear, appears by the Ninevites plainly. Nay, it
goes not only to *omni gente,* but even to *omni animante* too,
to beasts and all, yea to the dullest beast of all, to Balaam's Nu. 22. 33.
beast; he could not get her (smite her, spur her, do what he
could to her) to run upon the point of the Angel's sword;
that they are in worse case than beasts that are void of it.
So first it riseth of all, and farthest it reacheth of all.

And this fear, I would not have men think meanly of it.
It is, we see, "the beginning of wisdom;" and so both father Ps. 111. 10.
and son, David and Solomon call it. But if it have his full Prov. 1. 7.
work, to make us "depart from evil," it is wisdom com- Job 28. 28.
plete, and that from God's own mouth, Job the twenty-
eighth. Therefore Esay bids us make a "treasure" of it; Isa. 33. 6.
and, "Blessed is the man" that is ever thus wise, "that Prov. 28. 14.
feareth always"—it is Solomon. For howsoever the world
go, "this I am sure of," saith he, "it shall go well with Eccl. 8. 12.
him that feareth God, and carrieth himself reverently in
His presence."

And care not for them that talk, they know not what, of
"the spirit of bondage." Of the seven Spirits, which are Rom. 8. 15.
the divisions of one and the same Spirit this day here sent
down, the last the chiefest of all is "the Spirit of the fear Isa. 11. 2.
of God." So it is the Alpha and Omega, first and last,
beginning and end. First and last, I am sure, there is
sovereign use of it.

SERM. XII. Nor regard them not that say it pertains not to the New Testament, fancying to themselves nothing must be done but out of pure love. For even there it abideth, and two sovereign uses there are still of it, those two which before we named; 1. one to begin, 2. the other to preserve.

1. To begin. We set it here as an introduction, as the dawning is to the day. For on them that are in this dawning,
Mal. 4. 2. "that fear His name, on them shall the Sun of righteousness arise." It is Malachi saith it, it is Cornelius here sheweth it. As the base court to the temple; not into the temple at first step, but come through the court first. As the needle to the thread, it is St. Augustine, that first enters and draws after it the thread, and that sews all fast together.

Where there happens a strange effect, that not to fear the next way is to fear. The kind work of fear is to make us "cease from sin." Ceasing from sin brings with it a good life; a good life, that ever carries with it a good conscience; and a good conscience casts out fear. So that, upon the matter, the way not to fear is to fear; and that God That brings light out of darkness, and glory out of humility, He it is That also brings confidence out of fear.

2. This for the introduction. And ever after, when faith is entered and all, it is a sovereign means to preserve them also. There is, as I have told you, a composition in the soul, much after that of the body. The heart in the body is so full of heat, it would stifle itself and us soon, were it not God hath provided the lungs to give it cool air, to keep it from stifling. Semblably in the soul, faith is full of spirit, ready enough of itself to take an unkind heat, save that fear is by God ordained to cool it and keep it in temper, to awake our care still, and see it sleep not in security. It
Ps. 30. 6. is good, against saying in one's heat, *Non movebor*, saith the
Mat. 26. 33. Psalm. Good, against *Etsi omnes, non ego*—St. Peter found
Rom. 11. 20. it so. Good, saith St. Paul, against *Noli altum sapere.* And these would mar all but for the humble fear of God; by that all is kept right.

Wherefore, when the Gospel was at the highest, "work
Phil. 2. 12. out your salvation with fear and trembling," saith St. Paul;
1 Pet. 1. 17. "pass the time of your dwelling here in fear," saith St. Peter. Yea, our Saviour Himself, as noteth St. Augustine, when He

had taken away one fear, *Ne timete,* "Fear not them that Mat. 10. 28.
can kill the body, and when they have done that, have done
all, and can do no more;" in place of that fear puts another, [Vid. S.
"but fear Him That when He hath slain the body, can cast August.
soul and it into hell fire; and when He had so said once, Serm. 161.
comes over again with it to strike it home, *Etiam dico vobis;* *al.* 18. de
"Yea, I say unto you, fear Him." Verb. Apost. c. c. 5. 8.]

So then, this of fear is not Moses' song only, it is "the Rev. 15.
song of Moses and the Lamb" both. Made of the harmony 3, 4.
of the one as well as the other. A special strain in that "song of Moses and the Lamb" you shall find this, "Who will not fear Thee, O Lord?" He that will not may *sibi canere,* make himself music; he is out of their choir, yea the Lamb's choir; indeed, out of both.

This have I a little stood on, for that, methinks, the world begins to grow from fear too fast: we strive to blow this Spirit quite away; for fear of *carnificina conscientiæ,* we seek to benumb it, and to make it past feeling. For these causes, fear is, with God, a thing acceptable, we hear; and that the Holy Ghost came down where this fear was, we see. So it is, St. Peter affirms it "for certain, of a truth:" so it is, St. Peter protests it. Let no man beguile you, to make you think otherwise. No, no; but *Fac, fac, vel timore pœnæ, si nondum potes amore justitiæ;* 'Do it man, I tell thee, do it, though it be for fear of punishment, if you cannot get yourself to do it for love of righteousness.' One will bring on the
other; *A timore Domini concepimus Spiritum salutis*—it is Isa. 26. 18.
Esay. By it we shall conceive that which shall save us. Acts 10. 6.
These very words shall save us, said the Angel, and so they did; here in Cornelius, we have a fair precedent for it. And so, now I come to the other.

2.
But works withal; "and worketh righteousness." [Ps. 111. 10.]

For, I ask, is God all for within? accepts He of nothing without? Yes, that He doth. Of a good righteous work too, if it proceed from His fear in our hearts. Fear is not all then: no, for it is but "the beginning," as we have heard; God will have us begin, but not end there. We have begun with *qui timet Eum;* we must end with *et operatur justitiam,* and then comes *acceptus est Illi,* and not before. For neither fear, if it be fear alone; nor faith, if it be faith alone, is accepted of Him; but *timet* and *operatur* here with Peter, and Gal. 5. 6.

SERM. XII. *fides quæ operatur* there with Paul; fear and faith both that worketh, and none else. If it be true fear, if such as God will accept, it is not *timor piger*, 'a dull lazy fear;' his fear
Mat. 25. 18. 30. that feared his Lord, and "went and digged his talent into the ground," did nothing with it. Away with his fear and him "into utter darkness!" God will have his talent turned, have it above ground. He will not have his religion invisible
Jas. 2. 18. within. No; "shew me thy faith," saith St. James; "thy fear," saith St. Peter here, by some works of righteousness. Else, talk not of it. He will have it made appear, that men may see it, and glorify Him for it, That hath such good and faithful servants.

And they observe that it is not, "that doeth," but "that worketh righteousness." Not *facit*, but *operatur*. And what manner of work? St. Peter's word is ἐργαζόμενος here; and for ἐργαζόμενος, ἔργον will not serve; it must be ἐργασία,
Isa. 1. 17. which is a plain 'trade.' *Discite bene agere*, saith Esay, learn it, as one would learn a handicraft, to live by; learn it, and be occupied in it; make an ἐργασία, that is, even 'an occupation' of it. Christ's own occupation, Who, as St. Peter,
Acts 10. 38. tells us straight after, *pertransiit benefaciendo*, "went up and down, went about doing good," practising it, and nothing else; for that is ἐργάζεσθαι.

"Worketh righteousness." This "righteousness," to know what it is—besides the common duties of our calling, either as Christians in general; or particular, as every man's vocation lies—we cannot better inform ourselves of it, than from this party he speaks of, from Cornelius, and what the works were he did. And they are set down at the second verse, where, after St. Luke had said, "he feared God," to shew his works of righteousness he adds, 1. "he gave much alms," and 2. "prayed to God continually;" and at the thirteenth verse, that he was found 3. "fasting at the ninth hour," that is, three at afternoon. In these three, 1. "alms," 2. "prayer," and 3. "fasting," stood his works of righteousness—in these three; for besides these we find not any other. They be the same, and in the same order, as they were figured in the three oblations of the Magi, firstfruits of the Gentiles, there in the Gospel, as the Fathers allot them: 1. "Gold," that is, for "alms;" 2. "incense," that is, "prayer;" and 3. "myrrh," bitter myrrh, for works of mortification, as "fasting" and such like; as bitter to the flesh, as myrrh to the taste; both bitter, but wholesome both. But without all figure they are the same three, and stand just in the same order that here they do, where our Saviour teacheth them literally, and that, under the name of righteousness. 1. "Alms," first: that He begins with at the first verse, and so here it is first. 2. Then, to "prayer" next, at the fifth verse; 3. and after that, to "fasting," even as it is here too. Cornelius' works were these three: 1. "Gave alms;" 2. "prayed" duly; 3. was found at his "fast" by the Angel. This is all we find, more we find not specified; and these are enough, these would serve, if we would do them. These in him were, the same in us will be accepted. Mat. 6. 1, 5, 16. Acts10.2,3, 30.

III. Of God's acceptation. He, &c. "is accepted."

And now, of God's acceptation. Accepting is but a quaint term borrowed from the Latin. It is no more than receiving or taking. 1. First then, clear it is He will take them; but, where they be to take. But where they are not, take them He cannot. In vain shall we look for acceptation of that which is not. We are then to see there be some given, some for Him to take. Take us He cannot, if there be not Cornelius' hand to take us by; "come up in remembrance" they cannot, if none were done to remember; for *memoria est præteritorum,* and all ours are yet to come I fear, *in phantasiâ* rather than *in memoriâ.* Our "alms," alas they are shrunk up pitifully; "prayer," swallowed up with hearing lectures; and for the third, feast if you will continually, but "fast" as little as may be; and of most I might say, not at all. The want of these, the bane of our age. He stretcheth out His hand, to receive "alms;" He boweth down His ear, to receive "prayer;" He beholdeth with His eyes, to take us "fasting:" there is none to give them, and so He cannot receive them. But, by this *acceptus est* here, we see how we might be *accepti.*

It is beside the text; yet if ye ask, Here is fear, and here are works, where is faith all this while, "without which it is impossible to please God," or "to be accepted of Him?" Had he no faith? Yes, he would not have spent his goods, or chastened his body, without some faith; at least, "call" upon God he could not, on Whom he "believed" not. Heb. 11. 6. Rom.10.14.

Therefore he believed sure, the Gentiles' creed at least, that

SERM. XII. a God there is; that sought He will be; that He will not fail them that seek Him, but both regard and reward them.

The Ninevite's creed at least, in whose fear there was faith
[Jonah 3. 9.] and hope too. *Quis scit*, "Who can tell, whether God may not turn" and spare, and accept of a poor Gentile? There is nothing known to the contrary, and there be precedents for it. And so he turned and set himself to seek God, by the three
Ps. 9. 10. ways we remembered. "And Thou, Lord, never failest them
2 Cor. 8. 12. that seek Thee," but "acceptest them, not according to that they have not, but according to that they have," though it be but a "willing mind" they have. God forbid but concupiscence should be of equal power to good, that it is to evil. If you will reach it further to faith in Christ, living in garrison among the Jews he could not choose but have heard somewhat of Him, to move him to throw himself down before Him, and He took him up, *Acceptus est Illi.*

Isa. 42. 3. The flax did but "smoke," Christ "quenched it not." Cracks there were in the reed, but "He brake it not" though, but kindled the one, and bound up the other; and in that little strength he had, took him as He found him, and took order thus to bring him nearer the ways of His salvation.

And but "accepted." But now, lest one error beget another, and the last prove worse than the first, take this with you. When all is said that can be said, all is but accepting, for all this. That he was, and we shall be "accepted," that gives us some heart; and that it is but "accepted," that takes away all self-conceit of ourselves. For I know not how, if we be but "accepted," we take upon us straight, and fall into a fancy, that well worthy we were, or else we should not. *Altum sapere* comes, and we swell straight; insomuch as we cannot be gotten to accept of this *acceptus est*, to accept of any acceptation, but grow to a higher strain of merit and condignity, and I wot not what. To prick this bladder, all is shut up with this δεκτός. Out of which word, we are to take notice of this; it is neither our fear, nor our works, all is but God's gracious acceptation.

And it is not, as they well observe, δεκτέος, but δεκτὸς, not δεκτέος, *acceptandus*, 'is to be accepted' of Him, as if God could neither will nor choose; no, it is δεκτὸς only, that is, but *acceptabilis* at most, but a capacity that he may be; lays no necessity that he must be accepted.

The Schoolmen express it well at times by *non deerit Deus*, 'God will not be wanting' to such, will accept them; but *non tenetur Deus*, 'He is not so bound' but, if He would, He might refuse; and that He doth not, it is but of His mere goodness: all are but "accepted."

The Fathers thus:—I name St. Augustine for the Latin. *Hoc habet, non pondus humani meriti, sed ordo consilii divini;* 'that thus it is, it is no weight or worth of man's merit, it is but the very order and course of God's dealing,' His favourable dealing, that and nothing else, that there is any accepting at all. The Greek Fathers, thus;—I name Chrysostom for them. It is *καταξίωσις*, not *ἀξία*, that is, *dignatio*, not *dignitas; dignatio acceptantis*, not *dignitas operantis. Digni habebuntur*, saith the Gospel, and the Epistle both: the Gospel,
Luke the twentieth; the Epistle, second of Thessalonians, Lu. 20. 35.
the first chapter. God counts them worthy, and His so 2 Thes. 1. 5.
counting makes them worthy; makes them so, for so they are not of themselves, or without it, but by it so they are. His taking our works of righteousness well in worth, is their worth.

There was another centurion beside this in the Apostle, the centurion in the Gospel; the Elders of the Jews were at
dignus est about him, dignified him highly; but he indignified Lu. 7. 4, 6.
himself as fast, was at his *non sum dignus* twice, neither worthy that Christ should come to him, nor that he to Christ. And even thus it was ever with all from the beginning. Job,
another *timens Deum*, "his like was not upon earth," yet thus Job 1. 8.
he; *Etsi justus fuero, non levabo caput*, "All were he just, he Job 10. 15.
would down with his crest" for all that; and what? *Et depre-* Job 9. 15.
cabor Judicem meum, and plead nothing, stand upon no terms, but deal only by way of supplication; and that is the safest
way. And why so? For *verebar omnia opera mea*, saith he, Job 9. 28.
he durst not trust any of them. And why not? For the continual dropping of our corruption upon the web of our well-doing stains it so as, if he would stand straining them, He that now doth accept them, might justly except to them, for many exceptions there lie against them. He that takes them might let them lie, as not worth the taking up; for if He should ransack them, they would scarce prove worth the taking up; but yet take them up He doth, and reward them;

SERM. XII. both, for "the praise of the glory of His grace." To the glory
of the praise of which grace be all this spoken.

Eph. 1. 6. All which tends to this—for our work is this, our labour this, this is all in all, to get men to do well, and yet not ween well of their well-doing—to join first *timet* and *operatur*, to fear, and yet to do good; and when we have done good, yet to fear with Job for David's reason, *cognoscimus imperfectum nostrum*. Then to join again *operatur*, and *acceptus est*. For that is it, if we could hit on it. We cannot, but that is it though. For think you we can get men to this? No; do we evil, we will not know it, we excuse, we lessen it. Do we well, we know it straight; nay we over-know, and over-praise it. No remedy, merit it must be, and hire it must be; reward we cannot skill of. *Acceptus est* is nothing, "accepted" will not serve; we will know how we shall be "accepted," of merit or of grace. Fond men! so we be "accepted," though of "grace," are we not well? What desire we more, but to
Deu. 9. 4. be taken and not refused? The Law, that saith, "Say not, it
Ezek. 36. 22. is for my righteousness." The Prophets say, "It is not for
Rom. 10. 3. your sakes." The Apostle saith, "If you seek to establish your own righteousness," you are gone. Yea, Christ Himself
Lu. 18. 11, 14. saith, If you talk much of it with the Pharisee, "Lord," this I am, and this I do, there is not the poorest "publican" that goes by the way, but he shall be "justified" before you. And therefore be entreated, I pray you, to accept of *acceptus est*. That sets all safe, that brings all to God, and there leaves it.

For, if this fearer, this worker be "accepted," and not in himself, in whom then? who is it? The Apostle tells us
Eph. 1. 6. directly, "He hath made us accepted in His Beloved," His beloved Son:—so Paul. And St. Peter immediately in the very next words that follow upon these: "You know the word," the word of the Word That was in the beginning and made all, and "That in the fulness of time was sent and
Ps. 107. 20. healed all;" *misit Verbum et sanavit eos*. In Him and through Him all are "accepted" that have had, or shall have, the honour and happiness ever so to be. In Whom then we are "accepted," we see.

To what end "accepted." Now lastly, to what; and so an end. That being so "accepted" or received, whether you will, both or one, you may receive what? Plain it is, it follows, the Sacrament.

But they to receive the first Sacrament, that of Baptism; for they were yet in their Paganism, unbaptized. But they that are Christians already, and past the first, there remaineth for them to receive none but the second. And that then is it. And that bound they are to receive. For though by special privilege some are *aspersi Spiritu quos aqua mystica non tetigit*, 'sprinkled with the Holy Ghost, before they had the sprinkling of water,' of which number was Cornelius, and these in the text; though while they were at the sermon, the Holy Ghost came upon them, yet to the Sacrament they came though, we see. That was to them and is to us all the seal of God's acceptation. That first was theirs, but the chief and last is this of ours.

For this is indeed the true receiving, when one is received to the table, to eat and drink, to take his repast there; yea *ad accipiendum in Quo acceptus est*, to take, and to take into him "that body, by the oblation whereof we are all sanctified," Heb. 10. 10.
and that blood "in which we have all remission of sins." In Eph. 1. 7.
that ended they, in this let us end.

And this accepting we desire of God; and desiring it in an acceptable time, He will hear us; and this is that "acceptable time." [2 Cor. 6. 2.] For if the year of Pentecost, the fiftieth year, were "the acceptable year," as Luke the fourth and nineteenth, then the day of Pentecost, the fiftieth day, this day, is the "acceptable day" for the same reason. Truly acceptable, as the day whereon the Holy Ghost was first received, and whereon we may receive Him now again; whereon *acceptus est* is fulfilled both ways; we of Him received to grace, and He of us, His flesh and blood, and with them His Spirit. He receiveth us to grace, and we receive of Him grace, and with it the influence of His Holy Spirit, which shall still follow us, and never leave us till we be *accepti* indeed, that is, received up to Him in His kingdom of glory; whither blessed are they that shall be received.

A SERMON

PREACHED BEFORE

THE KING'S MAJESTY, AT WHITEHALL,

ON THE FOURTH OF JUNE, A.D. MDCXX., BEING WHIT-SUNDAY.

---

1 John v. 6.

That is that Jesus Christ That came by water and blood; not by water only, but by water and blood. And it is the Spirit That beareth witness, for the Spirit is truth.

Hic est Qui venit per aquam et sanguinem, Jesus Christus; non in aquâ solum, sed in aquâ et sanguine. Et Spiritus est Qui testificatur, quoniam Spiritus est veritas.

[*This is He That came by water and blood, even Jesus Christ; not by water only, but by water and blood. And it is the Spirit That beareth witness, because the Spirit is truth.* Engl. Trans.]

SERM. XIII.

"This is Jesus Christ;" "and it is the Spirit." So the verse, you see, linketh Christ and the Spirit together, is a passage from the one to the other. Linketh them, and so consequently linketh this feast of the Spirit present with those of Christ that are gone before; and under one, sheweth the convenience of having the Spirit an article in our Creed, and of having this day a feast in our calendar.

For though Christ have done all that He had to do, all is not done that is to do till the Spirit come too. We have nothing to shew, we want our test, a special part of our evidence is lacking; that when all is done, if this be not, nothing is done. "Christ" without "water," "water" without "blood;" His "water and blood" and He, without the Spirit, avail us nothing. The Spirit we are to have, and this day we have It; and for the having It this day, we keep a feast.

As those hitherto for Christ, *complementum legis,* so this for the Holy Ghost, *complementum Evangelii,* which was not complete *donec complerentur dies Pentecostes,* "till the days of Pentecost were fulfilled;" till this day was come and gone. [Acts 2. 1.]

St. John is every-where all for love. Here in this chapter, I know not how, he is hit upon faith. Which with him is rare; so the more to be made of. Specially in this age, wherein it is grown the virtue of chief request. And indeed Ἡ χαρίεν τι πίστις ἐστὶν, ἐὰν πίστις ᾖ, 'an excellent virtue is faith, if it be faith.' For as there is, saith St. Paul, γνῶσις ψευδώνυμος, "a knowledge falsely so called," so is there a faith; for faith is itself but a kind of knowledge. 1 Tim. 6. 20.

How shall we then make faith of our faith? Of itself it is but a bare act, faith, a thing indifferent, the virtue and the value of it is from the object it believeth in; if that be right, all is right. And that is right, if it have for this object, not Jesus Christ barely; but as St. John speaketh, "that Jesus Christ." "That Jesus Christ" is somewhat a strange speech, as if there were another. Is there so? Yes, ye have *alium Jesum,* and *aliud Evangelium;* not "that," but "another Jesus;" not "this," but "another Gospel." 2 Cor. 11. 4. Gal. 1. 6.

And as not "that" but "another Jesus," so Christ Himself tells us, you shall have not that, but another Christ. Another, nay many other; yet there is but one true. "Lo, here is Christ, lo, there He is." Go into the desert, there you shall have Him; get you to such a conventicle, and there you shall not miss of Him. Go but to one city I could name, you shall have Christs enough, and scarce a true one among them all. Mat. 24. 23.

Well then, what shall we do, "to sever the precious from the vile;" "that Jesus Christ, from others;" set the *hic est Ille* upon the right Christ? This, saith St. John, these two ways: 1. "That Jesus Christ" That comes "in water and blood" jointly, not in either alone, *hic est Ille.* If but in one, He is "another Jesus." 2. "That Jesus" That hath "the Spirit to bear Him witness," is the true; this witness if He want, *hic non est Ille.* Under one we shall learn Christ aright. For as one may learn a false Christ, so may he the true Christ falsely. "You have not so learned Christ," saith the Apostle, that is, not amiss you have not; meaning some Jer. 15. 19. Eph. 4. 20.

SERM. XIII. other had. And as learn Christ aright, so learn to do the Spirit His right; not to shoot Him off, but know He is to have a chief holy-day in our *fasti*, as He hath a part, and a principal part, in the test of whosoever shall be saved.

The sum. The sum is, three items we have: 1. That we take not *pseudo-Christum pro Christo*: 'the false Christ for the true;' that is, one that comes in His name, but is not He.

2. Neither when we have the true one, that we take not *semi-Christum pro Christo*, 'a moiety or part of Christ for the whole.'

3. When we have the whole, that we take Him not without His Test, and that is the Spirit, for as good not take Him at all.

The division. Three parts I would lay forth: 1. There is Christ's part; 2. there is the Spirit's part; 3. there is the Sacrament's part.

I. Christ's part: His double coming, in 1. "water," and 2. "blood." In it these: 1. that Christ was so to come; 2. that Christ did so come; 3. not only did, but doth so come daily to us. 4. As He comes to us in both, so we to come to Him for both; and ever take heed of the error of either alone, of turning *non solum* into *solum*.

II. Then the Spirit's part: 1. of His "witness;" 2. of the "truth" of it. 1. Of His witness: 1. that a witness there is to be; 2. that a witness there is; 3. nay not one, but three; 4. of which the Spirit is one and the chief witness. His witness to 1. "Jesus, 2. Christ That came;" 3. to the "water," 4. to the "blood," He came in. This of His "witness." Then of the "truth" of it; and withal, how to discern "the Spirit," that is, "the truth."

III. And last, the reversal to this. That as not these without the Spirit, so not the Spirit without these, that is, not without the Sacraments, which are the monuments and pledges of these. And so that we endeavour that the Spirit on this day, the day of the Spirit, may come to us and give His witness, that Christ is come to us, and come to us in them; in them both, to our comfort both here and eternally.

I. Christ's part: 1. That He was to come in "water and blood."

Thus it is written, and thus it behoved that He That was to come, Jesus the Saviour of the world, when He came, should come "in water and blood." His name was so called, Jesus, saith the Angel, to shew He should "save His people

from their sins." To save us from them, by taking them Mat. 1. 21.
away; for *hic est omnis fructus*, saith Esay, and it is a ground with us, "All the fruit we have, is the taking away of our Isa. 27. 9.
sin." Take that away, the rest will follow of itself; that, indeed, is all in all.

To take away sin, two things are to be taken away. For in sin are these two; 1. *Reatus*, and 2. *Macula*, as all Divines agree, 'the guilt,' and 'the soil,' or spot. The guilt, to which punishment is due; the spot, whereby we grow loathsome in God's eyes, and even in men's too. For even before them, shame and reproach follow sin. Take these two away, and sin is gone. And there is no people under Heaven, but have sense of these two; and no religion is, or ever was but laboured to remove them both.

To take away soil, "water" is most fit; to take away guilt, "blood." No punishment, for any guilt, goes further than "blood." Therefore had the heathen their lustrations for the soil, which were ever by water; (*donec me flumine vivo* [Virg. Æn. 2. 719. 20.]
Abluero;) and their expiations for the guilt, by shedding of [Æn. 2. 116.]
blood ever, (*sanguine placâstis*,) without which they held no remission of sins.

The Jews, they likewise had their "sprinkling water" for Nu. 8. 7.
the uncleanness; had their slain sacrifice, the "blood" where- Ex. 12. 22.
of done on their "posts," the destroyer passed by them, the guilt by it being first taken away.

But the Prophet tells us, no water—no, not "snow-water," Job 9. 30.
and put to it "nitre" and "borith" and fuller's "soap," never Jer. 2. 22. [Vulg.]
so much—can enter into the soul, to take away the stains of it. And the Apostle, he tells us, "it was impossible the blood of bulls or goats should satisfy for the sins of men." Heb. 10. 4.
The "water" had not the virtue to get out those spots; nor the "blood," the value, to make satisfaction to God, for man's trespass.

Donec venit Qui venturus erat, "Till He came That was to Gen. 49. 10.
come;" Shiloh, with a "blood," and a "water," which, because it was the "blood" and "water" of the Son of God, and so of God, by His divine power infused into both, gave the "water" such a piercing force, and gave the "blood" so inestimable high a value, as was able to work both; to put an end to that which neither the washings, nor offerings of

SERM. XIII. nature, or of the Law could rid us of. Thus, "in water and blood" was He to come, That was to take sin away.

2. That He did so come. Thus was He to come, and thus did He come; did come divers ways. "In blood," the blood of His circumcision; "in water," the water of His baptism. Began so, and so ended; "in water," the water of His strong crying and tears, whereby He made supplication to God for us; "in blood," the blood of His passion, the blood of Gethsemane, His bloody sweat; the blood of Gabbatha, of the scourges and thorns; the blood of Golgotha, of His hands and feet digged. Thus came He.

Mat. 26. 36, &c.

Joh. 19. 13, 17.

Yet is it none of these St. John pointeth to—these were at several times—but he points to His coming in both together at once. This place of the Epistle refers to that place of the Gospel, where at once, with one blow, His side being opened, "there came forth blood and water" both. Blood, *sanguis testamenti*, saith Zachary, the ninth, "the blood of His testament," whereby He set His guilty prisoners free. Water, saith the same Zachary, the thirteenth, *fons domui Israel;* "a fountain which He opened to the house of Israel, for sin, and for uncleanness." The one blood, the λύτρον, "the ransom" or price of the taking away the guilt; the other, water, the λουτρὸν, "laver" of our new birth, from our original corruption.

Joh. 19. 34. Zech. 9. 11. Zech. 13. 1. [Mat. 20. 28.] [Tit. 3. 5.]

[Vid. Tract. in S. Joan. 120.] *Hæc sunt Ecclesiæ gemina sacramenta,* saith Augustine. 'These are (not two of the Sacraments; so there might be more, but) the twin-Sacraments of the Church.' So but two of that kind, two famous memorials left us; in baptism, of the water; in the cup of the New Testament, of the blood He then came in.

3. That He comes so still. Thus did Christ come; did, and doth still. For the word is not ἐληλυθὼς, referring to the time past, but ἐλθὼν, which respecteth even the present also. Came not once, but still and ever cometh so. The water still runs, for He opened a fountain never to be drawn dry; and His *massa sanguinis* is not spent neither, for it is *sanguis æterni fœderis,* and so *æternus;* "of the everlasting covenant," and so itself lasting for ever.

Heb. 13. 20.

And that this His coming to us he means, the order sheweth. For when it came from Him, it came in another order; "blood" came first, and then "water;"—see the Gospel. But here in the Epistle, when He comes to us, "water" is first, and then "blood." "Blood and water," Joh. 19. 34. the order *quoad Se;* "water and blood," *quoad nos.* Ever to us, in water first.

But what means this, "not in water only, but in water and blood?" To say, "in water and blood," was plain enough, one would think. Our rule is in Logic, *Non sufficit alterum, oportet utrumque fieri in copulativis.* Our rule in Divinity, "What God hath joined, no man presume to sever." Yet Mat. 19. 6. when He had said, "in water and blood," He comes over with them again, with His *non in aquâ solum,* "not in water only, but in water and blood." What means this, but to make it yet more plain, that there might be no mistaking, no slipping of the collar? that one of them will not serve our turn? but, as once He came, so still and ever He is to come in them both?

4. That we are to come to Him for both.

And as He to come to us, so we to come to Him. He to us in both, we to Him for both. He not to us, in either alone; we not to Him, for either alone. For if for either alone, we make superfluous His coming in the other; we question His wisdom, as if He came in more than needed, as if any thing He came in, might well enough be spared. No, we need both, we have use of both, and so to come to Him for them both.

Among the *profunda Satanæ,* this was one: when he could Rev. 2. 24. not *κωλύειν,* 'keep Him out,' by a new stratagem he sought *λύειν τὸν Ἰησοῦν, solvere Jesum* (as the Fathers read the verse of the chapter next before) that is, 'to take Him in pieces.' When he could not prevail in setting up a false, he set some on work to take in sunder the true.

Was it not thus? Did they not *solvere,* 'dissolve,' take in sunder His natures; made Him come as only man, as Samosatenus; made Him come, as only God, as Sabellius? Dissolved they not His person; made Him come in two, as Nestorius? And is not this here a plain dissolving also? He coming entirely in both, to take Him by halves, take of Him what they list, what they think will serve their turns, and leave the other, and let it lie? So take *pars pro toto,* a piece of Jesus for the whole, as if they meant to be saved by synecdoche.

SERM. XIII. Which very taking Him in pieces makes Him that he is not the true. For if the coming in both twain make Him *Hic est Ille,* the taking away of either turns Him into *alium Jesum;* and so, *hic non est Ille.* This you may call Jesus Christ, but this is not that Jesus Christ, St. John His ἐπιστήθιος taught us. There was a sort of heretics in the Primitive Church were so all for "water," cared so little for His coming in "blood," as they ministered the Communion in nothing but water, and are therefore called *Hydroparastatæ,* or *Aquarii.* There were others—but it were a world to rake up old errors; what need we? Have we not now that frame to themselves a Christ without "water," or a Christ without "blood," and so seem to hold *aqua sola,* or *solus sanguis,* against St. John's *non in solâ,* flat?

1. See you some that pour out themselves into all riot, and
Eph. 4. 19. follow "uncleanness even with greediness?" Christ "in water" would do well for such, and they care least for it; by their good-will would have none come upon them, would not be clean, would be as they are, as swine in their wallow all their life long. No "water" they, but "blood," as much as you will. Frame to themselves a Christ without "water," all in "blood."

"This is that Christ That cometh." How comes He? what brings He? Comes He in "blood," brings He good store of that, that we may strike off the guilt of our old score? He is welcome coming so. But He comes with "water" too. Nay, they can spare that—with the Gergesenes, to pray Him to
Mat. 8. 34. be gone, "to depart from their coasts;" they love "blood" without "water," are all for comfort as they call it, nothing for cleanness of life. *In solo sanguine,* these.

2. See you some other, not many, yet some, careful to their weak power to contain themselves, yet through human frailty overtaken otherwhile? Christ in "blood" comes for these, for these in special, and alas! they dare not come near it, not His "blood," as utterly unworthy of it. These are but few, in comparison of those other, the *soli-sanguines.* Yet, some such there are, and for them hath St. John directed the letter of this text in this order which it stands; that Christ "came not in water alone, but came in blood too."

Timorous, trembling, consciences think they have never

"water" enough: if they find about them any unclean thing, they are quite cast down, utterly dejected straight; as if that Christ were John Baptist, that came in "water" alone; nay, [Mat.3.11.] were turned into Moses, that had his name of being "taken [Exod. 2. 10. *See Marg.*] out of the water," as if He came all "in water," nay were all "water," had not a drop of "blood" in Him. These seem to hold *in aquâ solâ*, whereas Christ hath both "water and blood," of each alike much, no less of the one than of the other; came in "blood," and came in it for them, and to them doth most readily apply it, that make most spare of it.

But the greater number by far are those in the other extreme, that are nothing timorous, far enough from that; dissolute, and care not how many foul blotches they have, so they may have the guilt and punishment taken away; hear there is remission of sins in His "blood;" so lie at His veins continually like horse-leeches, so as if it were possible they would not leave a drop of blood in Him. As for His "water," they have no use of it, nor desire not to have any, let that run waste; are all for "blood," would not care if all the "water" were drained from Him, nay if, as the "waters" of Egypt, all His were turned into "blood." Forgiven, that [Ps. 105. 29.] they would be; clean, they care not to be; as much "blood," as little "water" as you will. Both these would be looked to, but this latter more, as the predominant error of our age, wherein the "water" is even at the low water-mark. Now for these we return the *non solum*, as by good warrant we may, both ways; it is equally true, not in blood alone, hear you, but in blood and water. Will you have no "water?" then must you have no Christ, for Christ came "in water." And further we add, that as "in water and blood" both, so "in water" first, (for so it lieth in the text) and that which stands first we to pass through first. "Water," *quoad nos*, is the first, before "blood:"—there to begin in God's name. Take that with you too.

They then that have learned Christ aright, are to come to Him for both. With the woman of Samaria, "Lord, give us Joh. 4. 15. of this water;" with them of Capernaum, "Lord, give us of Joh. 6. 34. this bread," of this "Cup of the New Testament in Thy 1Cor.11.25. blood." To come to Him for "blood," for the forgiveness of our sins "through faith in His blood." To come to Him for [Rom. 3. 25.]

SERM. XIII. "water" as well, for the taking out of the stains. Yea, even as Esay said, *Haurietis aquas cum gaudio de fontibus Salva-*
Isa. 12. 3. *toris*, even "with joy to draw waters from the fountains of our Saviour;" with more joy so draw "water," than to draw "blood" from Him.

But indeed, to look well into the matter, they cannot be separate, they are mixed; either is in other. There is a mixture of the "blood" in the "water;" there is so, of the "water" in the "blood;" we can minister no "water" without "blood," nor "blood" without "water." In baptism we are washed with "water:" that "water" is not without "blood." The "blood" serves instead of "nitre." He hath
Rev. 1. 5. "washed us from our sins in His blood"—"washed." They
Rev. 7. 14. made their robes "white in the blood of the Lamb." No washing, no whiting by "water," without "blood." And in the Eucharist we are made drink of the blood of the New Testament, but in that blood there is water, "for the
1 Joh. 1. 7. blood of Christ purifieth us from our sins." Now to purify, is a virtue properly belonging to water, which is yet in the blood; and purifying refers to spots, not to guilt, properly. So, either is in other; therefore, the conceit of separation, let it alone for ever.

To take heed then of draining Christ's "water" from His "blood," or abstracting His "blood" from His "water;" of bringing in the restringent, *solâ*, into either. Every one of us, for his own part, thus to do. But howsoever men frame fancies to themselves—as frame they will, do what we can—that our doctrine be looked to; we are not to teach Jesus Christ, but "that Jesus Christ" That thus came in both. That our divinity then on the one side be not waterish, without all heart or comfort, presenting Christ in "water" only, to make fear where none is; nor on the other, that we frame not ourselves a sanguine divinity, void of fear quite, and bring in Christ all in "blood," blood and nothing else; with little "water," or none at all, for fear of *ex nimiâ spe desperatio*.

Gal. 3. 8. "Faith," as it "justifieth," saith St. Paul,—there is
Acts 15. 9. "blood;" so it "purifieth the heart," saith St. Peter,—
Rom. 8. 24. there is "water." "Hope," as it "saveth," saith St. Paul
1 Joh. 3. 3. —"blood;" so it "cleanseth" saith St. John,—"water." In vain we flatter ourselves if they do the one and not the

other. Do we make "grace of none effect?" That we may Gal. 2. 21.
not. "Do we make the Law of none effect by faith?" that Rom. 3. 31.
we may not neither, not this day specially, the feast of the Law and Spirit both; but rather "establish" it. Best, if
it could be set right, "the song of Moses and of the Lamb;" Rev. 15. 3.
it is the harmony of Heaven. If we teach *Ne peccetis*—
"water;" to teach also—"blood"—*Si quis autem pecca-* 1 Joh. 2. 1.
verit, with St. John. If we say *salvus factus es*—"blood;" Joh. 5. 14.
to say *Noli amplius peccare*—"water"—withal, with Christ Himself.

This is that Jesus Christ, and the true doctrine of Him; neither *diluta,* and so evil for the heart; nor *tentans caput,* and so fuming up to the head; neither scammoniate, tormenting the conscience; nor yet opiate, stupifying it, and making it senseless. And so much for Christ's double coming.

II. The Spirit's part.

Well, when Christ is come, and thus come, may we be gone, have we done? Done! we are yet in the midst of the verse; before we make an end of it, it must be Whitsuntide. The Spirit is to come too. So a new *Qui venit,* That comes in both those, and comes in the Spirit besides. And a new *non solum;* not in "water and blood" only, but in the Spirit withal.

Joh. 19. 30. 1. His "witness."

Not that Christ saith not truly, *Consummatum est,* that He hath not done all. Yes, to do that was to be done, Christ was enough, needs no supply; the Spirit comes not to do, comes but to testify. That, *inter alia,* is one of His offices.

A witness there is to be.

And a witness is requisite. There is no matter of weight with us, if it be sped authentically (especially a testament,) but it is with a test. And God doth none of His great works but so; of which this coming is one, even the greatest of all. Neither of His Testaments without one. As God in
nature "left not Himself without witness," saith the Apostle, Acts 14. 17.
so neither Christ in grace. As then in the Old Testament,
ad legem et testimonium, saith Esay; so in the New, *ad Evan-* Isa. 8. 20.
gelium et testimonium, 'to the Gospel,' to Christ 'and the testimony,' calls St. John here. Christ also to have His test, we to call for it; and if it be called for of us, to be able to shew it.

A witness there is:

A witness there needeth then, and a witness there is. One,

SERM. XIII.

nay three. *In ore duorum;* that is, in every matter nothing without two at least. But in this so main, so high a matter,

nay, three. Deu. 17. 6.

God would enlarge the number; have it *in ore trium*, have it few—no fewer than three; three to His part, three to ours.

[1 Joh. 5. 7.]

At the ordering of it in Heaven, three there were, "the 1. Father, the 2. Word, and 3. the Spirit;" that the whole Trinity might be equally interested in the accomplishment of the work of our salvation, and it pass through all Their hands. And at the speeding it in earth, three more: 1.

[1 Joh. 5. 8.] [Isa. 6. 3. Rev. 4. 8.]

"the Spirit, and 2. water, and 3. blood," to answer them, that all might go by a Trinity, that "Holy, Holy, Holy," might be thrice repeated. The truth herein answereth to the type. For under the Law nothing was held perfectly hallowed, till it passed three: the 1. cleansing water, first; the 2. sprinkling of blood, second; 3. and last, that the holy oil were upon it too—the holy oil, the Holy Ghost's type; but when any thing anointed with all three, then had it his perfect halidom, then it was holy indeed. And even so pass we through three hands, all. 1. God's, as men: water notes the creation; the Heavens are of water, and if they, the rest. God's, as men; 2. Christ's, as Christian men—blood notes the redemption; 3. and Spirit's, as spiritual men, Which

Gal. 6. 1.

pertains to all. If any be "spiritual," He knows this; and you that be spiritual do this, saith the Apostle. For Chris-

Jude 19.

tians that be *animales, Spiritum non habentes,* St. Jude tells us, there is no great reckoning to be made of them.

"The Spirit" a Witness. 1. To "Jesus Christ That came."

To let the other go. "The Spirit" is a Witness to Jesus Christ, "That came in water and blood;" Witness to Jesus Christ "That came," Witness to His "water and blood" He came in. In a witness it is required he be *testis idoneus:* will you see *quam idoneus,* 'how apt,' how every way agreeing? "The Spirit" and Jesus agree: Jesus was conceived by the Spirit. "The Spirit" and Christ agree: in the word

2. To the "water and blood" He "came in."

Christ is "the Spirit," for Christ is anointed. Anointed with what? With the Holy Ghost, the true unction, and the truth of all unctions whatsoever. "The Spirit" and "water"

Gen. 1. 2.

agree; "the Spirit moved on the face of the waters." "The

Lev. 17. 11.

Spirit" and "blood" agree: the spirit of life is in the blood; the vessels of it, the arteries, run along with the texture of the veins, all the body over.

To His coming, this Spirit agreeth also. When He came as Jesus, the Spirit conceived Him. When He came as Christ, the Spirit anointed Him. When He came in water at His baptism, the Spirit was there; "came down in the shape of a dove, rested, abode on Him." When He came in blood at His Passion, there too: it was "the eternal Spirit of God, by Which He offered Himself without spot unto God." So the most fit that can be to bear witness to all; *præsens interfuit, et vidit, et audivit,* 'was present, heard, and saw,' was acquainted with all that passed; none can speak to the point so well as He. **To His coming.** **Joh. 1. 32.** **Heb. 9. 14.**

The Spirit is a Witness, is true every way; but why is it said, "It is the Spirit That beareth witness," seeing they both, "water and blood," bear it too? it is "water," it is "blood," that bear witness also. They indeed are witnesses; but it is the Spirit, He it is That is the principal witness, and principally to be regarded, before the rest. Here, He comes in last, but He is indeed first; and so as first is placed at the eighth verse, where they are orderly reckoned up. And good reason. He is one of the Three, both above in Heaven, and beneath in earth; third there above, first here beneath; a Witness in both courts, admitted *ad jus testis* in both, for His special credit in both; the *medius terminus* as it were between Heaven and earth, between God and man. **"The Spirit" the chief Witness.**

Besides it is said, "It is He, He it is That beareth witness." For it is neither of the other will do us any good without Him; the whole weight lieth upon Him. Not the "water" without the Spirit, it is but *nudum et egenum elementum.* Not the "blood" without the Spirit, no more than "the flesh" without "the Spirit," *non prodest quicquam,* as said He, Whose the flesh and blood was, Christ Himself. **Gal. 4. 9.** **Joh. 6. 63.**

Will you see a proof without it? Christ came to Simon Magus "in water"—he was baptized; Christ came to Judas "in blood"—he was a communicant; but Spirit there came none to testify, they were both never the better. The better? nay the worse: Simon perished "in the gall of bitterness;" *Judas bibit mortem de fonte vitæ,* from "the cup of blessing" drank down his own bane. All for want of *et Spiritus est.* So is it with the word, and with any means else. **Acts 8. 13.** **Mat. 26. 26.** **Acts 8. 23.** **1Cor.10.16.**

But let the testimony of "the Spirit" come, the "water"

SERM. XIII. becomes "a well," springing up to eternity; the flesh and
Joh. 4. 14. blood, "meat that perisheth not, but endureth to life ever-
Joh. 6. 27. lasting."

And even in nature we see this: water, if it be not *aqua viva,* have not a spirit to move it and make it run, it stands and putrifies; and blood, if no spirit in it, it congeals, and grows corrupt and foul, as the blood of a dead man. "The Spirit" helpeth this, and upon good reason doth it. For Christ being conceived by "the Spirit," it was most meet all of Christ should be conceived the same way. That Which conceived Him, should impregnate His "water," should animate His "blood," should give the *vivificat,* the life and vigour, to them both. It is "the Spirit then That giveth the witness."

2. The truth of His witness.

Now, in a witness, above all it is required, he be true: the Spirit is so true, as He is the Truth itself. The Spirit, the
Joh. 14. 6. Truth? Why Christ saith of Himself, "I am the Truth." All the better; for, *verum vero consonat,* one truth will well sort with, will uphold, will make proof one of another, as these two do prove, either other reciprocally. The Spirit,
1 Joh. 4. 3. Christ's proof; Christ, the Spirit's. Christ, the Spirit's. "Every spirit that confesseth not Christ," is not the true Spirit. The Spirit Christ's: Christ, if He have not the test of the Spirit, is not the true Christ. Always, the truth is the best witness. And, if He be the Truth, on His test you may bear yourself. Not so on "water," or "blood:" without Him, they may well deceive us, and be *falsa* and *fallacia,* as wanting the truth, if He, if "the Spirit" be wanting.

That truth to be known.

It will then much concern us, to be sure, "the Spirit" on Whose testimony we are thus wholly to rely, that the Spirit be the Truth. And it is the main point of all, to be able to discern "the Spirit," that is, the Truth; because as there is
1 Joh. 4. 6. a "Spirit of truth," so is there a "spirit of error" abroad in the world—yea many such spirits; and the Apostle who tells
2 Cor. 11.4. us of *alium Jesum,* in the same verse tells us of *alium spiritum* too. We be then to try which spirit is the truth; that so the Spirit on Whose witness we rest ourselves, be the Truth. How take we notice of the Spirit? How knew they the Angel
Joh. 5. 4. was come down into the pool of Bethesda, but by the stirring and moving of the water? So by stirring up in us spiritual

motions, holy purposes and desires, is the Spirit's coming known. Specially if they do not vanish again. For if they do, then was it some other flatuous matter, which will quiver in the veins, and unskilful people call it the life-blood, but the spirit it was not. The spirit's motion, the pulse is not for a while, and then ceaseth; but is perpetual, holds as long as life holds, though intermittent sometime, for some little space. By His spiritual motions.

Yet hold we it not safe, to lay overmuch weight upon good motions, which may come of divers causes, and of which good motions there are as many in hell as in Heaven. The surest way is to lay it on that our Saviour and His Apostles so often lay it, that is, on *Spiritus vivificat.* The life is ever the best indicant sign of the spirit. *Novum supervenisse Spiritum, nova vitæ ratio demonstrat,* 'that a new Spirit is come, a new course of life is the best demonstration.' By newness of life. Joh. 6. 63. 2 Cor. 3. 6.

Now life is best known by vital actions. Three the Scripture counteth: 1. *Spiritus ubi vult spirat,* by breath; 2. *Spiritus manifeste loquitur,* by speech; 3. *Omnia hæc operatur unus idemque Spiritus,* by the work;—these three. The notes of that life. Joh. 3. 8. 1 Tim. 4. 1. 1 Cor. 12. 11.

1. The nearest and most proper note of the Spirit is spiration, or breathing. In breathing there is a double act: 1. there is a *systole,* a drawing in of the air, and that is cold, agreeth with Christ in "water;" there comes a cool breath ever from the water. 2. And there is a *diastole,* a sending forth of the breath; and that we know is warm, and agreeth with Christ "in blood." For blood is it, that sendeth a warm vapour into all the limbs. 1. Breath.

Agreeable to these two, have you the two Spirits, which upon the matter are but the two acts of one and the same Spirit: 1. Inspired, "the Spirit of faith"—the fear of God. Isa. 11. 2.
2. Out-breathed, "the Spirit of faith"—faith in Christ. 2Cor. 4. 13.
Fear comes "in water:" so saith Solomon, "The fear of God is" *fons vitæ,* "the well-spring of life," that is, "water." Prov. 14. 27.
Faith comes in "blood;" *per fidem in sanguine Ipsius,* Rom. 3. 25.
"through faith in His blood." "So is every one that is born of the Spirit." [Joh. 3. 8.] And to blow out faith still, and never draw in fear, is suspicious, is not safe. The true spiration, the breathing aright, consisting of these two, is a sign of the right Spirit.

SERM. XIII. The next sign in the same verse too: "and you hear the noise of it." For so the Apostle saith, "the Spirit speaks
2. Speech. evidently;" that is, His noise and speech is evidently to be
Joh. 3. 8. [1 Tim. 4. 1.] distinguished from those of other spirits. His coming in tongues this day, sheweth no less. Which sign of speech doth best and most properly sort here, with a witness. For a witness, what he hath to testify, speaks it out vocally.

What noise then is heard from us, (What breathe we? What "speaks the Spirit manifestly" from our mouths?) if cursing and bitterness, and many a foul oath, if this noise
Acts 9. 1. be heard from us; if we breathe *minas et cædes*, "bluster
Eph. 4. 29. out threatening and slaying"—that noise; if σαπρὸς λόγος, "rotten, corrupt, obscene communication" come out of our
Mark 14. 70. mouths? we are of Galilee, and our very speech "bewrayeth"
[Mat. 26. 73.] us. This is not the breath of the Spirit, this He speaks not; evidently He speaks it not. It is not the tongue of Heaven
Acts 2. 4. this: not *sicut dedit Spiritus eloqui*, no utterance of the Spirit's giving. Some of Christ's water would do well to wash these out of our mouths. The speech sounding of the Spirit, is a sign of the true Spirit.

3. Action. The last, but the surest of all, *Omnia hæc operatur Spiritus.*
1 Cor. 12. 11. And the work is as clearly to be distinguished as the speech. Each spirit hath his proper work, and is known by it. No man ever saw the works of the devil come from the Spirit of God. Be not deceived, the works of uncleanness come from
Mat. 12. 43. no spirit, but "the unclean spirit." The works of Cain,
Jas. 4. 5. from "the spirit of envy;" the works of Demas, from "the
1 Cor. 2. 12. spirit of the world." All the gross errors of our life from the
[Joh. 15. 26.] spirit of error. But this, this is "the Spirit of truth;" and the breath, the speech, the operations of Him, bear witness that He is so. Now if He will depose that "the water and blood" Christ came in, He came in for us, and we our parts in them; in them, and in them both; and so deposing, if we feel His breath, hear His speech, see His works according, we may receive His "witness" then, for His "witness" is true.

Now, that upon this day, the day of the Spirit, "the Spirit" may come and bear this "witness" to Christ's "water and blood," there is to be water and blood for "the Spirit" to bear witness to. So was there ever as this day, in the

Church of Christ. "Water:" a solemn baptism in memory of the first "three thousand," this day baptized by St. Peter. Acts 2. 41. And "blood:" never a more frequent Eucharist than at Acts 20. 16. Pentecost, in honour of this Spirit, to which St. Paul made such haste with his alms and offerings. Witness the great works done by Pentecostal oblations; which very oblations remain in some Churches to this day.

III. The reversal. So are we now come to the reversal, to the last *non solum;* and here it is. Not in the Spirit alone, but "in water and blood," *reciproce.* As not these without the Spirit, so neither the Spirit without these, that is, without the Sacrament wherein these be. So have we a perfect circle now. Neither "in water" without "blood," nor in "blood" without "water;" nor in them alone without "the Spirit;" nor in the Spirit alone, without them.

This day Christ comes to us "in blood," in the Sacrament of it so. But as we said before, either is in other. "Blood" is not ministered, but there is an ingredient of the purifying virtue of "water" withal in it: so He comes in "water" too. Yea, comes in "water" first—so lie they in the text; "water" to go before with us. So did it, at the very institution itself of this Sacrament. The "pitcher of water," and he that Mark 14. 13. carried it, was not in vain given for a sign; went not before them that were sent to make ready for it, for nothing.

It had a meaning, that water, and it had a use. Their feet were washed with it, and their feet being clean, they were "clean every whit." Many make ready for it, that see Joh. 13. 10. neither water nor pitcher. It were well they did, their feet would be washed; so would their "hands in innocency," Ps. 26. 6. that are to go to His altar. "In innocency," that is, in a steadfast purpose of keeping ourselves clean:—so to come. For to come and not with that purpose, better not come at all. To find a feeling of this purpose before, and to mark well the success and effect that doth follow after. For if it fail us continually, Christ did not come. For when He comes, though it be in "blood," yet He comes with "water" at the same time. Ever in both, never in one alone.

His blood is not only drink to nourish, but medicine to purge. To nourish the new man which is faint and weak, God wot; but to take down the old, which is rank in most.

SERM. XIII. It is the proper effect of His blood; it doth "cleanse our
Heb. 9. 14. consciences from dead works, to serve the living God."

Which if we find it doth, Christ is come to us as He is to come. And the Spirit is come, and puts His test. And if we have His test, we may go our way in peace; we have kept a right feast to Him, and to the memory of His coming.

[Rev. 22. 20.] "Even so come, Lord Jesus," and come, O blessed Spirit, and bear witness to our spirit, that Christ's water and His
Zech. 13. 1. blood, we have our part in both; both, "in the fountain
Mark 14. 24. opened for sin and for uncleanness," and "in the blood of the New Testament," the legacy whereof is everlasting life in Thy kingdom of glory. Whither, Christ That paid the purchase, and the Spirit That giveth the seisin, vouchsafe to bring us all.

A SERMON

PREACHED BEFORE

THE KING'S MAJESTY, AT GREENWICH,

ON THE TWENTIETH OF MAY, A.D. MDCXXI., BEING WHIT-SUNDAY.

JAMES i. 16, 17.

Err not, my dear brethren.
Every good thing and every perfect gift is from above, and cometh down from the Father of lights, with Whom is no variableness, neither shadowing by turning.

Nolite itaque errare fratres mei dilectissimi.
Omne datum optimum, et omne donum perfectum desursum est descendens a Patre luminum, apud Quem non est transmutatio, nec vicissitudinis obumbratio.

[*Do not err, my beloved brethren.*
Every good gift and every perfect gift is from above, and cometh down from the Father of lights, with Whom is no variableness, neither shadow of turning. Engl. Trans.]

AND, if "every good giving and every perfect gift," what giving so good, or what gift so perfect, as the Gift of Gifts, this day's gift, the gift of the Holy Ghost? There are in it all the points in the text. It is "from above," it "descended" [Lu. 3. 22.]
visibly this day, and from "the Father of lights"—so many "tongues," so many "lights;" which kindled such a light in [Acts 2. 3.]
the world on this day, as to this day is not put out, nor shall ever be to the world's end.

First, the Holy Ghost is oft styled by this very name or title, of "the Gift of God." "If ye knew the Gift of God," Joh. 4. 10.
saith our Saviour to the woman at the well's side. What gift was that? It is plain there, "the water of life." That

SERM. XIV. "water" was the Spirit. "This He spake of the Spirit,"
Joh. 7. 39. saith St. John, who knew His mind best, as then "not yet given;" but since, as upon this day, sent into the world.

Secondly, this "gift" is both "good" and "perfect"—so good, as it is *de bonis optimum*, 'of all goods the best;' and of all perfects, the most absolutely perfect, the gift of perfection, or perfection of all the gifts of God. What should I
Acts 8. 20. say? Not to be valued, saith St. Peter; not to be uttered,
Rom. 8. 26. saith St. Paul: as if all the tongues that were on earth before, and all that came down this day, were little enough, or indeed were not enough, not able any way to utter or express it.

Thirdly, nay it is not one gift among many, how complete soever, but it is many in one—so many tongues, so many gifts; as so many grapes in a cluster, so many grains in a
Ps. 68. 18. pomegranate. In this one gift are all the rest. "Ascending up on high," *dona dedit*, "He gave gifts:" all these *dona* were in *hoc Dono*, all those gifts in this Gift; every one of them folded up as it were *inclusive*. The Father, the Fountain; the Son, the Cistern; the Holy Ghost, the Conduit-pipe, or pipes rather, (for they are many,) by and through which they are derived down to us.

Fourthly, and lastly, not only in Him, and by Him, but from Him too. For He is the Gift and the Giver both.
1 Cor. 12. 4. "There is great variety of gifts," saith St Paul, "but it is one and the same Spirit That maketh distribution of them to every man severally, even as Himself pleaseth." Both the thing given, and the Party that giveth it, all derived to us from Him, wrought in us by Him, and by us to be referred to Him.

At the time of any of God's gifts sent us by Him, to speak of Scriptures of this nature, cannot seem unseasonable; but of all other, at the time of this gift, most properly. *Dona dedit hominibus;* what day was that? even this very day. *Dies donorum hic;* so many tongues, so many gifts. This day, I say, whereto *Donum Dei* and *Donum diei* fall together so happily. We have brought it to the day.

The sum. It will not be amiss to touch the end a little, which the Apostle aimeth at in these words. It is the old, it is the new
1 Joh. 2. 7. commandment, *mandatum vetus et novum*, to make us love God. The point whereto the Law and the Prophets drive,

yea the Gospel, and the Apostles and all. We cannot love him well, whom we think not well of. We cannot think well of him, whom we think evil comes from. Then to think so well of God, as not to think any evil. Not any evil? no, but instead thereof, all good cometh to us from Him. So thinking, we cannot choose but we must love Him.

And to this end, at the thirteenth verse before, St. James had told us plain, God is not the Author of evil; not tempted Himself, not tempting any to it. As at that verse, not the Author of evil, so at this, the Author of all, and every good. Men, when their brains are turned with diving into God's secrets, may conceit as they please; but when all is said that can be, no man can ever entirely love Him Whom he thinks so evil of as to be the Author of evil. We are with St. James to teach, and you to believe that will procure you to love God the better; not that will alien your minds, or make you love Him the worse. That therefore St. James denies peremptorily. No evil; *nemo dicat*, "let no man speak it," let it not once be spoken. But let this be hardly[1], [[1] *i.e.* strongly insisted on.] that all the good we have or hope for, descends down from Him. And that St. James here affirms as earnestly; "Err not, my dear brethren." It is to "err," to think otherwise; for that absolutely, "every good giving," and again over, "every perfect gift," there is not one of them all but from Him they come. And so we in all duty to love Him from Whom all, and all manner good proceedeth. This is His end, love; and that falls fit and is proper to this feast, the feast of love. For love is the proper attribute and proper effect of the Spirit, (*per charitatem Spiritûs*,) "the love of Rom. 15. 30. God is shed abroad in our hearts by the Holy Ghost" this [Rom. 5. 5.] day "given unto us."

The verse, to the chapter, is a clear and a strict proposition, The division. but hath in it the force or energy to make a complete argument. For if all good from God, then no evil. St. James lays it for a ground: salt or "bitter water and sweet cannot Jas. 3. 11. issue both from one fountain;" nor the works of darkness, from "the Father of lights," never.

But we take it only as a proposition, with a little item at the end of it. If we ask the questions of art concerning it, *Quæ, quanta, qualis? Quæ?* It is categorical. *Quanta?* It

SERM. XIV. is universal. *Qualis?* First, it is affirmative: then true—"err not" goes before it. So true, as to think the contrary is a flat error.

I. The rules of logic divide a proposition to our hands, into the fore-part, (in schools they call it *subjectum,*) and into the after-part, which they call *prædicatum.* 1. The *subjectum* here is *omne datum, &c.* The *prædicatum, desursum est, &c.* The subject is double: 1. *datum bonum,* and 2. *donum perfectum,* with an universal note to either. "Every good and every perfect," to be sure, to take in all, to leave out none. 2. The *prædicatum,* that stands of three points: 1. whence? 2. how? and 3. from whom? "from the Father of lights."

II. Then comes the item I told you of, provisionally, to meet with an objection, a thought that might rise in our hearts peradventure; that is, It may be as the lights of the world, or the children, have their variations, their changes, so the Father also may have them. But that he puts us out of doubt of too, with as peremptory a negative. Be it with the lights as it will; with "the Father of lights," with God, there is no variation, no change, no not so much as a shadow of them. In effect, as if he should say: From "the Father of lights," Which is unchangeable; or, From the unchangeable "Father of lights;" and so it shall be mere affirmative, but that there is *major vis in negatione,* 'denial is stronger.'

And all these he brings in with a *nolite errare;* and that not without just cause. For, about this verse and the points in it, there are no less than seven sundry errors. I shall note you them as I go, that you may avoid them, together with such matter of duty as shall incidently fall in from each; specially touching the gift of the day, the gift of the Holy Ghost.

I. Of the proposition: 1. The subject thereof double, 1. *datum,* and 2. *donum.*

To take the proposition in sunder. The subject first, and that is double; 1. *datum,* and 2. *donum;* and either of them his proper epithet; 1. "good," and 2. "perfect." Jointly, of both together first; after, severally of either part.

1. Of *datum* and *donum* jointly.

Datum, and *donum,* they both come of *do,* given they are both. Where first, because it is the feast of tongues, to set our tongue right. For the world and the Holy Ghost speak not one language; not with one tongue both. There should not else have needed any to have been sent down. The world talks of all, as had; the Holy Ghost, as given. Look to the *habendum,* saith the world, the having:—that is the spirit of the world. Religion; look to *donum* and *datum,* the giving: —that is His. The heathen calls his virtue *ἕξις* 'a habit;' [Aristot. Eth. 2. 5.] that comes of *habendo.* The Christian, by St. James here, *δόσις, δώρημα, datum* and *donum;* all which come of *dando.* Thus doth the Holy Ghost frame our tongues to speak, if we will speak with the tongues of this day. They that do not, they are of Galilee, and their speech "bewrayeth" them [Mat. 26. 73.] straight.

Will you hear one of them? You know who said, "Soul, Lu. 12. 19. thou hast enough"—"hast," and you know who spake otherwise, *Quid habes quod non accepisti?* "What but that you 1 Cor. 4. 7. have received?" Receiving and giving you know are relatives, which the other little thought of. You may know each by their dialect.

From the beginning. Esau he said, *Habeo bona plurima* Gen. 33. 9. *frater mi,* "I have goods enough:" that is his phrase of speech, that the language of Edom. What saith Jacob at the same time? Esau asking him, what were all the droves he met, They be, saith he, the good things that "God hath given me." "Have," saith Esau; "given me," saith Jacob. Gen. 33. 5. *Nonne habeo?* "Have not I power to crucify thee, and have Joh. 19. 10. not I power to deliver thee?" You may know it, it is Pilate's voice. But our Saviour, He tells him, *non habes potestatem;* Joh. 19. 11. power should he have had none, if it had not been "given him," and "given" him "from above." St. James' very phrase here from Christ's own mouth. So must we speak, if we will speak as Christ spake.

The first error.

This then is the first error. To have our mind run and our speech run, all upon having. Men are all for having, think and speak of what they have; without mention of whence, or how, or from whom they receive it, or that it is given them at all. *Nolite errare,* "be not deceived," for all that you have is *datum* or *donum,* all; and they both are of free gift, given all. Thus the tongue that sat this day on St. James' head, taught him to call them. Thus far jointly; now severally.

Or each severally: 1. *datum.*

For there is a cleft in these tongues. The cleft is *datum* and *donum.* Would not wrap them all up in one word, but

SERM. XIV. expresses them in two. Somewhat there is in that. We may not admit of any idle tautologies in Scripture. Two several sorts then they be, these two, not opposite, but differing only in degree, as more and less. "Every gift" is a giving; not every giving a gift. Every "perfect," "good;" not every "good," "perfect." We are not to think, either

[Mat. 25. 15. Lu. 19. 13. Mat. 22. 19. Lu. 21. 2.] all our sins, or all our gifts to be of one size. St. Matthew's talent is more than St. Luke's pound; Cæsar's penny, than the widow's two mites, yet good money all, in their several values. Of these two, 1. *datum* and 2. *donum*, 1. *bonum* and 2. *perfectum*, one is greater or less than another.

1. *Datum.* He begins with the less, *datum.* Weigh the word, it is but a participle; they have tenses, and tenses time. So that is only temporal.

2. *Donum.* But *donum* imports no time: so, a more set time, hath more substance in it, is fixed or permanent. One, as it were, for term of years; the other, of the nature of a perpetuity. A *datum*, that which is still in giving, that perishes with the use, as do things transitory; and be of that sort

Job 1. 21. that Job spake, God "hath given," and God "hath taken away." *Donum* is not so, but of that sort that Christ speaks,

Lu. 10. 42. in Mary's choice, so given as it "should never be taken from

[2 Cor. 4. 18.] her." So one refers to the "things which are seen, which are temporal;" the other, to the "things not seen, that are eternal." One to the body, and to this world; the other to the soul rather, and the life of the world to come.

1. *Bonum.* We shall discern it the more clearly, if we weigh the two adjectives, 1. "good," and 2. "perfect:"—they differ. Every

1 Tim. 1. 8. "good" is not "perfect." We know, "the Law is good,"

Heb. 7. 19. saith the Apostle, but we know withal, "the Law bringeth nothing to perfection:"—so not "perfect." Nature, *quà natura*, is "good," yet imperfect; and the Law in the rigour of it not possible, through the imperfection of it. Nature is not, the Law is not taken away—"good" both; but grace is added to both to perfect both, which needed not, if either

1 Joh. 3. 17. were "perfect." This "world's good;" so doth St. John

Mat. 7. 9, 10. call our wealth. Nay, "bread," "fish," and "eggs," we

[Lu. 11. 12.] give our children, our Saviour Himself calleth "good gifts." But what are these? not worthy to be named, if you speak of *donum Dei æternum*, and the perfections there.

Before I was aware, I have told you what is "perfect." 2. *Perfectum.*
The glory, the joys, the crown of Heaven. "For when that 1 Cor. 13.
perfect is come, all this imperfect shall be done away." But 10.
St. James seems not to speak of that; he speaks in the present, and of the present, what now is, what "perfect" in this life. And this, lo, brings us to *donum diei*, the gift of the Holy Ghost. For to "be partakers of the divine nature," is 2 Pet. 1. 4.
all the perfection we can here attain. No higher here. Now to be made partakers of the Spirit, is to be made partakers "of the divine nature." That is this day's work. Partakers of the Spirit we are, by receiving grace; which is nothing else but the breath of the Holy Ghost, the Spirit of grace. Grace into the entire substance of the soul, dividing itself into two streams: 1. one goes to the understanding, the gift of faith; 2. the other to the will, the gift of "charity, the Col. 3. 14.
very bond of perfection." The tongues, to teach us knowledge; the fire, to kindle our affections. The state of grace is the perfection of this life, to grow still from grace to grace, to profit in it. As to go on still forward is the perfection of a traveller, to draw still nearer and nearer to his journey's end. "To work to-day and to-morrow as Christ said, and Lu. 13. 32.
the third day to be perfect, perfectly perfect."

Now as we are to follow "the best gifts,"—it is St. Paul's 1 Cor. 12. 31.
counsel,—"the best," the most "perfect;" so are we to take *Omne datum*, as well as *omne donum.*
notice too of the "good," though not all out so "perfect," as St. James adviseth us; knowing this, that be it "giving," or be it "gift," be it "good," or be it "perfect," he puts an *omne* to both; comes over twice, 1. "every good," 2. "every perfect:" both we receive, both are given us. Set down that. There was among the heathen one that went for wise that said, to become rich he would pray and sacrifice to Hercules; but to be virtuous or wise, he would do neither, neither to Hercules nor to any god of them all, he would be beholden for that to none but himself. Look, in this cleft he took to himself the more, left God the less. This was a gross error; so gross, I will not bid you take heed of it. But The second error.
there be, that will not stand with God for the greater; but for the less, that they may be bold with, and take those to themselves. This is an error too:—err not this. No, *datum* hath his *omne* as well as *donum;* the "good," no less than

SERM. XIV. the "perfect;" given both, one as well as the other. St.
1 Cor. 4. 7. Paul puts us to it with *quid habes?* that is, *nihil habes.* "What have you?" that is, you have nothing, "but you have received it," but hath been given you; λῆψις and δόσις are relations, one confers the other.

Away then with this second error. He That made the elephant, made the ant; He That the eagle, the fly; He That the most glorious Angel in Heaven, the poorest worm that creeps on the earth. So He That shall give us the kingdom of Heaven, He it is That gives us every piece of bread and meat, and puts us to acknowledge it, in one and the same prayer making us to sue for *regnum Tuum,* and for *panem nostrum.* Be not deceived to think otherwise. And
Zech. 4. 10. hear you, you are to begin with *datum,* "not to despise the day of small things." It is the Prophet's counsel, to learn
Mat. 22. 21. to see God in them. "Cæsar's image," not only in his coin of gold, but even upon the poor "penny." See God in small, or you shall never see Him in great; in "good," or never in "perfect." This for the subject. There is a cleft, all are not of one sort; some less, some greater: greater or less, both are given. Not less had, and great given, but given both. And every one of both kinds, of the one kind as well as of the other.

2. The *prædicatum,* 1. Whence they come, *Desursum.* Ps. 4. 6. We have talked long of "good:" "Who will shew us any good?" there be many that will say, nay there is not any but will say. That will St. James here. And first, to shew us, turns our eye to the right place, whence it comes. That is ἄνωθεν "from above." There are two in this ἄνωθεν:— 1. θεν "from," 2. and ἄνω, "above." "From," that is, from somewhere else, not from ourselves; from without, and not out of us, from within. *Aliunde,* ἔξωθεν, and that *aliunde* is from ἄνω "above," not from κάτω, those lower parts upon the earth.

The third and fourth errors. Err not then, either of these two ways: 1. First, not to reflect upon ourselves, to look like swans into our own
Eph. 2. 8. bosoms. It grows not there, out of yourselves, "it is the gift of God," saith St. Paul. The very giving gives as much. Of our own we have it not.

2. If we look forth, let it not be about us, either on the right hand, or on the left, or any place here below. Look up,

turn your eye thither. It is an influence, it is no vapour; an inspiration, no exaltation; thence it comes, hence it rises not: our "spirit lusts after envy," and worse matter. "Why should thoughts arise in your hearts," saith Christ? If they "arise," they are "not good;" if they be "good," then they come down "from above." St. John Baptist is direct: "A man can receive nothing, unless it be given him, and given him from above." And, of all other, not the gift of this day; the Dove, the tongues, came from on high both. From ourselves, is one error; from any other beneath here, is another. Err not then, the place is *desursum*, without and above us.

Jas. 4. 5.

Joh. 3. 27.

Next, the manner how, that it descends; for even that word wants not his force. Descending is a voluntary motion; it concludes the will and the purpose of him that so descends. It is no casualty, it falls not down by chance; it comes down, because it so will. A will it hath, *et ubi vult spirat*, "it blows not, but where it will;" and it distributes to every one the Spirit, but *prout vult*, "as it pleaseth Himself," not otherwise.

2. How they come, *Descendens.*

Joh. 3. 8.

And this you may observe; the Scripture maketh choice ever of words sounding this way. He gives it, He casts it not about, at all adventure. He opens His hand, it runs not through His fingers. *Sinum habet facilem, non perforatum*, 'His bosom is open enough, yet hath no hole in it,' to drop through against His will. He "sent His Word," it came not by hap, that is, Christ. And, "I will send you another Comforter," that is, "the Holy Ghost." Nor He neither "Of His own will He begat us"—they be the words that follow.

Acts 10. 36.

Joh. 14. 16. 26.

Jas. 1. 18.

It is the fifth error, to ascribe to fortune either *datum* or *donum*. Err not then: as the place is from above, so the manner, *descendens*, not *decidens*; they come, they are not let fall.

The fifth error.

Whence, we see, and how; now, from whom. The Party, in a word, is God. He had said as much before, verse the fifth, "If any lack wisdom, let him ask it of God:" how comes He here to use this somewhat unusual term, "the Father of lights?" It had been, to our thinking, more proper to have said, from God the Author of all good things. No,

1. From whom. *A Patre luminum.* Why *luminum*, "of lights."

SERM. XIV. there is reason for it. For say, they are, they came down from above: when we cast up our eyes thither, we can see no farther, our sight can reach no higher than the lights, than the lights there above. And so, some you have that hold they come from them, *de luminibus*, 'from the lights;' that such a conjunction or aspect of them, such a constellation, or horoscope, such a position of such and such planets, produce very much good. This is in astrology, but not in theology. *Μὴ πλανᾶσθε*—of which word come the planets—saith St. James, wander not after the wandering stars; *de luminibus* is not it, *de Patre luminum* is the right. So, "the Father of lights" was purposely chosen, to draw us from the "lights." That not they, they are not,—not the children; "the Father," He it is, from Whom they come, the "lights." No, them He
Heb. 1. 14. made to do service. Nay, the "Angels" above them, He
The sixth error. made to be "ministering spirits" for our good. Be not deceived with this neither; to lift up our eyes to the host of Heaven, and no further; but beyond them to "the Father" of them all, and then you are where you should be.

This may be one reason. But further if you ask, why not rather of all good, as He began; why is He gone from that term to this of light? The answer is easy. If we speak of
Gen. 1. 3, 4. gifts, light it is *princeps donorum Dei*, the first gift God bestowed upon the world, and so will fit well. If of "good," the first thing of which it is said, *vidit Deus quod bona*, was "light;" and so, fit that way too. If you speak of "perfect," so perfect it is as it is desired for itself, we take comfort in seeing it, we delight to see it, though we see nothing by it,
Eccl. 11. 7. nothing but the light itself—observed by Solomon.

And for "good:" such is the nearness of affinity, such, I may say, the connaturality between "light" and "good," as they would not be one without the other. All that good is,
Joh. 3. 21. loves the light, would "come to the light," would be "made
Mat. 5. 15. manifest," desires no "bushel" to hide it, but "a candlestick" to shew it forth to all the world. That they might be searched with lanterns; to have the secrets, the hidden corners of their hearts looked into, that "the Father of lights" would grant them so to be.

For "perfect:" so "perfect" a thing is the light, as God
[1 Joh. 1. 5.] Himself is said to be "light." His Son our Saviour, to be

light of lights, "the true light that lighteneth every one that Joh. 1. 9.
cometh into the world." His Spirit, "light"—so is our collect: "God Which as upon this day hast taught the hearts of Thy faithful people, by sending to them the light of Thy Holy Spirit." The Angels that be good, be "Angels of light." Yea, whatsoever here on earth is perfect; the King 2 Sam. 21.
is called "the light of Israel;" the Apostles called, *luces* 17. Mat. 5. 14.
mundi; and the Saints of God, wherever they be in the world, shine as lights in it. That upon the matter, Father of good, and "Father of light," is all one.

Pater luminis would have served, if we respect but this, but Why *luminum*, not *luminis.*
the nature. What say you to the number? it is *luminum:* why, of lights in the plural? that is, to give light to what we said before, of the divers degrees of the givings, and of the gifts of God. In the firmament, there is one light of the sun, another of the moon, and yet another of the stars; and in the stars, "one differeth from another in glory." "Good" 1 Cor. 15.
every one, though not "so perfect," one as another. He That 41.
made the bright sun in all his glory, He made the dimmest star; all alike from Him, He alike the Father of all.

Besides, He sets them down in the plural, "lights," for that the opposite, *tenebræ,* is a plural word, and indeed hath no singular, for there are many, and so need many "lights" to match them. There is the senses' outward darkness, there is the darkness of the inward man; both the darkness of the understanding by ignorance and error, and the "darkness" 1 Joh. 2. 9.
of the will and heart by hatred and malice. There is the darkness of adversity in this world, the hither darkness—there is some little light in it; and there is "the blackness Jude 13.
of darkness," the utter darkness of the world to come—no manner light at all. Nothing to be seen, but to be heard; nor to be heard, but "weeping and wailing and gnashing Mat. 8. 12.
of teeth."

To match these so many darknesses, there behoved to be as many "lights;" and so *Pater luminum* comes in, not *luminis.* As to match the many miseries of our nature, there were as many mercies requisite; and so He, *Pater misericordiarum,* 2 Cor. 1. 3.
not *misericordiæ,* with the Apostle; of many, not of one alone. We need the number as well as the thing; to have a multitude, a plurality of mercies, to have "plenteous redemption," Ps. 130. 7.

SERM. XIV. to have χάριν πολυποίκιλον, "great variety of grace," and
1 Pet. 4. 10. that "over-abundant grace," that we might rest assured
1 Tim. 1.14. there is enough and enough, in "the Father of lights," to master and to overmatch any darkness of the prince of darkness, what or how many soever.

Shall I shew you these lights? Not the visible, of the sun, moon, and stars, or fire or candle; I pass them. Besides them there are two in us; 1. the light of nature, for rebelling against which, all that are without Christ suffer
Prov. 20. 27. condemnation. Solomon calls it "the candle of the Lord searching even the very bowels," which though it be dim and not perfect, yet good it is; though lame, yet, as Mephi-
[2 Sam. 4. 4.] bosheth, it is *regia proles*, 'of the blood royal.' 2. There is
Prov. 6. 23. the light of God's Law: *Lex lux*, saith Solomon, *totidem*
Ps. 119. 105. *verbis*; and his father, "a lantern to his feet." Nay, in the nineteenth Psalm what he saith at the fourth verse of the "sun," at the eighth he saith the same of "the Law of
2 Pet. 1. 19. God"—lights both. 3. The light of prophecy, as of a "candle
1 Pet. 2. 9. that shineth in a dark place." 4. There is the "wonderful light" of His Gospel, so St. Peter calls it, the proper light of this day. The tongues that descended—so many "tongues," so many "lights;" for the tongue is a light, and brings to light what was before hid in the heart. 5. And from these
2 Cor. 4. 6. other is the inward light of grace, whereby "God, Which commanded the light to shine out of darkness," He it is "That shineth in our hearts;" by the inward anointing, which is the oil of this lamp, the light of His Holy Spirit, chasing away the darkness both of our hearts and minds. 6. There is the light of comfort of His Holy Spirit,
[Ps. 97. 11.] "a light sown for the righteous" here in this life. And 7. there is the light of glory which they shall reap, the light where God dwelleth, and where we shall dwell with
Col. 1. 12. Him; even the "inheritance of the Saints in light," when
Mat. 13. 43. the righteous shall shine as the sun, in the kingdom of
Ex. 25. 32. their Father, "the Father of lights." Moses' candlestick with seven stalks and lights in each of them. Of all which seven "lights" God is "the Father," acknowledges them all for His children, and to His children will vouchsafe them all in their order.

Now this only remaineth, why He is not called the Author,

but the Father of these? In this is the manner of their descending. And that is, for that they proceed from Him *per modum naturæ,* as the child from the father; *per modum emanationis,* as the beams from the sun. So both "Father" and "light" shew the manner of their coming. Proper and natural for Him it is, to give good. Good things come from Him as kindly, as do they: therefore said to be, not the Author, the Lord and Giver, but even the very Father of them. It is against His nature to do otherwise, to procreate or send forth aught but good; His very loins, His bowels are all goodness. Father of darkness He cannot be, being "Father of lights," nor of aught that is evil. For they two, dark and evil, are as near of kin as light and good. This is the message, saith St. John, that we heard of Him, and that we declare to you, that "God is light, and in Him is no darkness at all." Neither in Him, nor from Him; *nemo dicat,* let never any say it, let it never sink into you; "tempted" He is not "with evil," "tempt He doth not to evil." Ascribe it not to *Pater luminum,* but to *princeps tenebrarum;* to "the prince of darkness," not to "the Father of lights." But ascribe all "good," from the smallest spark to the greatest beam, from the least "good giving" to the best and most perfect gift of all, to Him, to "the Father of lights." So we see 1. why "light," 2. why "lights," 3. why "the Father of lights." So much for the predicate and whole proposition.

3. Why *Pater,* not Author.

1 Joh. 1. 5.

Jas. 1. 13.

Eph. 6. 12.

1 Joh. 1. 5.

II. The item. The seventh error.

And all this may be, and yet all this being, it seems, some reply may be made, and stand with the Apostle's term of "lights" well enough. That what befalls the "lights," the children, may also befall "the Father" of them. The great and most perfect light in this world, is the sun in the firmament; and two things evidently befall him, the two in the text. *Παραλλαγὴν,* "variation," he admits, declines and goes down, and leaves us in the dark;—that is his parallax, in his motion from east to west. And turning he admits, turns back, goes from us, and leaves us to long winter nights;—that is his τροπὴ, in his motion from north to south. One of these he doth every day; the other every year. Successively removing from one hemisphere to the other; when it is light there, it is dark here. Successively turning from one tropic

SERM. XIV. to another; when the days be long there, they be short here. And if we shall say any thing of the shadow here, that way we lose him too in part, by interposing of the clouds, when the day is overcast. So the night is his parallax, the winter his *τροπὴ*, dark weather his shadow at least. Shadows do but take him away in part—that is not good. But darkness takes him away clean—that is perfectly evil.

That it may be even so with "the Father of lights," as with this it is. Good and evil come from Him *alternis vicibus*, 'by turn;' and, as darkness and light successively from them. That it may fare with Him as with the heathen Jupiter; who had, say they, in his entry, two great vats, both full, one of good, the other of evil; and that he served them out into the world, both of the good and of the evil, as he saw cause; but commonly for one of good, two of evil at least.

It was more than requisite he should clear this objection. So doth he, denieth both—all three if you will. That though
Job 14. 2. of man it be truly said by Job, "he never continues in one stay;" though the lights of Heaven have their parallaxes;
Job 4. 18. yea, "the Angels of Heaven, he found not steadfastness in them;" yet, for God, He is subject to none of them. He is
Ex. 3. 14. Mal. 3. 6. *Ego sum Qui sum*; that is, saith Malachi, *Ego Deus, et non mutor*. We are not what we were a while since, nor what we shall be; a while after, scarce what we are; for every moment makes us vary. With God, it is nothing so. "He is that He is, He is and changeth not." He changes not His tenor, He changes not His tense; keeps not our grammar rules, hath one by Himself; not, Before Abraham was, I
Joh. 8. 58. was; but, "Before Abraham was, I am."

Yet are there "varyings and changes," it cannot be denied. We see them daily. True, but the point is *per quem*, on whom to lay them. Not on God. Seems there any recess?
Jer. 2. 17. It is we forsake Him, not He us. It is the ship that moves, though they that be in it think the land goes from them, not they from it. Seems there any variation, as that of the night? It is *umbra terræ* makes it, the light makes it not. Is there any thing resembling a shadow? A vapour rises from us, makes the cloud; which is as a penthouse between, and takes Him from our sight. That vapour is our lust, there is the *apud quem*. Is any tempted? It is his own lust doth it;

that entices him to sin, that brings us to the shadow of death. It is not God. No more than He can be tempted, no more can He tempt any. If we find any change, the *apud* is with us, not Him; we change, He is unchanged. "Man walks in a vain shadow;" His ways are the truth. He cannot deny Himself. Ps. 39. 6.

Every evil, the more perfectly evil it is, the more it is from below; either rises from the steam of our nature corrupted, or yet lower, ascends as a gross smoke, from the bottomless pit, from the prince of darkness, as full of varying and turning into all shapes and shadows, as God is far from both, Who is uniform and constant in all His courses.

Shall we now cast up all into one sum, the errors by them[1], and the verities by themselves, and oppose each to each? The first error: to be all for having—never speak of it. The verity: that all is giving, or gifts—to be for it. The second error: to think great matters only are given, the meaner we have of ourselves. The verity: "perfect" as well as "good," and "good" as "perfect," they be given both. The third error: to think they are from us, not elsewhere from others. The verity: they are *ἔξωθεν,* they grow not in us, we spin them not out of ourselves. The fourth error: they be from below, we gather them here. The verity: they be from *ἄνω,* that is "above," not here beneath. The fifth error: to think that from thence they fall *promiscue,* catch who catch may, hap-hazard. The verity: they fall not by chance, they descend by providence, and that regularly. The sixth error: they descend then from the stars or planets. The verity: not from them or either of them, but from the Father of them. The seventh and last error: to think that by turns He sends one while good, other while bad, and so varies and changes. The verity: He doth neither. The "lights" may vary, He is invariable; they may change, He is unchangeable, constant always, and like Himself. Now our lessons from these.

[[1] themselves?]

The duty.

1. And is it thus? And are they given? Then, *quid gloriaris?* let us have no boasting. Are they given, why forget you the Giver? Let Him be had in memory, He is worthy so to be had. 2. Be the giving as well as the "gift," and the "good" as the "perfect," of gift, both? Then ac- [1 Cor. 4. 7.]

SERM. XIV. knowledge it in both; take the one as a pledge, make the one as a step to the other. 3. Are they from somewhere else, not from ourselves? Learn then to say, and to say
Ps. 115. 1. with feeling, *non nobis Domine, quia non a nobis.* 4. Are they from on high? Look not down to the ground then, as swine to the acorns they find lying there, and never once up to the tree they came from. Look up; the very frame of our body gives that way. It is nature's check to us, to have our head bear upward, and our heart grovel below. 5. Do they descend? Ascribe them then to purpose, not to time
Isa. 65. 11. [Vulg.] or chance. No table "to fortune," saith the Prophet. 6. Are they from the "Father of lights?" then never go to the
Jer. 10. 2. children, *a signis cœli nolite timere;* "neither fear nor hope
Rom. 11. 29. for any thing from any light of them all." 7. Are His "gifts without repentance?" Varies He not? Whom He loves
Joh. 13. 1. doth "He love to the end?" Let our service be so too, not wavering. O that we changed from Him no more than He from us! Not from the light of grace to the shadow of sin, as we do full often.

But above all, that which is *ex totâ substantiâ,* that if we find any want of any giving or gift, good or perfect, this text gives us light, whither to look, to Whom to repair for them; to the "Father of lights." And even so let us do. *Ad Patrem luminum cum primo lumine;* 'Let the light every day, so soon as we see it, put us in mind to get us to the Father of lights.' *Ascendat oratio, descendet miseratio,* 'let our prayer go up to Him that His grace may come down to us,' so to lighten us in our ways and works that we may in the end come to dwell with Him, in the light which is φῶς ἀνέσπερον, 'light whereof there is no even-tide,' the sun whereof never sets, nor knows tropic—the only thing we miss, and wish for in our lights here, *primum et ante omnia.*

But if we sue for any, chiefly for the best, the most perfect gift of all, which this day descended and was given. This day was, and any day may be, but chiefly this day will be
Lu. 11. 13. given to any that will desire, as our Saviour promiseth, and will be as good as His word.

Jas. 4. 5. Within us there is no spirit but our own, and that "lusts after envy," and other things as bad; from beneath it cannot be had. It is *donum cœleste:* Simon, if he would give never so largely for it, cannot obtain it. It descended *ad oculum* this day; it was seen to descend, and so will.

Which descents from on high, from the "Father of lights," there in the tongues of light, light on us, to give us knowledge, a gift proportioned to light, and to give us comfort, a gift proportioned to light; by faith to lighten, by grace to stablish our hearts!

A SERMON

PREPARED TO BE

PREACHED ON WHIT-SUNDAY,

A.D. MDCXXII.

---

1 Cor. xii. 4—7.

Or, *divisions.*

Now there are diversities of gifts, but the same Spirit.
And there are diversities of administrations, but the same Lord.
And there are diversities of operations, but God is the same, Which worketh all in all.
But the manifestation of the Spirit is given to every man to profit withal.

[*Divisiones vero gratiarum sunt, idem autem Spiritus.*
Et divisiones ministrationum sunt, idem autem Dominus.
Et divisiones operationum sunt, idem vero Deus, Qui operatur omnia in omnibus.
Unicuique autem datur manifestatio Spiritûs ad utilitatem. Latin Vulg.]

[*Now there are diversities of gifts, but the same Spirit.*
And there are differences of administrations, but the same Lord.
And there are diversities of operations, but it is the same God Which worketh all in all.
But the manifestation of the Spirit is given to every man to profit withal. Engl. Trans.]

SERM. XV.

A text read at this feast, of the Church's own choice, who I will ever presume best knoweth what text will best fit every feast; and so this. It begins, you see, and it ends in "the Spirit," Whose proper feast this is. "The Spirit" is in the first verse, and again "the Spirit" is in the last; first and last here we find Him.

And if we will look well into it, we shall in effect find that which happened this day, though in other terms. Here have you in this text "gifts," as it might be the tongues, which came from Heaven this day; for what were those tongues but "gifts?" And here have you again "divisions," as it might be clefts, in the tongues; for what is to cleave, but to divide? And if you lack fire, here have you in the last verse "manifestation," which is by light. For the use of light is to make manifest. So have you the Holy Ghost "in cloven tongues of fire," in some more general terms: the "gifts," the tongues; the "division," the cleft; the "manifestation," the fire. Those gifts, first divided, then made manifest, and that by the Spirit, amounting to the substance of the feast; that there can be no question but the text suits to the time, fully.

The use we have of the whole text is, that in all humble thankfulness we are to acknowledge the great goodness of the whole Deity entire, and of every Person in it; so seriously taking to heart the Church's, that is all our good, as we see they do in a sort meet here, and assemble Themselves, all Three, each for His part to contribute; one, gifts; another, callings; a third, works. And then commit over "the manifestation" of all to the Spirit, *ad utilitatem*, "to the profit," that is, to the general good of the Church, in whose good is the good of us all. The sum.

Now albeit, to authorize and to countenance the feast the more, the whole three Persons do here present Themselves in a joint concurrence to this work of distribution; yet you see the Holy Ghost hath here a double part, and in that respect a prerogative above the other Twain. For the Spirit is in, at both. In, at the division; and so are the rest. And again, in at "the manifestation;"—so are none of the rest. But He there, and He alone. For the tongues are His, and they are to manifest; so to Him alone we owe the manifesting. So His, and so His the honour of the day, which is *festum linguarum*, 'the feast of tongues,' or if you will so call it, the feast of manifestation. In very deed, the Holy Ghost's Epiphany; allowing, as Christ one, so Him another.

The sum of all is, that Christ's errand being done, and He

SERM. XV. gone up on high, the Spirit this day visibly came down, for Him and in His name and stead, to take the charge, and to establish an order in the Church; which order or establishment is here set down. And think not it holds in the Church alone, but that in it is represented unto us a true pattern or mould of every other well-composed government. For happy is the government where the Holy Ghost bestoweth the gifts, Christ appoints the places, and God effecteth the work, works all in all.

And as *rectum* is *index sui et obliqui*, 'a straight rule will discover as well what is crooked as what is straight,' both; so under one have we here, as the lively image of a well-ordered society, (for the preserving of these three aright makes all well,) so withal the manifold obliquities and exorbitances in the Church, in the commonwealth everywhere; which arise from the errors about these three: 1. the gifts not regarded, 2. the places not well filled, 3. the works not workman-like performed. The not looking to of which three hath brought, and is like more and more to bring, all out of course.

The division. The text, if ever any, is truly tripartite, as standing evidently of three parts, every one of the three being a kind of trinity. A trinity, 1. personal, 2. real, and 3. actual.

I. I. Personal, these three: 1. "the same Spirit," 2. "the same
II. Lord," 3. "the same God." II. Real, these three: 1. "gifts," 2. "administrations," or offices, 3. "operations," or works.
III. III. Actual, these three: 1. dividing, 2. manifesting, 3. and profiting. Three divisions from three, for three. The three real, they be the ground of all; the 1. gift, 2. offices, and 3. works. The three personal, 1. "the Spirit," 2. "Lord," and 3. "God," are but from whence those come. The three actual are but whither they will: 1. divided; 2. so divided, as made manifest; 3. so made manifest, as not only 1. to make a show, but πρὸς to some end; 2. that end to be, not συμφορὰ, 'the hurt or trouble,' but συμφέρον, 'the good;' 3. the good, not private, of ourselves, but common, of all the whole body of the Church.

I. The Trinity personal. First, and before all things, we find here, and finding we adore the holy, blessed, and glorious Trinity; the Spirit in plain terms, the other Two in no less plain, if we look to but the sixth verse of the eighth chapter before, where the Apostle saith, "To us there is but one God, the Father, of Whom are all things, and we of Him; and one Lord Jesus Christ, by Whom are all things, and we by Him." So by "God" is intended the Father, the first Person; by "Lord" the Son, the second; by "the Spirit" the third, the usual term or title of the Holy Ghost, all the Bible through. These three as in Trinity of persons here distinct, so in Unity of essence one and the same. For though to each of these Three there is allowed a "the same;" yet come to the Deity, and they are not three "the sames" but one the—"the same;" one and the same Godhead, to be blessed for ever.

1. Once before, are these Three known thus solemnly to have met; at the creating of the world. 2. Once again, at the Baptism of Christ, the new creating it. 3. And here now the third time, at the Baptism of the Church with the Holy Ghost. Where, as the manner is at all baptisms, each bestoweth a several gift or largess on the party baptized, that is, on the Church; for whom and for whose good all this dividing and all this manifesting is. Nay, for whom and for whose good the world itself was created, Christ Himself baptized, and the Holy Ghost this day visibly sent down.

The Trinity personal I deal with first, that we may know where and from whom all the rest issue and proceed. All errors are tolerable save two, about Alpha, the first letter, and Omega, the last, about *primum principium*, and *ultimus finis;* 'the first beginning,' whence all flow, and 'the last end,' whereto all tend. We err against the first when we derive things amiss; we err against the second when we refer them amiss: divide them right, and refer them right, and all is right. And the right dividing is, as here, to bring all from the blessed Trinity.

From this Trinity personal comes there here another, as I may call it, a trinity real, of 1. "Gifts," 2. "Administrations," and 3. "Operations." I will tell you what is meant by each. 1. By "Gifts" is meant the inward endowing, enabling, qualifying, whereby one, for his skill, is meet and sufficient for aught. A particular whereof to the number of nine is set down at the eighth, ninth, and tenth verses after. 2. By "Administrations" is meant the outward calling, place, func-

SERM. XV. tion, or office, whereby one is authorized lawfully to deal with aught. Of these likewise you have a list to the number of eight, at the twenty-eighth verse after. 3. By "Operations" is meant the effect or work done, wrought, or executed by the former two, the skill of the gift and the power of the calling; but these are infinite works, no setting down of them, only so to be ranged as every calling to know his own proper work, and so to deal with it.

So have you three quotients from three divisors. 1. "Gift," 2. Offices, 3. Works, from the 1. Father, 2. Son, and 3. Holy Ghost, *referendo singula singulis*. 1. "Gifts"—they from "the Spirit;" 2. Offices[1]—they from Christ "the Lord;" 3. Works[2]—they from "God the Father." The Spirit, He gives wherewith; Christ, He appoints wherein; the Father, He works whereabout. The Spirit gives all to all; Christ, He appoints all for all; God the Father works all in all.

[[1] *or*, "administrations."]
[[2] *or*, "operations."]

You are not here to think these three so limited as that all and every of them, every of the Three, come not from all and every Person of the Trinity. They come, all from all. Our rule is, the works of the Trinity, all save those that reflect upon and between Themselves inwardly, all outward, to any without them are never divided. What one doeth, all do.

To make it plain in these. "Gifts" are here ascribed to the "Spirit;" but St. James saith, "Every one of them comes from above, from the Father;" and St. Paul, he saith, "Christ, when He ascended up on high, He gave gifts unto men." So the "gifts" come from the other two Persons, no less than from "the Spirit." Offices are here assigned unto "the Lord," that is, Christ; yet, by and by, at the twenty-eighth verse, it is said of God the Father that He ordained Apostles, and so goes on there with other offices of the Church. And in Acts the twentieth chapter and twenty-eighth verse, of the Holy Ghost it is said, *posuit vos Episcopos*, that "He placed them Bishops;" and they are chief offices. So that offices are from the other Two, as well as from Christ. Works, they are here appropriate to God, that is the Father; yet in John the fifth, with one breath Christ saith, "My Father worketh hitherto, and so do I work as well as He;" and in this chapter, straight after, at the eleventh verse fol-

Jas. 1. 17.
Eph. 4. 8.
Joh. 5. 17.

lowing, thus we read, "All these things worketh one and the same Spirit." So works, as they are from the Father, so are they from the other Two. And so all and every of the Three Persons equally interested, in all and every of the three.

How is it then? How come they thus to be sorted? Sure, rather in a kind of apt congruity than otherwise; only in a fit and convenient reference to the peculiar, and, if I may so call it, the personal attributes, which most properly suits with each Person whence they flow, as thus. The Spirit is the essential love of the Father and the Son. Love then is His personal property, and love is bounteous; and from bounty come "gifts." So the "gifts," they from the Spirit. Christ, He is the essential "Wisdom" of the Father; and *sapientis est ordinare*—that is wisdom's office, saith the philosopher. So the ordering of places or offices falls to Him. God, we call Him the Father, Almighty, which sheweth might or power is His proper attribute, and power it is that worketh; so the work is His peculiar. And thus come they, thus sorted. And so well we may repair to each severally for his several, yet with no exclusive to the rest; but to all for all jointly, for all that. This needs not trouble any.

No more needs their order in standing—the Holy Ghost first, and the Father last—otherwise than in Baptism or in the Doxology. The works appropriate to the Father, though they be in execution last, yet are they in intention first. It is, as in a solemn train, *novissimi primi*, "the last go first," and [Mat. 19. 30.] *primi novissimi*, "the first come last;" and yet are first in order, though last in place. It is sure, the work is the end of both the rest, and of all. *Unumquodque propter operationem suam;* 'Every thing, be it what it will, gift or place, is and hath his being for the work it hath to do.' So the work is the chief of the three, and He the chief Whose the work is, let His standing be where it will.

II. The trinity real.

To the doing whereof there be required three things. And where there be more than one required, our books teach us, ever to consider them, first *conjunctim*, 'jointly altogether;' then *seriatim*, 'each in order' as they stand; and lastly, *seorsim*, every one 'asunder' by itself.

I. Of them jointly.

Jointly then. To the doing of aught there is requisite,

1. ability of the party, 2. authority for the party, 3. and diligence in the party. 1. Meet and sufficient men; 2. they, orderly called and placed; 3. diligent and painful at their business. To supply these here are 1. a gift wherewith, 2. a place wherein, 3. a work whereabout to employ both; and none to take on him the work except first in a calling, nor to take on him a calling except he first have a gift meet for it. The Spirit is free of His gifts, by which ability; Christ He invites us to some calling, wherein authority; God He calls upon us to be at work, wherein diligence is to be shewed.

Our duty it shall be to come, to be at these three doles or divisions, to have our share in them. Out of the first; 1. every one to get himself furnished with some gift. 2. Out of the second; to see himself bestowed in some calling. 3. Out of the third; having both these to apply himself to some work; and namely, that work that belongs to his calling. In a word, every one to find himself with a gift, in a calling, about a work. Not having the gift, not to affect to enter the calling; nor having the calling, not to venture upon the work.

By all means we are to avoid to frustrate this meeting of the trinity. To do them this honour, to think all the three absolutely needful, and not any of the three more than needs. The wisdom of God, as it is never wanting in any thing that needs, so neither is it lavish in any thing more than needs. And indeed, to hold any of the three superfluous, is in effect to call in question, whether some Person in the Trinity be not superfluous; namely, that Person Whose division we seem to set so light by. All three then are to be had, we cannot miss any of them. If we miss the gift, all will be done unskilfully; if the calling, all disorderly; if the work, all unprofitably, and to no purpose. Then, not to leave out, or to leap over the gift—that is a contempt of the Spirit; nor the calling—that is a trespass against Christ; nor the work—that is an affront to God Himself. So much for *conjunctim:* now for *seriatim.*

2. Of them *seriatim,* 'in their order.'

All to be had, and in this order to be had, as here they stand marshalled. The gift first; then the calling, to authorize, then the work, to make up all. But the gift before the calling, and the calling after the gift; the gift and calling both, before we be allowed to take any work in hand. The number not abated, the order not inverted. Neither the calling before the gift, nor the work before the calling and gift both be had. But every and each, in his order and turn. This order kept, the Church will flourish, the commonwealth prosper, and all the world be the better. We have done with *conjunctim* and *seriatim;* and now we fall to *seorsim*, to the several divisions. And first, to the Spirit's, that is, the "gifts," and the nature of them.

3. Of each severally. 1. χαρίσματα. The "gifts." [Aristot. Eth. 2. 5.]

The word is *χαρίσματα*. It is a word of the Christian style; you shall not read it in any heathen author. We turn it, "gifts." "Gifts" is somewhat too short, *χάρισμα* is more than a gift. But first, a gift it is. It is not enough with us Christians, that a thing be had; with the heathen man it is, he cares for no more, he calls it *ἕξις*. Sure he is he hath it, and that is all he looks after. The Christian adds further, how he hath it; hath it not of himself, spins not his thread as the spider doth, out of himself, but hath it of another, and hath it of gift. It is given him. *Unicuique datur*, it is the eleventh verse. "To every one is given." So instead of Aristotle's word, *ἕξις*, habit, he puts St. James' Jas. 1. 17. word, *δόσις*, or *δώρημα*—it is "a gift" with him.

Free gifts.

And how a gift? Not, *do ut des;* give him as good a thing for it, and so was well worthy of it. No, but of free gift. And so to St. James' word *δώρημα*, which is no more but a gift, he adds St. Paul's here, *χάρισμα*, wherein there is *χάρις*, that is, "grace," and so a grace-gift, or gift of grace. This word the pride of our nature digests not well, *φύσις* and *φυσίωσις* touch near, nature is easily puffed or blown up; but *χάρισμα* hath a prick in it for the bladder of our pride, as if either of ourselves we had it and received it not, or received it but it was because we earned it. No, it is *gratis accepistis* on our part, and *gratis data* on His; Mat. 10. 8. freely given of Him, freely received by us; and that is *χάρισμα* right.

Given by the Spirit.

Freely given by Him; who is that? "The Spirit." The natural man feels he hath a soul, and that is all the spirit he takes notice of, and is therefore called *animalis homo*, that is, nothing but soul;—that is all his spirit. The Jude 19.

SERM. XV. Christian takes notice of another Spirit That is not his own, that is, God's Spirit, the Holy Ghost; and that he is beholden to Him, Who is "one and the same Spirit." Else, so many men, so many spirits. But this is but "one and the same Spirit."

1 Cor. 12. 11. Which "one and the same Spirit" makes also against Paganism. For they had nine muses and three graces, and I wot not how many gods and goddesses besides. We go but to one. All ours come from one, from "the same Spirit." All our multitude is from unity. All our diversity is from identity. All our divisions from integrity; from "one and the same" entire "Spirit." A free gift, from the free Spirit; a gift of grace from the Spirit of grace. So from God, not from ourselves; for Christ, not for ourselves; by the Spirit, not by either our nature or industry—not alone: For without the Spirit, all our nature and industry will vanish, and nought come of them.

Thus it stands. The heathen man thanks his own wit and study for his learning, and we seclude them not; but this we say, when all is done with all our parts natural, and all our acts habitual, if the Holy Ghost come not with His graces spiritual, no good will come of them. Therefore, we to seek after spiritual gifts, and *ζηλοῦσθαι*,—it is the Apostle's word
1 Cor. 14. 1. —"zealously to seek them." For though the Spirit give, yet
Zech. 12. 10. we must sue and pray for them. Zachary makes but one "Spirit" of these two, 1. "grace," and 2. "prayer." "Prayer," as the breathing out: "grace," as the drawing in; both make but one breathing. To pray then, and more than to pray,
[2 Tim. 1. 6.] "to stir them up;" the word is *ἀναζωπυρεῖν*, "to blow them" and make them burn, as is used to be done to fire; and as is to be done to the fiery tongues of this day: else you will have but a blaze of them; and all else, but cinders, cold and comfortless gear, God knows. But so all are to be suitors, and to labour to have a part in this dealing.

By way of division. From the Spirit then they come, but by way of division. Not so, as some, all; some, never a whit, but by way of division. The nature whereof is, neither all gifts to one, nor one
1 Cor. 12. 7. gift to all; but, as it follows, *ἑκάστῳ*, *unicuique*, "to each" some: neither *donum hominibus*, 'one gift to all men;' nor
[Ps. 68. 18.] *dona homini*, 'all gifts to one man;' but *dona hominibus*,

"gifts to men;" every one his part of the dividend, for such is the law of dividing.

Which division is of two sorts: 1. either of the thing itself in kind, 2. or of the measure. 1. The kind: which the Apostle speaks of in the seventh chapter, and seventh verse, "To every one is given his special and proper gift;" to one in this kind, to another in that. God so tempering, as the natural body, that in it the eye should not have the gift to go but to see, and the foot not to see but to go; and as the great body of the world—in it, Hiram's country should yield excellent timber and stone, and Solomon's country good wheat and oil, which is the ground of all commerce: so the spiritual body; that in it Paul should be deep learned, Apollos should be of better speech—one need another, one supply the need of another, one's abundance the other's want.

1. In kind. [1 Cor. 7. 7.] 1 Kings 5. 8, 11.

But division is not of the kind only, but of the measure also. Divers measures there be in one and the same kind. Every one, saith the Apostle, "according" not to the gift, but "to the measure of the gift of Christ." For to some gave He "talents," saith St. Matthew; to some but "pounds," saith St. Luke:—great odds. And of either "to one gave He five, to another three, to a third but one;" in a different degree sensibly. To each, his portion in a proportion: his homer, the Law calls it; the Gospel, his *dimensum*. And remember this well. For not only the kind will come to be considered, but the measure too, when we come to see who be in, and who be out, at the Spirit's division. And so much for the Spirit.

2. In measure. Eph. 4. 7. Mat. 25. 15. Lu. 19. 13.

If we have done with the gifts, we come to the places; for where the Spirit ends, Christ begins. So as, if no gift, stay here and go no further; never meddle with the calling or work. But what, if we have a gift, may we not fall to work straight? No, but a calling is first to be had, ere we put forth our hand to it. Which *nemo sibi sumit, nisi qui vocatus*, "no man, to take on him, unless he be called." Though a gift then, though a good gift, not *eo ipso* to think himself sufficiently warranted to fall a-working. There goes more to it than so. We must pass Christ's hands too, and not leap over His head. For after the Holy

2. The places or calling. Heb. 5. 4.

SERM. XV. Ghost hath done with us, Christ will appoint to every one of us his calling.

Which are divided for order. 1 Cor. 14. 40. Of which division the ground is, that every man is not, hand over head, confusedly to meddle with every matter; but all is to be done κατὰ τάξιν, "orderly." Each to know his own. The very word "division" implieth order. Where we read "divisions," some read "diversities." But it is not so well that. Things that are diverse may lie together confusedly on heaps, but each must be sorted to his several rank and place, else are they not divided. So as "division" is the better reading; and "division" is for order.

And order is a thing so highly pleasing to God, as the three Persons in Trinity, we see, have put themselves in order, to shew how well they love it. And order is a thing so nearly concerning us, as break order once, and break
Zech. ii. 7. both your "staves," saith God in Zachary; both that of "beauty," and that of "bands." The "staff of beauty;" for no εὐσχημοσύνη, no manner of 'decency or comeliness' without it, but all out of fashion. The "staff of bands;" for no στερέωμα, no kind of 'steadiness or constancy,' but all loose without it. All falls back to the first *tohu*, and
Gen. 1. 2. *bohu*. For all is *tohu*, "empty and void," if the Spirit fill
תהו ובהו not with His gifts; and all is *bohu*, "a disordered rude chaos of confusion," if Christ order it not by His places and callings. Every body falls to be doing with every thing, and so nothing done; nothing well done, I am sure. Every man therefore, whatever his gift be, to stay till he have his place and standing by Christ assigned him. It is judged needful, this, even in secular matters. Write one never so fair a hand, if he have not the calling of a public notary, his writing is not authentical. Be one never so deep a lawyer, if he have not the place of a judge, he can give no definitive sentence. No remedy then, there must be division of places; of "administration," no less than of "gifts."

What the places be. Will you know what those places be? Eight of them are reckoned up at the twenty-eighth verse. Not to trouble you with those that were erected, as needful at first, but were not to endure but for a time; those that were to endure are reduced to three, and stand together, 1. "teachers," 2. "helpers," 3. "governors." A threefold division, taught

even the heathen by the light of nature, in their religion. They had them all three in their 1. Ἱεροφάντας, their 'teachers;' 2. Ἱεροδούλους, their 'helpers;' 3. Ἱερομνήμονας, their 'governors.' The very same prescribed by God to His people: 1. their "teachers," the Priests; 2. their "helpers," the Levites; 3. their "governors," the sons of Aaron, called *nesiim*, as true and proper Hebrew for prelates as *prælati* is נשיאים
Latin. The same is known in the Church of Christ through all antiquity: 1. *Presbyteri*, to teach; 2. *Diaconi*, to help; 3. *Episcopi*, to govern. And never any other.

All these three here go under the name of *Διακονίαι*, the proper term of the lowest of the three. We turn it "administration"—it is indeed ministry or service, and that on foot, and through the dust; for so is the nature of the word. An ill word for pride, who had rather hear of words sounding of dominion than of service, specially this service; for it is but the order of Deaconship, and pride would be at least more than a Deacon. Yet so we are all styled here, and no other name for any. The very highest are but so. The king
himself twice made "a Deacon," God's Deacon;—no other Rom. 13. 4.
title. The best king that was, David, is said but to have
"served" his time. "Served," that was all. The glorious Acts 13. 36.
lights of Heaven are said to be created *in ministerium*, Deu. 4. 19.
but "for our service." The Angels of Heaven are but
"ministering spirits;" nay, Christ Himself is styled no other- Heb. 1. 14.
wise, but that "He was a Minister of the circumcision." Rom. 15. 8.
He That is Lord of all, and gives all the offices, calls His own but so.

These places, we said before, are divided for order. Now I add further, they are divided, not scattered, or let fall; for that is casual. Dividing is not so; but, as it is in the eleventh verse, *prout vult*, a voluntary act. He that distributes, knows what, and to whom he doth it. Places therefore are to be divided by knowledge; not scattered or scrambled for, by hap and hazard. The wind is to blow Ps. 75. 6.
no man to preferment. It is the Lord That is to dispose of them.

Divided they be; not scattered.

And how to dispose or divide them? According to the former divisions of the Spirit. That these should first take place; the second depend upon those first; none taken to

SERM. XV. the second, till he have past the first. For Christ's places are for the Holy Ghost's gifts. Without inspiring with the grace, no aspiring to the place there should be. The Holy Ghost is by His gifts to point out those that should be taken into these "administrations." And where Christ placeth, so it is. For He placeth none, but whom the Holy Ghost
John 10. 7. commends. Christ is "the door;" of which door the Holy
[3.] Ghost is "the porter." No man passeth through the door, but whom the porter openeth to. No man to Christ, but by and through the Holy Ghost; nor to the calling, but by and through the gift. They that come not that way, by the door, get in by some other back way, *per pseudothyrum,* 'by some false postern:' that mars all. This is the true order,
Mat. 25. 15. *Vocavit servos, et talenta dedit*—so is the Gospel; whom He calls, He gives talents to. If he have none given him, he came uncalled, at least by Christ—He called him not; he came unsent, at least by God—He sent him not. Though he answer, "Here I am," Christ spoke not to him. Though he came running never so fast, God sent him not. Esay
Isa. 22. 16. asketh two questions, *Quis tu hic?* or *Quasi quis tu hic? Quis,* if by Christ; *Quasi quis,* if otherwise. And many a *Quasi quis,* God-wot, have we among us.

Each one to have a calling. What is then to be done that Christ be not neglected, and His call? That every one betake himself to some calling or other. In the Ministry, all: all Ministers; Ministers, either of the Church, or of the state and commonwealth; but all Ministers. Those that are not, that dispose not themselves
Lu. 13. 7. so to be, to be holden for superfluous creatures, for *inutilia terræ pondera,* "that cumber but the ground," and keep it barren; with whom the earth is burthened, and even groans
Ps. 58. 4. under them. "Deaf adders" they are, at Christ's call "they stop their ears," Who calls every one to a calling, to do some service some way.

According to his gift. To be in some calling; but withal, to have a gift meet for that calling. But if not at the first dole, the Spirit's, not at the second, Christ's; no gift there, no place here. Can any man devise to speak with more reason, than doth the Apostle
1Cor. 14. 38. in the fourteenth chapter following? "If any man be ignorant, let him be ignorant;" that is, hold himself for such, and not take on him the place, or work of the skilful. It is

against God's will, if he do. "Have you refused to gain knowledge? then have I refused you for being any Priest of mine." It is God Himself, in Osee the fourth. Have you not used the means? Have you misspent the time when you should have laboured for the gift? Christ hath no place for you. Whom the Spirit furnished with gifts, for them it is Christ provideth places; for them, and none else. Hos. 4. 6.

1. And yet, not every place for every gift neither; but to have a calling proper to his gift. Proper to it for the kind, not to be missorted into a place no ways meet; his gift lying one way, his place another. But put the right gift in the right place. In kind.

2. Proper for the kind, and proper for the measure also; for as there be measures in gifts, so there be degrees in places to answer them. And one is not to thrust himself into a place disproportioned to the portion of his gifts—the Apostle calls it *ὑπερεκτείνειν*. *'Εκτείνειν*, is 'to extend,' to stretch himself to the full of his measure; *ὑπερεκτείνειν*, is "to stretch himself beyond it," to tenter[1] himself far beyond his scantling[2]. But if a mean gift, a mean calling to content him. *Durus sermo*, for there is none so mean in gift, that he undervalues his gift for any place, yea even of the best worth. You may see these two, 1. the kind, and 2. the degree. The kind in Uzziah: he had no calling to his work of "incense," of burning incense—not at all. What became of him? You may read in his forehead. The degree in Uzza: he had a calling, was of the tribe, went only beyond his degree, pressed to touch the Ark, which was more than a Levite might do, and was strucken dead for it by God. God no less angry with him that went beyond the degree of his calling, than with Uzziah that had no kind of calling at all. None that is in therefore, to overreach or presume above his degree, but to keep him within compass. In measure. 2 Cor. 10. 14. [1 *i.e.* stretch.] [2 *i. e.* certain proportion.] 2 Chron. 26. 16. 2 Sam. 6. 7.

Now the gifts be dealt and the places filled, the Spirit's gifts put into Christ's, that is, into right places. Now fall we to the third, to God's division, to set them to work. Every thing, we said, hath his being for the work it is to do. Gifts, calling, and all for the work. For if the work follow not, the gift is idle, you may cast it away; the calling is idle, you may cast it off. A vocation it might be, a vocation it

SERM. XV. is not. The gift is for the calling; the gift and calling both are for the work.

And will you observe the proceeding here of the Spirit first? The Spirit is nearest resembled to breath; *spiro*, whence it comes, is to breathe. Breath, you know, is in the nostrils: they be two; through and from them both, the spirit proceeds. To answer these, God the Father, Christ the Lord, are two; from them both, by way of spiration, comes the Spirit, the sacred Breath of them both.

Now then secondly, as the Father doth beget the Son, and from Them both proceeds the Holy Spirit; so the gift to beget the calling, (of right so it should,) and they both to produce the work. And as no man comes to Christ but by the Holy Ghost, so no man to the calling but by the gift. And as no man comes to the Father but by Christ, so no man to the work but by the calling.

3. The work ἔργον. 1. Not ἀεργόν. Not to the work. The very word work, *ἔργον*, at once condemns three, *ἀεργὸν, πάρεργον, περίεργον*. *'Αεργὸν* first. Such as are idle-bodies, do no work at all, spend their days in vanity, consume whole years in doing just nothing. This, of works, is God's division; Who is not Himself, would not
Joh. 5. 17. have us idle. *Usque operatur*, "still He works;" still He
Jon. 4. 6. would have us so to do. Not as Jonas; get us "a gourd," and sit under it, and see what will become of Nineveh, but
Ezek. 11. 3. stir not a foot to help it. Not to lie soaking in the broth, as Ezekiel said of the great men in his days; the city is the cauldron, the wealth is the broth, and in the broth they lie
2 Cor. 11. 8. soaking, and all is well. St. Paul calls them the lolligoes of the land. His word is *κατενάρκησα*. The six days, and the seventh, to them both alike; holyday Christians. The poet
[Theocr. Idyl. 15. 26.] said, *'Αεργοῖς αἰὲν ἑορτὰ*, 'every day is holyday with idle people.' Out of this division, out of operations, they.

Not πάρεργον. The next sort, they will not be idle, but it were as good they were. They will be doing, but it is *πάρεργον* all they do, nothing to any purpose; from and beside it quite. *Opus quo nihil opus*, some needless work; *quæ nihil attinet*, as good let alone; leaving undone, that they should and are to do, and catching at somewhat else, and mightily busying them-
Ps. 90. 9. selves about that, and all to no end. *Anni eorum meditati sunt sicut aranea*, saith the Psalm: very busy they be, but it

is about weaving cobwebs; nobody shall wear them, or be the warmer for them; to no profit in the world.

And as these deal with *quæ nihil attinet,* so the last, περίεργον, with those *quæ nihil ad eos attinet,* 'that concern not them at all.' That will be doing, but it is with that they have nothing to do. There are divisions of works, and they work out of their division; love to be busy, to be dealing with any body's work save their own. Which is lightly the busy-body's occupation, condemned by the Apostle, not in men only, but in the other sex too. For they also will be meddling; πολυπράγμων is of both genders. Not περίεργον. 2 Thes. 3. 11.

I told you before, the callings were founded upon order, and to keep them so, have their ὁροθεσίας, 'limits or bounds.' And they do all ἀτάκτως περιπατεῖν, "walk out of order," disorderly break the pales and over they go; that leaving their own, become, as St. Peter's word is, ἀλλοτριοεπίσκοποι, "bishops of other men's dioceses;" do no good in their own, spend their time in finding fault with others. A thing not to be endured in anybody. Take the natural body for example, wherein the spirit, blood, choler, and other humours are to keep and contain themselves, to hold every one in his own proper vessel; as blood in the veins, choler in the gall. And if once they be out of them, the blood out of the vein makes an apostume; the choler out of the gall makes a jaundice all over the body. Believe it, this is an evil sickness under the sun, that the division of works is not kept more strictly. They are divided according to the callings; every work is not for every calling. For then what needs any dividing? But as the calling is, so are the works to be; every one to intend his own, wherein it is presumed his skill lies, and not to busy himself with others; for that is περίεργον. And these are the three errors about "operations." [1 Thess. 3. 11.] 1 Pet. 4. 15.

It will not be amiss if we look yet a little further into this word. For it is ἐνέργημα, which is more than ἔργον. For ἐνέργημα, is not every work; it is an 'in-wrought work.' A work wrought by us so, as in us also. And both it may be. For ἐνέργεια and συνέργεια take not away, one the other. So then by ourselves, as by some other beside ourselves; and that is God, Who is said here to "work all in all." [1 Cor. 12. 6.]

SERM. XV. "All in all." If we take it at the uttermost extent it will reach, then we must be well aware to sever the defect or deformity of the work from the work itself; as well we may. Moving is the work, halting is the deformity. Moving, that comes from the soul, is wrought by it; halting, the deformity, not from the soul, whence the moving comes, but that is caused by the crookedness of the leg. So is the evil of the work; the defect from us, the work from God, and that His.

But, of all good, all our well-wrought works, of them, we
Joh. 15. 5. say not only, *Sine Me nihil potestis facere,* "We can do none of them without Him;" but further, we say with the Prophet,
Isa. 26. 12. *Domine, omnia opera nostra operatus es in nobis.* In them He doth not only co-operate with us from without, but even from within; as I may say, in-operate them in us; *ποιῶν ἐν ὑμῖν,*
Heb. 13. 21. "working in you." Then, if there go another workman to them beside ourselves, we are not to take them wholly to ourselves. But if that other workman be God, we will allow Him for the principal workman at the least. That, upon the whole matter, if our ability be but of gift; if our calling be but a service; if our very work but *ἐνέργημα,* "a thing wrought in us;" *cecidit Babylon,* pride falls to the ground: these three have laid it flat.

But besides this, there are three points more in *ἐνέργημα.* I will touch them first. 1. "In us," they are said to be "wrought," to shew our works should not be screwed from us; wound out of us with some wrench from without, without which nothing would come from us by our will, if we could otherwise choose:—*ἐξεργήματα,* these properly. But *ἐνεργήματα,* from within; hath the *principium motûs* there, and thence; and so are natural and kindly works.

2. Next, from within; to shew they are not taken-on works, done in hypocrisy; so the outside fair, what is within
Ps. 51. 6. it skills not. But that there be "truth in the inward parts," that there it be wrought, and that thence it come.

3. And last, if it be an *ἐνέργημα,* it hath an energy, that is, a workmanship, such as that the gift appears in it. For energy implies it is not done *utcunque,* but workman-like done. Else there is an aërgy, but no energy in it. And even the very word "of division" comes to as much. Dividing implies skill to hit the joint right; for that is to divide. To

cut at venture, quite beside the joint, it skills not where, through skin and bones and all; that is to chop and mangle, and not to divide. Division hath art ever. And this for God's division, the division of works. And so now you have all three.

We have set down the order. Will you now reflect upon it a little, and see the variation of the compass, and see how these divisions are all put out of order; and who be in, and who be out at every one of them? First, whereas the gift and the calling are, and so are to be, relatives, neither without the other; there are men of no gifts to speak of that may seem to have come too late, or to have been away quite, at the first of the Spirit's dealing—no share they have of it; yet what do they? Fairly stride over the gifts, never care for them, and step into the calling over the gifts, and so over the Holy Ghost's head. Where they should begin with the gift, the first thing they begin with, is to get them a good place. Let the gift come after, if it will; or if it do not, it skills not greatly. They are well, they lie soaking in the broth in the mean time. This neglect of the gift, in effect, is a plain contempt of the Spirit, as if there were no great need of the Holy Ghost.

Thus it should be. As one speeds at the first division, so he should at the second. If no grace from the Spirit, no place with Christ. If some one, but a mean one, let his place be according. He with the two mites, not in the place of him with the "five talents:" or as one well expressed it, not little-learned Aurelius, Bishop of great Carthage, and great-learned St. Augustine, Bishop of little Hippo. This is a trespass sure against the first division, which respecteth not only the gifts *in specie*, but in measure too. Proportion the places to the proportion of the gifts; which proportion we know is both ways broken, whether a low gift have a high place, or a rich gift be let lie in a poor place; contrary to the mind of Christ, Who would have the degree of the place as near as could be to the measure of the gift.

There should be but one God. In the text there is no more. But here is another. The Apostle calls him "the god of this 2 Cor. 4. 4.
world;" who hath his ἐνεργουμένους, who works too; and his works tend to deface and damnify the Church all he may.

SERM. XV. Nor, there is but one Lord here, to divide places. But by a *jure patronatûs*, other lords there are, that make divisions and subdivisions of them; of whom the poor subdivided
Isa. 26. 13. places may say, with Esay, "O Lord, other lords besides Thee" have had the disposing of us.

So there is but "one Spirit." But another spirit there is abroad in the world. He that carried Christ up to the
Mat. 4. 9. top of the mountain, and talked of *Tibi dabo,* as if he had gifts too.

I shall be sorry to make any other division of gifts than those of the Holy Ghost. But made it must be, which the world hath made, and makes daily; and makes more account of them than of these here in the text. And indeed such account, as the Holy Ghost may sit still, and keep His gifts undivided well enough. The other spirit divided other manner gifts than the Holy Ghost hath any. The gifts of the Holy Ghost are *dona pectoris,* come out of the breast: you would think the others come out of the breast too, but they come but out of the bosom. And in speculation we say, The Holy Ghost's gifts are far above these; but in practice they are daily found to be far above them in power. For the
Prov. 18. 16. Wise Man saith, *Dilatant viam hominis,* these gifts have a power to make a way through never so thick a press; power to make any door fly open before them. They speak of graces; they make any that come with them more gracious than these of St. Paul. Nay, they will disgrace them, and mar their fashion quite.

But then those gifts hold not of this feast, not of Pentecost; but hold of the feast of Simon and Jude, they. The Church hath joined those two Saints in one feast; and the devil, in many things else God's ape, hath made a like joining of his too, in imitation of the true. His Simon is Simon Magus, not Simon Zelotes; and Jude, Judas Iscariot, not Judas the brother of James—no kin to him. Simon, he came
Acts 8. 18. off roundly, *προσήνεγκε χρήματα,* offered frankly, would come
Mat. 26. 15. to the price. And Judas, he would know what they would give, how thankful they would be; and it was done, and there goeth a bargain. These two are like enough to agree. And thus is the Holy Ghost defeated; bought out, He and His gifts, by Simon still. And thus is Christ betrayed in

His places, and that by Judas still. This wicked fraternity of Simon and Jude are the bane of the Church unto this day. Judas that sold Christ, like enough to make sale of Christ's places. Simon that would buy the Holy Ghost, had He been to be sold, as like to buy out the Holy Ghost's gifts, as the Holy Ghost Himself. And this fault in the first concoction, is never after amended in the second. For with such as these God will never co-operate; never comes there any fruit of such. Enough, if any thing were enough. But thus Christ's places go against Christ's will.

Thus have ye a calling without a gift. What say you now 2.
to a gift without a calling? Those are not for the Holy Ghost; these care as little for Christ. Some such there are, no man must say but gifts they have, such as they be; but they care not greatly for troubling themselves with any calling. They are even as well without. Hop up and down as grasshoppers, hither and thither, but place they will have none; yet their fingers itch, and they cannot hold them, doing they must be; and if they have got but the fag end of a gift, have at the work; be doing they will of their own heads, uncalled by any so that have right to call; and for default of others even make no more ado, but call themselves, lay their own hands upon their own heads, utterly against Christ's mind and rule. And so over Christ's head they come, from the gift to the work, without any calling at all.

Well in these two they have somewhat yet; either a call- 3.
ing without a gift, or a gift without a calling. What say you to them that have neither, but fetch their run for all that, and leap quite over gift and calling, Christ and the Holy Ghost both, and chop into the work at the first dash? That put themselves into business, which they have neither fitness for, nor calling to? Yet no man can keep them, but meddle they will and in Church matters specially—there soonest of all; and print us Catechisms and compose us treatises, set out prayers and new psalms, as if every foreigner were free, and might set up with us. Good Lord, what the poor Church suffers in this kind!

Yet have you a fourth, no less ill than any of these. And 4.
these be such as have gifts and callings both, it cannot be

SERM. XV. denied, yet fall short at the work; work not at all. Wrap
Lu. 19. 20. up their talent, fold it up fairly in a napkin, and lay it by
Jonah 4. 9. them. Let their calling lie fallow, get them into Jonas'
Ezek. 11. 3. gourd, and sit gazing there; or into Ezekiel's cauldron, and lie soaking there. Work who will, and work God in whom He will, in them He shall work nothing; nothing so to any public good. These have great account to make to God, for thus treading under their foot His division. Nay, to all Three; to Christ also for the contempt of His calling, and to the Holy Ghost too for burying His gifts.

So have you 1. a calling and no gift; 2. a gift and no calling; 3. neither gift nor calling, but work for all that; 4. both gift and calling, and no work, not for all that. All awry, all in obliquity, for want of observing the order here established. These obliquities to avoid.

III. The trinity actual. 1. Dividing. It is the will of God that this trinity real should meet, and grow into unity, as the personal Itself doth; that so this here on earth beneath may grow and be conformed to that there in Heaven above. The former three divisions in the former three verses all meet in the unity, and manifestation, in this fourth verse; which is the Spirit's unity. And so come we now about to the Spirit again. For all this dividing is not enough; but when the doles and divisions of all three
2. Manifesting. is done, then begins the Spirit anew. For these must not be concealed, but be all manifested. And that must be by the tongues of this day. Which is it that giveth the Holy Ghost a more special interest than the rest, and makes the feast to be His. For hitherto they had as good a part as He.

If you mark it, dividing and giving is a kind of inspiring, or breathing in; uttering and manifesting, a kind of breathing out again of that was inspired. And these two are two natural and kindly acts of the Spirit in us: by breathing in, to receive; by breathing out, to utter it out or manifest it.

And it hath good coherence, and follows upon the work well, this "manifestation." For every man's work is to make him manifest. No better way to take true notice of any than by it. It is not *loquere*, it is *operare ut te videam*. Christ
Joh. 10. 38. saith not, *auribus* or *sermonibus;* but *operibus credite,* that is, *oculis credite*. For works be manifest, and may be seen.

It follows well likewise upon division. For 1. first, division doth make manifest. Things that are propounded in gross, *eo ipso* are obscure; and are therefore divided, that they may more distinctly and plainly appear. 2. And second, "manifestation" itself is nothing but dividing. For what is divided unto us by the three Persons, it is required that we should divide unto others; and our dividing it among others is that which here is called manifesting. That which we receive when we make manifest, we are said to divide, and to distribute that which came unto us from the former three divisions.

But this is sure: without manifesting, all divisions avail nothing, all the *πολυποίκιλος χάρις*, all "the manifold variety 1 Pet. 4. 10.
of the graces" are to no purpose, no more than a treasure divided into never so many bags, if it be hidden and not manifest, is to any profit, or any the better for it. Nay it holds in all three. 1. In the gifts. We are not to rake them up, but to stir them up and make them burn. 2. In the calling. We are not to be ashamed of it, but to profess it manifestly, as he did, *Non me pudet Evangelii.* 3. In the Rom. 1. 16.
work. We are not to work inward, in a back room, but to open our shop, set out our wares and utter them. Divided and not manifested—that is, the tongues are cloven, but they have no fire, nothing to give light by. And light it is that maketh manifest. Which light is not to be hid "under a bushel," but to be set upon "a candlestick;" or, Mat. 5. 15.
as this feast gives, not to be kept in the shadow, but brought out into the sun, the bright and white sun of this day.

3. Profiting.

Manifested then. And why? for *μηδὲν εἰκῇ*, 'nothing is to be done in vain:' but in vain, if to no end. To some end then. For *πάντα πρός τι*, and *πρὸς* is here in the text. It falls not into a wise man, much less into the only wise God, to keep all this dividing and manifesting, and all to no end. To know that end then, that we run not in vain, labour not in vain, have not the gifts, take not on us the calling, do not the works in vain, "receive not the grace of God in vain," 2 Cor. 6. 1.
nay, receive not our own souls in vain. Else, we fall upon the other capital error about Omega, about our *ultimus finis.* To know our part then. For, *ignoranti quem portum petat, nullus secundus est ventus*, 'He that knows not whither he is bound, no wind in the sky is good for him.' To know our

SERM. XV. end then, whither to refer all. The gift is for the calling, and they both for the work, and they all three are for "manifestation."

But then take heed of making "manifestation" the end of itself, and go no further. There are that make that their
[εὐπροσωπῆσαι. end, that do it, *φαινοπροσωπεῖν*, the Apostle's word, "to
Gal. 6. 12.] make a fair show;" to spread their feathers, is all the use some have of their division. Christ's kindred would have made it Christ's end, and shouldered Him forward to it: If
Joh. 7. 3. you can do, as they say you can do, then get up to Jerusalem, seek to manifest yourself there, that you may be known for such; win credit, and become famous. But Christ came to another end. And the Christian's rule is,
[Phil. 2. 3.] "nothing for vain-glory," either by provoking, or by emulation. It is but Omicron this, it is not Omega.

Wherefore then are we to manifest? *Πρὸς τὸ συμφέρον.* Here is our part, this is our end, "to profit withal." Whether Paul, Apollos, or Cephas; whether gifts, places, or works; all are for this. This is the end of all.

Far they are from this end, that have use of all three. But *πρὸς συμφορὰν*, not *συμφέρον*, that is not to do good, but to do a shrewd turn withal, now and then. Nay that will not stick to boast (one there was that did so; of whom
Ps. 52. 1. the Psalm, *Quid gloriaris?* was made) how they are able to do one a displeasure by their place, and pay him home, if need be. As if *officium* came of *officiendo,* of standing in another man's light, of doing other men hurt. Otherwise, I trust, themselves take no hurt by their offices. But take this for a rule, the Apostle gives it two several times: There
2 Cor. 10. 8. is no power given to any "to destruction," or to do harm;
2 Cor. 13. 10. "for edification" it is, all that is; to do good with, and
Isa. 59. 5. therein to be made manifest. We may not "hatch cockatrice' eggs" to do mischief unto any, as they do to such as eat them.

But all *πρὸς τὸ συμφέρον.* It is a compound word, and we will take it in pieces. First, *φέρον*, which is to 1. bring, to 2. bring in, to 3. bring forth, to 4. bring with. To bring
Ps. 30. 9. in what? "What profit is there," saith the Psalm; to bring in some profit. To bring forth what? "What fruit
Rom. 6. 21. had you?" saith the Apostle; to bring forth some fruit.

To bring with it what? "that I may receive mine own with Lu. 19. 23.
advantage," saith he that gave the talents; to bring with
it some advantage. A way withal, saith Elihu in Job, of
which it may be said, "it did me no good, no good came of Job 33. 27.
it." These same *vana et non profutura*,—away with them, שוה לי
saith Samuel, never look after them. But what saith God ולא
by His Prophet? *Ego sum Deus tuus docens te utilia;* He 1 Sam. 12. 21.
teacheth us nothing, but that which will do us good. And Isa. 48. 17.
what by the Apostle? "These things are good and pro- Tit. 3. 8.
fitable for men," when he was in the theme of good works.
For, as we are forbidden to "hatch cockatrice' eggs," things Isa. 59. 5.
that will do harm; so are we also in the same place, to
weave spiders' webs, things very finely spun, but for nobody's
wearing; none the better for them. Our ἐνεργήματα must
be εὐεργήματα, 'works tending to profit with,' else are they
not the right works.

But φέρον is not enough, to bring in. "Bring in, bring Prov. 30. 15.
in," cries the horse-leech's two daughters, till their skin crack;
but it is only for themselves, and that is not the right. For
it is not *singulare commodum*, 'this profit our own private
gain.' Here is yet another part. Here is σὺν, that is, *con*,
which ever argues a community; a profit redounding to more
than ourselves. For συμφέρον properly is *collatitium*, where
there be a great many; bring every one his stock, and lay
them together, and make them a common bank for them all.
Just as do the members in the natural body. Every one confers his several gift, office, and work, to the general benefit
of the whole. Even as they did in the Law. Some offered
gold, and others silk, others linen, and some goats' hair; and
all to the furniture of the Tabernacle. And semblably we to
lay together all the graces, places, works, that we have, and
to employ them to the advancement of the common faith,
and to the setting forward of the common salvation.

For the common salvation is the "profit" here meant.
The Apostle himself saith it plainly; "Not seeking mine 1 Cor. 10. 33.
own profit or benefit, but the profit of many." And how?
that they may have lands or leases? No, but "that they
may be saved." Which is the true profit, redounding of all
these, and which in the end will prove the best profit; which
if any attain not, "what will it profit him, if he win the Mat. 16. 26.

whole world?" To which port we be all bound; to which port God send us!

And into this, as into the main cistern, do all these "divisions," "manifestations" and all, run and empty themselves. All gifts, offices, works, are for this. Yea, the blessed Trinity Itself, in their dividing, do all aim at this. And this attained, all will be to *Pax in terris*, the quiet and peaceable ordering of things here on earth; and to *Gloria in excelsis*, the high pleasure of Almighty God.

So come we about, and return again, to the first point we began with, that is, to the blessed Trinity. From Them are these; and if from Them, for Them: if from Their grace, for Their glory—the glory of Them that gave, ordered, and wrought; gave the gifts to us, ordered the places for us, wrought the works in us. If we the profit, They the praise: the rather, for that even that praise shall redound to our profit also, the highest profit of all, the gaining of our souls, and the gaining of them a rest in the Heavenly kingdom with all the Three Persons.

END OF VOL. III.

Made in the USA
Las Vegas, NV
04 August 2022